MEN OF
TROY

Also by Monte Burke

Rivers Always Reach the Sea

Lords of the Fly

Saban

4th and Goal

Sowbelly

Leaper (co-editor)

Atlantic Salmon Treasury,
75th Anniversary Edition (co-editor)

MEN OF TROY

The Legendary Afternoons, Wild Nights, and Enduring Legacy of Pete Carroll's USC Trojans

MONTE BURKE

GRAND
CENTRAL

NEW YORK   BOSTON

Grand Central Publishing
Hachette Book Group
1290 Avenue of the Americas
New York, NY 10104
grandcentralpublishing.com
@grandcentralpub

First Edition: January 2026

Grand Central Publishing is a division of Hachette Book Group, Inc. The Grand Central Publishing name and logo are registered trademarks of Hachette Book Group, Inc.

The publisher is not responsible for websites (or their content) that are not owned by the publisher.

The Hachette Speakers Bureau provides a wide range of authors for speaking events. To find out more, visit hachettespeakersbureau.com or email HachetteSpeakers@hbgusa.com.

Grand Central Publishing books may be purchased in bulk for business, educational, or promotional use. For information, please contact your local bookseller or email the Hachette Book Group Special Markets Department at Special.Markets@hbgusa.com.

Library of Congress Cataloging-in-Publication Data has been applied for.

ISBNs: 978-1-538-77258-4 (hardcover); 978-1-538-77260-7 (ebook)

Printed in Canada

MRQ-T

10 9 8 7 6 5 4 3 2 1

For Heidi and
Hansell

Palman qui meruit ferat ("Let whoever earns the palm bear it.")
—Motto of the University of Southern California

When she fell, a hole opened in the human world that may never be filled, save in memory. Poets must sing the story over and over again, passing it from generation to generation, lest in losing Troy we lose a part of ourselves.
—Stephen Fry, *Troy*

Contents

CONTENTS

Introduction

In media res . . .

The fourth evening of the year 2006. Sixty-eight degrees. The Rose Bowl, that low-slung concrete and metal Myron Hunt colossus, his nod to the Yale Bowl and the premodern era of this game that now clutches the country in its violent, balletic grip. A crowd of 93,986, alert, buzzing, now nearly four hours in, waiting for the resolution to an unscripted cliffhanger in this land of scripted ones.

The University of Southern California Trojans football team in its signature cardinal and gold. The University of Texas in all white, a garnish of burnt orange on the uniform letters and numbers and the Longhorn silhouette on their helmets. Night game, with no glorious midwinter California sunshine, no dusty rose-brown cresting wave of the San Gabriels in the background to distract the eye. The pitch-black darkness frames the brightly lit field, narrowing and focusing the aperture, the game and its players on the field seemingly apart from the rest of the world, a separate piece.

Two minutes and thirteen seconds left. USC 38, Texas 33. A USC fourth down and two at the Texas forty-five-yard line. Pete Carroll, USC's coach—once on career life support as a twice-fired NFL coach, but now a two-time defending collegiate national champion—decides to go for it, to ice the game, living up to his nickname: "Big Balls Pete."

Handoff to LenDale White, USC's bruising 235-pound tailback. Dark visor, face inscrutable save for his mouth. Same play that had worked all game, all year.

But this time it breaks down. A USC lineman misses a block. A Texas defender sneaks in and staggers White at the line of scrimmage and then is joined by another defender and another, a pride of lions on a wildebeest. White falls to the cropped Bermuda grass, short of the first down marker. Maybe by six inches.

Turnover on downs. Texas's ball on their own forty-four-yard line. Two minutes and nine seconds left on the clock.

Number ten in white jogs onto the field, six-foot-five, 233-pound Vince Young. He is Sirius, the brightest in the constellation of stars gathered on this night, which includes two Heisman Trophy winners and a total of fifty-two players who will go on to the National Football League. Young is on his way to 267 yards passing and 200 yards rushing, for three touchdowns, the singular performance on the sport's biggest stage.

First down. Pass play. USC cornerback Justin Wyatt blitzes from the left, forcing Young to dump the ball to his running back Ramonce Taylor, who is smothered by USC defensive end Frostee Rucker (his eye black: "Ice Cold"), for a two-yard loss.

One minute and thirty-eight seconds.

Carroll paces the sidelines, his face a stone, no trace of worry. He wears pleated khakis and a white Trojan polo shirt over a white long-sleeved T-shirt. He is fifty-four years old, his hair prematurely silver since his forties, his long face, adorned with a prominent zigzagging nose and anchored by his founding-father chin, preternaturally young. He is known as a players' coach and a defensive genius. He needs every bit of the latter he can conjure on this evening. His defense, battered and lacking experience at key positions, has had no answer for Young, who is torturing them with his arm and his legs. Young is somehow bigger and faster than he was on tape. USC tacklers learn the hard way that they must bring their legs with them and not just use their arms.

Carroll's Trojans have not lost since their fourth game of the 2003 season. Two years and three months ago. Thirty-four straight victories, including two straight national titles. And they'd just been six inches away from clinching a third straight tonight, something never done in the modern era of college football (1970 and on). Six inches from immortality. No one at the time—not Carroll, his players, the fans, the media—knew that this incredible era, the *Pax Troiani*, which still had another four years to go, was already in its decline.

Six inches.

On second and twelve, a blitz from an undersized former backup USC safety, Brandon Ting, who helplessly reaches for, and then grapples with, Young's legs. Young easily steps from his grasp but rushes the throw, bouncing it into the grass.

Third and twelve. One minute and forty seconds.

Pass play. The Texas line picks up the USC pressure. Young hits his receiver, Quan Crosby, on a shallow crossing route. He is stopped after a seven-yard-gain. USC has forced a fourth and five.

Except there's a flag. Another USC safety, Darnell Bing, had grabbed Crosby's face mask when making the tackle. It's ruled incidental and not intentional, a five-yard penalty. Which is good enough for a first down on the USC forty-six-yard line.

The book on Young, in this season and in the one before, was that he struggled to read complicated defenses and could be pressured into making mistakes with his quirky side-armed throwing motion. So his coaches had simplified his reads. Send the wide receivers deep on each side of the field to spread out the defense, thus forcing it to cover more area. Then run a tight end, like the talented David Thomas, into the open space in the middle, right in Young's sightline, for a short-to-medium gain, or provide him with a quick bailout to a running back flaring out of the backfield. But the final instruction of Young's coaches was the most important: if he was ever in doubt about a pass or felt pressure, *run!*

The strategy had worked all season, well enough for Young to earn the prominent chip affixed to his shoulder for finishing second to USC running back Reggie Bush in that season's Heisman Trophy balloting.

And Young had done all of it perfectly in this game. Except once.

Moments before, on Texas's second-to-last drive, Carroll's defense had finally gotten to him, had finally broken through to create that pressure point that could cause a mistake. With five and a half minutes left in the game, and the Trojans up, 38–26, Young dropped back to pass at the USC thirty-seven-yard line. On the play, two USC linemen—Travis Tofi and LaJuan Ramsey—broke through the right edge of the Texas offensive line and flushed the right-handed Young to his left. There, he found another USC lineman, Sedrick Ellis, holding down the gap. Young had nowhere to go. Instead of throwing the ball away or just running out of bounds, he corkscrewed his body back to the right and, falling away, threw the ball across the field to the right sideline, in the direction of his tight end, Thomas. The ball floated, no zing on it. Its high arc gave Ryan Ting—twin brother of Brandon and also an undersized former backup—enough time to get in front of Thomas and box him out, like a basketball player positioning himself for a rebound. Ting leaped as the ball finally came down out of the night sky. Instead of trying to catch it, though, he batted it down to the turf. An interception would have very likely ended the game, one of many near misses for the Trojans that night.

A few plays later, Young ran seventeen yards for a touchdown to cut USC's lead to five points.

One minute and eighteen seconds.

And now Young was back on track. Quick slant pass to receiver Brian Carter for nine yards to the USC thirty-seven. Ball pops out of his hands at the end of the play. Carter is called down, thus no fumble, and it's pretty evident right away that it's the correct call, but the referees stop the clock for a video review. The call is upheld. It's a good break for Texas. The review stopped the clock, serving as a quick timeout to gather wits.

Second and one. One minute and four seconds.

Young drops back and then scrambles, slipping through the tackle of USC linebacker Collin Ashton for a first down. Nothing new for the USC defense. They've been seeing ghosts—and grasping fruitlessly at them—all night long. Carroll, through his linebacker coach Ken Norton Jr., who relays Carroll's plays in from the sidelines, is trying to keep Young off balance by mixing and switching up his calls: he runs blitzes and man-to-man coverage on one play, a three-man rush and a drop-back zone on another. The tactic slows but does not stop the progress of Young and the Longhorn offense. All it would take at this point is for one special play from one of USC's gifted defenders—Rucker, Ellis, or Lawrence Jackson on the line; Brian Cushing or Keith Rivers from the linebacking crew; or Bing in the secondary—to end the game. But they are gassed, running on emotion, pride, and what's left of their adrenaline.

First and ten from the USC thirty-yard line. Fifty-three seconds.

No pressure on Young, who delivers a perfect pass—in stride—to Carter on a crossing route. Seventeen-yard gain.

Everyone in the stadium is now on their feet. Crescendo of noise, brassy top with deep basso undertone. The ABC broadcast crew has done their homework, finding their marks in the crowd.

Kobe Bryant, Henry Winkler, Will Ferrell, Nick Lachey, all there to cheer on the Trojans. Snoop Dogg is on the USC sideline. Dennis Quaid, Lance Armstrong, Roger Clemens, and a buzzed Matthew McConaughey are there for the Longhorns.

Those in the stadium are joined by what seems like the rest of the country. Number one USC versus number two Texas in what will go down as the most-watched national title game in history—35.6 million viewers, three out of every ten American households with a television—and one thought of by some as the greatest college football game ever played.

First and ten at the USC thirteen. Forty-five seconds.

Young throws a jump ball for receiver Limas Sweed, deep in the back right corner of the end zone. USC freshman cornerback Kevin Thomas—almost half a foot shorter than the six-foot-five Sweed—has him covered perfectly and gets a hand on the ball as Sweed tumbles out of bounds. Incomplete.

Second and ten at the thirteen. Thirty-nine seconds.

Young drops back to pass but feels pressure on the edges. He runs right up the middle for five yards.

Third and five at the USC eight-yard line.

On ABC's national telecast, Keith Jackson, in his last game as a broadcaster, and his play-by-play man, Dan Fouts, sound like they are out of breath. They have done a fine job with the most important but also hardest task for a sports broadcast team: getting out of the way of the game.

Timeout Texas with thirty seconds left. ABC stays with the game rather than break away for commercials. The USC marching band strikes up "Fight On!," the university's battle song, composed by a dental student in 1922.

Young saunters to the sidelines in the way that Michael Jordan used to walk to the bench during timeouts—unhurriedly, methodically, almost dragging his toes on the ground, as if consciously forcing himself to slow it all down to save his energy for some great last burst. Young finds his head coach, Mack Brown.

Ashton, the middle linebacker and signal caller on the USC defense, trots toward his sideline. He is a fifth-generation Trojan who has been to every USC football game since his birth. He is a former walk-on who earned a scholarship before his junior year and now plays ahead of former five-star prospects. He is exactly the type of player—a glue guy, a leader by example, and someone who outplays his supposed lot in the football life—that forms the connective tissue of any championship roster in any team sport (think: Steve Kerr on the 1990s Chicago Bulls, Scott Brosius on the late 1990s New York Yankees, Mike Vrabel on the early 2000s New England Patriots).

Ashton glances up at the clock. He spots Carroll on the sidelines and picks up his pace. He tries to stay locked in, focused on his duties. Texas is driving. The USC defense is exhausted. This is it. Backs against the wall. Three-peat championship on the line. Time to concentrate.

Ashton expects Carroll to be intent, curt, and to the point, ready with the defensive call on the next play and any that might follow. To put a hand on his shoulder pads. To remind him to stay in his gap and to use not just his arms but also his body and legs to get Young to the ground. He expects maybe a quick pep talk, "You got this," that sort of thing.

Instead, when Ashton reaches his head coach, the man is looking around in the stands at the fans and up past the lights, to the sky. He has a huge grin on his face.

Ashton is taken aback, befuddled by all of this. *This is the national title game. There are thirty seconds left!*

But before Ashton can say anything, Carroll looks down from the sky and the stands and turns his ice-blue eyes on him, his smile growing wider.

"Isn't this the coolest fucking thing ever?"

A captivating era. Nine years, one fewer than the actual Trojan War. It starts with a failed program, decades removed from the type of success it believed was a birthright, even when it wasn't earned. Then the arrival of an unexpected coach, motivated by his own failures, who became the right man in the right place at the right time, who became the Prince of LA.

The employment of a radically new way of doing things. The faltering start. The use of key old parts in the eventual build. The winning. The championships. Two in a row and very nearly a third in the game of the century.

The only relevant football team in town, filling the vacuum left after the departure of the professional teams from the City of Angels. The leveraging of the location. Everything the city had to offer—the beautiful weather, the beautiful people, the glamour, the self-reinvention, the hype, the power of make-believe, the money, the access, the celebrities who showed up not just for the games but at the open practices, the players who, themselves, would outshine those stars, like an electric running back from San Diego, a soft-spoken Polynesian safety who turned into a destroyer on Saturdays, and a quarterback who went from a chubby cross-eyed kid to national heartthrob. But also: the nightlife, the temptations, the illicit, and the shady men who operated in the shadows of a multibillion-dollar game trying to make money off kids who were prohibited from making a dime themselves.

The near misses in the years after the game of the century, the failure to live up to expectations, the departures of key coaches, the belief in their own hype, the misfires.

Then, the consequences of that great strength becoming the great weakness. The scandal involving the era's best player and one of the best to ever play the college game. The scandal that looks ludicrous from the vantage point of today, but one that nearly spiraled out of control into something darker, something bigger. The scandal that caused the implosion, the inglorious fall that the program has yet to recover from, even two decades later. The scandal that dropped scales from eyes and exposed the college game's governing body and member schools for what they were: hypocritical, bloodthirsty, nakedly avaricious. Modern-day slaveholders.

It was an era made up of different parts, the result of the work of many in tandem. But the primary driver, what made it all possible, was one man.

Wasn't it the coolest fucking thing ever?

CHAPTER ONE

The Education of a Coach

Just a little more than five years prior to that game against Texas, that man was at home, out of football, his avant-garde persona and philosophy publicly and humiliatingly invalidated twice.

Pete Carroll was a failure as a football coach.

He was in his late forties at the time, the supposed prime head coaching years. Young enough to have the requisite energy, old enough to know some things.

But no team wanted him. He was damaged goods. He was a players' coach—that cutting epithet—who allowed the inmates to run the asylum. He did not command respect from his assistants or his players. He was made fun of by the media and the fans. He embarrassed his bosses.

The journey to get to that point had been long, and he was far away from where he started. But, in a sense, he'd never left.

We start with him as a young boy. We will end with him pretty much the same way, because Pete Carroll is one of those men who never grew up, a Peter Pan figure, some mischief included.

Carroll was born in San Francisco and raised in Marin County, the younger of two boys. His father, Jim, was a liquor salesman, his mother, Rita, a homemaker.

The Carrolls' rambler-style house in Greenbrae was the de facto clubhouse for the neighborhood kid group, a place where Carroll's best friends—John Boro, Jim Peters, Skip Corsini, Henry Diaz, Ken Roby—all gathered, and a place where his older brother, also named Jim, brought his friends as well. "All Pete had to do was pick up the phone and say 'ballgame,'" says Corsini. "That was all we needed to hear, the signal to get over to his house."

"Men are born for games. Nothing else," says the judge in Cormac McCarthy's *Blood Meridian*. "Every child knows that play is nobler than work." The Carroll house and neighborhood were where Carroll and his friends acted out their noble endeavors. Carroll set up pillows in the living room, tucked a football under his arm, and jumped up and into them, headfirst, a running back leaping over a pile of linemen at the goal line. The group gathered on Sundays to watch football and, at halftime, headed outside for their own tackle game. They played low-hoop basketball, whiffle ball, or a game they made up, like "dead ball," in which they put a baseball in a sock to slow it down. They biked and skateboarded, and they surfed down a grassy hill on pieces of cardboard.

Carroll loved the constant motion, the total absorption that came with every game. He taught himself how to surf and learned the piano. He loved practical jokes. One of his favorites involved sitting in the passenger seat of his red Valiant convertible, working the pedals with his feet and keeping his left hand on the bottom of the steering wheel, so it appeared no one was driving.

Carroll idolized his brother, Jim Jr., who was five years older. He also wanted to beat him at everything he did, the seed of an obsession with competition that would carry Carroll through the rest of his life. Jim and his friends marveled at how much effort the younger brother put into trying to win and how frustrated he would become when he didn't—when he burst into tears, lashed out in anger. Occasionally, Carroll would take it too far. After one particularly aggravating encounter with his brother, Carroll took a swing at him. He landed the punch but, afterward, noticed something strange about his right hand: the ring finger was disobediently cocked at an angle. "I thought I'd just sprained it, so I ignored it," says Carroll. "But it turned out it was dislocated." The finger remains crooked to this day.

Carroll's father resembled his two sons, with a long skinny face and a prominent jaw. Like many fathers of that era, he wasn't too involved in the blocking and tackling of child-rearing, working long hours during the week and playing golf on the weekends. When he did interact with his sons, it was usually through some sort of contest—cards or a board game—in which he gave no quarter. "He was tougher than shit," says Carroll. "Always trying to win, to beat you at anything." Jim Sr. managed fifty employees and set them up in a competitive atmosphere, constantly pitting them against one another and measuring sales output.

Rita was the glue of the family. One friend of Carroll's described her as "like a madam, but not in a pejorative way." She managed the household with seemingly effortless aplomb, discreetly maintaining order, and doing so with a charming touch of irreverence, an ever-present cigarette in her hand. She doted on her sons and their friends and made hot dogs and macaroni and cheese when they were hungry but didn't hover unless necessary. A benevolent adult figure. "Pete really had a strong bond with his mother," says childhood friend Dave Perron. "All the other kids did, too."

Rita gave shape and coherence to the cultivation of Carroll's competitive nature. Faith is the cornerstone of being competitive— one must believe that one *can* win, that there's good reason to keep pushing. "She taught me to believe in myself and to be an optimist," says Carroll. "Her favorite thing to say was 'something good is about to happen.' I believed her and I still do."

As Carroll grew older, organized sports became the primary outlet for his competitiveness. "Pete ate, slept, and dreamt sports," says Perron.

Carroll was, by his own estimation, the best player on his Little League and Pee Wee football teams. But by the time he reached Redwood High School, he had a problem: his body had yet to catch up to his desire. At five foot four and 110 pounds as a freshman, he had to get a doctor's note to play football. His size resulted in a rather large chip on his shoulder, one that manifested itself on the field. By the time he reached the varsity team, he played a variety of positions — safety on the defense, running back, wide receiver, and, occasionally, quarterback on the offense. He ran and blocked and tackled with ferocity and little regard for his own well-being. His coaches loved him for his passion and work ethic and his understanding of the game.

At Redwood High, Carroll also lettered in basketball and baseball. After making all-state in football as a senior in 1969, he was voted the school's Athlete of the Year.

But sports weren't the only thing that molded a young Carroll. During his four years in high school, antiestablishment fervor swept the country. The civil rights movement converged with anti-Vietnam protests. In 1967, the Summer of Love sprang from San Francisco. Counterculture figures and hippies flocked to that city and many of them eventually found havens in the surrounding area.

Marin County, as it turned out, became a magnet for psychedelic-rock musicians. Janis Joplin, Carlos Santana, and members of Jefferson Airplane and the Grateful Dead moved there from San Francisco.

Carroll saw Joplin in concert and attended Dead shows. The music he witnessed was an expression of culture, and the culture at that time was non-hierarchal and questioning. "It reached all of us by osmosis and direct contact," says Perron.[*]

By the time Carroll graduated from high school he was, like all kids that age, a budding amalgam of his many different influences: someone who loved competition and sports, and someone open to new ideas and new ways of doing things.

Despite the accolades coming out of high school, Carroll didn't receive any offers to play Division I football. He enrolled instead at the College of Marin, a junior college just a few miles from his home. There, he finally grew into his body and, after two seasons as the starting safety, he earned a scholarship to the University of the Pacific, located in California's Central Valley. The school played in Division I,[†] and had some pedigree—Amos Alonzo Stagg, one of the winningest college football coaches of all time, coached there from 1933 to 1946, and longtime Oakland Raiders coach Tom Flores had both played and started his coaching career there.

At Pacific, Carroll made the All-Pacific Coast Conference team as a safety in his first season. He did it again the next year, under a new coach, Chester Caddas, a native Tennessean who had a folksy charm off the field and a tough-guy demeanor on it. Carroll would later write in his book *Win Forever* that his two years at Pacific gave him "a chance to reclaim my identity as a real athlete and performer."

In fact, Carroll believed in himself so much by that time that he was determined to play football professionally.

---

[*] That era would also affect a classmate of Carroll's at Redwood High, a drama student and cross-country runner named Robin Williams.

[†] Until 1995, when the sport was dropped because it was losing money.

No NFL teams came calling, so he turned to the Hawaiians, a brand-new team in the brand-new—and, as it turned out, short-lived (season and a half)—World Football League. Carroll was one of 111 hopefuls who showed up for the team's open tryouts at the University of California, Riverside.

And though Carroll made it through many days of the camp, his lack of size and a shoulder injury sustained during a drill ended his dreams of playing professionally.

"I was trying to play forever," says Carroll. He never really got over it. During his coaching career, Carroll would often tell his players, "You're doing what I always wanted to do."

His football-playing career over, Carroll returned home, directionless. He had no idea what he was going to do, but he knew he had to do *something*. He was a husband now, having married a woman named Wendy Pearl. In the end, Carroll followed in his father's footsteps, becoming a salesman at a roofing supply company.

He was miserable. Sitting at a desk provided him with no outlet for his boundless energy. He had nothing to center him and corral his attention.[†] He missed the sweat, the tears, the grass and mud, the way the game of football taxes you physically and mentally. "He was totally miscast in that job," says Perron.

He was also unhappy at home. "He played a lot of basketball after work during that time," says Corsini. "I mean *a lot*."

And then one day, he got a call from his old Pacific coach. Caddas needed a graduate assistant to help coach the wide receivers. Carroll says now that he had not even considered coaching at that point in his life. But he took the job, and enrolled in classes on the side, pursuing a master's in physical education.

[†] Carroll has self-diagnosed attention deficit disorder.

As significant as Caddas's hiring of Carroll to his first football coaching job was, what took place off the field during those three years as a graduate assistant at Pacific turned out to be far more important to Carroll's career and life.

During his academic study at Pacific, Carroll fell under the spell of one of the world's first real professors of applied sports psychology, Glen Albaugh, who believed that sports were as much about the mind as they were the body. Albaugh introduced Carroll, who was already predisposed to new ideas, to some of the new discipline's most intriguing voices.

One of the first thinkers studied in Albaugh's class was Abraham Maslow, the psychologist who dedicated much of his work to doing something completely different from his peers: instead of concentrating on the sick and depressed, he studied happy people and tried to figure out how they became and stayed that way.

Maslow was most well-known for a theory he devised in the 1950s, known as the "hierarchy of needs," which he detailed in his 1962 book, *Toward a Psychology of Being*. His idea was that human life could be seen as an ascending pyramid, or ladder, with five levels. On the bottom level are the necessities for survival, what he called the "physiological needs," things like food and shelter and sleep. The next step: what he deemed "safety and security," which included health, family, and property. Then: "love and belonging," which led to self-esteem. Each level built off the one below it, and the only way to ascend the pyramid was to achieve each level, one by one.

The level that intrigued Carroll the most was the topmost and final one. Maslow called that level "self-actualization," which is where purpose and full potential are reached and creativity springs, what Maslow described as "peak experiences."

Albaugh introduced Carroll to two more thinkers who would also have a profound effect on his life. One of them was Timothy Gallwey, the author of the groundbreaking book *The Inner Game of Tennis*, which had been published in 1974 to great acclaim. Its central thesis was that in order to maximize performance in sports, one must play them with a quieted mind, without distraction, and in the absence of fear. As the title implies, the book was written about tennis, but its applications were much greater than just that sport. Gallwey wrote about when peak performance happens and what it feels like:

> Reflect on the state of mind of a player who is said to be "hot" or "playing in the zone." Is he thinking about how he should hit each shot? Is he thinking at all? Listen to the phrases commonly used to describe a player at his best: "He's out of his mind"; "He's playing over his head"; "He's unconscious"; "He doesn't know what he's doing." The common factor in each of these descriptions is that some part of the mind is not so active. Athletes in most sports use similar phrases, and the best of them know that their peak performance never comes when they're thinking about it.

Gallwey's idea was that this state—the "zone" as it's sometimes described—is achievable through the learning and practicing of certain skills, first and foremost the letting go of self-judgment.

The other was a man named Michael Murphy, who had written a best-selling novel in 1971 called *Golf in the Kingdom*, in which the eponymous narrator, on his way to India to study with a spiritual leader, stops in Scotland to play a round of golf and meets a mystical golfing guru who urges him to eschew traditional thinking about the game and discover a higher, Zen-like level. The novel, which has since sold more than a million copies, was influenced by Murphy's studies of the concept of Zen, which he learned during an eighteen-month-long meditation retreat in India. After publishing the novel, Murphy cofounded a humanistic retreat center called the Esalen Institute, which focused on human potential.

All heady stuff for a phys ed class and a graduate assistant coach. But Carroll was entranced. Maslow wasn't writing about sports, but Carroll recognized that a coach could bring out the best in his players by creating an atmosphere that satisfied the various levels of the pyramid and allowed them to find purpose and creativity. Gallwey made Carroll think about how he could help get rid of outside distractions for his players. And Murphy's Zen-like teachings could help them get into the zone. Murphy also introduced Carroll to the Native American concept of the "long body," which was originated by a researcher named W. G. Roll, who studied Iroquois tribes. The idea was that there were times when an entire tribe created a consciousness, when it operated "as a single entity, functioning, sensing, and feeling as one," as Roll wrote, which Carroll believed could be achieved with a football team.

Carroll was perplexed about, and disheartened by, the fact that what he was learning from Albaugh was in direct contradiction to the manner in which the Pacific football players were being coached. On a visit to Albaugh's office, Carroll asked why the coaches grinded players down instead of trying to teach them. Why were the players seemingly constantly berated? Why weren't they ever asked for their opinions?

So one night during a meeting with his position group of players, Carroll decided to flip the script. Instead of standing at the chalkboard and telling them what to do, he solicited their input, asking them how they thought they could improve and learn the system better, and how he could help them accomplish that. "And all of a sudden these guys started, I mean, I filled up a chalkboard with ideas and things they wanted to do," Carroll told Adam

Grant in his *ReThinking* podcast. "It was like the best meeting I'd ever had because all of a sudden they were interacting, and we're going, and we're working."

Energized by that meeting, Carroll ran back to the coaches' offices. There, he ran into Caddas and had this conversation, as recounted in *Win Forever*:

"Coach, you won't believe what a great meeting we just had."

Caddas asked what happened. Carroll told him that he'd asked his players what they thought *they* needed.

But Caddas cut him off. "Don't you ever ask the players what they need. Don't you ever tell the players that you'll plan practice the way they want it, not as long as you're here on this staff coaching the game of football."

It was the first, but certainly not the last time that Carroll would face resistance for his style of coaching.

Carroll walked away, disheartened. But then he says he remembered the feeling in that player meeting room that night, the energy. He decided then that he would continue to ask his players what they wanted, to create a two-way relationship and an atmosphere of support that would allow his players to reach Maslow's self-actualization level. He would just do it when Caddas wasn't around.

"We did the drills that [the players] were talking about and, from that point forward, you know, I realized that I was on a different wavelength than the guy I was working for. It was a really big moment," Carroll told Adam Grant. "It was just that moment of when you connect with people and they communicate with you and they realize that you care enough that you could ask them, and then you'll act on it, and you'll back it up and you'll come through for 'em. The relationship just skyrocketed."

By Carroll's third year at Pacific, with his master's degree done, he was ready for a change. The program had been mired in losing seasons, and he came to realize there wasn't much of a future at

Pacific. "Our resources were bottom of the barrel," he says. He had divorced Wendy Pearl ("Not a great marriage," says Corsini) and gotten remarried to a woman named Glena Goranson, a volleyball player at Pacific who'd been the first woman to receive an athletic scholarship from the school. Glena would play an integral role in Carroll's future success as a best friend, a true believer, a sounding board, and even, once, a healer—a coach for a coach.

And that future began in 1977, when Carroll took a job at the University of Arkansas as a graduate assistant under head coach Lou Holtz, which kicked off the itinerate life that pretty much every football coach with the itch of ambition—for bigger jobs and paychecks—goes through. Over the next sixteen years, Carroll would bounce around as an assistant at Iowa State, Ohio State, North Carolina State, Pacific (again), the Buffalo Bills, the Minnesota Vikings, and the New York Jets. Each stop would prep him for what he'd begun to realize was his ultimate goal: to become a head coach.

Carroll had many mentors during those years—Holtz and the Vikings' Bud Grant and Jerry Burns, among them. But by far his biggest influence was Monte Kiffin, a defensive genius who was an architect of what became known as the Tampa-2 defense, a bend-but-don't-break scheme that relied on players who were fleet of foot and mind.

Carroll first met Kiffin at Arkansas, where Kiffin was Holtz's defensive coordinator. In 1980, after Kiffin took the head coaching job at North Carolina State, he hired Carroll, then twenty-nine, to run his defense, Carroll's first job as a coordinator. The two men became close. Carroll even babysat Kiffin's two young sons—Lane, who had already earned the nickname "the Helicopter" because he stirred everything up when he toddled into a room, and Chris.

Kiffin coached for three years at NC State. He did not find big success on the field. But he provided great entertainment off it.

For this first pep rally at the school, Kiffin—wearing a red suit topped with a red ten-gallon hat—rode a horse through the middle of campus while the "William Tell Overture" played on loudspeakers. At one point his horse, spooked by the crash of cymbals, nearly careered into a window of the student center.

On another occasion, Kiffin jumped out of a helicopter at a pep rally. And, perhaps most famously, he brought the boxer Joe Frazier in to speak to his team before the annual game against archrival North Carolina. "Frazier stood up in front of the team, bobbing and weaving," says Carroll. "And then he started to speak but the guy couldn't complete a frickin' sentence. All that came out was 'fuck 'em up, fuck 'em up.'"

Kiffin later entered a makeshift ring with Frazier in the jam-packed basketball arena, where the two men were supposed to playfully box. But the old boxer actually took a hard swing at Kiffin and connected, knocking the head coach to the ground. "Man, Kiff was wacky," says Carroll.

Kiffin was let go from NC State after three seasons. He never worked again as a head coach. Instead, he went on to become a legendary defensive coordinator in the NFL. He and Carroll later worked together at the Vikings and the Bills, where Kiffin continued to practice his defensive genius while maintaining his status as a merry prankster. While at the Vikings, Kiffin pretended to get in a fight with a linebacker on the roof of a building and threw a mannequin—dressed in his clothes—off the roof, terrifying some of the onlooking players. It was a prank that Carroll paid particular attention to.

Carroll would employ a version of Kiffin's defense for the rest of his career. But it might have been the personal that had a more significant influence on Carroll, who noticed that the gags and stunts not only provided Kiffin with enjoyment but also made the players looser and broke up any monotony. It reinforced what would become Carroll's overriding coaching mantra: yes, the game of football requires discipline and consistency but, at its essence, it was also meant to be *fun*.

After the 1993 NFL season, Bruce Coslet, head coach of the New York Jets, was fired. Hired to replace him: Pete Carroll, who had been Coslet's defensive coordinator there for the past four seasons. It was Carroll's first job as a head coach. He was forty-two years old and had spent half of his life as an assistant coach.

Carroll roared into the job full throttle, no governor. He installed a basketball court in the facility and played nearly daily games of three-on-three. He constantly had a basketball in his hand—his secretary knew when he was walking to his office because of the *thump-thump-thump* in the hallway. He hosted a teamwide home run derby. He taught himself the harmonica on his commute to work. He played James Brown throughout the team offices and on the practice field. He stood on serving trays and "surfed" down the aisle of the team plane as it landed.

His coaches and players didn't seem to know what to make of the whirling dervish of a coach, and held back a bit, to see if this would all work out when it came to the real test: the season.

One key person who seemed wholly unimpressed by the manner and methods of his new coach was the Jets' seventy-nine-year-old oil baron owner, Leon Hess.

In Carroll's first meeting with the team, he bounded into the room like a golden retriever, all smiles, bouncing on his toes. He pronounced at that meeting that there would be no rules for the team. *No rules!*

He happened to glance at Hess, who was in the front row, at that very moment. Hess sat motionless, his arms crossed over his conservative brown suit, a frown furrowing his face. "It was clear from his expression that he was not a fan of the somewhat unorthodox approach I took," Carroll wrote in his book.

The season started well—going into the twelfth game, the Jets were just one game out of first place in the AFC East.

And then disaster struck. In that twelfth game, Miami Dolphins quarterback Dan Marino executed what became known as the "fake spike," pretending to down the ball to stop the clock but instead throwing a touchdown pass behind an unsuspecting Jets defense in the game's waning moments for the win.

That one play derailed the entire season. The Jets lost their last four games of the season by a combined 87–36 and finished 6–10.

The New York media were ruthless with Carroll, blasting him for being a players' coach, for playing basketball, and for throwing passes with locker room attendants on the sidelines before games.

Carroll was fired at the end of the season, the rare one-and-done head coach. A few days after his firing, his basketball court was removed from the facilities. Someone had stuck a sign on the backboard that read: 6–10.

Carroll found a home for the next two years as the defensive coordinator of the San Francisco 49ers under head coach George Seifert, on a team that featured Steve Young, Jerry Rice, Ken Norton Jr., and Merton Hanks. In Carroll's last season with the 49ers, the legendary coach Bill Walsh came back to the franchise as an offensive analyst, and Carroll constantly picked his brain for coaching advice. "It was like talking to Yoda," says Carroll.

By the end of the 1996 season, with the 49ers' defense among the best in the league, Carroll, once again, was a hot head coaching prospect. And he ended up in an unlikely spot.

The New England Patriots had just come off an appearance in the Super Bowl after the 1996 season, losing to the Brett Favre–led Green Bay Packers. The success of the Patriots team was primarily due, many believed, to its larger-than-life (literally) and short-tempered bully of a coach, Bill Parcells.

But in a highly unusual move, Parcells, clashing with the Patriots' relatively new owner, Robert Kraft, over personnel decisions, decided to leave after the season.

As he searched for a new coach, Kraft says, "Given how complicated the Parcells situation was, I wanted a complete break."

He got his wish.

Kraft flew in Carroll and the two men met for an eleven-hour interview. "We talked about everything. Our families. Our kids," says Kraft. "Pete loved football and had an energy and a positivity that was infectious."

And in February 1997, Carroll was hired as the new head coach of the Patriots. He inherited a talented team led by Drew Bledsoe, Curtis Martin, and Willie McGinest. But he was also replacing a legendary, two-time Super Bowl–winning coach in Parcells, a coach who was the oldest of old-schoolers, who led by intimidation. Carroll, on the other hand, was on the vanguard of a new way of coaching football, one that had neither caught on nor proven itself yet. He wanted to lead by inspiration.

Carroll, as he had with the Jets, dove into the job with vigor. He met with every player individually in his office, his sandaled feet on the desk, working a pink wad of gum in his mouth, tossing a football or basketball in his hand. Once again, there would be no rules. He blasted Motown tunes throughout the building and on the field. He played basketball with his assistants. He stood in the end zone as his kicker practiced field goals, rifling spirals at the kicked balls, trying to knock them out of the air.

The Boston media, just like their New York brethren before them, were skeptical. They made fun of the basketball games and the fact that Carroll rode a ten-speed bike to practices. They nicknamed him "Poodle Pete," "Peter Prep School," and "Petesy."

He partially won over the media and some of the fans, though, when he went 10–6 in his first season and won a playoff game. After that season, the Patriots lost star running back Curtis Martin to the Jets (then coached by Parcells), even though Carroll had begged Kraft to keep him. The next season, New England made the playoffs again with a 9–7 record, but lost in the first round, with Bledsoe out with an injury.

And then things began to fall apart as Carroll's third season descended into mediocrity. A player told the media that the team had been "outplayed and outcoached" after one loss. Someone placed a "For Sale" sign in the front yard of the Carrolls' Medfield, Massachusetts, home. And he lost respect in the locker room from how he handled the talented but troubled wide receiver Terry Glenn.

Glenn was a generational talent on the field (he once had 214 receiving yards in a game) and generational cancer in the locker room, missing practices and meetings and pretending to be hurt. He had been a headache for Parcells, as well. Parcells had handled him with intimidation and ridicule, once referring to him to the media as "she." Carroll did the opposite, trying to save and not discipline him. "I went too far with Terry," says Carroll. "He was so troubled, and the other players gave up on him and thought I was babying him, which I was. Parcells tried to break him. I didn't think that was the right way. But maybe doing that at least made everyone else feel better. I failed in that one. I really failed. And the whole team and the coaches were watching."

The Patriots finished 8–8 in 1999. Kraft fired Carroll after the season. Carroll's style had not worked—neither with the owner nor the players. "If you're an immature player or didn't conduct yourself the right way, you could get away with it more with Pete," Willie McGinest, a team leader, told ESPN. "He would discipline you, but you didn't fear things. Bill was totally different."

Even Carroll's coaches at New England agreed. Steve Sidwell, Carroll's defensive coordinator there, told *The Athletic*: "Pete's players respected him but did not fear him."

Though Sidwell was not being complimentary, this was exactly what Carroll wanted. Not to be feared. But to be loved. Inspiration over intimidation. Humanistic over militaristic. Authoritative over authoritarian.

As he left the Patriots, a thought crossed Carroll's mind and terrified him. What if his way didn't work? What if football players, by their nature, desired the authoritarian, militaristic coach? After all, Kraft went right back to that model, replacing Carroll with Bill Belichick, a Parcells devotee.

What if he'd done this all wrong?

But no, he decided. It wasn't that the philosophy was wrong. Part of it was circumstance. The old ways were deeply entrenched. Change was uncomfortable. The owners weren't ready. And neither were the media and the fans, particularly in the cynical Northeast.

It was more than that, though. Carroll realized he still had shortcomings as a coach. He was not yet fully realized. He had trouble communicating and implementing his philosophy. He needed to better know it—and himself—before he could be truly effective.

He needed someone to give him another chance. Another NFL team? Unlikely, at least right away. Though he had an overall winning record as a pro coach (33–31), he'd been fired twice. He was branded as a failure.

A college team and its more impressionable players?

Maybe.

The problem was that no one called him for a coaching job. No one from the NFL. No one from college.

CHAPTER TWO

The Wilderness

Pete Carroll was forty-eight years old when he was fired by the New England Patriots in January 2000. He knew all bad coaches get fired. He also knew good coaches got fired sometimes, too. Belichick, his successor at New England, had been fired by the Cleveland Browns after the 1995 season. One of Carroll's old bosses, Lou Holtz, had been fired by Arkansas early in his career and, years later, won a national title as the head coach of Notre Dame. Nick Saban had been fired as the secondary coach at Ohio State but then moved on to a successful five years as the head coach at Michigan State, before being hired in late 1999 for the same job at LSU.

But none of those men had been fired twice.

So was Carroll a bad coach? Or a good one? Now, out of football for the first time since 1973, he had some time to dwell on that question.

Carroll first took some time to process and feel the cold rock bottom of his repudiation from the game he loved, then began trying to pick himself up. Seven years later, he'd finally open up to *Los Angeles* magazine about this period in his life, with some words that felt right out of a spaghetti western. "I've already been dead," he said. "You can't kill a dead man." He was still under contract with the Patriots for two more years and was owed $2 million. But the money would run out eventually. And pride had no price.

He spent time that winter at his house in Medfield. He ventured to the family lake house in New Hampshire. Snow on the ground. Thick layer of ice on the water. "I had no plan," he says. "I didn't know what was going to happen."

Carroll tried a few different things. Pat Kirwan was a longtime NFL coach and scout who had worked at the Jets when Carroll was there, as a player contract negotiator and salary cap guru. He and Carroll had become close. Kirwan, at this point, was also out of the NFL, having left the Jets after the 1997 season. The two men came up with an idea, which they called Real Football. They wanted to provide around-the-clock news about the game, like CNN had done for the news. The concept was a very good one—the NFL would use that same idea when it launched the NFL Network in 2003—but they could not get it off the ground. "We knew there was an appetite for something like that," Carroll says. "But we didn't know what we were doing, and we had no resources."

Carroll penned a few articles for the website CNNSI.com, and he became an ambassador and spokesperson for NFL Youth Football. But neither of these things were longtime gigs, and neither of them came close to his deepest desire—to become a head coach again.

One day on a whim, Carroll picked up a book written by the legendary UCLA basketball coach John Wooden, called *Wooden: A Lifetime of Observations and Reflections On and Off the Court*, which had been published in 1997. The book was revered by coaches and was known by shorthand as "The Blue Book" (the color of its cover). Carroll had, of course, known about Wooden for years, and he'd even skimmed through the book when it first came out. But on this read, something about it truly moved him.

Under Wooden, in the twelve seasons between 1963 and 1974, UCLA had won ten national titles, which included a stretch of seven in a row. But Wooden's book was less about the "how" when it came to becoming the best college basketball coach of all time, and much more about the "why." The axioms Wooden laid out made Carroll feel he was being directly spoken to:

"The man who is afraid to risk failure seldom has to face success."

"Failure is not fatal, but failure to change might be."

"Promise to forget the mistakes of the past and press on to greater achievements."

Wooden talked about the importance of positivity, as Carroll's mother had:

"Promise to wear a cheerful appearance at all times and give every person you meet a smile."

He talked about looking inward:

"Know that valid self-analysis is crucial for improvement."

One of the axioms hit Carroll the hardest, harking back to something he knew but had not yet manifested as a head coach:

"You must know who you are and be true to who you are if you are going to be who you can and should become."

The eureka moment for Carroll came when he realized something that he'd completely missed when he'd first read the book: Wooden coached at UCLA for *fifteen* seasons before he won his first national title. "But from that point on," Carroll says, "it seemed like he won forever."

And that success only came, Carroll surmised, after Wooden fully figured himself out. Wooden had internalized and lived his beliefs and philosophies and, importantly, then learned how to communicate them to everyone—to his players, coaching staff, trainers, and cafeteria workers, but also to the people who were, effectively, his bosses: the boosters, athletic director, and school president.

Carroll saw similarities between himself and the great coach. No, Wooden had never been fired (much less twice), but he had not had immediate success. And that was the reassurance that Carroll needed.*

In his book, Wooden had talked about how important it had been for his career to sit down and actually write out his core philosophies and his plan for winning. So Carroll did the same, thinking back to what he had learned as a graduate student at the University of the Pacific, to Maslow, Gallwey, and Murphy.

Carroll holed himself up in the late cold and colorless winter of New England, tamping down his innate restlessness to make himself sit and concentrate for hours on end. He jotted down paragraphs, sentences, fragments, words. He had been coaching football at various levels for twenty-seven years, and though he had some ideas and philosophies about the profession, this was the first time that he had truly thought them through. Though he says he didn't necessarily realize it fully as it was happening, he says now that "it was such a crucial time for me, that time to step away from the game. I concentrated and really dug in, and it became a tremendously rich time for learning and growing. Everything kind of came together."

The core of Pete Carroll's philosophy, he realized, was *competition*. It had been the animating trait in his life, handed down to him from his father, cultivated in trying to beat his brother and playing unorganized and organized sports, and manifested, finally, in trying to get a team to work together and win. He studied the concept, going back to the Latin root of the word — *competere* — and

---

* After arriving at USC, Carroll met Wooden and says he "formed a real relationship" with him. "He was really nice to me and kind of took me under his wing, a UCLA guy helping out a USC guy."

finally found what he was looking for. "Competing," as commonly viewed, was about triumphing over others. But the word had drifted from its roots. *Competere*, Carroll discovered, meant "to strive together, not against." Therefore competition, he came to believe, was not about trying to beat someone else. It was, really, about competing with yourself, to grow, to win, to improve, which dovetailed with what Carroll viewed as Gallwey's central message, that "the only competition that matters is the one that takes place within yourself."

With competition as the core of his philosophy, Carroll filled out the rest with some good solid football clichés—the competitive mindset would be fed by "great effort, great enthusiasm, great toughness" and "playing smart" and "doing things better than they've ever been done before." And he devised three simple rules that his next team would abide by, if he ever got the chance to coach again:

Always protect the team.

No whining, no complaining, no excuses.

Be early.

Rules. He now had them. And he knew he had to focus on them. Discipline was important. He and his coaches and his players would always have freedom—he would cultivate it, in fact. But it all had to be done within the framework of some hard and fast rules.

All of this would form the basis of the competitive mindset and would allow his players and team to play with Gallwey's "quieted mind" and reach Maslow's "full potential," allowing them to "win forever," as he believed Wooden had.[†] Carroll didn't think that there was an offensive or defensive scheme that could win

---

[†] *Win Forever*, of course, became the title of Carroll's book, written with Yogi Roth, and his short-lived business, also founded with Roth, that set out to coach coaches.

championships. Not on their own. They always had to fit into something bigger, a strong belief system that permeated through the program.

A pertinent question: Was all this a bit (or more than a bit) . . . *corny*? It all rang of self-help and self-improvement. And most books and talks within that genre are, indeed, corny, filled with aphorisms that are simple and plain and true (and self-evident?) and easy to remember. But all of that may be the very point.

Football is a complicated game, with many parts moving, sometimes synchronously and sometimes asynchronously. Having a simple and easy-to-understand philosophy can help make at least one part of the game easier and more digestible. To many elite athletes, these maxims are not the trite clichés they appear to be to most—they help clear and focus the mind. And one of the tricks pulled by the best motivational speakers is that when they speak these things into existence and repeat them over and over, it not only keeps their audience focused, but it also acts as personal reinforcement as well. "The sort of words a man says is the sort he hears in return," wrote Homer in *The Iliad*.

Though Carroll now believed he had his philosophy for winning down, he still had to deal with his practical reality: he was not a football coach. Rather, he was stuck in football purgatory.

He did not have anywhere he needed to be, no meetings, no playbook installations, no film time, no practices or games to prepare for. The forced respite had some benefits. Carroll spent some real time with Glena and his younger son, Nate, at home. He went to see his older son, Brennan—a tight end at the University of Pittsburgh—play in person, something that would have been nearly impossible to do if he'd been coaching.

But the year off had some unexpectedly tough moments. His mother, the original beacon of positivity and unconditional love, died, and then, eight months later, his father died, too. Carroll's

Patriots money had one year left. And Kraft, he says, was encouraging him to take a job he did not want—the defensive coordinator position at the Washington Redskins—presumably so he wouldn't have to pay him anymore.

Summer began to wane. Just for fun, Carroll and Kirwan attended college football's Kickoff Classic in Giants Stadium in late August and watched USC, with Carson Palmer at quarterback and Troy Polamalu at safety, defeat Penn State, 29–5.

And then it turned to fall, the new football season in full swing. Nothing was happening on the job front. "I didn't know where my next paycheck was coming from," he says. "I felt antsy for the first time." As the football season came to its conclusion, he made some calls. North Carolina had a job opening. Carroll believed he'd be a great fit, having spent time in the Atlantic Coast Conference (ACC) at NC State. "But they didn't call me back," he says.[†] He made more calls, a sense of desperation creeping in, the prospect of going two seasons in a row without a job—a probable death knell for his head coaching prospects—becoming a real possibility. "*No one* called me back," he says.

Still, the year off had been a productive one. Carroll had, he says, figured himself out. He no longer would care if people called him a players' coach, that pejorative term in coaching circles. Hell yes, he *was* a players' coach. But also, hell yes, he would coach with discipline, more than he had shown at the Jets and the Patriots. And there would be accountability and no more Terry Glenns.

But mostly, it would be about passion and compassion. He knew himself. That allowed him to be better at knowing others. He would get to know his coaches and players on a personal level,

---

[†] North Carolina ended up hiring John Bunting, who coached there for six years and posted only one winning season.

try to divine their likes and dislikes, and, more important, figure out what made them tick, what motivated them. The traditional way of coaching football was Old Testament, an immature and vindictive God who demanded loyalty through intimidation and fear and, if that loyalty was not given, lashed out. Those coaches humiliated their players, bullied them, and then built them back up just enough so they could, in turn, bully other teams. Carroll saw himself as all New Testament—inspirational, forgiving (to a point), empathetic, and, yes, loving. *Was it all a bit self-serving? Was it psychological manipulation for his benefit?* Of course, that was part of it. That's part of it for all coaches. It would help him win, help him reach the mountaintop. But it would also benefit others. They would win with him. And they would do it in a different way: it would be fun.

He had it all down. He was ready.

The question was: Would anyone care? Would anyone ever call him? Would he get a chance to put all of this into practice?

Carroll knew very few coaches got a third shot at a head job after being fired twice. He also knew if he did get that shot and he didn't succeed, it would certainly be his last.

CHAPTER THREE

Persona Non Grata

The first college football game ever played took place just four years after the conclusion of the Civil War. On November 6, 1869, some students from the College of New Jersey (later known as Princeton) traveled by carriage seventeen miles north and east to New Brunswick, New Jersey, to play a game against Rutgers University in front of one hundred spectators. The game had very little in common with the one played today. Twenty-five players on each team lined up against each other; there was no tackling and players couldn't pick up the ball but rather attempted to kick or bat it into the opposing team's goal, a sort of hybrid of rugby and soccer.* In 1875, after continual tweaking and evolving of the rules, the game came to resemble its modern iteration, when Harvard and Tufts played against each other. They had eleven players on each side, blocking, tackling, and trying to advance the ball by running with it.†

The popularity of the game grew in the late 1870s and throughout the 1880s, and it spread from the Northeast to the large state schools of the South—which took great pleasure in exacting tiny modicums of revenge for the Civil War by beating the teams of the elite Northeastern universities—and the Midwest. By the late

---

* Rutgers won, 6–4.
† Tufts won, 1–0 (a touchdown was worth one point).

1880s, the sport had completed its own manifest destiny, finding a foothold on the shores of the Pacific Ocean.

Football's professional version — the National Football League — has always been a game of the city (with the Green Bay Packers being the sole exception). College football, on the other hand, is mostly the game of the more rural, small-to-medium-sized towns, like Tuscaloosa, College Station, State College, Norman, Lincoln, Ann Arbor, and South Bend. There are exceptions to this, too, of course. The most prominent one is the University of Southern California.

Robert Maclay Widney was born on a farm in Ohio in 1838. He left home as a teenager, hunting and trapping his way out to California, which, at the time, was a frontier state. He went to the University of the Pacific, got a law degree, and settled in Los Angeles, where he became a judge and rose in prominence as a real estate promoter and developer, oftentimes accepting land in lieu of his legal fees. In the late 1870s, along with some other prominent Angelenos, Widney headed up efforts to establish a university in the city, then home to around 30,000 citizens. He formed a board of trustees, wrote up articles of incorporation, and, in 1879, talked three landowners into donating 308 lots of undeveloped mustard fields in south central Los Angeles, as a home for the university. The next year, the University of Southern California, a school of Methodist inclination, officially opened, with fifty students and ten faculty members.

Eight years later, USC — then known as the Methodists — fielded its first football team, coached by two Latin professors (who also played) and quarterbacked by a man named Arthur Carroll (no relation to Pete).[‡] The Methodists went 2–0 that

---

[‡] USC would become the "Trojans" in 1912, thanks to a sportswriter named Owen Bird, who came up with the nickname. At the time, apparently, USC

season, defeating the Alliance Athletic Club twice. It wasn't until the 1920s, under the school's first full-time coach, Elmer Henderson, that the football program became nationally relevant. Henderson was known to the local media as "Gloomy Gus" because of how he poor-mouthed his own team before games. But he went 45–7 in his six years as the head coach, won the school's first Rose Bowl, joined the Pacific Coast Conference, and moved the team into the then 75,000-seat Los Angeles Coliseum.

USC won its first national title in 1928, under coach Howard Jones, who had taken over for Henderson after Knute Rockne had turned down the job. Under Jones, USC would win three more national titles and begin to play against what would become their two biggest rivals—Notre Dame (in 1926) and the crosstown University of California, Los Angeles (in 1929).[§] After Jones died of a heart attack in the summer before the 1941 season, there followed a twenty-year fallow period in which the Trojans finished in the top ten nationally in only three seasons, an era that many Trojan fans seem to forget, perhaps because of the glorious twenty-two years that ensued under the program's following two coaches.

The first—John McKay, an Air Force tail gunner in the Pacific Theater in World War II—was hired in 1960. After a tough first two years, McKay's Trojans went undefeated during the 1962 season to win the national title, the first of four during his tenure.

---

was frequently smaller than and not as well-equipped as their opponents, but, as Bird wrote: "'Trojan' as applied to USC means to me that no matter what the situation, what the odds or what the conditions, the competition must be carried on to the end and those who strive must give all they have and never be weary in doing so." That the Trojans of Greek mythology actually lost the Trojan War seemed immaterial, I guess.

[§] Marion Morrison, who later became known as John Wayne, attended USC on a football scholarship and played for Jones for a season. His football career was ended when he broke his collarbone bodysurfing and was cut from the team and lost his scholarship.

McKay was a fan of a strong running game, in general, and the I-formation (a tailback lined up behind a blocking fullback in the backfield) in particular, frequently employing toss sweeps to either side of the field (which, depending upon the direction, was referred to as "student body left" or "student body right"). In 1963, he recruited a smallish running back who grew up in a Los Angeles housing project and ran with the anger and determination of someone trying to overcome a bad lot in life, seeming to seek out contact with defenders. That running back was Mike Garrett, who would become known as "Iron Mike," and he made McKay's I-formation hum. Garrett became a two-time All-American and won the university's first Heisman Trophy after the 1965 season. Then, in 1967, McKay recruited a junior college transfer named Orenthal James Simpson, who would also become a two-time All-American and win the school another Heisman Trophy in 1968.

McKay won his last national title as the head coach of the Trojans in 1974, then left for the Tampa Bay Buccaneers in the NFL after the next season. He was replaced by a man named John Robinson, who had been the offensive coordinator for two of McKay's national championship teams. Robinson kept the good times rolling, continuing the "Tailback U" legacy that McKay had created by coaching two more Heisman-winning running backs, Charles White (in 1979) and Marcus Allen (in 1981). Robinson coached for seven seasons, winning one national title in 1978. After the 1982 season, he left to become the head coach of the NFL's Los Angeles Rams.

And then USC entered the darkness. Robinson's replacement, Ted Tollner, lasted four seasons, going 26–20–1 overall and finishing only one of those seasons ranked in the top twenty. His replacement, Larry Smith, got off to a decent start, finishing in the top ten in two of his first four seasons, before bottoming out with a 9–13–1 record in his last two.

Robinson was then brought back to USC to try to recapture the past glory, but it didn't work out as planned. Second stints rarely do. Robinson did lead the Trojans to two PAC-10 championships in his first three seasons but never sniffed a national title (number twelve was his highest ranking in five seasons), and USC plummeted to 6–6 and 6–5 records in his last two seasons.

In January 1993, after USC athletic director Mike McGee had left the school for the other USC (the University of South Carolina), the Trojans turned to a familiar face to fill his role: its own Heisman-winning running back, "Iron Mike" Garrett.

Garret had been drafted by the Chiefs—then members of the American Football League, before the merger with the NFL—in 1966 after his playing career at USC ended. In his rookie year in the pros, he made the All-AFL team and played in the first-ever Super Bowl, which the Chiefs lost to the Packers. Three seasons later, Garrett and the Chiefs returned to the Super Bowl and won. He was eventually traded to the San Diego Chargers and finished his eight-year pro career there in 1973. He later got a law degree, worked in business development for the Great Western Forum (where the Los Angeles Lakers played), worked for the San Diego district attorney, dabbled in real estate, and did some television commentary work for USC football games.

When he was hired by USC, he was twenty years removed from his playing days. He was still lean, with a brushy mustache that seemed to prop up his bulbous nose. The frown lines between his eyes gave off a determined, almost angry, look. He was very much still Iron Mike, still appearing to relish contact. At his introductory press conference, he promised to get USC athletics back on track. Everyone knew what he was really talking about was the football team.

Garrett inherited Robinson as the team's football coach. But when it became clear that the coach's second stint wasn't working out, Garrett began to contemplate the hiring of a new head coach. And he believed he'd been watching him every Sunday afternoon on television.

Daryl Gross had been hired by McGee as a sports administrator at USC in 1991. After McGee left, Garrett kept Gross on and promoted him to the position of senior associate athletic director. The two men became friends, to the point where, nearly every Sunday during the NFL season, Garrett had Gross over to his house to watch his old team, the Kansas City Chiefs, play football.

While watching the Chiefs, Garrett became enamored with the team's offensive coordinator, Paul Hackett.

Hackett was considered a savant of the offensive side of the ball. He had some Trojan pedigree—he'd coached the quarterbacks and wide receivers for four years during Robinson's first, more successful head coaching stint at the school in the 1970s and 1980s. He had head coaching experience—he'd led the University of Pittsburgh for three years (two of them losing seasons). He'd spent time in the NFL with some of the best franchises, including the Dallas Cowboys, the San Francisco 49ers (where he was Joe Montana's quarterback coach), and now the Chiefs (where he coached Montana again).

Garrett told Gross that Hackett would be a good fit when the time came to replace Robinson.

Gross agreed, but as they watched NFL games during the 1997 season, he also couldn't help pointing out another NFL coach, one he had worked with for two years before coming to USC, when he was a scout for the Jets. "When Patriots games would come on during those Sundays, I'd point to Pete and tell Mike, 'I worked with this guy. He's so dynamic. He'd be great in college,'" says Gross.

At the end of the 1997 season, Garrett decided to fire Robinson. The process of doing so was messy and, many believed, disrespectful to the aging but once legendary USC coach. Garrett kept Robinson in limbo for three and a half weeks after the season and then, according to Robinson, merely left a message on his answering machine when he fired him. (Garrett says he tried to get Robinson on the phone many times and even spoke to his wife, who told him he was unavailable.)

Gross knew his boss was locked in on Hackett as Robinson's replacement, what with his Chiefs pedigree and ties to USC. But he decided to make a Hail Mary phone call anyway . . . to Carroll.

Carroll was just finishing his first season with the Patriots, the 10–6 campaign that would include a division title and a playoff win. "I actually offered Pete the job on the phone," says Gross. "I thought I'd take a shot. I told him one million a year." Gross says Carroll declined right away. "He told me, 'We're having success. Why would I walk away from this?'"

So Garrett hired Hackett, and Carroll stayed in New England. But Gross never passed up an opportunity to point out the New England head coach whenever an update on a Patriots game interrupted Garrett's viewing of a Chiefs game.

On paper, Hackett looked like a good hire—NFL pedigree, offensive guru—and his tenure started well in the 1998 season, with three straight wins and the emergence of a gifted true freshman quarterback named Carson Palmer, who split time early in the season before eventually earning the starting job. That first season ended with an 8–5 record, and a loss in the Sun Bowl. It would be Hackett's only winning season at USC.

Hackett brought a hard-nosed NFL approach to coaching the Trojans. During camp, he worked the team mercilessly, sometimes forcing them to endure three practices a day. He did not have much of a relationship with his players. Omar Nazel, a defensive end, says Hackett was "cold and professional." Running back Sunny Byrd says he saw Hackett one day when walking to class and excitedly called out to him. "But he didn't say anything back, just a slight nod and he kept walking."

Hackett also had a complex system for this offense. Too complex, according to center Norm Katnik. "We were just flopping around, either because the concepts were just too hard to coach well, or because we weren't being coached well enough," he says. Palmer suffered the most from the complexity. He was a natural athlete and an intuitive quarterback, but Hackett's playbook—several inches think—caused hesitation and overthinking on the field, which led to mistakes.

Hackett's second season started well again, with two victories and a number sixteen ranking in the country. But early in the third game against Oregon, Palmer broke his collarbone to end his season, and the team lost six of the next seven games and finished 6–6.

And then the wheels came off. Despite the return of Palmer and a bright 3–0 start, the 2000 season descended into misery with a five-game losing streak. The games at the Coliseum began to feel funereal, with less than half of the 92,000-seat stadium filled. Hackett attempted to save the season by changing things up and trying to become a rah-rah coach. "It just felt inauthentic," says David Newbury, a kicker. "There was one time he was trying to get everyone fired up and he punched a hole in the whiteboard. But we all knew that a graduate student had made the whiteboard weaker so he could punch all the way through it. It just wasn't who he was."

Hackett's players began to tune him out. He and his coaches appeared to reciprocate. "We'd be working out on the practice field with no supervision from the coaches," says Marcell Allmond, a cornerback. "Nobody was going to class. People were showing up to practice drunk. There was no discipline because no one was watching us."

And any concept of playing as a team flew out the window. "Guys were just focused on their own stats," says Nazel. "We tried in those first two seasons with Hackett. But in that last one, if we got down, we'd just give up. There was a real coldness on the team, no togetherness. We weren't teammates or friends."

Palmer had a miserable year, throwing for sixteen touchdowns but also eighteen interceptions, which tied a school record. The Trojans finished that season an abysmal second to last in the country in turnover ratio.

And yet USC beat rival UCLA, 38–35, in the second-to-last game of the season to bring their record to 5–6 and stave off the possibility of finishing with a losing record, which hadn't happened to USC since 1991, and had only happened four times in the previous four decades. The last game of the season was at home, against the Trojans' other rival, Notre Dame, which was ranked number eleven at the time. An upset win may have saved Hackett's job, at least for another year. But it was not to be—USC was beaten, 38–21, and they tied for last place in the PAC-10.

Hackett was fired by Garrett two days later.

The storied USC football program was no longer among the upper echelon in the country. In truth, it had been a long while— since the glory years of the 1960s and 1970s—since it had been. Yes, the program had nine national titles, but the last of those was won twenty-three years earlier. In the eighteen years since the end of Robinson's first stint as head coach, they hadn't come close to winning a national championship, finishing the season ranked in the top ten in only three of those seasons. They had only made a bowl game once in the last five years.

Other factors added to a general sense of degeneration. The area surrounding the USC campus, once prosperous, had declined severely and gained a reputation as a dangerous place, especially after the riots there in 1992.[1] There was an earthquake in the city in 1994. Later that same year, the school got unwanted attention when OJ Simpson, the former star USC running back, was arrested and charged with the murder of his ex-wife and another man, which was followed by his circus-like trial in 1995. More immediate and relevant to the program, the USC football practice facilities and locker room, and even the legendary Coliseum itself, were dilapidated and outdated.

In years past, when the team was winning, any and all of these things could be overlooked and overcome. But now, they just added to the lack of appeal. The USC head coaching job was no longer among the most prestigious in the country. Big-name coaches, like Notre Dame's Lou Holtz, declined to even be interviewed for it. The USC program had always relied on the vestiges of the glories of the past. But now it was hopelessly mired in the inglorious present.

And the pressure was on Garrett, the man who, in a way, represented the foundation of the last golden age, now more than two decades gone. His tenure as the athletic director had been mired in mediocrity, with the football team posting a 31–29 record in the previous five years. Home game attendance had become embarrassing—the *thwack* of punted balls reverberated off the empty seats in the old stadium during games. Garrett had ungracefully fired a fallen legend. He had then hired a man unfit for the program, hit rock bottom with a last place finish in the PAC-10, and then fired him, too. Another bad hire would have surely ended his career at USC. Garrett had one more shot. He was hoping the third coach was the charm.

————————

[1] The riots had been in response to the acquittal of the policemen who had been charged with assaulting and beating Rodney King.

The city of Los Angeles has long been a place of new ideas, a place with a sense of optimistic freedom. It is where the real and the fake intermingle, in the movies produced by Hollywood and the bodies produced by plastic surgery. It is a city in a desert, born from the imagination, made manifest by the redirection of river water. It is a place of transplants—even the city's palm trees aren't native—where people move to chase a dream, to free themselves from the puritanical shackles of the Northeast, the windswept, stunting normality of the Midwest, the lethargic, swampy caste system of the South.

It is a place of self-improvement and self-reinvention, two things Pete Carroll happened to have been working on during his year of exile from the game he loved.

Carroll had actually visited the USC campus a few times in 2000. His daughter, Jamie, played for USC's very good women's volleyball team, and he attended some of her games, sometimes tacking on an extra day to the trip to get in some surfing at Redondo.

Even though Gross had reached out to him in 1997, Carroll says he never considered USC as a possible place to coach, even as he visited Jamie. "I just didn't have that job in mind," he says. Hackett, he thought, would certainly get at least one more year. And the conventional wisdom was that, even if Hackett left, the school would not want another former NFL guy in the head spot.

But someone never forgot Carroll.

Mike Garrett says that during the coaching search after the 2000 season, though he talked to a few other coaches, he "only had one man in mind" and that any rumors to the contrary were just "reporters filling space" and that "we made moves to make it look like we were looking at others, but there was only one man we wanted." That man, he says, was Pete Carroll.

Well, maybe. What Garrett details may be a bit of revisionist history because according to Daryl Gross, the man who ran the search, Carroll wasn't the only coach USC considered. And he wasn't the first choice.

Media reports of the search painted a picture of a program in desperation. The school, reports said, talked to four or five coaches before finally finding someone who actually wanted the job. Dennis Erickson, a two-time national title–winning coach at Miami, a former NFL coach and, at the time, the coach at Oregon State, was one name. Mike Riley, a former Oregon State coach and, at the time, the head coach of the NFL's San Diego Chargers, was another. Mike Bellotti, the coach at Oregon at the time, and Sonny Lubick, then coach at Colorado State, were also mentioned.

All these men reportedly turned down the job.

But that wasn't the case, according to Gross.

"We branded the search and said we were looking for a proven college coach, that's true," says Gross. "Erickson fit that, of course. And he was our choice. And we offered him the job."

And Erickson took it, according to Gross, just a few days after Hackett was fired. But then, just a few days after that, Gross says he was leaving a USC men's basketball game at Anaheim Arena when he got a call in the parking lot. It was Erickson. "He said, 'Hey, Daryl, I can't take this job.' And I said, 'What do you mean? You've already taken it,'" says Gross. "And he told me he couldn't do it. He couldn't look his players in the eye. I talked to him for a long time. I was the last car in the parking lot when we finished. He was out."

Riley says he met with Gross and Garrett, and they wanted him to meet the USC president, to further along the process. "But I kinda said no," says Riley. "I was coaching the Chargers at the time, and I felt bad."

Gross says he spoke to Bellotti and Lubick on the phone. No one appeared to want to be the USC head coach. And an unnamed college coach had gone so far as to tell the *Los Angeles Times* that it was a "mediocre job."

About this time, Gross says, "I told Mike, 'We have to get Pete into the mix.'"

Carroll flew to Los Angeles a few days after Erickson declined the job, meeting Garrett and Gross at the LAX Marriott hotel. "I brought a whiteboard so Pete could talk with it and diagram stuff," says Gross. "I needed Mike to see and feel what I had seen with Pete at the Jets."

Carroll walked into the meeting wearing a sharp blue suit. He was prepared. He had learned to do interviews, he says, from the late basketball coach Jim Valvano, who had been at NC State when Carroll was on Kiffin's staff there. "He told me that I had things I believed in and knew best and could talk about best, and that no matter what someone asked me, I had to answer the questions the way I wanted to, with what I knew," says Carroll. "He told me that no one really cared what my answers were, they just wanted to see how I answered them and how I came across." Carroll had used that advice to get the jobs at the Jets and the Patriots. And he was about to use it again, for what was the most important interview of his career to date.

"I had spent a year getting my act together," Carroll says. "By the time I did that interview with Mike and Daryl, I was friggin' jacked, so excited about the stuff I had to share. It was all a blur. I don't even remember what they asked me. I just told them what I needed to tell them."

Garrett and Gross wanted a coach with a strong defensive background. "I played on offense, and I knew that side of the ball sold tickets," says Garrett. "But the old saying is true: defense wins championships." Gross says that back then, the PAC-10 lacked a defensive identity. "It seemed like defense didn't matter and whoever had the senior quarterback won the conference," he says.

In truth, the entirety of West Coast football was in a funk at the time. And the PAC-10 in particular was viewed as West Coast flaky, a conference that emphasized high-flying offenses and was allergic to defense. In the twenty-three years since USC's last national title, the West Coast had barely made an appearance on the national stage. BYU won what was considered a fluky title in 1984.[**] Colorado shared a title in 1990.[††] And Washington shared one in 1991.[‡‡] The left coast had produced only two Heisman winners since USC's Marcus Allen won the trophy in 1981.[§§] And that was it. USC was, in many ways, the lynchpin of West Coast college football. When it fell on hard times, so did the rest of the region, a reality that would be emphasized again in ten years' time.

In his interview, Carroll delivered on Garrett and Gross's hopes for a defensive mind, describing his own philosophy, which had worked in the NFL, and detailing how he would attack some of the better PAC-10 offenses, which he had scouted in preparation. "I'd done my homework," says Carroll.

"Pete was so energetic and dynamic, like a pied piper, and it was infectious," says Gross. As they walked out of the hours-long interview, Garrett turned to Gross and said, "Damn, I get it now."

Garett and Gross asked Carroll to accompany them to campus so he could tour the football facilities at Heritage Hall. They

---

[**] BYU was undefeated but did not play a team that season that ended up in the top twenty-five.

[††] With Georgia Tech.

[‡‡] With Miami.

[§§] BYU's Ty Detmer in 1990 and Colorado's Rashaan Salaam in 1994.

waited until off hours, trying to be stealthy, so that no players, students, or members of the media would see him. "We get him in there and just as we're walking up the stairs we pass [defensive back] Darrell Rideaux and he gives me a look like, 'Oh, I see what's going on here,'" says Gross.

Rideaux wasn't the only person to see Carroll on that trip. Katnik, the center, and his fellow offensive lineman Lenny Vandermade were at the facility that day. "We were just hanging out," says Katnik. "Lenny was playing the piano when he saw Garrett walking with this guy through the basement of Heritage Hall. I didn't recognize the guy, but he came over and said hello. He was nice, very personable. Then he left and Lenny says, 'Do you know who that was?' I had no idea. And he says, 'That was Pete Carroll.'"

Another person saw him the next day. Haruki "Rocky" Seto had walked onto the USC football team as a college transfer in 1997 under Robinson.[¶] He played for Hackett for a year and then became a graduate assistant and an administrative assistant on his staff. "I was pretty down at the time," says Seto. "I thought I was getting fired with Hackett." His girlfriend convinced him to go watch a USC women's volleyball game to try to lift his spirits. "We get there, and Pete Carroll was sitting right behind me," says Seto. He was there to watch Jamie play in the NCAA Regionals. "I thought, 'Well, maybe he's a candidate?'" says Seto. "So I introduced myself and told him that I'd been on Hackett's staff."

A week later, Seto would meet Carroll again.

After the interview and Jamie's game, Carroll stayed in Los Angeles for a bit, watching some high school football games and hanging out at the beach, surfing and swimming. He was on the beach

---

[¶] His parents named him after the boxing great Rocky Marciano.

when he received the call from Garrett and Gross officially offering him the job. He accepted and flew home to Massachusetts for a few days.

Garrett and Gross were cognizant that some fans, alumni, and members of the media would not view the hiring in a positive light because of Carroll's lack of recent college experience and the lack of success he'd had at his most recent coaching stops. Garrett waited a few days before calling the introductory press conference, so he could prepare. And when he finally called it, he scheduled it on December 15, 2000, a Friday, a day of the week often used to dump unpleasant or controversial news that the dumper hopes will be dissipated by the distractions of the upcoming weekend. "I knew there would be hell to pay," says Garrett.

He wasn't prepared for how much hell.

Rocky Seto was sitting in his apartment that Friday when he got a call from a USC associate athletic director named Steve Lopes. "I need you to come with me to the airport," Lopes told him. They drove out to LAX in Lopes's Ford Explorer. "When we got there, I got out and there was Coach Carroll," says Seto. "He reached out to shake my hand and said, 'Good to see you again.' I was like, 'Wow, he has a great memory.'"

Carroll got into the Explorer with Lopes for the ride back to campus. Seto's job was to drive Carroll's rental car—an orange Pontiac Firebird—and follow them. All went well until they reached the athletic department's parking lot at USC. "There's an arm there at the entrance of the lot," says Seto. "And Steve only had one card. So he and Coach Carroll go in and I try to follow them closely, to sneak in with them. But the arm comes down on the hood of the Firebird. And I get out and manually push it up. I really wanted to keep working for the football team. And now I'm thinking, 'That's it. I'm not getting hired.'"

Carroll's introductory conference was in Heritage Hall, where the university's then-four Heisman Trophies were prominently displayed. Everyone gathered in a small conference room known as the Varsity Lounge. "Just a ton of media there," says Tim Tessalone, who was USC's sports information director at the time. Some security guards were there as well, a precaution taken because of the expected negative reaction.

Before the press conference, Garrett had taken Carroll aside and warned him, "I don't think they're going to like this." As a preemptive measure, the school had hired a public relations firm to speak to reporters beforehand about Carroll's virtues as a coach. Carroll says he wasn't worried. "My mentality was that I wouldn't be bothered by what everyone else thought."

Carroll jumped up to the front of the room. He smiled. And then he went off, gushing enthusiasm, speaking so quickly that he occasionally stuttered, leaving some members of the media wondering if he was mental. "I've been an unpopular choice at many places," he said. "It's a challenge. I would say to [Garrett] and [USC president Steve Sample] that I'm going to prove them right."

As he walked out of the conference, he stopped to introduce himself to the reporters, smiling, shaking hands, clapping backs. And then he went upstairs to his office.

Most media members left then, but some milled around the room for a bit. "I was standing near the door, near the exit, with Daryl," says Tessalone. T. J. Simers, the famously acidic sports columnist for the *Los Angeles Times*, walked to the exit and stopped. "Simers looked at us and said, 'We'll see you back here next year, same place, same time.'"***

***"T. J. has nine toes over the line," John Carroll, Simers's editor at the *Los Angeles Times*, once said. "And it's our job to keep him from using that last toe."

That was only the beginning. Whatever small amount of good-will and patience Garrett had after firing two coaches in four years instantly vanished when it was announced that he'd brought in a mediocre NFL coach who hadn't even coached at the collegiate level in seventeen years. Significant alumni were less than enthused. "I wasn't super bullish," says David Bahnsen, a longtime booster. Brian Kennedy, a Los Angeles promoter for whom the football practice field was named, says, "All I knew about him was that he had not done well in the NFL and was out of a job."

Immediately, two decades' worth of pent-up anger was unleashed on USC's athletic department. Gary Foster, a Hollywood producer and USC alum, told Gross to stay away from the sports blogs. Jim Hardy, a legendary USC quarterback from the 1940s, wrote Garrett a scathing letter suggesting that he should have hired Sonny Lubick instead. The offices at the athletic department were flooded with outraged calls, emails, and faxes, close to 3,000 by one estimate—one of the fax machines broke from overuse. Garrett was defiant. "The backlash from the alums and fans told me the hiring was perfect because they didn't know shit from Shinola," he says.

Splashed across the *Los Angeles Times* sports page the day after the press conference was the headline "For Pete's Sake, USC, Why Did You Do It?" The article was written by the influential sports columnist Bill Plaschke. Within the piece, he joined his brethren in New York and Boston, poking fun of Carroll for dribbling basketballs in the football offices. He questioned why USC officials would hire "somebody non-traditional to lead a tradition" and asked if they "forgot this was college football." He ended the piece with this: "I'm not mad at a guy for being in a position where the players are uncertain, and the fans are angry, and administration is worried. I'm mad at USC for putting him there."

Letters also flooded the news desk of the paper. One in particular seemed to sum up the collective sentiment perfectly:

Mike Garrett, what was it about Pete Carroll that made you want to hire him for the head coaching job? Was it his lifetime record of two games over .500? His complete lack of recruiting ties to the West Coast? His limited college coaching experience? His reputation for being soft on players and not a good motivator? You must like those qualities in your coaches, Mike, you hired Paul Hackett, after all. . . . The only bright side to this story is that it's only 1,095 days from today until you and Carroll probably are both out of a job. Until then, it's more misery as another NFL retread realizes he doesn't understand the college game or its players while learning on the job.

Even the former coach of the program believed Carroll stood no chance. In the head coach's office in Heritage Hall, Hackett reportedly left Carroll a written list of twenty reasons why he couldn't win at USC.

If it felt like an extremely desperate situation, it's because it was. Desperate for USC, and for Garrett, the old running back possibly facing a three-and-out.

But the most intense and important desperation was that of the new head coach. Carroll was damaged goods. He'd been run over and run out of town twice. His philosophy didn't seem to work. He was a failure as a head coach. Carroll was not the savior riding into the City of Angels on a white horse. He was a man, dusty and bruised, running to catch up to the white horse that had bucked him, as the jeering crowds who gathered along the road all told him to go home.

If Carroll failed here, he was likely looking at a lifetime as a coordinator, something that fit some men, like his mentor, Monte Kiffin. But it didn't fit Carroll. He'd gotten a taste of being the leader, calling the shots, garnering the attention. He craved it. He believed he had the tools to succeed, even though those tools were outside of the mainstream. He believed being a head coach was what he'd been born to do.

What he needed to succeed was to complete what seemed to be the impossible trifecta—to be the right man in the right place at the right time.

The obvious question was: Could Carroll save USC?

The other, perhaps more pertinent question: Could USC save Carroll?

CHAPTER FOUR

O Come All Ye Faithful

November 26, 2000

The day after Paul Hackett's USC Trojans lost embarrassingly at home to their rival, Notre Dame, 38–21, their defensive line coach, Ed Orgeron, was at home. He was thirty-nine years old, already well into the itinerate life of an up-and-coming assistant football coach. The USC job was his seventh. He was hardened, accustomed to tuning out any noise above his paygrade. He was going on a recruiting trip the next day and had his list of targeted players, guys he thought—no, *knew*—would help Hackett turn around the sleeping giant that was USC. It was then that he got a phone call.

"Hey, man, what are you doing?" It was Hue Jackson, USC's thirty-five-year-old offensive coordinator.

"I'm getting ready to go on the road recruiting."

"No, you're not."

"What happened?"

"We're having a meeting with Mike Garrett at seven."

"What's wrong?"

"We're getting fired, you dumbass."

Orgeron has a wide face, substantial, as if made from granite. He himself is a substantial man, his six-foot-two, 240-pound, large and powerful body nearly equal in size to those of the defensive linemen he coached. His voice sounds like that of a man who had gargled Tabasco sauce since birth and then, at some point, swallowed a bullfrog, low and guttural and to some, indecipherable. He is from a small parish south of New Orleans, the bayou. He is of Cajun descent. He shoveled shrimp on the boats in the summers. He played football and received a scholarship from Louisiana State University but lasted only a few weeks there because of homesickness, though Baton Rouge was only one hundred miles away from his parents. He went home and shoveled more shrimp for a year and then enrolled in Northwestern State in Natchitoches and played football for four years. His coaching career began there, the year after he graduated. Three stops later, he was the defensive line coach at the University of Miami under Jimmy Johnson and then Dennis Erickson. He was part of two national title–winning teams and coached star defensive linemen including Warren Sapp, Russell Maryland, and Cortez Kennedy.

Orgeron seemed destined for bigger things, perhaps next a job as a defensive coordinator and then, eventually, a head coach. Some personal demons had held him back a bit, though. In 1991, while at Miami, he had a restraining order filed against him by a woman. A year later, he was arrested for allegedly head-butting a bouncer during a bar fight. Both the restraining order and the charges were eventually dropped, but he took a leave of absence from Miami and never returned. He went home, back to the bayou, got some help and got his life back in order. After a year out of the game, a volunteer job at Nicholls State led to a three-year gig as an assistant at Syracuse. And then, in 1998, Hackett, the incoming USC coach, hired him to coach his defensive line. And now, that job seemed over. Orgeron wasn't sure what to do.

He reached out to the prominent booster Brian Kennedy. "I told Ed to work through his contract, which ran through January 2001," says Kennedy. He also talked to Gross. "I told Ed, 'Just keep recruiting, brother, and when the new staff comes in, I'm going to make sure they interview you,'" Gross says. "We had to have someone out there to salvage whatever we could from that recruiting class."

So, with nothing else to do, Orgeron did one of the things he did best: he went recruiting.

Nearly two weeks later, on the early evening of December 9, 2000, Orgeron was at Citrus College in Glendora, twenty-five miles east of Los Angeles, to watch the Division VII high school championship game, Los Altos versus Charter Oak. There was a player on Los Altos that Orgeron had fallen in love with, an absurdly athletic six-foot-five, 255-pound defensive tackle named Shaun Cody, who had a combined fifty-seven sacks in his final two years of high school.

Orgeron spotted Cody's family in the stands. Cody's father, who went by Big Mike, was an Irishman and a big fan of Notre Dame. In fact, there was a Notre Dame coach currently sitting to his left. And on his right, a coach from UCLA. Cody's mother and grandmother saw Orgeron and greeted him with big hugs. They loved him. Big Mike? Not so much. Orgeron walked over to shake Big Mike's hand, but the Irishman blew him off as the Notre Dame and UCLA coaches who flanked him broke into laughter.

Orgeron told Big Mike that he was going to remain a coach at USC and that he would coach his son, and then he turned and walked away.

In truth, Orgeron had no idea what his future held. He left the game at halftime and missed Cody being installed on the offense as a fullback and scoring two touchdowns, the last of which won the state championship with thirty-two seconds left in the game.

Orgeron headed home to Aliso Viejo down state route 57, disheartened and done with this recruiting trip and done with his recruiting for USC for good. And then he got a call from a friend, Barry Sher, who coached at Los Alamitos High School. Sher told him to come to the Division I championship game. It was a banger, a tight one between Long Beach Poly and Loyola. Orgeron knew many of the Poly players well and the game was right on his way home.

So he went. It was 10:30 at night when he walked in. Twelve thousand fans. Game in overtime. He then spotted a familiar face on the sidelines. It was Pete Carroll. They had met once before, briefly.

Carroll walked over.

"Hey, Coach, what are you doing here?" Carroll asked.

"I'm recruiting," replied Orgeron, though he had, an hour before, actually stopped recruiting and pretty much given up hope.

"Who are you recruiting for?"

"USC."

Carroll smiled and pointed to the field.

"You know those guys out there?"

Orgeron nodded. "Yeah, there's Darnell Bing. There's Hershel Dennis. Winston Justice . . . wait, what are you doing here?"

"I'm getting hired by USC next week."

There were reasons to believe Carroll could succeed at USC, easier to see now in hindsight, of course. The college game fit his youthful personality well and, with its captive audience of young players who were more suggestible than the pros, it served as a good training ground to test his philosophy.

Football games are defined, somewhat, by *when* they are played. High school games are associated with Friday nights, a time of liberation and release at the end of the school week. The NFL plays most of its games on Sundays, that day of the blues, the scaries that come with the knowledge that Monday morning and work and responsibility beckon with a cold finger.

College games, though, are played on Saturdays, that more optimistic day of the weekend, with its promise of carefree fun and the built-in cushion of a recovery day to follow. The brassy bands, the alumni returning to a place where they'd spent perhaps the happiest time in their lives, the youthful exuberance of the students in the stands, the veneer of innocence and purity of the student-athletes on the field and the promise they held all played into the feeling of a college game and was perhaps the reason that the fourteen largest stadiums in the US are found on college campuses.

That optimism fit Carroll well.

There was also the factor of Los Angeles itself. It was college football's unrealized mother lode at the time. The city contained, and was surrounded by, some of the best high school football talent in the country. Los Angeles was, objectively, a fun, beautiful, and electric place. The sun and weather. Hollywood and the celebrities. The music scene. The club scene. The beach. The bikinis. There were no professional football teams to compete for attention—the Rams and Raiders had left six years before Carroll took over USC. The city's other professional sports teams were in or very near downcycles—Wayne Gretzky had left the NHL's Kings during the 1996 season. The Dodgers made the playoffs but never really threatened to make the World Series. The Angels did win a World Series during the Carroll USC era, but they always played second fiddle to the Dodgers and were in the midst of an identity crisis.* The NBA's Clippers were perennially one of the worst teams in sports. Even the glitzy Lakers, who did win titles during Carroll's USC reign, ran into a bit of a lull around that time. In 2003, star player Kobe Bryant was caught up in an

---

* They were the California Angels and then the Anaheim Angels and then the Los Angeles Angels of Anaheim and now are the Los Angeles Angels.

icky scandal for alleged rape and his fellow star Shaquille O'Neal left the team a year later.

The sports fans of the city were notoriously fickle and fair-weather. LA was an attention economy, and there was a lot more to do there than root for a losing football program. But the city loved nothing more than a winner.

In other words, there was a vacuum in Los Angeles sports at the time. And Carroll would fill it.

The first thing a new coach at a program must do, of course, is deal with the staff of his predecessor. Carroll got right on it, asking for all of Hackett's assistants to meet him in the staff room directly after his introductory press conference.

It so happened that on that morning, Orgeron was at Los Altos, still courting Shaun Cody. While there, he had called Carroll and put Cody on the phone. The high schooler and coach talked briefly, and then Cody handed the phone back to Orgeron.

"Eddie, I forgot to tell you about the meeting after the press conference," Carroll said. "Can you be there?"

Orgeron said yes, but he wouldn't have time to go home and change.

The gaggle of Hackett assistants filed into the staff room. None of them, save for Orgeron, had been really working for the last two weeks, since Hackett had been fired. And all of them, save for Orgeron, were dressed up as if they were doing a job interview, coats and some ties. Orgeron still had on his USC hat and golf polo.

Orgeron took a seat in the back of the room. Carroll gave a brief speech, ending with this: "Guys, I know there are some good coaches in this room but, look, I'm just going to start with a clean slate, okay? I'm not hiring anybody."

Orgeron's jaw went slack. He'd been sure that he was going to be on the new staff—he'd been communicating with Carroll regularly and, for God's sake, had just put the coach on the phone with one of the biggest recruits in the country that very morning. *Are you kidding me?*

Because of where he was sitting in the room, Orgeron was the last man to get to the door to leave. And just as he was about to walk by Carroll and out of the door and out of the USC program, Carroll stopped him. "Oh, except for you, Eddie," he said. "Let's get to work."

When it came to filling out the rest of his staff, Carroll opted for the familiar, those with deep ties to the college game who would help fill in for his lack of recent experience in the game, and two young, unproven kids, one of whom he used to babysit.

DeWayne Walker was Carroll's first hire, as the secondary coach. He had been the defensive backs coach under Carroll at New England and had ten years of college experience. Nick Holt, who had played at Pacific when Carroll coached there and had fifteen years of experience in college, was hired to coach the linebackers. Wayne Moses, a running backs coach, had spent twenty-two years in the college game, including a year on Monte Kiffin's NC State staff when Carroll was there. Kirby Wilson had extensive experience at the collegiate level and in the pros as a receivers coach. Carroll kept Rocky Seto on as a graduate assistant, even though he had run his rental car into a parking lot boom gate. And Carroll would be his own defensive coordinator.

But Carroll's splashiest hire, by some margin, was a man who appeared to be his antipode—reserved, introverted, maybe a bit uptight, and a renowned genius of the opposite side of Carroll's football expertise: the offense.

Norm Chow grew up in Hawaii. His paternal grandfather was from China. His mother was Hawaiian. He attended the University of Utah and played football there, making all-conference as a guard, though he now claims, "I wasn't very good." He played a bit in the Canadian Football League, spent some time in the Navy during Vietnam, and then returned to the University of Utah to get a master's degree in special education. And then he went looking for a job in a sport that he may not have played at a high level but loved, nonetheless.

In 1973, Chow was hired as a part-time graduate assistant at Brigham Young University under head coach LaVell Edwards, who, during his twenty-nine-year stint at BYU, gained fame as an offensive innovator. But it was another BYU staff member—offensive coordinator Doug Scovil—who Chow says was "LaVell's secret." Scovil, Chow says, was the first coach to split the running backs in the backfield, which allowed for flexibility: in that formation, a running back could either get the ball on a draw play or check the protection and go out for a pass. "It was the precursor to the empty set [no running backs in the backfield] that we have now," says Chow. "I still have the notebooks where I wrote down everything Doug said."

Chow eventually worked his way up to coaching the receivers and quarterbacks. He began to make his own name in the latter position. He first tutored Marc Wilson, who went on to a ten-year NFL career. Wilson was followed by Jim McMahon, who set thirty-two NCAA passing records, including ones for yards and touchdowns. And then came Steve Young, who, in 1983, completed more than 70 percent of his passes and led an offense that *averaged* 584 yards a game. Robbie Bosco quarterbacked BYU to its only national title in 1984. Six years after that, Chow coached Ty Detmer, who won the Heisman Trophy.

In 1996, Chow was elevated to offensive coordinator. That year, a little-known junior college transfer named Steve Sarkisian threw for 4,321 yards and thirty-five touchdowns while leading BYU to a 14–1 record. During his time at BYU, Chow coached with fellow offensive wunderkinds Mike Holmgren, Andy Reid, and Brian Billick.

After the 1999 season, when it became clear that Chow was not the BYU administration's choice to replace a soon-to-be-retiring Edwards, he left to become the offensive coordinator at NC State under Chuck Amato. There, he inherited a freshman quarterback named Philip Rivers who had a javelin-throwing passing motion. In his one season under Chow, Rivers threw for 3,054 yards and twenty-five touchdowns.[†]

In December 2000, Chow received his first phone call from Carroll. The two had never met, but Carroll wanted him to become his new offensive coordinator. But Chow was comfortable at NC State and liked what he had in Rivers. "I turned down Pete a couple of times," he says.

But Carroll seemed almost desperate to hire Chow, a sign of how badly he wanted—and needed—to win at USC right away. So he turned to DeWayne Walker, who had coached with Chow at BYU, to work on the offensive coach.[‡] "DeWayne said 'Get on a flight,'" says Chow. To further entice Chow, Carroll had received permission from USC to take the money he would theoretically be slated to make as the defensive coordinator and add it to Chow's salary.

Chow finally relented and flew to Los Angeles. Carroll hired him right away. "He is arguably the best offensive coordinator in

---

[†] Rivers went on to break nearly every NC State passing record and had a very productive seventeen-year career in the NFL. While still at NC State, he remained close to Chow and would check in with him on a weekly basis and often send him tape to review.

[‡] Walker was the first Black coach in BYU's history.

the history of college football, certainly in terms of championships and wins and people he has coached," Carroll said when he
announced Chow's hiring. His high opinion of his new assistant
coach would change over time, though.

Carroll allowed Chow to hire some coaches for his staff. He
brought in Keith Uperesa, who had played under him at BYU, to
coach the offensive line. And he hired one of his former quarterbacks at BYU who had a quick and creative mind—Steve Sarkisian, who was twenty-six and had been selling computer cubicles
at the time. Chow urged Carroll to keep Kennedy Pola, who had
coached the running backs under Hackett and happened to be
the uncle of USC's defensive star, safety Troy Polamalu.[5] Carroll
did, and moved him to special teams until 2002, when he retook
his job as the running backs coach.

With the offensive staff nearly complete, Carroll then asked
Chow for a favor. "He wanted me to interview Lane, the son of
Monte Kiffin, [the coach] who had taken care of Pete," says Chow.
And so "the Helicopter"—short blond hair, baby face, sardonic
grin—was hired by USC at the age of twenty-five. The good news
was that he was part of a quasi-package deal. His father would
hang around the Trojans quite a bit over the years—a sounding
board for the head coach who sometimes sat in the booth during
games and conferred with Carroll at halftime.

Sarkisian and Kiffin, the young guns in their first real jobs in
football, started their coaching journey at USC in the summer as
assistants to Chris Carlisle, the strength and conditioning coach

---

[5] Kennedy Polamalu's family shortened their surname to "Pola" when they arrived in the US from American Samoa in the 1970s, and he used that last
name while at USC. In 2011, he legally changed his name back to Polamalu.
I will use "Pola" because of the time period, and to differentiate him from his
nephew.

who Carroll had hired away from Tennessee. That arrangement, according to Carlisle, lasted all of one day, a day in which they apparently spent their time sitting around and talking to the players, who weren't much younger than they were. "The next day I said, 'Why don't you go upstairs, and I'll call you if I need you,'" Carlisle told ESPN. "One day was enough."

Kiffin would end up coaching the tight ends, and Sarkisian—his tightly cropped black hair, steely eyes, and cocksure walk the remnants of his playing career—the quarterbacks. They carpooled to and from work together, so they could use the high-occupancy vehicle lane and get to work faster, an apt metaphor for their coaching trajectories.

Player-wise, Hackett had not left the cupboard completely bare. In fact, he had recruited two players who would become verifiable stars—Palmer at quarterback and Polamalu at safety—and others who would have good-to-great collegiate careers, like Keary Colbert (wide receiver), Jacob Rogers (offensive tackle), Alex Holmes (tight end), and Kris Richard (cornerback).

But there were some massive gaps, most notably on the lines. "During the first practice, I turned to Pete and said, 'Um, where are the offensive linemen?'" says Chow.

The 2001 recruiting class was unlikely to fill too many of the holes. With the downturn in the program, the coaching change, the skepticism of the Carroll hire, and the gap of two weeks or so when only Orgeron was recruiting, the class had little shot at being great or even very good. But Carroll saw a way in which it could, at the very least, offer something else, a blueprint for the ones to come.

With Orgeron as the director of recruiting and Pola playing a role in designing the recruiting methods the coaches would use, Carroll laid out a very basic idea: They needed to lockdown the state of California. Specifically, Southern California. It was by no means a novel idea—Barry Switzer, while coaching at Oklahoma, once quipped that a USC football coach "drives by more Division I football players than we've got in the whole state"—but it was something Hackett and his immediate predecessors had failed to do.

Carroll recruited, well, like his job depended on it. He and Orgeron went to nearly a dozen schools on some days, sometimes not even stopping to eat.

Carroll would eventually make good on his effort to dominate recruiting in the state. During his nine years at USC, nearly three-quarters of the prospects signed by USC were from California. Forty of them were rated in the top ten nationally. Four of them were named the state's best high school player.

But he'd have to endure a learning curve early on.

Carroll did not lack for energy and enthusiasm but because he'd been out of the college game for seventeen years, he still had some work to do on the finer points of the recruiting trade. Pola recounted a story to the *Los Angeles Times* about Carroll's first in-home visit to a recruit, a tight end named Joe Toledo who lived in Carlsbad. In the car on the way there, Pola offered to coach up Carroll on how to recruit college kids. Carroll blew him off, telling Pola that if he could deal with the media in New York and Boston, he could surely handle the parents of a high school recruit.

They went into Toledo's house, and "we just got our ass kicked," Pola said. Toledo's parents had asked about safety at USC and its surrounding area. Carroll stumbled around, never providing a suitable answer. He and Pola left. Toledo committed to Washington.

Afterward, Carroll asked to meet Pola in a coffee shop. He'd swallowed his pride. "Okay, what do I need to know?" he asked.

"You had the answer if you had just listened," Pola replied.

"What was my answer?"

"Your daughter goes to school there."

One Southern California recruit in the 2001 class is viewed as the cornerstone of Carroll-era recruiting at USC, the one who enabled everything else that followed to happen. That recruit: Shaun Cody, the player who Orgeron had never given up on even though he seemed like an impossible dream.

Cody was a high school All-American five-star recruit considered to be the best defensive tackle prospect and the fifth-best prospect overall nationally in the 2001 recruiting season. USC was far from his only suitor: he was coveted by UCLA, Ohio State, Miami, Washington, and, of course, Notre Dame, where his father, Big Mike, was pushing hard for his son to play and where he nearly signed during his recruiting trip and where all the recruiting agencies and experts expected him *to* sign. But Orgeron soldiered on. And now he had a secret weapon to deploy.

Carroll's first contact with Cody was the brief phone call he'd had with him on the day of his introductory press conference. His second came a few days later, when Carroll made the twenty-mile drive from USC to Los Altos High School. Cody was impressed by Carroll's high spirit. He liked his NFL pedigree. And he loved Carroll's vision for an aggressive and attacking pro-style defense, with him right in the middle of it.

Cody was still not totally sold, though. He went to a high school All-American game and floated the idea of not going to Notre Dame and choosing USC instead to some of his teammates there. They looked at him like he was certifiable.

On the night before National Signing Day, Cody called his family together. He also asked for the family's priest to be in attendance, which led Big Mike, the Irish Catholic, to believe his prayers had been answered. But Cody told them that he was signing with USC. He spent most of the rest of the night rationalizing the decision to his father.

The Cody signing was a significant one from an on-the-field standpoint—Cody would become a starter five games into his freshman season, the beginning of an excellent college career that would end up with him becoming a team captain, an All-American, and the PAC-10 defensive player of the year.

But the symbolism of the Cody signing had an even bigger impact. At the time, the USC football program was diminished and couldn't even lock down their own city in recruiting. Carroll was viewed as a retread. Notre Dame was . . . Notre Dame. Being able to sign a recruit like Cody signaled a change. "He gave us some notoriety, and we pumped it up as much as we could," says Carroll.

There were two other important recruits in that 2001 class. One was Mike Patterson, a stubby defensive lineman from Los Alamitos (where Orgeron's friend Barry Sher coached). Patterson was not a highly sought-after recruit, mainly due to his height, which, at six feet, was considered short for a defensive lineman. Oregon and Colorado State had shown mild interest, but that was about it. USC was late to recruiting Patterson, but Orgeron fell for him, and had to spend days trying to talk Carroll into him before his head coach finally relented. Patterson would start his final three seasons at USC, never missing a snap, an anchor on the defensive line that would become the foundation of USC's defensive success.

And then there was a quarterback who had won the Gatorade Player of the Year award in California at Mater Dei High School in Santa Ana. He had initially been recruited by Hackett and considered committing to Oklahoma after the coach was fired. But Carroll had wooed him back.

That quarterback was a kid named Matt Leinart.

CHAPTER FIVE

Turnover

March 20, 2001

In Carroll's initial meeting with the full team, the first thing he did was to hold up a football, that prolate sphere that can create legends, break hearts, and bounce any which way *and* loose.

"Fellas," he said. "It's all about the ball."

Carroll knew turnovers are often the single biggest determinant factor in the football game, that the team that wins the turnover margin wins the game close to 70 percent of the time. This wasn't some secret—every coach and player and fan was privy to this information. But Carroll also knew the team he'd inherited finished the previous season with the second-to-worst turnover ratio in the nation. So his first and most simple goal for his new team: minimize giveaways and maximize takeaways.

He then told the team that "competition" would be at the core of everything. He announced that beginning with the first practice, there were no starters. Every position was up for grabs and had to be earned, no matter who the player was. (This was not entirely true—Palmer and Polamalu would not be fighting for their places on the field.)

Carroll outlined how every week of practice would be handled, with a theme for each day, something he'd worked on during his year away:

- "Tell the Truth" Monday: A day for reviewing film and for reckoning and responsibility for both mistakes and things that went well in the previous weekend's game.
- "Competition" Tuesday: A day for emphasizing competition between players, position groups, and the offense and defense.
- "Turnover" Wednesday: "It's all about the ball."
- "No Repeat" Thursday: A day when the game plan is gone over with the idea that it would be learned and run so well that there would be no need to do anything more than once.
- "Review" Friday: One last look at the game plan and day when any issues were addressed and any wrinkles ironed out.

And then Carroll laid out the three rules he had devised:

- Always protect the team.
- No whining, complaining, or excuses.
- Be early.

After the meeting, Carroll ran his first practice. It was relatively mellow—some conditioning drills and light running. When it was over, he gathered the players together and told them, "See you tonight at ten in the Coliseum."

In truth, Carroll admits now, he had no idea what he was going to do with the team that night at the Coliseum. But he knew he wanted to use the stadium in some way. It was a magical place filled with history, backdropped by the San Gabriels, and modeled after the great arenas of antiquity.* It had hosted the 1932 and 1984 Summer Olympic Games.† The Dodgers played there when they won the 1959 World Series. It had hosted two Super Bowls. Martin Luther King Jr. had given a speech there. John F. Kennedy had accepted the nomination as the Democratic Party's nominee on the field. Over the years, it grew weathered and slightly dilapidated in a way that gave it gravitas.

Carroll knew that there had been friction on the team before he got there. "The defense used to hate the offense under Hackett," says Omar Nazel, the defensive end who played under both coaches. "They never put up enough points." That knowledge gave Carroll an idea, as he recounted in his book. He went to a firehouse a few blocks from Heritage Hall and asked to borrow a large rope.

Carroll showed up at the Coliseum early. It was dark and empty, a bit spectral and unearthly. He laid down the rope at the fifty-yard line and waited. He wasn't totally sure if anyone was going to show up. But then he heard his players—just their cleats clacking on the concrete floor of the entrance to the field. It was a little before ten. They'd already adhered to one of his team rules.

Carroll gathered them around and asked Palmer to name his best eleven on offense and Polamalu to do the same on defense. And then he had the two sides play a game of tug-of-war. The sides each pulled, giving some ground and then taking it back. It was, for all intents and purposes, a stalemate. Carroll then abruptly stopped them and asked what they learned. No one said a word. He then told them that if they pulled against each other, they would never get anywhere. But if they pulled together, they would.

---

* The entrance of the Coliseum is flanked with actual stones from the Colosseum in Rome and the Altis Olympia in Greece.
† And will play a role in the 2028 Summer Olympics.

He then had the players stand shoulder to shoulder and back to back at the fifty, looking out at the stands, like the actual Trojans set to protect Troy.

"We are defending this stadium," he said. "This is our home. No one comes in here and beats us." He told the team that if they were really committed and ready to turn the program around, he wanted each of them, individually, to either come to his office or drop him a note and tell him "I'm in."

It was a moment that even Wooden may have found a bit corny and, indeed, afterward some of the players rolled their eyes at the entire evening. It was also the type of gesture that, had things gone sideways for Carroll at USC, would have been added to the list of seemingly unserious stunts that the players' coach pulled that didn't work. But history is written by the victors, as they say, and as the wins and conference and national titles piled up during the Carroll era, the evening became part of the team's lore, and players, like Polamalu, would later recount it with reverence. As Wooden wrote about supposedly naïve and corny gestures, "Think a moment about what they mean and who you become if you abide by them."

All the players eventually did tell Carroll "I'm in." He would later put the two words on top of the gate that led to the practice field.

Carroll was different. That much was for sure. And most of the players—especially those who had been under the stoical Hackett—allowed themselves a bit of belief. And why not? They wanted to succeed, too. "It started to seem then like he might be the immediate shift we needed," says Alex Holmes, a tight end who had played under Hackett.

"We wanted to be good. We wanted to win," says Palmer. "But we just didn't know how. And Pete had a plan."

———

Carroll says now that he didn't consciously do anything different from Hackett. But things indeed did change, quickly and rather dramatically.

Carroll's first conditioning drill was a double-elimination, three-on-three basketball tournament. He evened out the teams among the players as best he could. The winner of the tournament played a team of coaches—Carroll, Kiffin, and Sarkisian. The two young coaches were good athletes—both were former college quarterbacks—and Carroll was a deadly shooter. "It was fun and kind of tore down the wall between the players and the coaches," says David Newbury, the placekicker on the 2001 team. "The coaches were out there showing us their athleticism and competitiveness. And it was like, 'Things were going to be a little different around here.'"

While there wasn't much Carroll could do about USC's notoriously subpar facilities, he did set out to update and modernize the football offices at Heritage Hall. For decades, USC coaches had paraded recruits through the foyer of the building, where the trophies of the school's four Heisman winners were prominently displayed. Carroll believed this made the place feel like a museum and served as a reminder of the program's recent mediocrity, especially since the most recent Heisman—Marcus Allen's—was won all the way back in 1981. Even the coaches' offices on the second floor were stale and joyless—and beat-up. Chow says that when he first moved into his office, "All of the drawers were busted." Carroll got new office furniture and, more important, changed the decor. He sent Trojan gear to every USC player in the NFL, got them to send back pictures of themselves wearing it, framed those pictures, and displayed them in offices. He also framed their NFL jerseys and hung them in the hallways, which gave the offices a less corporate and more vibrant feel. And the message they conveyed was simple, to the current players and to recruits: this program is a pathway to the next level.

Before his first game as the USC coach—against lightly regarded San Jose State—Carroll switched up a few other things. The team changed hotels, from the Biltmore in downtown Los Angeles to the Marriott. It had been a tradition for years for the team to go to Paramount Studios the night before a game to watch a movie together. But Carroll put an end to that, allowing players to watch whatever they wanted in their hotel rooms and saving them from sitting, sometimes for hours, in Los Angeles traffic going to and from the studio. And instead of having the team make the fifteen-minute walk from Heritage Hall to the Coliseum, or busing them straight to the locker room, he had the buses drop them off at the plaza at the entrance to the stadium. There, the students and fans gathered and made a pathway for the players, cheered them on, and gave them high-fives as they walked to the Coliseum. "That walk was awesome," says Newbury. "It definitely energized you." It quickly caught on and has been known since then as the "Trojan Walk."

On the evening before the first game, Carroll stepped out of a conference room where a defensive meeting was taking place. He wanted to clear his head. He wandered into the lobby and ran into Chow, who was sitting in a chair, going over his game plan notes.

Carroll walked over to him.

"They're just kids," he said.

Chow looked up, saying nothing, unsure of where Carroll was going with this.

"They have no idea how important these games are," Carroll continued. "They're just playing. They don't know what winning means, for the university, the administration, and the coaches who have everything riding on it. It's so vitally important."

Chow remained quiet. Carroll wandered back into the meeting. He likely knew, somewhere not even that deep down, that he was really talking about himself.

September 1, 2001

Sunny, high seventies. In the Coliseum, 45,500 fans, the stadium half full or half empty, depending on how you looked at it. San Jose State was outmanned from the beginning. USC running back Sultan McCullough ran for 167 yards. Palmer went 21–28 for 213 yards and an interception. Final score: 21–10, USC.

And then things got ugly.

The following week, the twelfth-ranked Kansas State Wildcats came to the Coliseum. The good news for the Trojans: the Kansas State quarterback threw for only twenty-six yards. The bad news: the Wildcats ran for 340 yards. A late Palmer fumble essentially ended the game, a 10–6 loss.

In the next game, against the seventh-ranked, Joey Harrington–led Oregon team, Palmer threw for 411 yards but was again plagued by turnovers: he threw three interceptions, one of which was returned for a touchdown. USC held the lead briefly in the fourth quarter, but ultimately lost, 24–22, on a late Oregon field goal. They then lost to Stanford, 21–16, the following week.

Next up: eleventh-ranked Washington, which had finished the previous season number three in the country at 11–1 and tied for the PAC-10 title. USC kept it close the entire game—Palmer threw two touchdowns and Polamalu had an interception return for a touchdown. But the Huskies won, 27–24, on a field goal as time expired.

On the field after the game, as Carroll shook hands with Washington coach Rick Neuheisel, he pulled him in close and leaned into his ear: "Don't get too comfortable at the top," he said. "You know it's not going to take us very long."

Carroll's bravado belied the fact that his team was now 1–4, the program's worst start in four decades, which provided Carroll's growing legions of naysayers more ammunition than they could have ever dreamed of.

But they had no idea that a cult hero was about to be born.

Sunny Byrd, a 220-pound fullback, had started his college career at El Camino,[‡] a junior college, and then transferred to USC in 2000 and redshirted. He was blond, a surfer, and had received his first name from what he described as his "hippie" parents back in Manhattan Beach. Prior to the sixth game of the 2001 season—against Arizona State—Byrd had never taken a handoff in a game.

That changed with fifty-four seconds left in the first half against Arizona State, when Byrd took the ball from Palmer and ran three yards for a touchdown, which gave USC a 21–10 lead going into halftime.

McCullough, the star of the first game of the season, was hurt and out of the game. Carroll told Chow to keep pounding the line with the surfer kid. And so he did. Byrd would end up with sixty-three yards on twenty carries. The 3.1-yard-per-carry was nothing to write home about, but the gritty way Byrd earned those yards—throwing himself into the line, keeping his feet churning even after the whistle had blown—endeared him to Carroll and the fans.

Byrd's day ended on a drive in the fourth quarter in which he ran the ball on *thirteen* of the team's fifteen plays, including a stretch of eight straight runs. On his last carry, he broke the collarbone of an Arizona State safety. As Byrd was tackled on the play, he grabbed his calf and screamed in pain. The stadium went silent. The trainers came out and told him it was just a cramp, but that didn't make it hurt any less. "They told me I had two options," says Byrd. "They could carry me off and I'd hear some cheering, or I could walk off on my own and hear the crowd roar." Byrd chose the latter, and as he limped off, the roar indeed came.

[‡] Sarkisian had played at El Camino, as well, before he enrolled at BYU.

The Trojans finished off the best game they'd played under Carroll, a 48–17 trouncing, which included three touchdown passes and no interceptions for Palmer, the clean game that he needed.

When asked about Byrd's performance in the game, Carroll told the media, "That was probably the greatest sixty-three yards I've ever seen."

Next up: Notre Dame.

Carroll says that in the lead-up to his first game against the Fighting Irish, he "had a lot of cronies at SC telling me that this was the biggest game of my life, and that it was the most important thing that will happen in the lives of all of these young men on my team."

So he made the occasion a big deal. He had the team fly in early for the game. They toured the Notre Dame campus, saw the statues and the portraits that intermingled the sacred (religious figures) with the profane (football coaches), lit candles at the Grotto of Our Lady of Lourdes, toured the College Football Hall of Fame,[§] saw "Touchdown Jesus." It even got to the point where "Mr. Trojan" himself, Marvin Goux, the former USC player and coach and the man for whom the entry gate to the Trojan practice field was named, called Carroll as he walked into Notre Dame Stadium for the first time. "He wanted me to feel the glory of the Notre Dame rivalry," says Carroll. "I was on the phone with him, walking through the tunnel, walking him through my experiences, 'Here's the field, oh I see the scoreboard,' that sort of thing. And then we go out and play like shit and get our asses kicked."

Byrd had another tenacious, if unspectacular game, gaining sixty-two yards on twenty-two carries, and Palmer threw for two touchdowns but also slipped into his old bad habits, throwing two interceptions. The Trojans lost, 27–16. "That was all on me. I totally blew it," says Carroll. "Never again would we arrive early and

---

[§] Then located in South Bend. Now located in Atlanta.

do those tours and all that we did there. I was still really learning how to be a coach at the time, still trying to figure things out. I learned that day that it doesn't matter who the fuck you play. It's never about them. It's about us."

The Trojans were 2–5.

Even Hackett, in his last year as the USC head coach, had a better seven-game start, at 3–4. The outside noise had begun the rise in volume again. Letters, emails, faxes. Internet message boards. Sports talk radio. All came to the same conclusion: Carroll wasn't it.

"People were not happy with me," says Daryl Gross. One of the least happy? Mike Garrett, who summoned Gross to his office.

"We're two and five!" Garrett said to Gross. He was agitated. His fate was inextricably intertwined with Carroll's.

Gross tried to talk him off the ledge. "Mike, all of our losses are to good teams, and we lost by just one score in all but one game. We've been in every game."

The logic didn't move Garrett.

"Everyone was skeptical," Orgeron said in a 2021 Harvard Business School case written about Carroll.

Even Carroll admits he was deeply worried. "Oh, hell yes I was," he says. "This was my last chance. I had to find a way to elevate so it wouldn't bother me."

The Parcellian maxim that "you are what your record says you are" is undeniable. And yet, there is some gray area. What Gross had told Garrett was true—the Trojans *were* in every game. Carroll's team just didn't know how to win, how to finish, yet. The difference was in the margins. And his quarterback, who had fumbled late in the Kansas State loss and had four multi-interception games, was arguably the margin at that point. It was all about the ball.

While preparing for the next game against Arizona, Carroll was ready to make a dramatic change. "I thought, 'Maybe Carson doesn't have it, maybe he's not good enough,'" he says. And he had another quarterback, a true freshman, who had flashed in practice: Matt Leinart. "I was thinking, 'Let's just bust Matt out, let him play.'"

But Chow pushed back. "I still had faith in Carson, and I didn't think Matt was ready," he says. As the week before the game wore on, Carroll left the decision up in the air, but he gave Leinart meaningful snaps in practice and told him to be ready to start the game.

The team flew to Tucson the day before the game against the University of Arizona. When they arrived, it was nearly one hundred degrees. From the airport, they went straight to the stadium, so they could see the locker room, get accustomed to the field, and run through the game plan. Carroll liked to make this a carefree and playful time, a chance to work out any pregame jitters. He would often organize a game of touch football with the linemen, which brought to mind a parade of elephants, or stage a field goal kicking contest among the non-kickers. "But we walked onto the field that day and there was absolutely no juice, no energy. It was as flat as could be," says Carroll. "Guys were sitting on the bench, sitting in the shade under a wall. It was a total disaster."

Back at the hotel, Carroll called an emergency gathering with his coaches before the traditional seven p.m. meeting with the team. "I told them, 'These guys are flat as a pancake. You're each going to get up in front of them tonight and tell the most inspirational, gut-wrenching story you can. I don't care what story you tell, and I don't care if it's true or not,'" says Carroll. "I was desperate."

At the team meeting, Nick Holt went first. When he felt like his story was not gaining any traction from the captive audience, he began to take off his clothes to kick it up a notch. But that didn't work, either. The players just stared blankly at him. Orgeron and Kirby Wilson got up and basically just yelled at the players. The quiet Chow somehow managed to bring the energy *down* even further. "It all seemed like a futile attempt," says Carroll.

He also had the unresolved quarterback situation to figure out. By the night before the game, Chow had talked him out of Leinart, but not completely. "Pete told me, 'I'll give Carson a half,'" says Chow. That meant that Carroll had to break the news to Leinart. He called the quarterback up to his room to tell him that they were starting Palmer. "Matt was heartbroken," says Carroll. "He told me that his dad was already on the road, driving down from LA [seven hours away]. It was just another young QB story. You can really fuck them up if you're not careful."

The game got off to a lethargic start for both teams. Deep into the first quarter, they were tied, 3–3. And then, suddenly, the nightmare situation for a quarterback on thin ice: Palmer threw an interception that was returned sixty yards for a touchdown. On the sidelines, Carroll shook his head. He thought ahead to the second half, about putting in Leinart. Perhaps his father's drive had not been in vain after all.

But then USC exploded, scoring twenty-eight points in the second quarter to go up 31–13 at halftime. Palmer's job was safe, at least for now.

USC, though, came out flat in the second half, and Arizona took advantage. And with just more than seven minutes left in the game, they had tied the score at thirty-four. The Wildcats quarterback Jason Johnson was shredding the USC secondary, throwing the ball all over the field, including a twenty-four-yard touchdown pass that USC cornerback Kris Richard just missed intercepting.

A familiar pit had lodged itself in the stomachs of the USC players and coaches. "It felt just like the other games where we'd been ahead and let the other team come back," says Carroll. "I was like, 'Oh shit, here we go again.'"

With just over two minutes left in the game, things were not looking good for the Trojans. Arizona had driven into USC territory.

On second and six at the USC forty-four-yard line, Johnson took the snap and quickly got the ball out, on a short route in front of his team's bench.

Richard, still smarting from his earlier near interception, instinctively jumped the route and picked the ball off. He turned up field, juked out Johnson, and scored a touchdown fifty-eight yards later to put the Trojans ahead, 41–34.

The game wasn't quite over—Arizona got the ball back and was threatening again until Shaun Cody ended the game with a sack.

Palmer didn't have a totally clean game—he tossed another interception to go with the pick-six. And the running game was still stuck, with Byrd leading the team with just sixty-seven yards. But the offense had played well enough. And the defense had not bowed under pressure—Polamalu had twelve tackles and one of the team's six sacks on the day—and they had intercepted Johnson four times, which had flipped the turnover margin in their favor.

But it was Richard's pick-six that would become etched in USC lore. "We finally made the play we had to make to win a game," says Carroll.

After the game, with the team gathered around him in the tiny visitor's locker room, Carroll told his team, "We don't have to lose anymore."

USC ran off two more wins in a row, over Oregon State and Cal, to get to 5–5. One more win in their last game of the season would make them eligible to play in a bowl game, something they'd done only once in the previous five seasons. UCLA came into the last game of the season ranked twentieth in the nation. But they never stood a chance.

USC's defense was all over the Bruins from the beginning. Cody had two sacks, Patterson one, and the Trojans forced three interceptions on their way to a 27–0 victory. USC's defense was so suffocating that the game was effectively over at the end of the first quarter when Trojan cornerback Antuan Simmons intercepted a deflected ball by trapping it between his legs and then ran it back for a touchdown.

Simmons's play was not as impactful as Richard's pick-six against Arizona, at least in terms of how it affected the outcome of the game. But it had its own significance. That Simmons, a well-liked member of the team, was even on the field was remarkable in and of itself. During a routine surgery on his back the year before, doctors had discovered a large tumor in his stomach. Simmons spent six weeks in the hospital after having it removed, losing forty pounds and, at one point, nearly dying. Carroll had made sure that Simmons was involved with the team as he worked his way back to the field. And as he high-stepped his way into the end zone that day against UCLA, his teammates and coaches went wild on the sideline.

Simmons's interception later became ESPN's college football play of the year, providing the Trojans with a small but important bit of positive national attention. And USC was on its way to the Las Vegas Bowl, the remarkable turnaround in their season complete, punctuated with the victory over UCLA. "That win was just so dominant," says David Bahnsen, a USC booster. "It just felt like something had turned."

There would still be a few growing pains, though.

The Trojans had more than a month to prepare for the bowl game against a solid Utah team. Carroll allowed his seniors to determine how the team would travel to Las Vegas. The players figured out that the NCAA was going to pay for their flights there and that, under the rules, if they drove instead, they got to pocket that money. So they decided to drive. Many of them went early.

The team stayed at the MGM Grand in Vegas (their opponents stayed in Utah until the day of the game). The seniors got their own rooms. And the players, flush—at least for a while—with cash, had a blast, doing everything but concentrating on their upcoming game. "We got away from ourselves," says Byrd. "We weren't disciplined. I remember late the night before the game seeing a starter at one of the tables. I said, 'Man, what are you doing?' He said, 'I'm on a roll.'"

The game was at 12:30 PST on Christmas Day, a mostly cloudy, fifty-degree day. The Trojans got manhandled. Polamalu, from his safety position, was forced to make *twenty* tackles as Utah runners kept shooting through the USC defensive line. Palmer threw for only 150 yards and was sacked four times. The Trojans' running game finally hit rock bottom: They ran the ball twenty-five times for a net one yard (which meant they averaged just under an inch and a half per rush). And they lost, 10–6, to finish the season at 6–6. "We didn't just play lousy," says Carroll. "There is no way to describe it."

In the locker room after the game, Carroll did something he says he'd never done before and hasn't done since: he completely lost his temper, screaming at his team and becoming, for a brief moment, exactly the kind of coach he never wanted to be. "I ripped them," he says. "I told them we would never again play a game like this, where we weren't the more physical team."

In reality, though, Carroll knew who was to blame. "I was so fucking pissed at myself," he says. "We didn't play the game in our image, and I lost track of it during the bowl process, and Utah embarrassed us, and we'd lost out on a winning season because of it. It was my fault, though."

And that was the moment, Carroll says, when everything changed.

CHAPTER SIX

Good Cop, Bad Cop

Pete Carroll *loved* practice. It was something he believed should be enjoyed, not endured. He liked it to be fun, high energy, sharp, not too long, and "competitive as hell." During practice, Carroll seemed high on his own supply. He darted around, smiling, high-fiving anyone within range, jawing at his assistants, trainers, and the waterboy. He looked happy. If he'd been a dog, his tail would have been wagging, furiously.

During his first training camp, Carroll approached his newly hired strength and conditioning coach, Chris Carlisle, with a small but revolutionary idea. What if the players didn't run "gasser" sprints at the end of practice, something that most, if not all teams, from Pee Wee to the pros, did?

Carroll knew the players—all of them—hated sprints. More than that, he believed most players held back some effort during practice to save some juice for them. And that seemed like a negative incentive, and something that defeated the purpose. So Carroll asked Carlisle: What if we just got our conditioning in *during* practice? What if we sprinted through each drill and then sprinted to the next drill? Those sudden bursts mimicked the real game better anyway.

Carlisle didn't know how to respond.

And from that point on, USC players did not run sprints after practice. Carroll never failed to mention that fact to recruits.

Carroll had two pre-practice rituals: Just before he walked onto the field, he would rub the bronze plaque of Marvin Goux, "Mr. Trojan," who had passed away in the summer of 2002.* And then he'd jump up and smack the "I'm In" sign that he'd placed at the top of the field's entrance gate.

The players also tapped the sign, a symbolic gesture. "You have homework and a girlfriend and everything else, but all of that stayed on the outside of the practice field when you tapped in," says Chris McFoy, a redshirt freshman receiver in 2002. "The focus was football and football only for the next two and a half hours. All that other stuff would be there when you're done. The tap-in was an affirmation, that you were locked in the moment."

After he tapped in, Carroll would sprint from the gate to the middle of the field, where the equipment manager, Tino Dominguez, awaited him with four packs of Bubble Yum in his hand. (Carroll chewed, on average, fifteen pieces a day. "I stepped in more gum in my career at USC than I have in the rest of my life. It was everywhere. Everyone had it in their shoes," says Alex Parsons, who played from 2006 to 2009.) In most practices, Carroll sprinted down the field with the kickoff team, despite persistent neck and knee pain from his own playing days. On his birthday every year, Carroll attempted to throw a ball as many yards as his age.

In one practice, Carroll inserted himself at running back on a fourth-and-goal-at-the-one drill—no helmet, no pads—finally getting to live out the play he'd practiced as a child in his living room. The ball was snapped and handed to Carroll, who

---

*Though Carroll believed that Goux had oversold the entire Notre Dame tradition thing, the two men were friendly.

approached the scrum of 300-plus pounders at the goal line and leaped—a la Herschel Walker or Bo Jackson or Eddie Vedder at Lollapalooza. But unlike Vedder, no one caught Carroll in the air, and he thudded to the ground. The players went quiet. And then he hopped up and spiked the ball. "I was like, 'What the hell is wrong with that dude?'" says Marcell Allmond. "But you know what? When your head coach is jumping around like a fool, guess what you want to do? He was just a big-ass kid."

But there was a method to Carroll's madness, intent behind it all.

Hackett had been notorious for his hard practices, those three-a-days before the season. But his practices weren't crisp. They seemed to lack purpose, and they left players beat-up for the season. Carroll had no desire to wear his players out. He wanted to keep it loose but fast and competitive.

He practiced quick-twitch situational football. Carroll ran the field goal unit onto the field with under ten seconds on the clock with no timeouts. He'd work on the four-minute, two-minute, and one-minute offense and defense and last-seconds-of-the-game goal line plays. He practiced sudden changes—a turnover deep in their own side of the field, a recovered onside kick. If things weren't going well in practice, he'd sometimes throw in a curve to get the team refocused.

"If we were dropping a lot of balls or the quarterback was throwing a lot of interceptions in a part of practice, I'd stop it and take them all to the locker room and tell them that this is halftime, and we've played terrible, and we were down." Then the team would go through their halftime routine, with players getting their talks from their position coaches. After a few minutes, they'd head back out to the field. "And I'd tell them, 'Okay, we're gonna put together a comeback and this is what it will feel like,'" says Carroll.

He drilled the fundamentals. The 2001 Kansas State game had been lost primarily because of a late fumble by Palmer. Initially, a

USC player had his hands on the ball. But a Kansas State player wrestled it away from him under the dogpile. So Carroll, on every Turnover Tuesday, began to practice dogpile drills, where the players worked on covering the ball, covering one another, stealing the ball from the opponent, and pulling players off the pile.

He created as competitive an atmosphere as possible. He kept score on every drill, oftentimes manipulating it to enhance the tension and keep the players hungry and on edge. He liked to turn the intensity all the way up to the point where the players wanted to fight one another, but never further.

Mark Sanchez, the quarterback who joined the team in 2005, likes to tell the story of a near fight that broke out in one practice:

> One day Chilo Rachal [a six-foot-five, 300-pound offensive guard] and a defender were going at it and tempers flared and helmets hit the ground, and they were literally about to go at it. And I was like, "Oh shit, these are two huge dudes, and this is going to be bad. Someone is going to have his face rearranged and there will be collateral damage because they are so big." But then, out of nowhere and just when the first blow is about to happen and the benches are about to clear, here comes Pete, sprinting. He doesn't try to break up the fight. He just jumps into Chilo's arms. Chilo is forced to catch Pete, and he holds him like a baby, and Pete's saying, "Easy, big guy. Hang in there." And he's bought time for the other coaches to get over there, to help break it up. And Pete goes, "I love it, I love it," and calls everybody in. "This is what I want, this is as far as it goes. We walk with the opponent to the edge and let them throw the first punch." Pete was a psychological ninja. He made it into a teaching moment.

Carroll also emphasized best-on-best in practice, with the Palmer-led offense squaring off against the Polamalu-led defense. "Our practices were harder than anything we did in a game," says

Jacob Rogers, the offensive tackle. The defenders were instructed to not take an offensive ball carrier all the way to the ground—Carroll wanted to avoid lower-leg injuries. But they were instructed to hit and hit hard.

In many ways, Carroll hadn't changed much as a coach. He still played basketball at lunch. He competed at everything. "We were doing a Sunday night media call once, and while he was on the phone, we were throwing a baseball back and forth," says Tim Tessalone, the sports information director. "And as we went on, Pete started to put spin on the ball and throwing knuckleballs, trying to get me to drop it."

He was voluble: Carroll would see one of his players walking on campus and call out his name and say, "See you at practice!" loud enough so that everyone around him—especially the co-eds—would know the kid played football.

He still had unconventional and memorable ways of getting a point across: Carroll once had Kennedy Pola make a dramatic entrance into a meeting with the players while wearing a Michael Jordan jersey that was all burned up.

"The jersey doesn't make you," Carroll said, pointing at Pola. (Pola later complained: "I paid a lot for that jersey.")

And he still loved pranks: During a practice in the 2001 season, right before the game against UCLA, Carroll borrowed a page out of Monte Kiffin's book. He pointed to the roof of a nearby building, where a man was standing. "That's a UCLA spy!" Carroll said. Suddenly, a USC equipment manager appeared by the man. The two men wrestled and disappeared out of sight and then the "UCLA spy" was tossed over the side.

The mannequin nearly hit an unsuspecting student who was walking by.

To some on the team, the Full Carroll Experience felt like a bit much early on. "There was a lot of 'Whoa, what are we doing now?'" Palmer told ESPN. "He ruffled some feathers for sure. There were definitely some guys that were used to the old-school football mentality—the John Robinson guys, the Paul Hackett guys."

Though the Trojans had improved in 2001, Carroll still had some worries. A 6–6 record was not going to cut it in this, his third go-round as a head coach. And the way the season ended, with the desultory loss in the Las Vegas Bowl, still gnawed at him.

After the 2001 season, Carroll made some small tweaks to his staff, taking Keith Uperesa off the offensive line and putting him on the offensive tackles and the tight ends with Kiffin, much to the chagrin of Uperesa's good friend Chow.[†] Carroll replaced Uperesa with Tim Davis from Wisconsin. Carroll liked the fact that the Badgers played unabashedly smashmouth football—Davis's line had blocked for Ron Dayne, who had set the NCAA record for career rushing yards in 1999. Secondary coach De-Wayne Walker, Carroll's old friend from the Patriots, left for a job with the New York Giants. He was replaced by Greg Burns, who was assisted by Rocky Seto, who'd been promoted from a graduate assistant role.

But for the most part, the USC coaching staff stayed intact. In putting it together, Carroll had set aside his ego. He knew he had to win now. The staff was filled not with disciples and yes-men, but with big personality, fully formed coaches with extensive experience in the game.

Culture over scheme. That was Bill Walsh's mantra. And culture in the college game comes from the head coach, who has most of the power, and runs downhill, filtered through the assistant coaches. Carroll had only a few rules for his coaches and gave them creative freedom. They could be themselves, within parameters.

[†] Uperesa would be fired after the 2002 season.

The parameters were fairly straightforward. He demanded energy from his assistants, especially at practice. "He wanted us to be jacked up for every minute of practice, or else we weren't doing our jobs," says linebacker coach Nick Holt. Carroll brought breakfast to the facility on most days, to make sure his staff had fuel to burn. He encouraged his coaches to go home early on Thursday nights after the game plan had been installed, to get refreshed and see their families. He also encouraged them to get in a workout every day, to stay fit, physically and mentally. The younger coaches played basketball. Chow, the oldest assistant, went for walks. "I even saw Holt running around in a Speedo once," says Lee Webb, who played linebacker and running back. "I almost vomited. But all of those coaches came out to practice fired up every day." (Holt says he doesn't exactly recall the Speedo, but admits it was in line with his personality.)

Carroll occasionally got into the details during practice, helping the defensive backs refine their man-to-man technique, or demonstrating to a defensive lineman how he wanted him to rush the quarterback. "But mostly he was a master of telling us what he wanted done," says Holt. Chris Carlisle once described Carroll as a "microleader not a micromanager."

The freedom he gave his coaches was critical because Carroll had basically upended the traditional football coaching model. On most teams, the head coach is the disciplinarian and the assistants fill in on the other side—he would, for instance, scream at a player and then an assistant would move in on cleanup duty and try to explain the reasoning behind the outburst, try to put it in context and maybe soften the blow.

But on Carroll's team, *he* was the good cop. That meant most of the discipline was left up to his assistants. And on his early USC teams, they were very good at it.

Kiffin and some of the younger coaches still had some work to do as disciplinarians—they merely yelled a lot, as if to establish their authority. And Kirby Wilson, with his pro experience, could sometimes go a bit too far with his receivers and, early on, would kick them out of practice for dropping a pass. (Chow would have to tell Wilson that if the receivers were kicked out of practice, they'd have no opportunity to learn how to catch the ball better.)

The other coaches, though, relished the bad cop role. Holt, according to the fullback Brandon Hancock, was "a total psychopath and did crazy locker room stuff."

Perhaps Holt's most famous stunt is known as the "Kentucky Derby" story. Near the end of one season, when there were only a few teams left in the race for the PAC-10 crown, Holt told an impassioned story to the team about the horses in the Derby coming around the final stretch. As he told the story, his voice rose, and the veins began to pop in his neck. Finally, as he became totally overcome by the story, he began to strip off his clothes. "He was talking about that last furlong, about the horse that was coming from behind, and then his shirt is off, then his pants, and then he was naked," says Hancock. "He was always piss and vinegar. He'd chest bump you, headbutt you. He had great energy."

Kennedy Pola implemented a new chant, initially for the unit he coached. He'd split his special teamers into two groups and one side would chant "ST!" (for "special teams") and the other would respond "Wild Bunch!" They would repeat it until the room went wild. The chant was eventually tweaked and utilized by the entire team, which would end meetings before games chanting:

"SC!"

"Wild Bunch!"[‡]

[‡] There may be some well-adjusted football coaches out there, but the profession is filled, by and large, with high-functioning crazy people.

But Carroll's greatest enforcer, his best "bad cop," was Orgeron. The duo was yin and yang. Orgeron was Carroll's hammer.

Orgeron liked to show up early in the morning at the football facilities. He'd often make his way into the office of another early riser, Chow. "Ed would just come in on those mornings and just talk and talk," says Chow. "I'm guessing it's something he did because of the counseling he'd had earlier in his career. Eventually, I'd have to stop him and say, 'Uh, Ed, I have to work.'"

Counseling may have helped Orgeron, but he had little patience for the psychological theories about performance Carroll had learned from Gallwey, Maslow, and Murphy. Carroll once brought a psychologist into a coaches' meeting, who eyeballed Orgeron as he took notes. Orgeron informed Carroll that he was not going to participate in the exercise and left the room.

So Carroll let Orgeron be Orgeron, which, in the end, was exactly the right move.

"The thing with Pete is that he was a master psychologist," says Tim Tessalone. "He could punch different buttons with players and coaches."

Carroll used that psychology all the time, to his advantage. He once told one of his coaches that appearing to be nice was something that allowed him to get things he wanted done.

Of course, being a master psychologist implies the existence of patients upon whom the psychology is practiced. Some of his players got hip to that use of psychology on them. "We always called him 'Sneaky Pete,'" says LenDale White, the running back who joined the team in 2003. "He always knew what he was doing, and he would find a way to get what he wanted done."

Orgeron was the head of recruiting and was excellent at that part of his job. He spent the recruiting period relentlessly chasing down potential players, using his considerable personal charm in doing so. But when the players signed with USC and showed up on campus, his tone changed. "Ed always had a first meeting with the new recruits in the fall, and he was like, 'All right you moth-erfuckers, your asses are mine now. We're going to work.' And the kids were like, 'Holy smokes, a month ago you were kissing our asses,'" says Chow. "I never missed that meeting."

The receiver Mike Williams told ESPN about one evening when he and his fellow new 2002 recruits were on their way to study hall when Orgeron suddenly stopped a defensive lineman named Van Brown, who was six foot five and 255 pounds. Brown happened to be wearing a green shirt. "O walks up and puts two hands on his chest and rips the dude's shirt off. 'Don't wear that Notre Dame shit around here!' We're like, 'Holy shit, are we at the right school?'"

Along with his recruiting and defensive line duties, Orgeron was also in charge of bed checks on the evening before games, a job usually reserved for the orneriest coach on the staff. Hancock, no small man himself (six foot one, 240 pounds), recalls a time he was late for bed check his freshman year:

> I was maybe one minute later getting back to the hotel. I put my key in the door and Orgeron turns the corner [in the hall-way] and gets down in a three-point stance about seven yards away from me. And then he charges. "What the fuck, you freshman piece of shit?" I'm shellshocked, standing against the wall. He rips my shirt off and uppercuts me. "Fuck you. I'll send you back home." I go into my room. My roommate, Her-shel Dennis, is there. Orgeron comes back five minutes later with his shirt still off. He comes in and does a bunch of push-ups on the floor. "You still want to go?" he says. "No, Coach. It's all good, you win." He was a dude you did not want to cross.

Orgeron was notoriously tough on his defensive lineman. "Mike Patterson was fat and lazy when he came in," says Lee

Webb. "And Orgeron went all *Full Metal Jacket* on him, just on him all the time." Patterson dropped weight—from 306 pounds to 276—and became perhaps Orgeron's most reliable player on the defensive line, even earning an endearing nickname from his position coach—"Baby Sapp," after the Pro Football Hall of Famer Warren Sapp, whom Orgeron had coached at the University of Miami. "Coach O was so demanding on his guys, no days off, no excuses," says Palmer. "I played with guys later in the NFL who'd been coached by him and every single one of them said he was the best coach they ever had."

Carroll sometimes played the good cop/bad cop role with Orgeron without first letting him in on it. Defensive lineman Manny Wright was a player with unlimited potential who was held back by a lack of discipline. One day, after Wright had missed a series of classes, Orgeron brought him into his office and brutally dressed him down. Wright started to cry. Carroll heard the commotion and walked into Orgeron's office and began to chew *him* out for being too harsh on Wright. When Wright left the room, Carroll smiled at Orgeron and winked.

Early on, Carroll says, "We had to come on really strong and be tough, aggressive, and demanding. That's how you turn it around. Everyone was really crazy, so it was really fun. I did have to sometimes calm down the guys."

The only coach on the USC staff who he didn't have to calm down was Chow, who wasn't a rah-rah guy because, he says, "I didn't have to be."

The job of a head football coach occupies a singular place in American culture. The most successful of them—Vince Lombardi, Bill Walsh, Knute Rockne, Bill Belichick, Nick Saban— are regarded as some of the most effective leaders the country has ever produced. The head football coach's job demands that he be, at once, a priest, psychologist, teacher, father figure, military tactician, salesman, politician, CEO of a medium-sized company, and, on many teams in the NFL and at the larger programs in college, a media celebrity.

In the college game, unlike the more player-driven NFL, the teams are mostly affiliated with their coaches. A casual football fan would likely know that, say, Bear Bryant was once the coach at Alabama, and Joe Paterno was once the coach at Penn State, but they also might have difficulty naming more than five players from those coaches' eras with their respective teams.

One reason for this is that college coaches are the lone constant in a sea of change, annually greeting an incoming tide of fresh recruits (and now, transfers), and annually bidding farewell to an outgoing tide of both graduating seniors and any underclassmen who have opted to leave the program early to turn pro (and now, departing transfers).[5]

There is another reason for that strong affiliation, though. College coaches have more power over their teams than most coaches in NFL do over theirs. The reason: in the pros, authority over a team is typically split among the coach, personnel people, and the owner. At some college programs, though, the coach gains nearly complete control of his programs.

Carroll was one of those coaches. At USC, he finally had the absolute authority he had always desired. "I was the GM [general manager] and the head coach," he says. "Garrett had like twenty other sports he had to look after." Nominally, Garrett and the USC president and its board of trustees were Carroll's bosses. But as Carroll began to win—and, in the process, help generate positive publicity and huge amounts of revenue for the school—he unquestionably became the most powerful figure at USC. Even when Garrett tried to stick his nose into the football program,

---

[5] A similar version of this riff appeared in my book *Saban: The Making of a Coach.*

Carroll would exert his authority. Garrett once dressed down a few of Carroll's players after a game. Carroll confronted him. The two engaged in a shouting match. And Garrett backed down.

Carroll hired his own coaches, recruited his own players, set the practice schedule, and designed the training table diet. He even gained access to the academic files of his players to help his coaches figure out how they learned so they could tailor their teaching.

But even the most powerful figures cannot avoid some of the prosaic problems that come with management.

There was some tension on Carroll's early staff at USC, mostly between the head coach and his offensive coordinator. Norm Chow was quiet, reserved, bespectacled, and he never had a hair out of place. He chewed pumpkin seeds. He was a natural worrier. That manifested itself on the nights before games, when his anxiety about the game plan prevented sleep, and he would sometimes either walk or drive around all night before returning to his hotel room to shower, eat breakfast, and dress for the game. Chow was a devout Mormon and didn't drink alcohol, which meant he missed out on the biweekly or monthly evenings when Carroll and many of the coaches went out for beers. He was beloved by his players and by the media, which wrote often about his glowing track record as an offensive coach.

Chow and Carroll each separately went to Seamus Callanan, the football operations assistant who was close to their age, to vent their frustrations. Chow's main issues had to do with Lane Kiffin, the son of Carroll's mentor, who had been plopped into Chow's lap and was untouchable. Kiffin, at the time, was still very much learning on the job. The other coaches knew not to talk much around Kiffin—he was thought of as Carroll's snitch. But it was the skin of Chow—who sometimes referred to Kiffin as "Pete's little guy"—that the young tight ends coach got under the most.

Kiffin could be brash at times and spoiled at other times. "We were riding into work one day when Lane turned to me and said, 'Coach, why are you so uptight all the time?'" says Chow. "I told him, 'Lane, if we don't win, I can't feed my kids.' Lane didn't have to work a day in his life, so he could be a little flippant." Kiffin sat next to Chow in the booth during games, as Chow relayed the called plays to Sarkisian, who was on the sidelines and was in charge of signaling them in to the quarterback. Kiffin would sometimes mock Chow about a play call. In one game, Chow told Carroll he wanted to punt on a long fourth down. Kiffin chided him: "You're losing your courage, man."

Kiffin knew that Chow didn't love recruiting and, because of his shy, introverted personality, wasn't one of the staff's recruiting stars. And he liked to make sure that everyone else knew that, too. At one recruiting event, Kiffin, standing with some of the younger coaches, spotted Chow, who was shyly trying to make small talk with a recruit. "Look at Norm," Kiffin said. "He has no clue. He's never recruited a kid in his life."

According to several assistant coaches, Carroll's issues with Chow were manifold. He didn't like that Chow was reserved, taking it as a lack of enthusiasm and buy-in. He was wary of Chow's reputation as an offensive savant and, especially as time went on and the USC offenses improved, didn't like that Chow got much of the credit. But, early on, Carroll's biggest problem with his co-ordinator was the offensive scheme.

On paper, Carroll's decision to bring in Chow to run his offense looked brilliant. Chow was, after all, the man who groomed Heisman-winning, future NFL quarterbacks who helmed offenses that racked up 500 yards a game. He may not have been a great one-on-one recruiter, but his name and reputation alone were recruiting tools. And his players loved him.

At BYU, Chow had designed big, high-yardage offenses that were executed by many players (outside of the quarterbacks) who were not top-tier college athletes. The big idea at USC was that he would be able to marry those brilliant schemes with what, presumably, would be a group of much better athletes. It seemed fail-safe.

But it had not worked in the 2001 season. Palmer was sacked frequently and was still throwing too many interceptions. And the running game—Sunny Byrd's heroic sixty-plus-yard games notwithstanding—was not working.

So Carroll decided to intercede on the offensive side of the ball. "After that first season, I drilled into the philosophy of how I wanted the offense run," says Carroll.

The one big change was the installation of an outside running scheme, something done most effectively by the Mike Shanahan–coached Denver Broncos and engineered by their running game coordinator, Alex Gibbs. The scheme favored agile linemen who, after the snap and handoff, stepped laterally instead of bulling straight ahead. On any given outside running play, the linemen at the front of the surge were responsible for blocking the defenders in front of them or, if uncovered, for helping a fellow lineman out with a double team or working their way downfield to take on linebackers and safeties. The backside linemen flowed in the same direction. Their job was to stop any pursuing defenders, which, in theory, opened up cutback lanes for the running back, if needed. The running backs in the scheme had to be quick—of foot and mind. They had to discern whether the frontside linemen were doing their jobs correctly and follow them if they were. If things broke down, they were coached to immediately look for a cutback lane (hopefully) created by the backside linemen.

Carroll sent Kiffin and Sarkisian to Tampa to study the concept from Buccaneers head coach Jon Gruden, who also ran it, and to pick the brain of Shanahan's son, Kyle, who worked for Gruden and knew the system well. And Carroll brought in Gibbs to coach it to his team. "I asked Alex if he'd always be on call for us," says

Carroll. "And I told the guys on staff, 'I don't want anyone trying to solve a problem. If we have a problem, we'll call Alex.'"

Carroll's idea was that once the USC offense got the stretch running game going, it would open up the passing game, creating one-on-one matchups on the receivers, who would run primarily slants and fades. "That offseason was my favorite one ever," says Carroll. "We got the running game and the passing game structured in a way that I stayed with for the next twenty years. It was designed with balance, throwing the ball quickly, play action, moving the quarterback. We were never the same after that. I was never the same coach after that."

Chow, to his credit, learned the system and called the games as his coach desired. And the change was welcomed by others on the offensive staff. "I think that's where Pete was ahead of his time, and unique," says Lane Kiffin. "He was a defensive genius, but he had a creative offensive mind. Offensive minds see everything moving around. Defensive coaches are a little more tunnel vision and a little more uptight, like Saban. You'd think Pete was an offensive guy by his personality."

One way in which Carroll exerted his near absolute power over his team came in the form of an institutional accountability for his players. This marked a change from his days as an NFL head coach, where he left much of the accountability up to the players themselves. It helped that college players, especially at that time, were pretty much a captive audience.

Carroll was strict about his players' academics, which, ostensibly, was beneficial for their own growth as young adults. But he also wanted to keep them eligible to play. Players in danger of getting into academic trouble had advisers who waited for them outside of the actual classrooms. "They'd be there to make sure you were on time and make sure you had your backpack and pencils and notebooks, so that you weren't just going through the motions," says Sunny Byrd. Any players who did not maintain at least a 2.3 grade point average had to attend a team study hall, which was run by the assistant coaches. "Coach Holt would run it, and it was brutal," says Lee Webb. "He'd say, 'You better study your ass off. We're just waiting to use your scholarship on someone else.'"

The occasional missed class was usually ignored by the coaching staff. But if players consistently missed them, or missed time with their tutors, they were enrolled in a five a.m. running/sprint class with Orgeron. The same fate awaited any player who consistently broke any of the three team rules. "Pete was a players' coach, and there is a stigma that comes with that," says Jacob Rogers. "People see it as soft. But he wasn't soft. If you showed up late for practice a few times, you didn't practice. You ran."

Carroll kept the players accountable in another way, too. Every day, during film review, he'd show their mistakes for everyone to see. But even that he handled in a different way. When he showed film of a player getting beat one-on-one, he wouldn't get angry and berate him. Instead, he would talk to him in a manner that expressed disappointment, putting the onus on them. "You were afraid to let Pete down," says Pat Ruel, USC's offensive line coach from 2005 to 2009.

But perhaps the person Carroll held most accountable was himself. He knew this was his last shot, after all. He worked his ass off. He slept at least three nights a week at the office. "The basketball coach once tried to beat Pete into the office in the morning," says Webb. "He got there at 6:30 but Pete's car was already there. He tried 5:30 the next morning, same thing. He tried 3:30 the morning after that, same thing. He finally realized that Pete didn't leave."

Carroll never seemed to run out of juice. He had a hustler's verve that felt genuine. To most, anyway. "He was amazing in terms of his energy," says Tim Tessalone. Says Palmer, "Pete had consistent energy. It didn't grow; it didn't dissipate. It just stayed the same, which made it easy to follow." Though he did drink a lot of Mountain Dews then, Carroll says his energy "is just natural. I don't have to be pumped up by anybody." He recharged, he says, by taking advantage of what he calls "the spaces between the spaces."

"It could be thirty seconds here or there. I just take a pause and regain focus on what's at hand, what's going on. And then I'm back, always trying to churn the energy, trying to keep the players and coaches tuned in and turned on, so that they're lit up and their awareness is heightened, and they can take advantage of it and have a chance to catch every single morsel of opportunity in the moment."

Carroll also recharged sometimes in another way. "He'd come in some mornings a little later than the rest of us because he'd been out in the ocean boogie-boarding," says Callanan.

His quick-twitch attention span, which was well-known and well-tolerated by everyone around him, became a useful tool. It gave him an excuse to make practices as up-tempo as possible, mimicking the actual games. "He hated stopping practice and repeating plays," says Rocky Seto. "He wanted players in and out of the huddle crisply, and the defense swarming around. Even the walk-throughs were done with tempo."

Carroll sometimes changed the direction of a practice so fast it caused whiplash. He called off practice one day and took the team to the nearby Olympic Swim Stadium, where he climbed the ten-meter diving platform and jumped off.

His attention span allowed him an excuse to quickly get through things he knew he had to do but would rather not dwell on. He was never rude—he always had time for someone, always bestowed at least a little bit of attention. "He was always available to me," says Tessalone. "But I knew I had a small window with him, as far as asking three things—*boom, boom, boom*—and there wasn't a lot of chitchat because his mind was off to something else in about a minute."

Chow says the best illustration of Carroll's short attention span happened during the annual recruiting rules test that the NCAA forced coaches to take. "It was open book, so you couldn't fail," says Chow. "I knew some guys who got the test early and would have all the answers, which were just A or B. Carroll would come by my office and ask, 'You got the test yet?' We'd get the answers, and he would go in and finish the test in two seconds. The rest of us would at least try to act like we were taking it." Chow says Carroll even ate in a hurry. That attention span, he says, "was not a drawback for Pete. It was a plus." And Carroll could extend his focus when needed. "On game days, on the headset, he was calm and collected," says Chow.

One day in 2002, a USC assistant coach took Carroll's car to run an errand. It was sunny, so he pulled down the visor. Out fell a card. It had something written on it:

"I will coach this team with discipline today."

It was in direct response to the perception, somewhat true, that Carroll was too loose during his time with the Jets and the Patriots. There would be no repeating of that mistake at USC.

Affirmations are very important, Carroll says. They help you stay on track. "And they help you avoid regret," he says. "It's really hard to equate just how valuable it is to get your ass kicked and have stuff happen that jerks your head around. It forces you to figure stuff out. I hate learning the hard way, but some of the best lessons I've learned have come that way."

CHAPTER SEVEN

Rattling the Cage

USC opened the 2002 season with a marquee game: a Monday night primetime clash with the Auburn Tigers in the Coliseum. The Trojans went into the game with a preseason ranking of twenty. Auburn was unranked but had talent, particularly at the running back position, which featured two promising sophomores, Ronnie Brown and Carnell "Cadillac" Williams.

Williams ate up USC in the first half, rushing for ninety-seven yards. But the Trojan defense clamped down on him in the second half, in which he rushed for a total of minus-three yards.

Palmer had 302 yards passing and two interceptions. The latter stat was worrisome—cutting down on his interceptions was a point of emphasis coming into the season. But he was only sacked once and, most important, he was sharpest when he needed to be, leading a long drive late in the fourth quarter that culminated in his game-winning one-yard touchdown run over a team that would finish number fourteen in the country. Palmer wasn't satisfied, though. "I expect to be perfect, and I should be perfect," he told the media after the game.

He was closer to that in the next game, against the eighteenth-ranked Colorado Buffaloes in Boulder. The game was the first to demonstrate the balance Carroll hoped the outside running scheme would provide his offense. Sultan McCullough ran for

110 yards, including a sixty-two-yard touchdown on an outside run to the left. Palmer threw for 244 yards and one touchdown and no interceptions and was not sacked. The defense stifled the Colorado attack all day. In the end: a 40–3 USC beatdown.

USC then lost to Kansas State 27–20 and beat Oregon State 22–0. On October 5, they traveled to Pullman, Washington, to play Washington State. USC appeared to have the game won on a fifty-five-yard touchdown pass from Palmer to freshman receiver Mike Williams. But the Trojans kicker, Ryan Killeen, missed the extra point, which left them up only 27–24. Washington State drove late for a game-tying field goal. Killeen missed a field goal attempt in overtime and Washington State hit theirs and won, 30–27. The loss dropped USC to 3–2, not exactly the start Carroll had envisioned for this pivotal year.

But from that point until January 2006, the Trojans would lose only one more game.

Culture may trump scheme, as Bill Walsh said, but neither culture nor scheme means a thing if a team doesn't have talented players.

In the NFL, the game is rigged in the name of competitive balance. There is a hard salary cap. Teams are assigned draft pick spots based on the previous year's finish, with the worst team picking first and the Super Bowl winner picking last. One way to look at it: a team was penalized for success.

This was not the case in college football. Nick Saban left the Miami Dolphins to coach Alabama in 2007. One of the driving reasons: "In the NFL, you only get one first-round draft pick, and that's if it hadn't already been traded away. You couldn't really outwork anybody," he said. "In college, I could recruit ten players with first-round talent every year." In college, talent could be hoarded. And Carroll and his staff concentrated on outworking everyone else to do just that.

USC's 2002 recruiting class was ranked twelfth overall in the country, up from twentieth the year before. It included offensive lineman Winston Justice and running back Hershel Dennis, two of the Long Beach Poly players Orgeron had been recruiting when he ran into Carroll on the sidelines of that high school championship game.

The class was also the first of Carroll's at USC to feature impact players from outside of California. Tight end Dominique Byrd came from Minnesota. And, perhaps most important, wide receiver Mike Williams was plucked from Tampa, Florida.

The Williams signing was impactful. The six-foot-five 200-pounder was a starter from the second game in his freshman season (Justice would also start in his freshman year), and he was an immediate star, setting school and PAC-10 freshman records for receptions (eighty-one) and NCAA freshman records for receiving yards (1,265) and touchdowns (fourteen).

Williams had a background that mixed tragedy with good fortune. He never met his biological father, and his mother left the family when he was eleven. Williams went to live with a great-aunt and then was taken in by a white couple for whom his great-aunt babysat.* The couple never officially adopted him, but Williams referred to them as his parents.

Williams grew up a fan of Florida State (his car in high school had a garnet exterior and a gold interior, the colors of the school), who had pursued him heavily and were believed to be his top choice. The couple who raised Williams wanted him to stay in-state for college, either at Florida State or Florida. But USC won out, thanks mainly to Lane Kiffin, who was his primary recruiter on the Trojan staff. Kiffin sold Williams on the opportunity to

---

* Sort of The Blind Side before The Blind Side.

play right away—USC needed talent at receiver—an opportunity Williams would grab. Though Kiffin was still viewed as impetuous and brash by some of his fellow assistants, the Williams recruitment earned him credibility and foreshadowed the recruiting phenom he would become as his career progressed. The Williams signing also signaled to the world of college football that Carroll's Trojans weren't satisfied with locking down just the state of California in recruiting—they would be a force nationally.

Carroll remained relentless on the recruiting trail. Mike Riley, who came back for his second stint as the coach of Oregon State in 2003, says he couldn't help but take notice of what was happening at USC. "I saw things taking shape for them. This was back when you could go on the road and recruit in the spring,[†] and I was actively going to schools and everywhere I went, Pete had already been there. And I thought, 'Oh no, this combination of the USC brand and Carroll out there working hard is bad news for the rest of us.'"

Carroll brought the same energy and enthusiasm he had in practice to the recruiting trail. "When he really wanted a player, he'd pour it on," says Pat Ruel. "He made us figure out everything about the kid, their girlfriend's name, their stats from games. He recruited the kid, his parents, his coach, his pastor." And, of course, he kept it fun. Tim Davis, USC's offensive line coach from 2002 to 2004, told ESPN the story of a day he spent recruiting a wide receiver with Carroll in the Bay Area. At one point during the visit to the receiver's high school, Davis lost track of Carroll. He went outside to look for him and found him in the middle of a basketball game with some of the students. "I said, 'Hey, we have to go on to the next school,'" said Davis. "And he said, 'No, I ain't done yet. I'm losing.'"

Carroll was also frank with recruits and didn't try to bullshit them. "I was a tight end when he came to recruit me," says Charles

---

[†] The NCAA prohibited football coaches from visiting recruits in the spring starting in 2008.

Brown, who played for the Trojans from 2005 to 2009. "He told me he saw me as an offensive lineman. Everyone else said they'd let me play tight end. But he was dedicated to his plan." (Brown became an All-American offensive tackle.)

And he didn't take himself too seriously. "Pete and Lane came to my house," says Michael Reardon, a center who joined the team in 2007. "My brother, who was nine, said he didn't feel good. But my mom made him go shake Pete's hand. And then my brother threw up all over Pete's shoes. Pete just laughed about it."

Carroll allowed his coaches creative freedom in recruiting, as well. "I'd call a recruit and tell him I was running late, that traffic was bad, and that I'd be there in thirty-five minutes," says Ruel. "The dad would say, 'Be safe, take your time.' In reality, I was in my car, just down the street. And then I'd knock on their door two minutes after I hung up and say, 'See, I told you that you were important!' No other coach would let you do that."

And Carroll was strategic. An assistant coach once took a recruit to a pier at the beach. The coach pointed at a man boogie-boarding in the waves and said, "Hey, there's Coach Carroll!" Carroll dragged himself out of the water to say hello to the recruit, an encounter that was intended to look serendipitous, though it was very much staged.

Defensive back Justin Wyatt met Carroll—unintentionally—at one of his football games during his senior year. Wyatt played at Dominguez High School in Compton. In the fourth game of the season, Dominguez played powerhouse Long Beach Poly. In the game, Wyatt matched up against Josh Hawkins, a hyped receiver who had committed to Oregon State, and held him to one catch for eight yards. After the game, Wyatt says he was headed to the sideline with his team when he saw a man jump the fence and run toward him. It was Carroll. "I didn't even know who Pete Carroll was," says Wyatt. Carroll introduced himself and told Wyatt that though he had been there to watch the Long Beach Poly players, he was impressed by how he'd played. "He said he'd love for me to be a Trojan," says Wyatt. "My recruitment was pretty much done at that point."

A little while later, Carroll would cement the deal. He and Orgeron went one night to meet Wyatt and his father and stepmom, who lived in what was considered a dangerous part of Los Angeles. "I'll never forget watching Carroll and Orgeron walking down the street at like, nine o'clock, with no worries. Just the two of them," says Wyatt. "It just proved to me that they were the real deals."

Chris McFoy, the receiver, says the little things Carroll's staff did went a long way, too. At the time, USC was perhaps the only school that had its coaches send handwritten letters to recruits—Pola's idea, according to Chow. "I got a handwritten letter from Chow," says McFoy. "Seems like a small thing, but it really stood out. Everyone else sent typed form letters."

Orgeron was particularly good at inserting a recruit into a vision, casting him as the hero in an action movie. "Orgeron came up to watch me practice and then had dinner with my family," says Hancock, who was from Fresno. "He's a crazy good storyteller with his crazy voice. He laid out a scenario for me—'Fourth and goal on the one, a few seconds left, we hand the ball to Hancock, who does a dirty dive right down the middle for the winning touchdown.'"

Hancock was the valedictorian of his class and had verbally committed to Stanford after being recruited hard by their coach, Tyrone Willingham. But then he met Orgeron and later met Carroll. "Pete had done his homework," says Hancock. "He knew my girlfriend went to Long Beach State and was like, 'Wouldn't you want to be near her?' He knew my uncle was a CPA for movie stars and that I was interested in TV and media. And he painted this elaborate picture of what my life would be like in LA. I bought it, hook, line, and sinker. When I stood up to leave, I had goosebumps. I said, 'I'll see you in the fall.'"

Hancock thought he should break the news to Willingham in person, so he and his father drove to Stanford. "Willingham had been this very polished guy when he was recruiting me but when I told him I was going to USC, he dropped the visage," says Hancock. "He said, 'Fuck you, you coward, you're not worth a shit' right in front of my father. I was blown away. And just a few days later, he announced he was leaving Stanford and going to Notre Dame. It stung me."

USC poured it on for recruiting weekends. They'd take the high schoolers to Universal Studios on Friday and then have a dinner that night, with some of the coaches going with the players and others going with the parents. Carroll was always in the latter group. "He was so good with them, especially the moms," says Callanan.

On Saturday, the recruits toured campus and then met with Carroll in his office, one at a time. That night, they were bused to the Coliseum, where the public address announcer called their names one by one as a picture of a Trojan jersey with their name on the back was displayed on a video board.[‡] And then they would reboard the buses and join their parents and go down to San Pedro to Papadakis Taverna, a Greek restaurant owned by the Papadakis family, which had deep ties to USC football. (John, the father and founder of the restaurant, played linebacker for USC in the 1970s. Taso, a son, played for the team in the 1990s, and Petros, another son, played fullback under Robinson and Hackett and was a team captain in his senior year.)

The dinner was festive, complete with wineglasses thrown into the fireplace. John would get up at one point during the dinner and give a talk, which usually included the line "Christ had his Peter, and he said on this rock we will build our church. At SC, we have our own Peter, and he is our rock."

[‡] Even though USC does not have names on the back of their football jerseys.

John would then ask for a volunteer to come up and learn how to do a Greek dance with his comely daughter or a belly dancer. Usually no one would raise a hand, so the coaches would choose someone—almost always their top recruiting target. The dinner and the dancing gambit were a great success with recruits.

There were, of course, other recruitable players in college football. California was awash with good junior college programs and Carroll and his staff recruited from them to help plug some holes (players like offensive lineman Deuce Lutui and safety Scott Ware, both part of USC's 2004 class, were good examples). Occasionally, they even found players from other four-year colleges. One in 2002 was the quarterback Brandon Hance, a former starter at Purdue. Another was a linebacker named Lofa Tatupu.

Tatupu was the son of Mosi Tatupu, a former USC player who was a fullback and special teams ace for fourteen years in the NFL, all but one of them with the New England Patriots. After his pro career ended, he fell on hard times for a few years before landing a job as a high school football coach in Massachusetts. One of the best players on his team was his son.

Though he had a stellar high school career, Tatupu—who played quarterback and linebacker—was considered short for both positions (five foot eleven) and thus was not recruited heavily. He ended up at the University of Maine, resigned to playing his college years at the I-AA level.[5]

But his father, who had been a star on John McKay's 1974 national title–winning Trojan team, never gave up. He put together a tape of his son's highlights and sent them to his alma mater.

---

[5] USC was a level up, in I-A. The nomenclature has since changed to FBS (Football Bowl Subdivision) for I-A and FCS (Football Championship Division) for I-AA.

Carroll and Orgeron watched the tape. In every clip, Tatupu looked dominant, though the two coaches were unsure of how exactly to judge what they were seeing, mainly because of the level of competition. But Carroll, mindful of the work ethic of Tatupu's father, took a flier on him anyway.

When Tatupu arrived on the USC campus, he came with two old-school 1960s-era pillbox suitcases. They contained pretty much all his worldly possessions at the time. Because of the NCAA transfer rules, he was forced to sit out the 2002 season. But he still made an impression on his teammates. "He was so hungry," says Omar Nazel, Tatupu's roommate. "He worked so hard at school and at football. People saw that, saw that he had a plan and was successful. He wouldn't stop running before the finish line and he didn't let others do it, either." Tatupu became an All-American in the 2004 season and was the first in a long line of spectacular linebackers who played under Carroll at USC.

Of course, recruits and transfers weren't the only players Carroll had to manage. There were also the players who were already there. "Pete was wary about those of us who came in under Hackett because he just wasn't sure of what he had," says Lee Webb.

In college football, the best programs often view the NCAA rule book in the way savvy corporate lawyers view the IRS tax rules—they look to "maximize their benefits," as Nick Saban once put it.

Carroll did the same, especially when it came to shaping his roster. "Pete kind of weeded out the guys who didn't buy in," says Palmer.

Technically, a scholarship given to a college football player is a one-year, renewable deal. But very few, if any, programs treat scholarships that way. Getting a reputation for yanking scholarships would be detrimental to roster building—potential recruits would see it and possibly shy away, and if they somehow missed it, rival coaches would certainly make sure they knew.

But there were ways back then for coaches to move aside players they no longer wanted. They could lean on a player who was not working out to transfer. Carroll did this with running back Chris Howard, who had started some games in 2001, but ran into some academic problems and was indifferent about conditioning. After Carroll intimated that he'd likely only play on the scout team, Howard left USC in 2002.

Medical hardship—essentially retiring a player from the team but allowing him to keep his scholarship—was another tactic and was particularly useful to the program because players who were moved to medical hardship scholarships were not counted against the normal scholarships.

When Carroll arrived at USC, the school's athletic compliance office fielded many questions about the sudden increase in medical hardships. "Normally a team might have two a year," says Keith Miller, USC's compliance officer from 2001 to 2005. "That first year we had them in double digits."

Miller says the reason for this was that many players under Hackett had suffered concussions that went untreated or undiagnosed. "I'd get questions from the NCAA like, 'Is he running off players he doesn't want?' And I'd tell them that no, the previous coach was playing players who probably shouldn't have been out there." Miller says they brought in an outside physician to evaluate the players with concussions. And while it's true that Hackett's notoriously over-the-top three-a-day practices likely resulted in more concussions, it's also true that two players with long histories of concussions—Troy Polamalu and linebacker Matt Grootegoed—stayed on the team and played . . . and were both All-Americans. Miller maintains that Carroll was not trying to sneak around the rules. "He wanted to tiptoe up to the line, but he didn't want to cross it."

Carroll had complicated relationships with some of the former Hackett players who stayed on, like Marcell Allmond, who had joined the team in 1999 as a wide receiver. "Pete came in and was all nice and cool and then something flipped when the entire coaching staff got in," says Allmond. "I loved playing for Pete, but we were not best friends. I don't think he realized that a lot of us on the team were from the hood. I grew up ten minutes from campus. You didn't fuck with us. We were tougher than he knew."

In 2001, Allmond got into a fight. "I got jumped by a frat guy and I won," he says. "Pete gave me no support, and the school decided they wanted to make an example out of a football player." Allmond was suspended for the fall semester and, thus, missed the football season that year. He came back in the spring of 2002 to find a crowded receiver room, with Mike Williams, Kareem Kelly, and Kerry Colbert, among others. Carroll asked Allmond to switch to cornerback. "I didn't trust Pete off the field. If he wanted to go to lunch with me, I'd tell him to fuck off," says Allmond. "But I did trust him on the field." So in the 2002 season, Allmond made the switch. "I listened to Pete and did what he told me to do," says Allmond. "I wasn't the most skilled player, but he put me in a position to be a good player."

There was one other factor involved. Allmond had a grandfather who was disabled and who had been a big part of his life. "And Pete accepted him, and made it easy for him to get to games, and had people watching out for him," says Allmond. "That meant a lot. And that's why I played as hard as I did."

One of the Hackett holdovers who gave Carroll the most trouble was Omar Nazel. "Pete's always been called a players' coach," Nazel says. "And that's true, but you had to be a player he liked, someone like Jacob [Rogers] or Sunny [Byrd]. When a new coach comes in, he must evaluate the team and see who can help push the new agenda. Carson and Troy, they were the easy guys. And then you go to the guys who were squeaky-clean and good in class. Anyone else who didn't come along or who were on the fence about the plan or didn't like it or didn't fit it, those guys he tried to replace. I was one of those guys."

Nazel says he was boisterous and eccentric. "I tested the boundaries and Pete didn't like that," he says. "He disciplined me a lot, used me as an example."

Carroll, Nazel believed, viewed him as too small to play defensive end. "So he tried to put me in a position to fail," he says. Nazel says that during practice, Carroll had Nazel play strong side defensive end with the first team and then weak side defensive end with the second team, essentially making him take all the snaps in practice. "He was trying to wear me down," says Nazel.

Carroll, as might be expected, views his early interactions with Nazel through a slightly different lens. "Omar was the type of guy who had been hollered at all his life, the type of guy who got kicked out of programs. He was late to meetings and didn't do the right stuff," he says. "I distinctly remember saying, 'Omar, I'm not going to throw you out of the program, so quit fucking trying. You have to survive this. If you don't, you'll be a jackoff all your life. This is your chance. You have someone on your side.'"

In the end, the two came to a détente of sorts. Like Allmond, Nazel began to buy into what Carroll was coaching. "He had us so focused on the details in practice, on our steps and hand placement, which made us better," says Nazel.

And Nazel says that Carroll's tactics helped him and the team as a whole. "Carroll and the coaches would try to play psychological games with me, trying to come at me and some others," he says. "And I was like, 'This is bullshit, they're just trying to break us,' and I got really vocal about it. And the more they did it, the more we barked back. It bonded us. They were playing a game with us pit bulls, rattling the cage. And we were biting at the bars."

The psychological games continued into the 2002 season. After the Trojans' fourth game against Oregon State, Nazel was notified before a team meeting by a coach that he and kicker Ryan Killeen had been chosen as PAC-10 players of the week, something Carroll always made a big deal of celebrating.

At that meeting, Carroll was about to dismiss the group when he stopped and, according to Nazel, said, "Hold on, we have a PAC-10 player of the week here. Shout out to Ryan Killeen!" He never mentioned Nazel. "That really solidified for me the psychology he would use in order to push his agenda," says Nazel. "At the end of the day, we were successful, but it wasn't without casualties."

Nazel, in the end, became a starter and a key component of USC's defensive line, coached by Orgeron. The group—Nazel, Cody, Patterson, and Kenechi Udeze—became known as the "Wild Bunch II," a callback to the original Wild Bunch, USC's defensive line in 1969, which helped lead that team to an undefeated season.[¶] And the defensive line became the dominant unit on defense that Carroll had desired. They led a defense that gave up an average of only eighty-three rushing yards per game in 2002, despite facing nine running backs who would rush for more than 1,000 yards that season. The defense created thirty-six fumbles and forty-three sacks and finished 2002 ranked fourth in the country.

The Wild Bunch II was so dominant, Nazel says, that they never even really thought of their opponents. And here he credits Carroll's coaching methods. "Pete helped everyone on the team figure out that it was about us and not the outside world," he says. "Look at what you can do to improve, focus on the inner things, and then inevitably the outside world will produce what you

---

[¶] The original USC Wild Bunch was named after the movie of the same name, a Western starring William Holden and directed by Sam Peckinpah. The group included Al Cowlings, a tackle, who would later become famous for driving OJ Simpson's white Bronco during the wild televised highway chase in 1994.

want. When you're focused on your job, you don't worry about what everyone else is doing. It's like an actor who doesn't see the camera."**

Nazel says that during games, he and his fellow linemen would only look to see where the opposing tight end was lining up. "Then we'd move accordingly, right or left, and put our hands on the ground," he says. "Then you know what time it was? It was time for me to unleash all of those times when the coaches yelled at me, when Pete was unfair to me, when he put me in two-a-days in two different positions. You are all about to pay for that."

** After his football career, Nazel became an actor.

CHAPTER EIGHT

Wonder Boy and the War Daddy

The two players who didn't need any real coaxing from Carroll or anyone else were, of course, Troy Polamalu and Carson Palmer. "Pete made it really easy for us to follow and roll with him," says Palmer.

Polamalu is of Samoan descent. He was born in Orange County but left as a child to live with an uncle in Oregon. There, he starred as a high school running back and safety. In 1999, he signed with USC, which seemed like fate, given his name. "I believe God named me Troy for a reason," he said on many occasions. "I was born to come here."

Polamalu became a starter in his sophomore season. He was known to his teammates as sort of a Jekyll-and-Hyde figure. He was deeply religious and, off the field, was soft-spoken, thoughtful, and polite, saying "Yes, sir" when speaking to his coaches. He didn't go to parties. He was an accomplished classical pianist, often sitting down to the piano located in Heritage Hall and playing Chopin or Mozart. DeWayne Walker, who coached the USC secondary in 2001, remembers stopping a meeting once to make sure his players were taking good notes. "I went over to Troy and looked at what he'd written down and the detail and the penmanship, I'm like, 'Oh my God, this dude,'" he says.

On the field, however, Polamalu was something completely different. "Troy was soft and gentle," says Palmer. "Until it was time to play football." He began his USC career with a buzzcut but eventually grew out his hair into the long dark mane that ferally cascaded from beneath his helmet and over his shoulders because he believed it could help ward off the many concussions he was sustaining. Other than that, though, he had little regard for his own body or the bodies of others. He was the Tasmanian Devil, cutting a path of destruction across the field. He loved to hit, even in practice. "My freshman year we were doing a power formation, and my job was to take out the first body I saw," says Brandon Hancock. "That happened to be Troy. I went at him, and he came in full speed. I squatted 620 back then. I thought I was going to plow through him. But he did a power clean through my chin and I went from running to a full stop, like I had run into a brick wall. I was knocked out. The buttons on my helmet popped. My chin strap was on my eyeballs. He smashed off me and made the tackle for no gain. He was so explosive, violent, and powerful."

Polamalu also liked to get down and dirty. "You hit that switch with him, and he wanted to kill you," says Hancock. "He'd choke you under the dogpile, bury your face in the mud, knee you in the back, and then get up and it was like he'd just come to after losing his mind. He'd pray for you, do the sign of the cross, like he was asking for forgiveness for destroying you."

Justin Wyatt remembers attending a USC practice in the spring before he enrolled. In one play, Polamalu was hit by a vicious crack block delivered by the receiver, Grant Mattos. "The block was so bad. The first thing that hit the ground was the back of Troy's neck," says Wyatt. Kevin Arbet, a cornerback, had failed to call out the crack block to Polamalu. "The first thing Troy did—the play was still going on—was bounce off the ground and go into a frenzy looking for Arbet. When he found him, he grabbed his face mask and twisted it in a figure eight and yelled, 'Call out the motherfucking crack!' Needless to say, when I came in and got my first reps, I was yelling 'Crack!' on fades, slants, whatever, just to cover my ass."

Carroll remembers another practice when Polamalu was blocked hard by a teammate. "He got all fired up and he just fucking flipped," says Carroll. "We had to call off practice after another ten or so plays because he was just going after everybody. He was just ferocious."

But it wasn't all fury. Polamalu was a smart, instinctive, and athletic player, and he was the focal point of the defense. "Our defense was predicated on the four down linemen holding their gaps and filtering runs to the linebackers and one down safety, which, thank God, was Troy," says the linebacker coach Nick Holt.

In the USC defense, Polamalu had freedom within the scheme. "He was an extraordinarily gifted guy in terms of feel for the game, and he would take his shots like great players did, like Willie Mays stealing an extra base. I trusted the shit out of him," says Carroll. "We'd put him in positions where he had the freedom to attack and he was so instinctive, he was rarely wrong."

"People ask me who was the best athlete I played with at SC, and they assume it's Reggie [Bush, who joined the team in 2003]," says Hancock. "But it was Troy. There was nothing he couldn't do."

At the Trojans' end-of-the-year awards ceremony in 2002, Carroll talked about the great safeties he'd coached in the NFL—Ronnie Lott, Merton Hanks, Joey Browner, Lawyer Milloy—and as he handed out the team's defensive MVP award to Polamalu, he described him as "the best safety my eyes have seen."

And after one particularly dominant game in Polamalu's All-American 2002 season, Carroll was asked to describe his wild-haired safety. He said just two words: "He's perfect."

Carson Palmer arrived at USC in 1998, a six-foot-six, 220-pound, highly touted high school quarterback from Orange County. He'd been tutored by Bob Johnson, the well-known quarterback guru, since the seventh grade. He had dusty blond hair, blue eyes, and a toothy grin, the quintessential California kid.

Palmer played a few games as a freshman, then began the 1999 season as a starter. When he broke his collarbone in the third game of that year—which knocked him out for the season—he gained an extra year of eligibility, which was the only reason he was on the 2002 USC team in the first place.

Palmer was an incredible athlete. He won the team pullup competition in 2001, a remarkable feat for a quarterback and for someone of his height. He had massive hands and was known for throwing good blocks for his running backs. He threw an interception against Oregon State one year, fell down, and then ran across the field and tracked down and tackled the cornerback who'd intercepted him. "He was an exceptional quarterback, had a cannon for an arm, and threw the tightest spiral I've ever seen," says one of his tight ends, Alex Holmes. Chow loved him. "If you were to make a movie of quarterback throwing technique, you'd just tape Carson," he says.

"He was a born leader," says Lee Webb. "Like Troy, he stayed out of trouble, didn't party, didn't engage in anything but getting better at all times."

Even after Palmer had healed from his injury, he had a bit of a tougher time than expected in the 2000 and 2001 seasons. The talent around him then wasn't great, especially at the offensive line positions, which led to him being sacked a lot. And oftentimes it was left to him, and only him, to win games, which made him try to force plays, which led to interceptions. Early in his USC career, he'd also lost faith in his coaches. In a game during the 2000 season, Hackett and his offensive coordinator, Hue Jackson, argued over the headset about a crucial play—to the point where it was never called in to Palmer and the play clock expired and resulted in a penalty. The two coaches continued to argue about who was at fault as the game went on, seeming only to care about who won the argument and not the game.

Palmer blossomed when Carroll and Chow showed up. The playbook under Chow was just a few inches thick, as opposed to the *War and Peace*–sized one under Hackett. "By 2002, Carson had the same coordinator and quarterback coach for two years and got familiar with the offense," says Chow. "The offense wasn't complicated, and it didn't need to be." His big talented freshman receiver, Mike Williams, helped, too. "Mike unlocked Carson," says Chow.

All of which set the stage for what would be Palmer's magical 2002 season.

In his second season, Carroll continued the work of getting his players and coaches and the rest of the staff to buy in to what he was trying to do. How?

> It's about how you respond, the way you discipline, the way you celebrate. Every expression you make is a statement about who you are and the standards. If you do it well, you don't miss many opportunities to make a statement about what your expectations are. I think I was really demonstrative when I got my chances to be. Like Troy going off in that one practice. I didn't punish him. I wanted the guys to see what it looked like to be a great war daddy and be so competitive. You don't always do it right, but you try to capture those opportunities, those teachable moments, when you can. If you're on your stuff and you capture them and make the most of them, you imprint the learning and the expectations. That's the whole thing.

It even began to work on those holdovers from Hackett. "There were some really talented players [under Hackett]," says Carroll.

"They just hadn't been put together where the talent could show up, where they could be part of something."

Hackett's former players knew pain. They'd worked out in the run-down weight room and used the sixty-gallon trash bins for ice baths that they had to fill up themselves. And they'd done it all for naught, worked hard and lost, lacking any purposefulness.

And now these players were beginning to find the trust in the new staff. "With Pete, you genuinely felt he cared about you, individually and collectively, and cared about the success of the program and winning games. You felt like there was a payoff for what he was asking you to do," says Norm Katnik. "With Hackett, you weren't sure there was a payoff. He'd ask you to do something and you'd think, 'Are we going to get anything out of this?'"

Even Carroll's antagonist Nazel agreed. "The mentality of us old Hackett guys was now we can see an actual plan to be successful."

And, of course, being successful—as in winning games—creates the best environment for getting complete buy-in.

The sixth game of the 2002 season got off to a horrid start for USC. Cal, led by quarterback Kyle Boller, jumped out to a 21–3 lead in the Coliseum. It looked like more of the same for the Trojans. They had not beaten Cal at home since 1994.

But the game began to turn when Palmer threw a six-yard pass to Kareem Kelly in the end zone late in the second quarter, which the receiver appeared to have trapped off the ground. But the officials signaled touchdown. Well after the game—and well after anything could be done about it—it was determined by the PAC-10 that Kelly had, indeed, failed to catch the ball. All great dynastic teams receive at least a bit of good fortune along the way.[*]

---

[*] See: The Patriots' 2001 AFC Divisional "Tuck Rule" playoff game.

In the second half, USC dominated. Palmer escaped from the pocket, scrambled, and threw on the run, ending the game with 289 passing yards and two touchdowns (and two interceptions). McCullough ran for a career-best 176 yards. Williams, the freshman, caught six passes for 103 yards and a touchdown. Still, the game came down to a Killeen field goal with one minute and forty-one seconds to play, which allowed the Trojans to escape with a 30–28 win. "I feel like if we had lost that game, the era might have gone differently," says David Newbury.

From that point on, the Trojans, led by its fifth-year senior quarterback, "caught fire," Palmer says.

They beat Washington, 41–21. (Palmer: four touchdown passes.)

They beat Oregon, 44–33. (Palmer: five touchdown passes.)

They beat Stanford, 49–17. (Palmer: four touchdown passes.)

They beat Arizona State, 34–13. (Palmer: two touchdown passes.)

Then came UCLA, away, at the Rose Bowl. By then Tessalone and his assistant, Chris Huston, had designed a Heisman campaign for Palmer, who had begun the season completely off the radar—he was not even listed among the top thirty players on the preseason Heisman odds betting sheet. With a nod to the great late-night host and to LA showbiz, Tessalone and Huston branded the campaign "The Carson Show."

On the Thursday before the game, after he'd watched hours of UCLA tape, Chow declared, "This is the worst defense we've seen all year. We are going to put up fifty on them." He turned out to be correct.

The rout was on after Palmer threw two touchdown passes in the first five minutes of the game. The USC running game produced 197 yards. The defense forced seven fumbles, recovering four of them. And when Palmer threw for his fourth and final touchdown on the day, with two minutes left in the third quarter, the home fans started streaming for the exits, leaving only the Trojan partisans, who alternated between chanting "Heiz-mannnnn!" and "Pee-turr Care-Rull!" *Clap, clap, clap-clap-clap.* The final score: USC 52, UCLA 21.

"I'm jealous of our freshmen," Palmer told the *Los Angeles Times* after the game. "Before they leave here, they're going to play in a BCS Championship [Bowl Championship Series] game. They are going to do a lot of special things under Coach Carroll."

After the game, USC rose to number six in the nation. And in the last regular season game of the year, they faced seventh-ranked Notre Dame, under its first-year coach, Tyrone Willingham, in what was one of the most hyped games of the year.

The primetime game kicked off at eight p.m. EST, and Notre Dame took an early 6–0 lead on two field goals. USC answered with a Palmer touchdown pass and a field goal. Late in the second quarter, Notre Dame blocked a punt for a touchdown and took a 13–10 lead. Those were the last points the Irish would score. During a halftime interview on the field with an ABC sideline reporter, Carroll said, "I hope everyone is having a blast. I am."

The game served as a breakout one for the USC running back Justin Fargas, who rushed for 120 yards. Williams continued his incredible freshman season with 169 receiving yards and two touchdowns. Polamalu had two tackles for a loss, a sack, and a forced fumble, leading a defense that held the Irish to 109 total yards on offense.

But this game was Palmer's. He'd had Heisman-type moments in previous games—against UCLA, after a twenty-two-yard scramble, he'd taken a huge hit, performed a complete flip, and landed on the goal line, only to pop right up, arms triumphantly in the air. But the Notre Dame game sealed the trophy. Palmer threw for 425 yards and four touchdowns, the capstone to a six-game stretch to end the regular season in which he threw for twenty-three touchdowns and only four interceptions. Against Notre Dame, USC ran off thirty-four unanswered points and won, 44–13.

After the game, Hancock—who never forgot the way Willingham had treated him during his recruitment—found the coach on the field. "I went up to him and grabbed my crotch and spat on his shoes and said, 'Fuck you! Remember me?'"

Two weeks later, Palmer would handily win the Heisman over Iowa quarterback Brad Banks and Penn State running back Larry Johnson, USC's first winner of the trophy since Marcus Allen in 1981. "It's back," *Los Angeles Times* columnist Bill Plaschke—the same person who published the "For Pete's Sake, USC, Why Did You Do It?" column—wrote that day after the game: "USC football, in all its 1960s and 1970s glory, has returned."

USC ended the regular season ranked fifth in the country and tied for the PAC-10 title with Washington State, which received the conference's Rose Bowl bid due to their head-to-head win over the Trojans.

USC, though, was headed to another BCS game—the Orange Bowl in Miami to face Brad Banks and the third-ranked Iowa Hawkeyes.

One day during the 2002 season, OJ Simpson showed up at the USC practice facility, just as the team was preparing to head out to the practice field. The former running back was, of course, one of USC's all-time great players, thirty-four years removed from winning the Heisman Trophy. He was also seven years removed from being controversially acquitted for allegedly savagely murdering his ex-wife and her friend. He was, in short, a potential distraction and a surefire public relations problem.

Members of the media, both from Los Angeles and the country writ large, were already perched on railing surrounding the field, in position to cover practice. This fact made Tim Tessalone anxious. Part of his job as USC's sports information director was to put out fires. Another part was to make sure nothing burst into flames in the first place.

Tessalone, aware that many eyes followed his moves, approached the compliance officer, Keith Miller, and asked if he could somehow deal with Simpson and make sure he didn't get out to practice, in front of the media and their cameras.

Miller approached Simpson. "OJ knew who I was and knew why I was coming over," says Miller. Simpson surrendered with much less resistance than he had presented the LAPD in 1994. "OJ just gave me a quick affirmative nod and followed me out," says Miller. "On our way out, I saw Pete. He raised his eyes, like 'Thank you.'"

But Simpson would prove to be the proverbial bad penny that season.

At a USC practice at Nova Southeastern University in Miami one week before the Orange Bowl, Seamus Callanan was standing next to the *Los Angeles Times* writer Gary Klein. They were chatting when suddenly Klein looked up.

"Oh my God," the reporter said. "I'm going to have to bury my lede now."

Klein had planned on leading his practice-day report with the news that Lou Holtz had come out that day to watch his former graduate assistant prepare for a BCS bowl game. But no longer.

Callanan looked at Klein and then followed his gaze to the practice field. There stood Simpson, watching from the sidelines. Justin Fargas, the running back whose father had played Huggy Bear on *Starsky & Hutch* and knew Simpson, had supposedly invited him to practice. Tessalone and Carroll could do little about his presence now. "It was kind of a spectacle," says Carroll. "I didn't really know how to handle it, so I just treated him like he was a ballplayer and tried to be as normal as possible. But it was awkward."

At the end of practice, Carroll called in his players and said, "Fellas, we have one of the all-time USC greats here with us today." Simpson spoke briefly, telling the team, "I'm the greatest, you're the latest." Carroll then led the team in a breakdown: "I want to hear 'OJ' on three . . . one, two, three . . . OJ!"

Carroll hoped that OJ would take the hint and leave after that. But he didn't. He followed the team into the locker room and mingled. "It was brutal, a weird feeling," says Brandon Hancock. "OJ's just lurking around, walking in that rickety way he did. He had huge hands and a thirty-three-gallon head, a fucking melon. The players either loved that he was there or they hated it, broken down roughly by racial lines." Simpson hung out a bit, signed a few shirts, and then, finally, left.

After Klein's story ran the next day, the phone lines at the USC hotel lit up and Carroll received faxes with death threats.

Simpson's visit was an indication of something, though. "It definitely brought a heightened level to what we were doing and let us know that this was a big stage and that all eyes were on us," says Hancock.

Iowa came into the game 11–1, a mirror, in a way, of the USC team. They had their own star quarterback in the Heisman runner-up Brad Banks. They had their own big-time safety in Bob Sanders. They had an excellent receiver in their tight end, Dallas Clark.

But USC was confident. "Walking into the Orange Bowl that night, we had no fear," says Marcell Allmond. "We knew we were going to win."

USC did receive some troubling news before kickoff, though. Polamalu had been battling a hamstring injury in the lead-up to the bowl game. And during pregame warm-ups, with the muscle still bothering him, he'd gone back into the locker room for a shot of Toradol, an anti-inflammatory. But when the shot was administered, it accidently hit a nerve, leaving him unable to feel his leg. Polamalu would only play two snaps in the game: he lined up to defend an early extra point and then limped onto the field for one play in the fourth quarter. But in the end, the Trojans wouldn't even need the contribution of their star safety.

Iowa started the game with a bang, running the opening kickoff back one hundred yards for a touchdown. After that, though, the first half grinded to a near halt and ended with the teams tied at ten.

The two teams made their way to the locker rooms. "They were walking," says Collin Ashton. "And we came sprinting by them. At that moment, I thought, 'We've got these clowns.'"

In the second half, USC exploded. After receiving the opening kickoff, they proceeded to work their way eighty yards down the field on a drive that ended with an eighteen-yard touchdown pass from Palmer to Williams. They scored touchdowns on their next two possessions as well, and the game was effectively over early in the fourth quarter, with USC ahead, 31–10.

With just over nine minutes to play, USC got the ball back and drove it down to the Iowa eighteen-yard line. On the sidelines, Carroll summoned Sunny Byrd and told him, "Sunny, you started it for me, you're going to end it for me."

Byrd was handed the ball on five straight plays. He ran like he always had for USC—two hard-won yards here, three hard-won yards there. On one of his runs, he trucked Iowa linebacker Fred Barr, who had spent the week telling the media how soft USC was and had almost started a fight between the two teams at a pre-bowl game dinner at a Miami steakhouse. And on his last carry as a Trojan, Byrd broke through the line and lumbered into the end zone for a six-yard touchdown.

Final score: USC 38, Iowa 17.

On the podium after the game, Carroll stood next to his warrior-chief Polamalu, one of the key players in USC's turnaround, someone who had bought into what Carroll was selling, had flourished, and, in turn, had helped the team flourish as well. The great safety was done with college, on his way to what would become a Hall of Fame career in the NFL. Carroll would miss him, but he wasn't looking back. He wasn't in the present, either. "We're just getting started," he told the crowd.

That night, back at the hotel, the team had what Tessalone described as "an epic party" in the ballroom, with the players, coaches, staff, family, and friends. "It went on until basically sunrise," he says.

As per custom, the coach of the Orange Bowl winner was supposed to appear at a press conference in the media hotel the morning after the game. "At about four a.m., I got Coach and said, 'Hey, I'll meet you in the lobby at 7:30 and we'll drive to the media hotel.'" But when Tessalone showed up at the appointed time, Carroll was nowhere to be found. He called Carroll's room. "I just remember his voice, how low and gone it sounded when he finally answered," says Tessalone. "I said, 'Pete, we have to go to the presser.' And he goes, 'Just tell them I'm not going to make it.' And he didn't."

"That was a great night," is how Carroll remembers it.

That same morning, Sunny Byrd awoke in his hotel room to a call from his girlfriend. He'd been up nearly all night. "I was like, 'I'm a senior, I don't have football anymore. Might as well go for it,'" says Byrd. His girlfriend asked if he was on the team's plane going home. He was not. And, he realized suddenly, the plane was leaving in twenty minutes.

In a panic, Byrd called Pola, his running back coach.

"Pola said, 'You're not on the plane?' and I was like, 'Nope,'" says Byrd.

Mark Jackson, the director of football administration, then called Byrd and told him to go immediately downstairs, where a policeman was waiting for him. "So I go down to the lobby and, yep, there's a cop," says Byrd. "And he's like, 'Sunny Byrd! You scored a touchdown last night! That's so cool!' And then he gave me a hug."

They went to the police car and Byrd tried to get into the back. After the night he'd had and the trouble he was presumably in, it's where he felt like he belonged. But the policeman insisted Byrd join him in the front. "He's got the sirens on, he's racing, going the opposite direction of traffic, hitting seventy in a thirty, and asking me all of these questions like, 'How does it feel to score a touchdown in the Orange Bowl?'" says Byrd. "And I'm just hanging on to the 'Oh shit' bar in the car for dear life."

They pulled onto the tarmac, just in front of the plane. "I can just feel everyone's eyes in the plane on me," says Byrd. "The boosters, alumni, coaches, wives, players." He got out and the policeman gave him one final hug. Byrd walked onto the plane and when he looked down the aisle, he saw Carroll and Garrett. The plane was dead silent. "And then Garrett stood up and smiled and said, 'We can't be mad at you, Sunny Byrd,' and gave me a hug and Carroll gave me a hug, and the plane went wild, everyone clapping," says Byrd.

A cult hero until the very end.

Palmer's Heisman Trophy and the resounding win in the Orange Bowl had given the Trojans a taste of the big time and a place in the national spotlight. They would be losing some key players after that season, Palmer and Polamalu foremost among them. But they had plenty of talent and depth coming back.

When Lou Holtz had visited the pre–bowl game practice, he'd marveled at the speedy running back, Hershel Dennis, and the way he hit his holes and sliced through the defense. He'd marveled even more when Carroll told him that Dennis wasn't even a starter and was, in fact, on the scout team for that practice. (Dennis would get two carries in the Orange Bowl.) "I think at that point, with players like Shaun Cody and Mike Williams, we realized we were pointed in the right direction talent-wise," says Jacob Rogers. Talent is the name of the game in college football. And talent attracts more talent, especially when it is well-coached and wins. And the talent USC had in 2002 was just a small taste of what was to come.

CHAPTER NINE

Split Decisions

In college football, there are two parts to recruiting. The first is evaluation—being able to identify talent and somehow figure out if that talent will hold or bloom in the years to come.

The second is the wooing, the coaxing, the selling—everything that goes into the delicate act of convincing a seventeen- or eighteen-year-old kid, his parents, his coach, and sometimes his grandparents and pastor that the school and football program is the right one for him.

Despite its utmost importance, recruiting is, always has been, and always will be an inexact science. Only 6 percent of high school football players play in college, at all levels (FBS, FCS, Division II, Division III, etc.). Some, but not all, of these players will be assigned ratings from specialized agencies. These ratings, like Wikipedia, provide a foundation from which to start research, but they aren't always reliable. Roughly half of the high school recruits who are assigned a five-star rating (the highest) will start at least half of their college games by their second year. According to a 2018 *Bleacher Report* study, 52 percent of the high school five-star players will be drafted by an NFL team, and only a little more than a third will be "retained" by a team (played for more than a season or two in the league). College teams are also given ratings for their collective haul of recruits at the end of the recruiting period. And sometimes, recruiting classes that garnered a top-ranking flameout.

Dealing with human beings—and especially young, still-developing human beings—is the main reason recruiting is an inexact science. Kids who look great in high school will often disappoint at the next level: a kid might be a physical specimen but not have the work ethic. Injuries happen. Another recruit might appear to be a worthwhile project—that muscly, 270-pound kid who only played a season of high school ball but appears to have all the tools—and never pan out. And then there are the kids who surprise and outplay their ratings—that two-star with the killer combination of late-developing talent and a chip on his shoulder.

But the 2003 USC recruiting class stands out as a repudiation of that inexactitude.

During his time at USC, especially early on, Carroll had on his staff some of the best college football recruiters in the sport's recent history. "Coach O is the best recruiter of all time," says quarterback Mark Sanchez. And "nobody could sling it better than Kiff," Carroll says about his young tight ends coach. Sarkisian, the other young gun, more than held his own. Holt was as dogged as they come. Pola was solid and straightforward. Chow, though not always the most eager road warrior, was a benefit by his presence alone—especially now that he had coached *two* Heisman Trophy–winning quarterbacks.

These coaches did much of the initial work—the information gathering and the first visits—and then Carroll would come in at some point during the process. "We didn't have some solemn pitch," says Carroll. "We were being as authentic as we could with the kid and family and told them that we'd take care of them, win, and have fun. We'd just try to overwhelm them, so they'd be like, 'I have to go there.' We didn't have to make anything up. We didn't have to do anything out of the ordinary. Frickin' great school, LA, the fun, the weather, the fans, the Coliseum experience, the Trojan Walk, all of the things we did we showed them and made them feel a part of it."

It helped that Carroll promised all recruits that they could compete for a job on day one. "And we meant that," he says. "We wanted guys to play early, and we gave them that chance, which played into the whole competition thing. The idea was to get them to play in the first half of their freshman season so they could be valuable as regular players by the middle of the season. That was the whole point, to get them ready to help us win." Carroll would end up having a freshman start at every position during his time at USC.

"His idea was to out-talent everyone, to have so much talent and depth as to be able to dominate," says Chris Huston, the assistant sports information director.

Carroll was the ultimate closer with the kids and their families, could "talk a dog off a meat truck," as Huston says, and "made it feel like he was going places and he wanted you on board," as offensive tackle Winston Justice puts it. At one point, as the team got rolling and the talent began to pour in, Carroll didn't have to work too hard on the wooing part. He once told a member of the staff, "We don't have a recruiting department. We have a selecting department. Our challenge is to select the right guys."

It helped, too, that Carroll had an unexpected ace up his sleeve in the recruiting game: one of his players, the tight end Alex Holmes.

Holmes was a star student at Harvard-Westlake High School, one of the top academic schools in the country. He was trained in the classical languages—he finished first three times in a national Latin exam—was a violinist and a tech savant. Football was never his abiding passion. "I'm not a football guy," he says. "Never have been." But he was good enough at the sport to be recruited to

USC in 2000 under Hackett. He began his career as a backup and then, under Carroll, became a starter.

And yet, football remained a secondary aim. "One of the main reasons I went to SC was for the networking," Holmes says. "It's a great network, especially in California." He networked well early on, and by his junior year, he says, "I was fully integrated into the entertainment and Hollywood community." That, his coaches came to realize, made him a valuable asset in recruiting.

In the Orange Bowl game against Iowa, Holmes caught three passes for twenty-seven yards. But he also broke his back, which forced him to miss the entire 2003 season. "So I poured myself fully into recruiting," he says. "It was kind of an unspoken thing. The coaches would come up to me and say, 'Could you help me with this guy?'" Holmes was in charge of every top recruit who visited during his time at USC, hosting Cody, Williams, Leinart, Reggie Bush, LenDale White, Dwayne Jarrett, Lawrence Jackson, and Keith Rivers, among others.

He talked to the kids and their parents about the school. "I always stressed SC's academics with the parents," says Holmes. "The kids were less interested in that." What they *were* interested in was another thing Holmes provided—a memorable weekend on the town.

Holmes struck up a relationship with Brian Kennedy, the Los Angeles promoter who was plugged into the food and fun scene in the city. "My offices are up on the strip," says Kennedy. "A lot of kids wanted to go there, and I could get them reservations at the best restaurants and the hottest clubs with Alex."

Through Kennedy, Holmes says, "we were able to go places and do things and not wait in line and not have to pay any money. I didn't have a dime to my name, and I was doing things executives weren't able to do. And I could apply that when I had a recruit. I would take them out and introduce them to celebrities and show them what could happen if they came here and played their cards right."

Holmes knew many of the celebrities in town and knew where they liked to hang out at night. When LenDale White came on his recruiting visit to USC, Holmes took him to the House of Blues, where the high schooler met Shaquille O'Neal and Jamie Foxx. "If it wasn't for Alex Holmes, I don't know if I'd be a Trojan," White told *The Athletic*.

Holmes says that though he never asked celebrities to explicitly tell a recruit to come to USC, their very presence was an implicit suggestion that it would be a wise decision. "Back then, clubs didn't make you sit down and get a bottle," says Holmes. "The recruits would run into the celebrities because people were standing and talking. And people like Jamie [Foxx] had no ties to SC. They'd just talk about the town." And just being noticed by a celebrity was a hell of a recruiting tool on its own. Chris Galippo, a five-star linebacker recruit in the 2007 class, says, "One of my fondest memories is when I went to the Brea Mall with some friends, and we were in line for a movie. In front of us was Snoop. And he turned around and said, 'Is that Chris Galippo?'" These types of interactions were not happening in State College, Pennsylvania.

At the end of the weekend, Holmes says, "I'd tell the recruit that no one can play football forever, it doesn't matter who you are. This is the place where you can network for after football." And then he'd issue his closing statement. "I really didn't talk about other schools," he says. "I'd just ask them, 'Do you want to go to an incredible school and live in a place that has great weather and beautiful girls and Hollywood and all this stuff? Or do you want to go somewhere else?'"

By the time he graduated after the 2004 season, Holmes had helped recruit *fifteen* All-Americans to USC. And he helped put together the Trojans' 2003 recruiting class, which may have been Carroll's masterpiece.*

There was a kid at Helix High School, nine miles east of downtown San Diego, who had a bit of a growing legend at the turn of the new millennium. He played all over the place for his team—running back, wide receiver, quarterback, kick returner, and even did some punting. The kid wasn't very big—maybe six feet and 180 pounds. He was quiet, polite. His mother was a prison guard. His stepfather a school security officer.

By his senior year, every program in the country knew about Reginald Alfred Bush III.

Nick Holt was Bush's primary recruiter from USC. He loved him. But his head coach had some reservations.

Carroll says he watched Bush's high school film "three times as much as any guy I ever looked at." The reason: "He would break away and there was no one else on the field, in the camera shot. I couldn't tell what was going on. Was it too easy for him? Were his opponents subpar? The funny thing is that his quarterback on that team was Alex Smith, who ended up going number one in the NFL Draft,[†] and I never once noticed him, and I watched that film a ton."

But Holt and other assistants finally convinced Carroll that Bush was worth going after and, from that point on, Carroll says, "We went hard." But they had competition. Texas, Washington, and Notre Dame were after him, as well. And the Irish seemed to have the upper hand.

But Bush came to visit USC on the weekend in late November 2002, when Notre Dame came to play USC in the Coliseum.

---

* Holmes's sister, Theodora, married Troy Polamalu.
† To the 49ers in 2005.

Holmes hosted him and took him out Friday night for dinner and some clubbing with Leinart and Williams. And then the next night, Bush stood on the sidelines as USC destroyed Notre Dame, 44–13, in front of a raucous, sold-out Coliseum crowd. The outcome of the game, it appeared, changed Bush's mind about where he was going to play football in college. "I always think of that," Lane Kiffin told ESPN. "Like how that changed college football. What if Reggie Bush would've gone to Notre Dame and had not been part of the Pete Carroll era? Would that era have been the same?"

The answer is a definitive "no," for more reasons than one.

Bush became part of USC's twenty-five-player class of 2003. It was the third-rated class in the country that year. But history has proven it to be one of the greatest of all time.

Bush was joined by two other top-rated running backs in that class, White and Chauncey Washington. The class wholly revamped the secondary with the three cornerbacks, Terell Thomas, Eric Wright, and Will Poole (from a junior college). Two defensive linemen—Lawrence Jackson and Sedrick Ellis—would help maintain the tradition of the Wild Bunch II. USC added a stellar receiver, Steve Smith, to join Williams. And the class produced two generationally talented offensive linemen in Sam Baker and Ryan Kalil.

In all, the 2003 class would boast a future Heisman winner and Associated Press player of the year in Bush, five first-team All-Americans, nine first-team all-PAC-10 players, and thirteen NFL players (four drafted in the first round, five in the second).

The class was not without heartbreak—the promising high school All-American linebacker Drean Rucker drowned the summer before the season after getting caught in a rip current at Huntington Beach State Park (Carroll and the team attended his funeral).

It also had a major flop.

During the process of putting together the 2003 class, back when Bush was no guarantee to commit, Carroll and his staff put a lot of effort into recruiting a player named Whitney Lewis. Lewis was the California player of the year who, during his senior season at St. Bonaventure High School in Ventura, became the first high school player in California to gain more than 1,000 yards in both running and receiving in the same year. He scored a touchdown once every 4.5 times he touched the ball. Carroll told his assistants that Lewis "could play in the NFL right now."

Some of those assistants had concerns, though. One of them echoed Carroll's concern about Bush: the game seemed almost too easy for Lewis. They worried about his work ethic and his general demeanor, too—Tim Davis, the offensive line coach, had described Lewis as "a pain in the ass." Maybe most important: it was fairly clear that Lewis really wanted to go to Florida State, but there was a sense that his parents were preventing that from happening. There was a rumor that before legendary Florida State coach Bobby Bowden showed up at the Lewis family's door on a recruiting visit, Lewis's mom had made sure her son was not at the house and at a USC basketball game instead.

Still, USC pulled out all the stops in recruiting him. On his official visit, Orgeron borrowed Marcus Allen's Heisman Trophy and slapped Lewis's name on it.

But because of the concerns, Lewis was not assured of an offer from the Trojans. He had competition within the coaches' offices from a player named Mark Bradford, a wide receiver. Bradford had starred at Los Angeles's John C. Fremont, a Title One school that served mostly low-income families.[‡] Carroll and his coaches loved Bradford, a tough and smart kid, and his father, who had raised Bradford alone after his mother died at a young age.

[‡] Dr. Dre, California congressman Henry Waxman, and the founder of the Crips gang, Raymond Washington, are among the school's notable alumni.

A few days before National Signing Day, Carroll had only one scholarship spot left.

The decision came down to Lewis or Bradford. Carroll gathered his staff in what was known as the War Room. He asked for a vote and went around the room. And one by one every coach — Chow, Kiffin, and Sarkisian among them — voted for Bradford. Carroll finally got to Orgeron, the last person to be asked for an opinion. "Coach, I have to disagree with everyone else," Orgeron said. "We have to get Whitney. He's a special player."

Carroll then turned to all his coaches. "He used an old John McKay line," says Seamus Callanan. "He said, 'Fellas, this ain't a democracy and I have to agree with Ed.'"

So USC let Bradford walk (he went to Stanford) and signed Lewis. Lewis showed up to his first camp overweight. He did not take well to the hard coaching, to the "bad cops" on the staff. In his freshman season, he had a total of three catches for twenty-seven yards and three carries for eleven yards. He missed his sophomore season because he was ruled academically ineligible. During his junior year, he did not catch a single pass. He ended up transferring to Division II Northern Iowa after that year, having ended his Trojan career without ever starting a game.

Bradford, on the other hand, set a Stanford school record for receptions as a freshman and would finish his career there as one of the all-time leaders in that category.[§] He would also come back to haunt Carroll and the Trojans in just a few years' time.

Coming into the 2003 season, the favorite to win the all-important quarterback job was a player named Matt Cassel. Cassel had joined USC in 2001, part of Carroll's first recruiting class. He was an excellent athlete who had played in the Little League

---

[§] He also played for two years on the Stanford basketball team.

World Series (and could throw a baseball ninety miles per hour) and had also starred at football and basketball in high school.

Behind Cassel was Brandon Hance, the transfer from Purdue who had started games there before he left and had sat out the 2002 season at USC because of the NCAA transfer rules. He was followed by Leinart, another member of the 2001 class, a left-handed former star at Mater Dei High School who had nearly had his moment in the 2001 season when Carroll considered inserting him for the then-struggling Palmer. Next came Billy Hart, who also played baseball for USC, and John David Booty, a freshman who had enrolled early at the school.

Going into spring practice that season, the coaches' opinions of the quarterbacks were all over the place. The race for the starting job had basically been narrowed down to three players. Some liked Cassel because of his athleticism. Chow preferred Leinart. And Carroll initially liked Hance. "Pete was smart enough to see what was on the horizon with quarterbacks, that mobility was going to be a thing," says Chow. "And Hance could really run around."

It remained a battle throughout the camp, to the point where, Chow says, the coaches screwed up. "I learned a lesson that spring. We tried to be fair and give them all equal snaps. But by being fair, we weren't fair to any of them, because no one improved."

Hance was the first man out. An ankle injury and a bout of viral meningitis cut into his practice time, and "he wasn't very big," says Carroll. The competition came down to the two Matts. "Cassel was a little wacky," says Carroll. "I used to think of him as Daffy Duck, silly and stuff, excitable. He was a really good athlete but a little hesitant." Wide receiver Chris McFoy says Cassel was "intense, a little uptight on the field." Leinart, he says, was a little more relaxed.

At the end of spring practice, Carroll told Chow it was time to choose a starter. In the end, Leinart won out. "I think Leinart's

smarts took him over the top," says Chow. "He'd sometimes annoy
Pete at practice. We'd be doing scripted plays in a scrimmage, and
Leinart would line up in the formation and then change the play
within the same formation, and Pete would say, 'Hey, you can't do
that!'" It also helped that Leinart was straight from quarterback
central casting. "He was a big good-looking kid who did everything well," says Carroll.

Leinart wouldn't have too much time to get adjusted. His first
game as a starter looked like a doozy—the preseason eighth-
ranked Trojans would be traveling to Alabama to play the sixth-
ranked Auburn Tigers.

The Tigers were confident going into the game, and for good reason. Their two superb running backs—Ronnie Brown and Cadillac Williams—were a year older and, presumably, better, and the
duo was joined in the backfield by quarterback Jason Campbell.
(All three would play in the NFL.) Auburn also had two preseason All-Americans at linebacker—Karlos Dansby and Dontarri-
ous Thomas. They would have home field advantage, as well,
with a packed stadium and a swampy game-time temperature of
eighty-eight degrees.

But maybe most significant to Auburn was the fact that they
were facing a quarterback making his first start. Leinart had appeared in three games in his Trojan career—always at the end
of a blowout—and had yet to throw a pass. Spencer Johnson, an
Auburn defensive lineman, told ESPN that he and his defensive
brethren were "drooling at the mouth" at the prospect of facing
Leinart.

Before the game, Carroll brought in two former Trojans to address the team. John Papadakis made a speech about USC football tradition. "He told us that our jersey color was cardinal so that
you couldn't see blood and talked about the Trojan network, the

brotherhood and sisterhood and all the Trojans loving the hell out of each other and how it wasn't just talk, it was real," says Justin Wyatt. "It hit you in the face."

Then Sam Cunningham stood up. Cunningham had played on USC's 1972 national title–winning team, but he was there to talk about another monumental episode in his life. In 1970 at USC, Cunningham was part of the first all-Black backfield in Division I college football history. In the first game of that season, the Trojans traveled to Birmingham to play the Alabama Crimson Tide. The Alabama football team was, at this point, all white, and the state itself was working through the still-hot embers of the end of segregation.

In that game, Cunningham (whose nickname was "Bam") ran all over the Alabama defense, gaining 135 yards and scoring two touchdowns in a convincing 42–21 win. Lore has it that Alabama coach Paul "Bear" Bryant went to his school's president after the game and convinced him to integrate the football team, which happened the following year.[1]

Omar Nazel says Cunningham's speech had a powerful effect, especially on the Trojan defensive line, which was intent on teaching another Southern school a lesson. "We had an agenda that day," he says. "We wanted to show these guys, 'Whatever you thought it was, it ain't.'"

In warm-ups before the game, the starting four members of USC's defensive line (aka the Wild Bunch II)—Cody, Patterson, Udeze, and Nazel—came out on the field with their shirts off. It was an idea that had originated with Kennedy Pola. "Coach Pola would always say, 'What's the first thing you do when you get in a

---

[1] Jerry Claiborne, who had been a Bryant assistant, famously said about that game, "Sam Cunningham did more for integration in sixty minutes than Martin Luther King did in twenty years."

fistfight? You take your shirt off,'" says Nazel. "He would lead us in the 'SC-Wild Bunch' chants, get us all riled up, and every time he'd do it, he'd take his shirt off and the whole meeting room would explode, people throwing chairs. So when we walked out at Auburn with our shirts off, the message was, 'Whoever wants some, come get it. We ready.'"**

Auburn, on the other hand, was not. Campbell was picked off on the third play of the game. Three plays later, Leinart completed his first official pass as a collegiate player, which went for a touchdown to Williams. And then the Trojan defense, led by the Wild Bunch II, took over. Auburn's hyped running game gained only a total of forty-three yards, and the entire offense was held to just 164 yards and lost two fumbles. The USC defensive line opened up gaps for Lofa Tatupu, playing in his first game for USC, who accumulated twelve tackles and two of the six sacks of Campbell on the day.

The USC offense, while not spectacular, played well enough. Leinart went 17 for 30 for 192 yards and that one touchdown. Hershel Dennis, the sophomore running back now off the scout team and starting, had eighty-five yards and a touchdown. And Reggie Bush and LenDale White got in the game late for their first snaps as college players.

USC easily handled its next two opponents, BYU and Hawaii, with Leinart throwing for a combined five touchdowns and the young running back duo of Bush and White scoring two touchdowns each. The Trojans rose to number three in the nation.

** Carroll used this gambit in recruiting, as well. Blake Ayles, a tight end who joined the Trojans in 2008, says at his high school recruiting gathering—with 500 or so of the top California recruits—Carroll stood up in front of the group and asked the same question Pola had. "And then Pete ripped his shirt off, and everyone in the room got so hyped and jumped out of their seats and started ripping their shirts off, too."

And then came the Cal game, one that would be remembered as among the most important in the Pete Carroll era at USC.

Cal came into its home game against the Trojans with a 2–3 record. The Golden Bears coach Jeff Tedford had been frustrated enough with the early season that he'd benched his starting quarterback, Reggie Robertson, for a junior college transfer named Aaron Rodgers, who would be making his second start of the season against USC.

The game did not start well for him—Rodgers tripped and fell on his first snap. But it got better. He ran for an early touchdown and threw for two more, leading Cal to a 21–7 lead at halftime.

The Trojan locker room was silent . . . until Carroll bounded in. "Okay, guys. I don't care about the score. Fuck the score," he said. "What I care about is how you respond. Show me how you're going to respond. Go out there and show me. Give me all your effort, focus on the details, and go out and have fun and see what happens."

The speech nearly worked. White ran for a six-yard touchdown midway through the third quarter and then, a few plays later, Tatupu ran back an interception for a touchdown. Suddenly, the game was tied. And Rodgers was out with an injured knee, replaced by Robertson.

After exchanging field goals in the fourth quarter, the game went to overtime. In the first overtime period's second play, Dennis fumbled the ball near the goal line. A few plays later, Cal lined up for what would be a game-winning twenty-nine-yard field goal. But the attempt was blocked—USC's second blocked kick of the game—by Gregg Guenther, a six-foot-eight tight end who also played on USC's basketball team.

In the second overtime period, the two teams traded touchdowns. And in the third, Killeen missed a thirty-nine-yard field goal, and Cal made a thirty-eight yarder, and the game was over. 34–31, Cal.

USC had plenty of places to look for blame. The running game was weak—Dennis only ran for fifty-three yards and had that crucial fumble. Leinart threw three interceptions. But perhaps the biggest reason that the Trojans lost was their inability to corral Cal's running game. Golden Bear back Adimchinobe Echemandu ran for 147 yards. The Wild Bunch was embarrassed. That they'd been run over by the very same outside zone running scheme that Carroll was trying to perfect at USC only made it worse.

"I remember looking around the locker room after that game," says Marcell Allmond. "It didn't look like we'd lost. It looked like we fucked up. When we lost with Hackett, we got our asses beat. Against Notre Dame one year, we didn't even cross the fifty in the second half. But when we lost to Cal, they didn't beat us. We fucked up. There's a big difference."

Hancock agreed. "It was an epiphany," he says. "The only team that could stop us was us. And that's only if we didn't prepare well, if we overlooked an opponent, if we didn't bring it every day."

A players-only meeting was called after the game. "I think there were some egos then, and those went out the window," says Justin Wyatt.

Carroll, for his part, didn't dwell on the loss. He told the team they'd watch film and get better. He made a few small scheme changes, emphasizing the run to give his still-inexperienced quarterback time to grow.

"That game was a huge turning point," says Allmond. "We knew then what we had to do."

"We got total buy-in from that point on, on team and scheme," says Wyatt. "From that point on, it was electric."

The Cal loss ended USC's eleven-game winning streak.

But it started a much longer one.

The Trojans went on a tear. In their last nine games of that season, they averaged forty-four points a game on offense and only gave up an average of seventeen on defense.

They destroyed Notre Dame in South Bend, 45–14.

The Wild Bunch took out their fury on then-sixth-ranked Washington State, with each of them getting at least one sack (Udeze had two) and holding the Cougars to minus-twenty-five yards rushing.

USC beat UCLA in front of a sellout crowd at home, 47–22, holding the Bruins to one yard rushing in the first half.

Bush and White, role players at the beginning of the season, began to come on. White rushed for 140 yards and two touchdowns against Arizona State. Bush began to show signs of the triple threat he would become, equally dangerous as a runner, receiver, or return man, and had a thrilling ninety-six-yard kickoff return for a touchdown against UCLA.

On the season, Leinart threw for 3,556 passing yards, thirty-eight touchdowns, and only nine interceptions. He finished sixth in the Heisman voting. Williams, who had ninety-five catches for 1,314 yards and sixteen touchdowns on the season, finished eighth.[tt]

With the winning streak came the vibes. Billboards featuring Leinart and Williams hovered above the highways. LA's fair-weather fans—from the worlds of Hollywood, music, tech—came flooding back to the now-sold-out games at the Coliseum, talking as if they'd never left and had always stayed true. Success attracts the successful. Tailgating tents—something not seen in years—popped up outside of the stadium. Thousands now showed up for

---

[tt] Sandwiched in between the two Trojans was Chow's old quarterback Philip Rivers.

the Trojan Walk. Students made their presence known at games, chanting "Big Balls Pete!" whenever their kinematic coach went for it on fourth down.

USC's practices, by tradition, had been open to the public for years, even under Robinson and Hackett. But, also for years, they'd only been attended by a handful of donors and media members. But now they were swarmed with hundreds of people—fans, kids from the neighborhood, even the occasional celebrity. Carroll, unlike most other coaches, liked the throngs at the open practices, never worrying about a scout from another team diagnosing the Trojan plays. Part of it was that he believed other teams could pretty easily divine what USC was doing from game film. And part of it was a growing confidence—he knew his team was so good that it didn't really matter if the other team had the entire play sheet. The practice crowds increased the buzz. They had become part of the community. Within three years of Carroll's arrival, the Trojans had become the city's team.

And at the center of it all was Carroll, the leading man. His recruiting visits became events. When he arrived on a high school campus, he was often greeted by the school band, which would break out an impromptu version of "Fight On!" as the high school kids cheered him on. Other coaches tracked his movements and did whatever they could to keep him at bay. "I remember going to recruit a receiver in Alabama and when I got to the high school, the kid wasn't there," says Carroll. "Alabama had gotten word and had sent someone to take him off campus." On one recruiting weekend at USC, Holmes took some of the players and their parents to the House of Blues. And, lo and behold, who stepped out onto the stage to play the piano to a packed house? Pete Carroll.

The LA media got caught up in and helped perpetuate it all. They were at the practices and the games, too, soaking up the growing excitement. But more important was the fact that the Trojan coach, unlike most other football coaches, didn't bemoan the intrusion of the media. He embraced it. "Carroll was such a breath of fresh air," says Ivan Maisel, a national college football reporter for ESPN at the time. "He didn't have his guard up and was a people person at heart. That was refreshing, because most of these guys viewed us as the enemy." It helped, too, that "he never came across as the football coach with the veins popping out of his neck," says Tessalone. "He was different."

Carroll had learned a thing or two after going through the media gauntlets in New York and Boston, which eviscerated the young, naïve, and unprepared. "Pete was great with the media," says Tessalone. "He's survived those tough media markets. LA had professional media, too, but it was different." Most college football coaches face the media three times a week. But Carroll in those early years at USC—with a Tuesday media brunch and availability as he walked off the practice field—was fielding questions sometimes five days a week.

This was calculated. He used the media to deliver his upbeat, energetic message—to the fans, his players, and recruits—and the daily access meant he could keep tabs on the media and some modicum of control on the message, as well. And he knew how to keep them at bay when needed. "Pete coached me up about that," says Keith Miller. "When there was something we didn't want to discuss with the media, he'd tell us not to talk within earshot of the reporters or to walk and act busy so they wouldn't approach us." Carroll also took the techniques he'd learned from Jim Valvano about job interviews back in the NC State days and applied them to interviews with the media—he didn't necessarily answer their questions, but he always told them what he wanted to tell them.

The local LA media was equal parts charmed—they weren't immune to the tonic of winning—and befuddled by the coach.

About Carroll, Bill Plaschke of the *Los Angeles Times* wrote, "He talks like a forty-five-year-old surfer dude who just happens to coach football."

Plaschke's colleague T. J. Simers called Carroll "my greatest challenge . . . one of the best at not answering a question."

Scott Wolf of the *Los Angeles Daily News* nicknamed Carroll "Caesar" for his total control of the program and the message.

Carroll was, in his own way, a difficult person to profile, hard to pin down because he was always in motion. "In one interview I did with him, he took swings with a baseball bat the entire time he was talking to me," says Maisel. The novelist/ghostwriter J. R. Moehringer wrote what is perhaps the most incisive profile of Carroll during his USC years, and even *he* felt like he only skimmed the surface. The piece, which appeared in *Los Angeles* magazine in 2007, was titled "23 Reasons Why a Profile of Pete Carroll Does Not Appear in This Space: An Attempt at Writing About a Football Coach."

Carroll still claimed that he didn't pay attention to what was written and said about him in the media. This was not totally true, at least according to some members of the media. Petros Papadakis— son of John and a former USC fullback who was the captain of the team in Hackett's last season—covered the team on a radio program after his playing days. "Pete would call me at night if I said something he didn't like and yell at me," he says. "And I'm like twenty-four years old, living in a one-room apartment."

It also helped that Carroll has immense personal charisma. He was like a skilled politician—a Bill Clinton type. His attention moved fast and shifted quickly, but when that attention fell on you, it felt like stepping out of the cool shadows into the warmth of the sun. Paul Salata, a former USC receiver and prominent booster, marveled at the fact that Carroll "knows your name and your wife's name." Carroll charmed some of the biggest boosters at his weekly

Monday Morning Quarterback meeting, where he would sit with them and walk them through game footage and provide them with glimpses of what went on behind the scenes in the locker room. "He was gifted at handling an audience," says booster David Bahnsen, who sat "eight feet away" from Carroll at the meeting every week. Carroll was the typical extrovert, providing energy for the crowds and drawing energy and nourishment as it was reflected back at him. "Pete was really good at the interpersonal and he understood how that affected the macro," says Rocky Seto.

Carroll fostered an atmosphere of inclusivity with the players, coaches, fans, media. Everyone. He had Brandon Hancock's mom break down the practice huddle. He would stay after practice and sign autographs for forty-five minutes. "No coach in the country did that," says Pat Ruel. "He always said it was part of his job to make everyone feel like they were part of the program." He gave seldom-used walk-on Spencer Torgan the nickname "Torch." "Pete would find a little role for everybody and help people see it and appreciate it," says Seto. Carroll would ask the trainers, the sports information staff, the ballboys—anyone—what they thought about a particular player or play call. Chris Huston remembers once walking into an interview with T. J. Simers with Carroll and Jim Perry, a former USC sports information director who was in an emeritus role at the time. "Perry was telling Pete about Simers, about how he could be tough," says Huston. "But Pete already knew this, and Perry was talking very slowly and taking up Pete's valuable time.

"Pete listened to him, didn't big-time him. After Perry left, I rolled my eyes and told Pete, 'That's Jim.' In my mind, I was protecting Pete. Hackett would have told me, 'Don't let that guy waste my time ever again.'"

Carroll did the interview. And as Huston walked him out, Carroll turned to him. "He told me, 'Don't roll your eyes at Jim. He's on our side, he's on our team.' The lesson was that Perry deserved polite consideration. It symbolized the way Pete talked to everybody. He was very much like that, especially early on. He made everyone feel like they were part of the program and had a key role and that their input was recognized and noticed."

That feeling of inclusion benefited the team in more ways than one.

USC, like Notre Dame and Stanford, had high academic standards for admission for student-athletes. "There was a gap between USC's academic standards and the NCAA's," says Huston. And, sometimes, the Trojans would lose out on a recruit because of those standards.

There were, however, something called university exemptions, in which a coach could go before a USC committee and make the argument for a player he wanted who hadn't achieved the required academic standard but wasn't too far off. During Hackett's years, Huston says, there were maybe eight players who were university exemptions. "But Pete came in and changed that."

That change happened, according to Huston, because of Carroll's ability to make people feel like they were part of the program. One of those people was the school's provost, who happened to be the person in charge of making academic decisions for athletes. "We'd give the provost four field passes and they'd be down there and feel like they were part of things and, lo and behold, we'd get an unlimited amount of exemptions," says Huston. One way to get those exemptions was through a loophole. According to Huston, a psychologist in Colorado was often used to evaluate recruits. "He found that some had dyslexia," says Huston, which meant they qualified as learning disabled and could take untimed tests and, generally, have an easier time getting into the school. "We got a lot of guys under Carroll that we didn't get before," says Huston.

That inclusion—that warmth of the sun—was felt most, of course, by his players. Carroll was still, through and through, a players' coach. "He was really outside the box when it came to his players, unlike the more military coaches, like Saban," says Kiffin, who coached under both men. "He was really creative and really moved things to the players. He moved practice plans and schemes around them. Most coaches don't do that. They're like, 'This is my system and scheme, and players have to fit in it.' He would give them leadership and give them plenty of rope."

Carroll made his first connection with an individual player during the recruiting process and then after signing them. He aimed to form a relationship and understand them, to get to know everything he could about them—their backgrounds, family life, motivations—learning his learners. He wanted to unearth their individual philosophy because he believed that would unlock something greater. "Philosophy is about figuring out who you are. Purpose is about connecting with a reason to put your philosophy in action," Carroll wrote in his book. "And if somebody feels you recognizing who they are and what they're all about, that they are truly being seen and being heard, you've opened up a connection to introduce them to the collective purpose."

"Being a psychology guy really helped Pete with all that," says Mark Sanchez. "It helped him understand what made people tick and what kind of buckets people's emotions and talents fell into. And he could immediately connect the dots, with speed and accuracy, not something a lot of people can do."

It wasn't just the personal relationships that did this, though. One of the most significant keys to Carroll's success at USC was something he did for his players and his coaches, something that seemed impossible: he created an atmosphere that enabled them to love the game in the way they'd first loved it as a kid, playing touch football in the backyard—the fun, the smiles, and the creative energy and concentration that came with total absorption.

"There were times when I felt like I was fifteen again," says Pat Ruel. Garrett Nolan, an offensive lineman, says, "You play your best when you're having fun."

"Football never felt like work with Pete," says Palmer.

Kiffin described it as an atmosphere of "want to" rather than one of "have to."

And this, to Carroll, was everything. "The illustration is the child at play," he says. "When a child plays, you can stand right next to them and they won't notice you, they're so into what they're doing. That's what I was trying to create. Be in the moment. A lot of Buddhist teachings are about judgment and how it gets in the way. But it's about being mindful in the moment. That's why Kobe [Bryant] and Michael [Jordan] played like they did. Nothing else existed. Just the moment. It might sound hokey to some, but that's really what it is."

"Pete brought energy and enthusiasm every day and I think about it often because I don't know how he did it," says John David Booty. "Everyone was drawn to it. Everyone was like, 'I didn't know football could be like this. Man, I want to play for that.'"

Carroll combined something unusual in an authority figure, a very useful dualism. His prematurely gray hair, and his decades-long coaching background in college and in the NFL, gave him the visage of a wise old sage, that gravitas. And yet he had the energy, the demeanor of a kid. "It felt like Pete was twenty-five," says Palmer.

It all set up an unusual dynamic between coach and players. Football coaches are often likened to father figures—"Pete was that to many of us," says Katnik. But Carroll was not the father who motivated by fear. He was the father who motivated in another way. "With the culture he set, the fun and everything else, you just never wanted to disappoint him," says the quarterback Matt Barkley.

———

All of this—the inclusivity, the vibes, the fun—was part of the journey. And, as we are told over and over again, the journey is paramount, it's what makes a life. This is undoubtedly true. But there is no such thing as a meaningful journey unless it has a meaningful destination. That destination is what gives shape, purpose, and relevance to the journey. It's what makes the journey possible in the first place.

And what made everything work for Pete Carroll—now at USC and not before in New York or New England—was the destination that gave definition and meaning to the journey.

That destination, simply put, was winning. Winning made it all possible, made it all work. Winning was the ultimate validation.

On Saturday, December 6, 2003, the Trojans completed the regular season with their eighth straight victory, 52–28, over Oregon State. Leinart threw five touchdown passes. Bush averaged nearly twelve yards a rush. Steve Smith broke out with a five-catch, 136-yard, one-touchdown performance. The defense forced four interceptions (including a pick-six) and a fumble.

USC entered that game as the second-ranked team in the nation. All logic said that they would be in the BCS Championship game that year, to be played in the Louisiana Superdome, home of the Sugar Bowl. As the Trojan players exited the Coliseum field after beating Oregon State, they were serenaded by Def Leppard's "Pour Some Sugar on Me" via the public address system. Wide receiver Keary Colbert held up a box of sugar. "We were sure we were headed to the Sugar Bowl to play in the championship," says Rocky Seto.

Until they weren't. Later that evening, in the Big 12 Championship game, Kansas State upset top-ranked and previously undefeated Oklahoma, 35–7.

That left three teams—USC, Oklahoma, and LSU—with identical one-loss records. Oklahoma's loss had been the embarrassing defeat to Kansas State. LSU had lost to a then-unranked Florida team at home, 19–7. USC had lost to Cal, away, by three points in triple overtime and had finished the season with eight straight big wins. The Trojans seemed like a shoo-in for the championship game. The AP voters and the coaches, who voted in the ESPN/ *USA Today* poll, agreed, ranking USC number one in the country.

But, somehow, when it was all said and done, the BCS rankings, which considered the human polls and a set of computerized metrics, left USC out of the game. The Trojans were to play Michigan in the Rose Bowl instead. Carroll put some spin on it—win the game against Michigan and USC had a really good shot at splitting the championship. Despite that, says Hancock, "People were angry."

Michigan had a very good team. They'd beaten five ranked teams and had a solid rushing attack and a huge offensive line that, as the media framed it, would control the game against a softer PAC-10 defense.

But the USC players were not in the least bit worried. "None of it mattered," says Nazel. "It's what Pete instilled in us. Play the game we've been practicing, focus on the details, and everything else will handle itself."

Carroll didn't seem to be worried, either. On the day before the Rose Bowl game, he and Orgeron and some other staffers were in Carroll's car together. At one point during the drive, Carroll said, "Guys, I want y'all to relax. We're going to play our best game tomorrow. Our guys are going to play great."

USC went into the Rose Bowl on January 1, 2004, with plenty of relaxed confidence combined with a shot of righteous fury.

In the run-up to the Rose Bowl, a practice was broken up one day by the appearance of a golf cart that had, in its passenger seat, someone in a full Trojans uniform. Carroll stopped the practice as the cart approached. He told the team that a fraternity boy was trying out at tight end. USC was hurting at the position — Holmes had been out all season with his back injury, and his replacement, Dominique Byrd, had torn up his knee in the sixth game of the season.

Out of the cart stepped a person in a number eighty-five jersey. He wasn't that big and didn't look very athletic. The players stood awkwardly, shifting from foot to foot. And then number eighty-five took off his helmet.

It was the actor Will Ferrell, whose movie *Old School* had come out that year. The players went wild. Some began chanting "Frank the Tank! Frank the Tank!"

Carroll sent Ferrell into the huddle. Leinart called "842 Amigo," a play in which all receivers and tight ends run "go" patterns. Ferrell took off down the sidelines, loosely covered by All-mond. Leinart heaved the ball downfield. "Kind of underthrew me," Ferrell told *Sports Illustrated*. But Ferrell caught it for a forty-yard gain. "It was silent for a second and then when I made my catch, I got a weird, pathetic cheer," Ferrell said.

Carroll and Ferrell had met at a Lakers game earlier in the year, and Ferrell had told the coach that he'd graduated from USC in 1990, had majored in sports information, and had even interned under Tessalone in USC's sports information department. He also told him he'd been a placekicker back in high school. Carroll invited him to practice. And a prank was born.

Ferrell would drop in to Trojan practices many more times as the years went on, sometimes participating in a prank and other times merely watching. He became a fixture on the sidelines at home games and bowl games, the first of many celebrities who would attach themselves to the USC football team. The beginning, really, of a deluge of publicity and attention, a phenomenon that Carroll would encourage and nurture, as it helped take the program to new heights even as it left it exposed to peril.

On the field before the Rose Bowl, Carroll, in pleated khakis and a red short-sleeved polo over a white long-sleeved compression shirt, tossed the ball back and forth with a staffer. At one point he caught the ball, held it, and stood still for a moment, a rarity for him.

"You know, in this very spot, a USC quarterback threw a bomb for a touchdown over my secondary."

Carroll was recalling the 1980 Rose Bowl, in which USC beat Ohio State, when he was the Buckeyes' secondary coach.

He smiled and pulverized the gum in his mouth and began tossing the ball again, as positive thoughts washed away the memory.

Michigan received the opening kickoff for a touchback and then drove the ball to the USC thirty-yard line. The Wolverines attempted a field goal, but Shaun Cody blocked it.

And that was as close as Michigan would come to being competitive in the game.

The game was a contrast in skill and style. USC was quick and creative, Michigan slow and mundane.

The vaunted Michigan offensive line was completely overwhelmed. The Trojans sacked Wolverines quarterback John Navarre *nine* times. The game was over early in the third quarter, when USC jumped out to what would turn out to be an insurmountable 21–0 lead.

Carroll even let Chow loose late in the game. With just under four minutes left in the third quarter and a comfortable 21–7 lead, Chow noticed that the Michigan defense was in man-to-man coverage. He decided to try a play, one that he had run with Rivers back at NC State, and one he had tried, unsuccessfully, in his very first scrimmage at USC, something called "trips right, 18 toss, reverse quarterback throwback."

Leinart snapped the ball and turned and tossed it back to the running back, Hershel Dennis. Mike Williams, one of the three receivers lined up to the right, ran behind the line of scrimmage back toward Dennis, who flipped *him* the ball. Without breaking stride, Williams threw a lofted pass to . . . Leinart, who had gone out on a route near the left-hand sideline. Leinart was not known as a fleet-of-foot quarterback, but because of the misdirection, he was wide open. He caught the ball and ran it in for a touchdown. A *Sports Illustrated* cameraman caught the moment he crossed the goal line, lifting the ball in triumph.[‡‡]

The play would turn out to be the last one of significance in a Trojan uniform for the ultra-talented sophomore receiver Mike Williams.

Michigan scored in the fourth quarter to get within shouting distance of USC, but they never threatened again, and USC won, 28–14.

At the postgame ceremony, Carroll told the crowd, "I think we just won the national championship."

Three nights later, in an ugly defensive slugfest, Nick Saban's LSU Tigers defeated Bob Stoops's Oklahoma Sooners, 21–13, which meant, by virtue of the fact that the game was the designated BCS Championship, that LSU had won a national title.

But so had USC. In the AP poll, the Trojans had finished in the top spot, with forty-eight votes to LSU's seventeen. The title was split, the only time that happened during the BCS era and the last time it ever happened, period.

LSU prevailed in the ESPN/*USA Today* coaches' poll because the coaches were supposedly obligated to vote for the winner of the BCS Championship game. But three coaches ignored the

---

[‡‡] When the Philadelphia Eagles successfully ran the play during their win in the Super Bowl at the end of the 2017 NFL season, it became known as the "Philly Special."

rules and voted USC number one, instead. One of those coaches was Lou Holtz, Carroll's old boss who was then the coach at South Carolina (the other two: Oregon State's Mike Bellotti and Illinois's Ron Turner).

It was split, but USC had its first national title in twenty-five years.

When Carroll was asked about his 2003 season and team, he didn't spend much time reminiscing. He was already looking ahead, echoing what he'd said after the Trojans' 2002 bowl win.

"I can't wait for next year," he said.

The Trojans had reached the mountaintop. But they wanted more.

INTERLUDE

A brief break from the football to catch up on the actual Trojans and the war they engaged in against the Greeks sometime in the twelfth or thirteenth century BC.

The story of the Trojan War, the writer Stephen Fry contends, is a mix of fact and fiction, "historical and imaginative" at the same time. It got its biggest boost from Homer, when he wrote *The Iliad* in the eighth century BC. The epic poem famously starts not at the beginning of the war but *in media res* (in the middle of things).

A little background: the city of Troy (located in present-day Turkey) had been left in ruins after a series of wars until King Priam ascended the throne and rebuilt it, turning it into, as Fry describes it, "the most marvelous kingdom in the world."

All was well until Paris—the prince of Troy, as a son of Priam's—stole Helen of Sparta from her husband, Menelaus, the king of Sparta. Helen was reputed to be the most beautiful lass in the world. The Greeks, angered by the theft, sailed to Troy to get her back. And thus began the Trojan War.

Paris, as the Byzantine author Malalas described him, was "charming," "eloquent," "sturdy," and had a "good nose" and a "long face." In this instance, Carroll can be seen as Paris. And

Helen? She would be college football, which Carroll and his USC teams completely hijacked for a while.

Some of the Greek gods chose sides during the Trojan War — Ares (war), Apollo (the archer god of harmony), and Aphrodite (love) protected the city of Troy. Athena (wisdom and warfare) and Hermes (the herald of the gods) were among those on the side of the Greeks.

Many gods stayed out of the fighting. Among them was Hades (god of the dead). He had his reasons: he just liked the carnage and wanted the bodies.

In this instance, Hades can be understood as the media, the fans of other college teams, or any of the various rubberneckers who slowed down to take a look as everything during the Carroll era at USC — the build, the championships, the near misses, and the inglorious and sudden fall — unfolded.

The Trojan War would last nine years and end with the destruction of Troy in the tenth, eerily similar to the timeline and fate of Carroll's Trojans.

The Trojans of Homer and other chroniclers fought valiantly and legendarily, which is why, I suppose, they are the mascot for roughly 400 high schools and nearly twenty-five colleges in the country, though none nearly as prominently and popularly as USC. The university really leans into its mascot and name. Before home games in the Coliseum, a man dressed in Trojan battle gear — cuirass (breast and back plates), greaves (shin protection), helmet and crest (that thing that looks like a brushy mohawk), and sword — rides a big white horse (usually an Andalusian) named Traveler around the field and dramatically plants the sword at midfield.*

But at the end of the tale of the Trojan War — in that tenth year — the Trojans were done in by excessive pride and negligence

---

* College football is the best.

and were caught by surprise. Odysseus, the cunning king of Ithaca, came up with an idea to defeat the Trojans. Outside of the city walls, the Greeks built a large wooden horse, and they left it there as they pretended to sail home, defeated. The Trojans rolled the horse into the city, a spoil of a war they believed they had won forever. But within the horse, of course, were around forty Greek warriors, who slipped out of it in the middle of the night, took the unsuspecting city, and, thus, won the war.

As Homer wrote in *The Iliad*:

> Troy has perished, the great city.
> Only the red flame now lives there.
> The dust is rising, spreading out like a great wing of smoke
>   and all is hidden.
> We now are gone, one here, one there.
> And Troy is gone forever.

CHAPTER TEN

The Hottest Ticket in Town

In March 2004, USC was invited to the White House to com-memorate the national title. LSU was invited, too. Same day, same time.

Both teams gathered in the East Room of the White House to wait for President George W. Bush. There wasn't much mingling or conversation between the two teams, who were simultaneously dismissing each other and sizing each other up.

Bush arrived and seemed to sense the odd tension in the air. And, as was often his wont, he tried to cut through the unease with humor. With a deadpan look, he struck a Heisman pose, which got some laughs, and then he suggested that the two teams hash it out once and for all with a game on the South Lawn, which he said was "a pretty good size."

On the bus to the White House, Carroll reminded his players to not approach Bush, to stay put in their lines and wait until the president called them up. Desmond Reed, USC's special teams ace, apparently didn't hear his coach. After Bush made his jokes, Reed broke from his spot and started walking toward him, extend-ing his hand with a big goofy smile on his face and saying, "Hey, Mr. President."

Two Secret Service members instantly stepped toward Reed, their hands moving—alarmingly—to their hips, where their guns presumably rested. Bush saw what was happening and called off his Secret Service. "It's okay, guys," he said. He said a quick hello to Reed—game recognizing game—and then sent him back to his spot.

Both teams did their photo sessions with the president. And then it was on to the next season.

The returning 2004 Trojan team had serious talent—twenty of its players would go on to the NFL.

Some of the players would be coached by new faces that season. Three USC assistant coaches—some of the staff stalwarts—left in the offseason. In what basically amounted to a swap, Kennedy Pola left to become the running backs coach for the Cleveland Browns, and Todd McNair left that position at the Browns to coach running backs at USC. Nick Holt left to become the head man at Idaho. He was replaced as linebacker coach by Seto, who was to be assisted by Ken Norton Jr., son of the former heavyweight boxer and a fearsome former NFL linebacker who had won three Super Bowls in his career (and played under Carroll at the 49ers). Carroll's son Brennan, who had joined the team as a graduate assistant in 2002, took on responsibility for the tight ends. And Sarkisian—at the age of twenty-nine—left for his first job in the NFL, as the quarterbacks coach for the Raiders.*

The offseason also had other tumult, the type that exposed the tiny cracks that often appear in the glossy veneer of success.

It started in March, when offensive lineman Winston Justice—a two-year starter and budding star—was arrested for suspicion of assault with a deadly weapon. Though the "deadly weapon" was reportedly a pellet gun that was pulled on a fellow student, Justice

---

* Sarkisian had left USC for about a month in 2002 to go to San Diego State but came back.

found himself in a jam—he'd been arrested for soliciting a prostitute the prior summer. The USC administration, left with little choice, suspended him for two semesters, which meant he would miss the season. "That was a dark time in my life," says Justice. During his time away, he trained on a near-daily basis with the famed boxing coach Freddie Roach.

Two months later, redshirt freshman quarterback Michael McDonald was arrested for drunk driving.

Two players on the 2003 championship team were also arrested in that offseason. Sandy Fletcher, a defensive back and wide receiver who had never quite lived up to his promise, was nabbed for having a loaded firearm in his car. And Will Poole, a cornerback, was charged with a DUI. Neither player had any eligibility left—Fletcher was out of football and Poole had been drafted by the Dolphins.

It didn't stop there. Before the season, receiver Whitney Lewis and running back Chauncey Washington were ruled academically ineligible to play the season, and running back Hershel Dennis was investigated for an alleged sexual assault. His case was eventually dropped for lack of evidence, but Carroll suspended him for two games, a costly punishment for the player who had been a starter in 2003. By the time Dennis came back in the 2004 season, he'd been supplanted by Bush and White and relegated again to taking snaps with the scout team.

But bad behavior wasn't the only problem facing the Trojans in that offseason. The team's vaunted wide receiver room appeared to be falling apart.

The Trojans had struck gold with Mike Williams. He was exactly the prototype receiver Carroll and Chow loved—a big guy who was adept at winning one-on-one situations, making him a perfect fit for the slants and fades favored by the USC passing attack. He was a starter from nearly day one, setting NCAA, PAC-10, and

USC records and earning a spot on the Freshman All-American team. In his sophomore season he got even better, finishing as a first-team All-American and garnering Heisman votes.

He was well-liked by his teammates, too. "Mike was hilarious," says his fellow receiver Chris McFoy. "He was an extrovert, very outspoken. He took care of business on the field and knew how to have fun off it." Williams frequently said things off the cuff that were either intentionally or unintentionally funny. "We'd be having a pregame lunch, and he'd turn to me and say, 'I love this sammich almost as much as I love my dick,'" says Lee Webb. He helped bond the team together by pushing back on some of the "bad cop" coaches, especially the ones who were only a few years older than the players they coached. "He used to mispronounce Kiffin's name on purpose," says Brandon Hancock. "He'd walk by him and say, 'Fuck you, Lance.'"

In February 2004, Maurice Clarett, the Ohio State running back who had been kicked off the Buckeyes team in 2003,[†] won a lawsuit that made him eligible for the 2004 NFL Draft, repealing the NFL rule that required a player to be at least three years out of high school to play in the league.

Williams—like Clarett, only two years out of high school— kept a close eye on the trial. He believed that his size and skill made him a first-round pick in the NFL. Most scouts agreed with him. So, shortly after the Clarett ruling, Williams hired an agent named Mike Azarelli to represent him. In doing so, he forfeited his remaining two seasons of collegiate eligibility.

That turned out to be a mistake.

In April of that year, just before the NFL Draft, a federal appeals court put the Clarett ruling on hold. And then, a month after that, the Second U.S. Circuit Court of Appeals formally

---

[†] For all kinds of reasons—reportedly receiving illegal benefits, fighting with coaches, publicly bad-mouthing the university, etc.

overturned it. That meant that Clarett would not be eligible for the 2004 draft and would have to wait a year. It meant the same for Williams. Because he had hired an agent, he wasn't eligible to play in college, either.

In June 2004, Williams decided that he would attempt to get reinstated by the NCAA. He fired Azarelli and began paying back the more than $100,000 he'd received in endorsements, from Nike and a playing card company. USC, on its end, worked feverishly to get him back.

One significant problem Williams faced was that he had dropped out of school when he had hired Azarelli back in February. The NCAA required that all athletes continue their academic progress while playing a sport. Williams entered summer school in an attempt to comply with that rule.

But in the end, the NCAA declared that Williams cleared neither of the "obstacles" facing him for reinstatement, "one related to academics and one related to amateurism," which meant he was set adrift and couldn't play in the NFL or with the Trojans. The NCAA's decision was handed down two days before USC's 2004 season opener, just as the team was boarding its flight to the game. Carroll was incensed. "To take it all the way to one hour before we leave?" he told the *Los Angeles Times*. "I couldn't be more disappointed. It's very cold and insensitive for them to deny him this opportunity."

The good news for the Trojans was they had a backup plan for Williams.

The bad news was that the backup plan was having his own serious troubles.

Dwayne Jarrett grew up in New Brunswick, New Jersey, raised by his strict mother and his grandmother. He was a star football player in high school, as a receiver and a defensive back. In his senior year, he was named to the *Parade* magazine high school

All-American team, won the New Jersey offensive player of the year award, and scored all three touchdowns in New Brunswick High School's 21–14 win over Long Branch High School in the 2003 state championship game.

Jarrett was nearly a Williams clone, tall (six foot five) and shifty with reliable hands, and was one of the gems of USC's top-ranked 2004 recruiting class, which included eight five-star players— tight end Fred Davis, offensive lineman Deuce Lutui, and linebacker Keith Rivers among them. (Jarrett was four-star.)

Carroll viewed Jarrett as a player who could come in and learn from Williams for a year and then take over, and, in fact, Williams had hosted Jarrett on his official visit to USC. But that process would now have to be sped up.

Jarrett enrolled in USC in June 2004, just a few days after his high school graduation. He was still just seventeen years old. And almost immediately, he became severely homesick.[†] He called his mother every night from his USC dorm, begging her to let him come home. When she repeatedly said no, he called his grandmother and aunts to lobby them to convince her to change her mind. The homesickness grew worse as August training camp neared.

Jarrett's teammates and coaches tried to help but, as shy and introverted as he was, they couldn't tell if their efforts were working. "I remember sitting on a bench with him and telling him, over and over, 'It's going to be okay,'" says Chow. The one teammate Jarrett connected with was Fred Davis, the tight end who had come from Ohio. "We bonded over the homesickness," says

---

[†] Homesickness among first-year college football players is an underrated and underreported phenomenon. One prominent former college coach estimated that 20 percent of his incoming recruits were negatively affected by it. And remember, Ed Orgeron, during his playing days, had left LSU because of it.

Davis. "We just hung out every day talking about back home, about what we'd be doing at that moment back there."

The coaches allowed Jarrett to go home for a weekend and were relieved when he actually returned. They decided to make Leinart his roommate, to help with the homesickness and, hopefully, establish a connection between the quarterback and receiver that could be taken to the field. Leinart's parents took Jarrett out to dinner and did his laundry. But Jarrett remained shy, removed, and homesick. And it affected his play.

During the offseasons at USC, the strength and conditioning staff, led by Chris Carlisle, usually came up with the slogan for the winter and spring workout period. They were usually your garden-variety sports clichés—like "Start Fast, Finish Strong" or "Go Hard or Go Home." They'd plaster the words on T-shirts, hoodies, and the walls.

The 2004 slogan: "Leave No Doubt."

Carroll grew up a fan of the Grateful Dead, and he liked to repeat a quote that he'd once read from the band's lead guitarist and vocalist. "Jerry Garcia said he didn't want his band to be the *best* ones doing something. He wanted them to be the *only* ones doing it. To be all by yourself out there doing something that no one else can touch—that's the thought that guides me, that guides this program: we're going to do things better than it's ever been done before in everything we do, and we're going to compete our ass off. And we're going to see how far that takes us."

In the 2004 season, it took them all the way to the top.

The Trojans began the season ranked number one in the preseason polls. Their first game, against Virginia Tech, promised to be a good test of that ranking. The Hokies were coming off a winning season and their coach, Frank Beamer, was a well-respected veteran of the college game.

USC began the game a bit lethargic and held back by some drops by Jarrett, who was still wrestling with his homesickness. At halftime, they trailed 10–7. But they came out after halftime and clamped down on the game, which they won, 24–13.

One of the signature traits of USC during the Carroll years was that they owned the second halves of games. That they fell behind occasionally in the first halves of games wasn't totally surprising—they were in the midst of becoming a big target, every other team's Super Bowl. "The other team would play carefree and give us their best shot and we'd have to absorb it," says Chow. "Pete would always tell our guys that the game wasn't won in the first, second, or third quarters, but in the fourth."

But the second-half takeovers mostly had to do with USC itself. The team's lines on both sides of the ball had become so physical and dominant that, as the game went on, they would inevitably wear down the other team. And both Carroll, on the defensive side, and Chow, on the offensive side, were masters of halftime adjustments. Carroll liked to ramp up the pressure on opposing quarterbacks after the half and confuse them by blitzing cornerbacks and dropping defensive linemen back into coverage. Chow liked to save his attempts at explosive plays for the second half, almost like a boxer setting up his opponents with jabs and then, eventually, coming in with an uppercut. "In the first half, we'd see what was going on," he says. "And then we'd show them something they'd already seen, like a curl route, and then make that route a curl and go."

USC next destroyed Colorado State (and head coach Sonny Lubick), 49–0, and then did the same to BYU in Provo, in what amounted to a homecoming of sorts for Chow, where Leinart threw for two touchdowns and Bush and White combined for 234 yards rushing and two touchdowns in a 42–10 win.

Away at Stanford, USC again fell into a first-half hole, down 28–17. But Stanford never scored again, and a thirty-three-yard punt return by Bush late in the fourth quarter helped set up the game-winning touchdown. USC 31, Stanford 28.

Then came the team that had ruined the Trojans' perfect season the year before.

Cal, which came into the game in the Coliseum ranked seventh in the country, was loaded, particularly in the backfield, which featured Aaron Rodgers and two excellent running backs—the speedy senior J. J. Arrington and the ferocious freshman Marshawn Lynch.

The Trojans scored early on a Leinart touchdown pass to White, which gave them a lead they would never relinquish, though they would never be comfortable.

Rodgers began the game completing his first of *twenty-three* passes, which tied an NCAA record. But his fourth down pass into the end zone at the end of the game fell harmlessly to the turf, and USC held on to win, 23–17.

The Trojans escaped, though not unscathed. Steve Smith, USC's leading receiver, broke his leg in the game. But there was also some good news that maybe would blunt the impact of Smith's absence: Jarrett had played significant minutes and had avoided drops and caught the touchdown pass from Leinart that provided the game's final margin. The next week, at home against number fifteen, Arizona State, Jarrett had his breakout, catching five passes for 139 yards and three touchdowns in a 45–7 win.

He had finally settled in at USC, enough so that his mother called off her plans to move out to Los Angeles to be near him. By the end of the season, Jarrett would be the team leader in receptions (fifty-five) and yards gained (849).

And as the wins piled up, so did the attention. By the midpoint of that season, USC football had become the hottest ticket in town. The Trojans set a home attendance record (511,373 people) and a PAC-10 home game average attendance record (85,229). They also helped other teams sell out their stadiums whenever their traveling circus came through town.

But it wasn't just the games. Attendance at Trojan practices went from hundreds to thousands. And the crowd of students, neighborhood kids, media, and players' family members had been joined by a different type of Los Angeles fauna: celebrities.

Ferrell, the first real celebrity to attach himself to the team, continued to show up. Snoop Dogg first came to a practice during an early bye week in the 2004 season. He would eventually become even more entrenched with the team than Ferrell, dressing out for practice and running routes, sitting in on film study, rapping his song "Drop It Like It's Hot" at team meetings, participating in a freestyle rap battle with cornerback Eric Wright, and becoming good friends with LenDale White off the field. "It was wild to have Snoop standing five feet away from me as I practiced punting," says USC punter Tom Malone. Snoop was even named the Trojans' "guest coach" during the week before the Notre Dame game. When asked why he gave Snoop that honor, Carroll replied, "Here we are in LA. Why not?"

Denzel Washington was there. So was George Lucas, Brad Pitt, Angelina Jolie, Henry Winkler, Kirsten Dunst, Jessica Simpson, Nick Lachey, Dr. Dre, Warren G, Spike Lee, Alyssa Milano, Arnold Schwarzenegger, Sean "Diddy" Combs ("That one feels weird now," says Lee Webb), members of the Red Hot Chili Peppers, Jamie Foxx, Christian Slater, Arsenio Hall, Jake Gyllenhaal, Keanu Reeves, Adam Sandler, Jerry Bruckheimer, Johnny Knoxville, Kiefer Sutherland, and Miley Cyrus. "It all became kind of glitzy," says Holt.

They came to the games and the practices, patted the players' helmets when they came off the field. They got autographs and photos. "It was electric on the sidelines," says Henry Winkler. "They had whatever that secret sauce was, when you meet someone, a real star, and you just go, 'Oh, that is the *it* person.' And that secret something was sprinkled over the entire team. It was just amazing."

"In LA, people don't care about you unless you're the best," says Jacob Rogers. "Pete always highlighted that, that there was a reason the celebs were here to watch us, that we were pushing in the right direction." USC football became a cultural phenomenon in Southern California. When the celebrities flocked to the Trojans, they found within them some semblance of a community and some sort of reflection—the players, in their own way, were doing what they did for a living, after all. Performing for an audience. Breathlessly running through scripts. Hearing the cheers after a good play, and the groans after a not-so-good one.

A-listers came because they were attracted to winning. The B-listers (*Hey, there's the guy who played the other Terminator!*) came to be seen with the A-listers. "I remember seeing Minnie Driver standing on the sidelines by herself and I was thinking, 'Why is she here?'" says Petros Papadakis. "And then it dawned on me that someone had told her she *should* be there, to get her picture taken, to be seen as part of the celeb crowd there."

"In a way, the celebrities could get their notoriety from us," says Carroll. "It was as much for them as it was for us."

The Trojans became the football version of the NBA's Showtime Lakers of the 1980s, the dynastic team of Magic Johnson, Kareem Abdul-Jabbar, and Pat Riley, and they filled the vacuum left by the struggles of the Lakers from 2004 to 2007. As if to drive the point home, at one USC game in the Coliseum, Luke Walton, a Laker star in the 2004–2005 NBA season, was asked to leave the Trojan sidelines because he didn't have a pass, and the security guards didn't know who he was.

"Having celebs there was a great way to build momentum and attention," says Carroll, who didn't just lean into it—he weaponized it. He made sure Tessalone provided the television producers with a list of celebrities in attendance for the games and where they would be, whether that was on the sidelines or in the stands. Carroll knew exactly what the celebrities meant for recruiting, that you couldn't even begin to place a value on Snoop Dogg high-fiving a high school senior on a recruiting visit, and the story that kid would have for his friends back home.

But practice is where Carroll made the most use of the celebrities. His practices were always designed to simulate actual games. The Trojans hit hard. Carroll piped in loud music and crowd noise. He stopped practice at random and waited to begin again, simulating a television timeout. He once even surprised the team before an important final preseason scrimmage with a trip to a beach volleyball tournament. "DJs, bikinis, all the things that come with the beach in Southern California," says Yogi Roth, an assistant quarterbacks coach. And then he bused the team back to play the scrimmage. Carroll did not intend the volleyball excursion as a break; rather, it was a chance to work on the skill of refocusing.

Carroll wanted to play in a state of zero distractions that Gallwey and Murphy had described. His practices became, undeniably, big events, for the fans and the players and coaches. The idea was that because the practices were big events, they helped make the real big events feel, well, normal, without distractions. If the players could handle Snoop and Arnold Schwarzenegger and Alyssa Milano watching them practice, then they could handle the Orange Bowl.

Carroll became the maestro of something you couldn't find in South Bend, Ann Arbor, Columbus, Tallahassee, Tuscaloosa, or even Miami. What was happening at USC—the wins, the buzz, the "it" that Winkler described—had never happened before in college football and, because of what resulted from it, will likely never happen again. The combination of the school, the location, and the coach made it possible, and made it so that no one else really *could* do it. UCLA was in the same city, but they didn't have the history, they didn't have the wins, they didn't have Carroll, they didn't have budding superstars in Bush and White.

And in the 2004 season, no one else had a quarterback who appeared as if he could slot right into a Hollywood production, with his good looks, skill at throwing the ball, poise, easygoing manner, leadership, and that intangible but very real thing known as "cool."

CHAPTER ELEVEN

Word Made Flesh

Matt Leinart didn't always possess those things. Far from it.

He grew up in Santa Ana, the younger of two boys in a middle-class family. His father, Bob—a former collegiate baseball player—sold giftware. His mother, Linda, worked at a local high school.

Leinart had a difficult childhood. He was chubby and was born with a condition known as "strabismus," which is, essentially, crossed eyes. He had surgery at the age of three to start the correction but was left with eyes that were still crossed and glasses that were bottle-thick.

Bullying was more tolerated back in the 1980s and early 1990s, not the openly addressed issue it is today. And Leinart—the literal fat kid with crossed eyes and glasses—was one of its sufferers. He cried nearly every day from the cruelty. But because of the times, he didn't talk to his parents about it. Though his older brother would occasionally step in and fight on his behalf, Leinart didn't get into any scraps on his own. He just internalized the pain.

And he eventually had the last laugh.

At the age of twelve, Leinart had a second surgery on his eyes, which allowed him to ditch the glasses. And near the end of eighth grade, he hit a growth spurt, and he would eventually become tall (six foot five) with lean muscles (200 pounds). He had always loved sports but had not been great at them. Until now.

By the time he entered Mater Dei High School, he excelled at baseball, basketball, and football. Baseball, his father's sport, was his first love—and he threw an eighty-mile-per-hour fastball. But he could also dunk a basketball and was a sharpshooter from three-point range. And he showed promise as a young quarterback, enough to be tutored by Steve Clarkson, the founder of the quarterback academy known as Air 7.* By that time, too, Leinart had also begun to flourish as a student—his mother claimed he had a photographic memory.

And then, late in his ninth-grade year, he tore his rotator cuff and damaged his labrum and was forced to sit out sports in his sophomore year. That injury was, in some ways, as difficult to endure as the bullying. He'd finally transformed into the swan, but he couldn't preen in the pond.

When he came back in his junior year, Leinart focused primarily on football. But Mater Dei already had a starting quarterback—a player named Matt Grootegoed, who was the team's do-it-all star, the leading rusher *and* tackler. Grootegoed, a senior, who would also attend USC and become a foundational player during the early Carroll era, started the first eight games of the 1999 season.

But everything changed in that eighth game, against Servite High School, when Leinart came on in relief of Grootegoed, as he had all season to that point, and threw for 281 yards and four touchdowns. Leinart led the team from that point on, all the way to a state championship. He was named the Gatorade Player of the Year in California.

---

* Clarkson also tutored Ben Roethlisberger, the Heisman winners Gino Torretta and Tim Tebow, and Matt Barkley, who would become USC's starting quarterback in 2009, Carroll's last season as the Trojans' coach.

Leinart was recruited heavily by Michigan and Oklahoma and by Hackett at USC. He committed to USC mainly because of the relationships he'd formed with Kennedy Pola and Hackett's offensive coordinator, Hue Jackson.

After Hackett was fired, Leinart briefly considered committing to Oklahoma. But when Chow, the quarterback guru, was hired as Carroll's offensive coordinator, he decided to stay, even though Palmer was firmly entrenched as the starter for the foreseeable future.

In his freshman year, Leinart languished on the bench behind Palmer, growing tentative, losing faith in himself, and going out a bit too much. Then came the week of the Arizona game in 2001, when Carroll dangled the possibility of him starting and Leinart's father, who was heavily invested in his son's career and often referred to him using the plural personal pronoun (as in "We threw for 2,870 yards in *our* senior season at Mater Dei"), drove to Tucson to watch. But then, of course, Carroll decided to stick with Palmer. Leinart took only a few snaps that season, never throwing a pass, and was redshirted.

In 2002, still behind Palmer, Leinart grew more frustrated. Palmer was a fastidious worker and only felt comfortable when he took nearly all the snaps in practice, which left very little to do for his backups, which also included Cassel and Hance. Leinart still felt the sting from having the rug pulled out from under him at the Arizona game the year before. And his father's heavy involvement—he attended most USC practices—only heightened the pressure. (Bob Leinart once referred to his son as "Tom Brady, only better.")

And after practice one day during the 2002 season, the young quarterback appeared to hit his boiling point.

He walked into the coaches' offices with his chin down. Seamus Callanan, the self-described "lowest man on the totem pole," was the only staffer present. Perhaps that's why Leinart felt like he could be candid. "I'm fucking transferring," he told Callanan. He would not lack for suitors—like Oklahoma—if he did.

Callanan had an idea. Pablo "Chick" Prietto, a USC graduate, had been the team orthopedist for many Mater Dei athletes and was a beloved figure in that high school's community and among its football players, especially. Callanan called him and put Leinart on the phone and left the office. An hour later, Leinart walked out. He'd decided to stay.

In the end, Carroll hadn't "fucked up" Leinart as he worried he might have back in 2001. And that would turn out to make all the difference for the future of the program.

When Carroll told Leinart that he'd beaten out Cassel and Hance for the starting job in the 2003 season, Leinart told him, "You're not going to regret this."

Leinart was different from Palmer. In many ways, he was an avatar for Carroll. He was affable. He liked to tell jokes in the huddle when he thought his offense needed a mental reset. He was competitive as hell, on the field or at the ping-pong table. In one practice, the team did a series of drills that pitted Leinart and his best receivers against the team's best cornerbacks. The cornerbacks won the session. And as they jogged off the field as a group, hyped about their win, Leinart fired a ball from thirty yards away that hit cornerback Justin Wyatt perfectly on the shoulder. "I was like, 'Who fucking threw that?'" says Wyatt. "And then I turn around and see Leinart laughing his ass off and I'm like, 'Why did I even ask that dumbass question?'"

Leinart was a lefty. He didn't have the physicality of Palmer, who could throw the ball with serious velocity into tight spots. "Matt was more of a tactician than Carson," says Alex Holmes.

Chow's first assignment at USC was to go meet and evaluate Leinart at Mater Dei. "He didn't throw very hard," Chow says. "I had to ask him to rip the ball. You could tell he was very smart, though. Bright as the day is long."

He was also tough. Perhaps the pivotal game of Leinart's USC career came in his first year as a starter, in 2003. USC was playing Arizona State in Tempe, one week after the deflating triple-overtime loss at Cal.

In that game, Leinart was sacked on USC's first drive of the second quarter and suffered a high ankle sprain and a knee bruise. Cassel came in for him and finished the half, playing just well enough to keep USC in the game, tied at ten at the half.

At halftime, as he was icing his ankle, Leinart told Carroll he wanted to go back in for the second half. Carroll didn't think it was possible but told him, "If you limp, you're not playing."

Carroll huddled with Chow and Sarkisian, who weren't thrilled with how Cassel had played (he'd completed only four of his ten passes and had a fumble). They decided to get Hance ready.

But as the team warmed up on the field for the second half, out came Leinart. He did not walk with a limp, gutting it out through gritted teeth. He came in, his team now down 17–10, and played the second half and led the Trojans to twenty-seven unanswered points and a 37–17 win. Some of his teammates nicknamed him "Lion Heart" after the game.

He may have been Lion Heart, but he also remained very much a "dude." He loved video games, especially *Halo*. He wore the same pair of lucky underwear in games. He took his laundry to his parents' house when he needed it done. In his early years, he earned a reputation for his romantic conquests on campus (some of his teammates called him the "bareback bandit"). "I was walking to lunch with him one day and all of these women were walking up and handing him pieces of paper with their numbers on them," says Keith Miller. "I was single at the time, and Matt turned to me and said, 'You need some of these?'"

Leinart dated the surfer and model Veronica Kay and then Jessica Simpson's personal assistant. But in the fall of 2004, he seemed to settle down a bit when he started dating Brynn Cameron, a freshman phenom on the women's volleyball team.[†]

But he also never forgot his childhood, never let it go. He was reminded of it twice a year when he had to go to his eye doctor to get checked to make sure there was no reoccurrence of strabismus. It kept him close to the pain, fueling him.

And it helped him become the best player in the college game in 2004.

Barbara Kingsolver, in her book *Demon Copperhead*, has a passage about the process of devising and learning football plays and then actually performing them on the field. "It's an act of magic to take an idea and turn it into bodies on bodies," she writes. "Like what's said about the Bible, the word made flesh."

The Trojan football team in 2004 had this incarnation down pat. The offense—and the offensive stars, like Leinart, Bush, White, and Jarrett—got most of the attention, as offensive stars do. And they deserved it. USC could beat you by passing the ball. They could beat you by running the ball. They usually beat you by doing both. There were many games in that season and the next when the Trojans were so far ahead the starters were routinely benched in the *third* quarter. In games like that, the offensive coaches—Chow, Sarkisian, and Kiffin—would ask who hadn't scored a touchdown yet. "And some third stringer would speak up and Kiffin would say, 'Watch this shit,' and they'd dial up a play and the next thing you know, the third stringer had a touchdown," says Hancock.

The defense played an equally important role, though. They stoned teams, holding opposing offenses to thirteen or fewer points eight times that season, which included two shutouts. They

---

[†] They would have a child together in 2006.

forced turnovers. They gave their high-powered offense extra possessions and short fields in every game. They ran what was, in essence, an NFL defense, Monte Kiffin's Tampa-2, which required smarts. They had their stars, too—Lofa Tatupu led the team in tackles and Shaun Cody led them in sacks. But they also had players who had come in under the radar and blossomed, like Mike Patterson and, in particular, Leinart's old co-quarterback at Mater Dei, Matt Grootegoed, who by then was a linebacker.

Grootegoed was a favorite of his teammates and coaches, an undersized, no-nonsense, throwback player who had long hair and resembled the singer Stephen Stills. "When Kiffin recruited me, he said, 'You'll have no problem starting; this guy ahead of you, Grootegoed, is like five foot ten, 200,'" says Keith Rivers, a linebacker who joined the team in 2004. "When I get there, I room with Grootegoed and he's sitting on the sofa, watching TV, and they're playing a classic high school game, Mater Dei versus Long Beach Poly. And there's Grootegoed, playing on both sides of the ball, an animal, the stripe of his helmet flapping off, and I'm like, 'Oh my God, this guy is a beast. Kiffin is such a liar.'"

In 2004, Grootegoed was named one of the team's captains. He'd been recruited under Hackett and had started his USC career as a safety. Though he was undersized for the linebacker position, Carroll had moved him there, and he flourished. "Grootegoed was just awesome," says his fellow linebacker Clay Matthews (a soon-to-be star who didn't see the field in a game in 2004). Holt, the linebacker coach, calls him "one of the best players on that 2004 team." Grootegoed led the team in interceptions that year and was named a first-team All-American.[‡]

[‡] Grootegoed's size caught up to him in the pros. He played a season for the Lions and then three seasons for the Canadian Football League's Calgary Stampeders.

The 2004 Trojans outscored their opponents, 496–169, with an average game score of 38–13.

And yet, it wasn't all as easy as it looked. They had some biblical moments, and some moments when the word made flesh didn't exactly go as planned and required some divine intervention.

They had the Cal escape in their fifth game of the season, when a red-hot Aaron Rodgers inexplicably went cold in the dying moments of the game. In their eighth game, against Washington State in Pullman, the Trojans were greeted with freezing rain and hail that pinged off their helmets (they won, 42–12). The next week, against Oregon State in Corvallis, the field was shrouded with a fog so thick that the players barely showed up on the television broadcast. "It was mystical," says Carroll.

Early in the second quarter of that game, USC fell behind, 13–0, and trailed 13–7 at the half, held back by a rare Bush fumble and a Leinart interception. But, as they so often did, the Trojans came out of halftime and scored an early touchdown to make it 14–13 in their favor.

But the game remained tight and very much in the balance until early in the fourth quarter when Oregon State was forced to punt from within their own territory. Bush—to whom, it was becoming very clear by now, no team should ever punt—was back to field the kick.

The punt arced high in the air, the ball obscured by the fog. Bush drifted to his right, tracking it. The ball hit the artificial turf in front of him at the USC thirty-five-yard line and he rushed forward to field it on one bounce. His momentum nearly took him out of bounds, but he executed a full 360—nearly a pirouette—juked out two onrushing Oregon State players, and then burst, laterally, to the left-hand sideline, out of the fog and into the open, an apparition come to life. He hopped over a dramatic dive by the Oregon State punter fifty yards down the field and ran into the end zone untouched, for all intents and purposes calling the game.

That game was followed by a 49–9 home win over Arizona. And then Notre Dame came to town. Wide receiver Steve Smith was back from injury. Leinart threw for 400 yards and five touchdowns in a 41–10 thumping, which sealed up his Heisman win and ended Tyrone Willingham's Notre Dame career.

For the last game of the regular season, USC traveled across town to the Rose Bowl to take on UCLA. The Bruins were by no means great that season—they were 6–4—but they featured a small, shifty running back named Maurice Drew (he would later change his last name to "Jones-Drew"), who led the team in rushing. Drew was UCLA's version of Bush, a Swiss Army knife back who could run, catch the ball, and return kicks. Carroll loved him coming out of high school and, at one point, believed he had landed him to join Bush and White after an intense recruitment that included a one-on-one meeting in an empty Coliseum. Though they had Drew, UCLA looked overmatched, at least on paper.

And yet, despite holding Drew to minus-five yards rushing in the game, and despite Bush running for 204 yards, and despite leading 23–10 midway through the third quarter, USC could not quite shake the Bruins. With just over two minutes left in the game, UCLA scored on a touchdown pass to Marcedes Lewis to close the gap to 29–24. They had one more chance to spring an upset—an onside kick. But the game essentially ended when the kick was recovered by . . . Matt Cassel.

Cassel, who had spent his entire Trojan career as a backup, was such a good athlete that Carroll sometimes used him on special teams. (He also played one year of baseball at USC.) He'd made one start on the football team, as an H-back (sort of like a tight end who lines up behind the line of scrimmage) against Cal in 2001. In his entire USC career, he attempted a total of thirty-three passes, completing twenty of them, with one interception and no touchdowns.

Yet, in his own way, Cassel was an important part of those USC teams. He was another classic glue guy—the player who doesn't see the field much but leads by example by giving it his all on the practice field and in the film room. Cassel would occasionally stand and give pep talks in the locker room. He was witty and excellent at impressions (the voluble Nick Holt was a frequent target). Carson Palmer would later serve as the best man at his wedding.

Cassel was also a vivid illustration of just how deep and talented those Trojan teams were during Carroll's era. He was taken by the Patriots in the seventh round of the 2005 NFL Draft and made the team as the backup to Tom Brady. In 2008, when Brady was injured in the opening game of the season, Cassel replaced him and led the Patriots to an 11–5 record. In 2010, with the Chiefs, he made the Pro Bowl. He ended up playing in the NFL for fourteen seasons.

USC had begun the season ranked number one in the country and remained there at the end of the regular season.

Oklahoma had begun the season ranked number two in the country and remained there at the end of the regular season.

The two teams would meet in the BCS Championship game in the Orange Bowl, billed as the "game of the century." The Trojans were favored by a point.

But before the game, there was a trip to New York City for Leinart. He had been the Heisman favorite since nearly the beginning of the regular season, which he finished throwing for twenty-eight touchdowns and just six interceptions and nearly 3,000 yards. Only a late push by Oklahoma's freshman running back Adrian Peterson, who ran for nearly 2,000 yards on the season, made it interesting. Peterson would end up second in the balloting. His quarterback, and the 2003 Heisman winner, Jason

White, finished third. Reggie Bush ended up fifth.[s] Leinart was Chow's third Heisman-winning quarterback.

At the ceremony the Heisman presenter took an entirely new tack with the pronunciation of the winner's name, announcing him as "Matt Line Heart."

Oklahoma appeared to be a formidable opponent. They had a Heisman-winning quarterback. They'd played in the BCS Championship game the year before (and bumped USC out of it). And they'd added a new notable weapon: the freshman Adrian Peterson. The same Adrian Peterson who had nearly signed with USC and created what would have been certainly the best running back trio in the history of the game.

Peterson, from Palestine, Texas, was considered the best high school prospect in the 2004 recruiting class (he had rushed for nearly 3,000 yards in his senior year in high school). Every big program in the country offered him—Texas, Texas A&M, UCLA, Miami—but early in the process he had narrowed his selection to two schools: USC and Oklahoma. And USC, it appeared, had the edge.

Alex Holmes hosted Peterson on his trip to USC. "Adrian had an incredible time," Holmes says. "I took him to Hollywood. He met a bunch of famous people, and the famous people recognized him." Peterson told the USC coaches that it didn't bother him that Bush and White, who would be entering their sophomore seasons in 2004, were already there. The thought of the potential three-headed monster at the running back position had Carroll's head spinning. "I tried really hard to get Adrian," he says.

At the end of Peterson's recruiting trip to USC, just as he was about to get into the car that would whisk him away to the airport, Carroll arranged to meet him at the Manhattan Beach Pier.

---

[s] Bush's old high school teammate Alex Smith finished one spot ahead of him.

Peterson walked out onto the pier into the sunshine, surrounded by the surfers, the sunbathers, the upscale restaurants and beautiful beachfront homes. It was everything Southern California promised to be. Carroll spoke to him, one last sales job. "He was really fired up," says Carroll. He thought he had him.

Then came National Signing Day. "Adrian had basically committed to us," says Holmes. "But then things started going crazy. Pete was running around, and he told me, 'We have to get Adrian on the phone. Something is going on.'"

They waited by the fax machine for his commitment letter. But it never came. "Adrian told us that his father was in prison and because of that, he couldn't watch his son play on TV if he went to USC," says Holmes. "The prison apparently only got Texas and Oklahoma games."

Carroll never bought that excuse. "I don't know, man. There just seemed to be some other variable there," he says, without elaborating on what that variable might have been.

In the week leading up to the BCS Championship game, the two teams were invited to a Rickey Smiley comedy show in Miami. The Trojans arrived first and took their seats. The Sooners came in just as the show was about to begin, moseying in one by one, a cock walk, almost as if choreographed. Jason White was the first in. Nothing much to look at. Not that big. But a Heisman winner. Then came Peterson. Bigger than he looked on film, all lean muscle. *That dude's a freshman?* Then Dan Cody, a big corn-fed linebacker, six foot five, 255 pounds. Larry Birdine, Oklahoma's loquacious defensive end, strutted by. Earlier in the week, Birdine had told the media that Leinart was "definitely overrated . . . he's a good quarterback but not a Heisman-winning quarterback." He also described USC as "an average team." And, last, Jammal Brown, the offensive lineman and winner of the Outland Trophy for the nation's best lineman on either side of the ball. An absolute giant at six foot six, 315 pounds, he blocked out the light as he walked by, a human eclipse.

Carroll saw the looks in his players' eyes as they watched the Sooners walk in. He gathered the team together at the Westin Diplomat hotel after the show. "Don't dial into what you saw tonight," he said. "Focus on your preparation for the game. This ain't about them. It's about us."

In the game of football, Carroll knew, every team had a weakness. Game plans were about optimizing your strengths and covering for your weaknesses while trying to blunt the strengths and exploit the weaknesses of the other team. But Carroll also knew that these tasks would be difficult for the Oklahoma Sooners in this game. Because his team had no real weakness.

On Monday night before the game—when players were susceptible to distraction and anxiety, with the game twenty-four hours away and their families and girlfriends there—Carroll asked Orgeron to lead what was known as a "Heartbeat Meeting." The team gathered in a hotel conference room. Orgeron told them to leave everything—all of those distractions—behind. Someone had a drum and started to beat on it, slowly at first, but gradually gaining in tempo. Orgeron paced the room. "We are going to play at a level that our opponent is unable or unwilling to match," he said. The beating of the drum began to sound like the beating of a heart. The players stood, clapping along. The beat got faster and faster. The players began to yell, martially, primally. "It became a full dance-off, people doing the worm, throwing chairs in the middle of the room, everyone on their feet," says Collin Ashton. "People yelling, 'Fuck 'em up, but play with poise.' Pete was right there in the middle of it all, dancing around. It was awesome, what playing for Pete was all about. I have been to parties that didn't go as hard."

At one point Orgeron got up on a table. "Tonight, you're gonna go to sleep and then we're going to go out there and kick their asses. Because every last one of y'all was born to be here."

Orgeron might not have liked all of the psychology stuff that Carroll did as a coach. But he'd played right into it, right into W. G. Roll's idea of the "long body," when a Native American tribe or, in this case, a football team, develops a "single consciousness" and operates as a "single entity, functioning, sensing, and feeling as one."

If Carroll and his coaches had a concern, it was about the health of LenDale White. The running back had sustained a high ankle sprain in the last regular season game of the year against UCLA and had not been able to practice at full speed. "I had fragments floating around my ankle," says White.

As great as Bush was, he was not an every-down back. White was, though. He was the bruiser who wore down defenses and allowed the Trojans to control the game from start to finish. He was the bully, the establisher of attitude. *This is what we're going to do to you and we're going to do it all . . . game . . . long.* When he played well, the Trojans generally rolled. When he didn't, or when he wasn't used much, the game sometimes grew a bit more difficult. In USC's only loss from 2003 to 2004—against Cal— White had only gotten two carries.

A few days before the game, White declared himself healthy. The ankle had healed . . . in a somewhat unconventional way.

White had been swimming in the hotel pool when some of his teammates asked him about his ankle. He told them that it was still bothering him. Carroll's wife, Glena, was nearby and overheard the conversation. "She swam over and told me to sit on the side of the pool," says White. "And then she prayed over my ankle."

Did it work? "Yeah, it did," says White. "The prayer and some injections. Toradol in the ass and pain medication right into the ankle."

Before the game, the USC coaches were confident. Even the usually anxious Chow was cautiously optimistic. "When I was leaving the hotel for the game, my wife asked me how we were going to do," he says. "I told her, 'I have no idea. But those other guys better be ready.'"

The players were more brazen. "I knew we were going to curb stomp them," says Holmes.

In the locker room, as game time neared, Carroll told his coaches and players what he told them every Saturday before a game: "We are a rock band, and this is our concert. Don't be uptight. Cut it loose. Do not miss this. We don't get this back."

Shaquille O'Neal did the pregame coin toss. Snoop, Henry Winkler, Kevin Hart, and Ferrell roamed the USC sidelines. "I drive freight when I'm not doing the movie thing," Ferrell deadpanned to a sideline TV reporter. "And my truck actually broke down here, and it's not going to be fixed until [Wednesday]. And I was able to hustle a couple of tickets."

And at 8:24 p.m. EST on January 4, 2005, Oklahoma kicked the ball off to USC. First play: a quick slant pass from Leinart to Bush—who had lined up at wide receiver—for twenty-seven yards. But the drive stalled three plays later, and USC punted the ball down to the Oklahoma eight-yard line.

And then Oklahoma proceeded to go on a methodical, ninety-two-yard drive—a mix of Peterson runs and White passes—and scored a touchdown.

The television cameras flashed to the USC sidelines for a reaction shot. Carroll was smiling, ear to ear. The rout was already on. Oklahoma just didn't know it yet.

The next seven Trojan drives ended like this:

- Thirty-three-yard touchdown pass, Leinart to tight end Dominique Byrd.
- Forty-four-yard punt by Tom Malone.
- Six-yard White touchdown run.
- Fifty-four-yard touchdown pass, Leinart to Jarrett.
- Five-yard touchdown pass, Leinart to Steve Smith.
- Thirty-three-yard touchdown pass, Leinart to Smith.
- Forty-four-yard field goal, Ryan Killeen.

At halftime, the score was USC 38, Oklahoma 10.

Carroll says he had one moment of worry during the game. At halftime, which was elongated because of the famously disastrous musical performance by Ashlee Simpson,[1] Carroll had his coaches walk around the locker room on a rotating basis, trying to keep the players focused and charged up. Finally, just as they were about to take the field again, Carroll called everyone together. The players began to chant: "We are all we got! We are all we need!"

"We were in this alcove and one of our players leaned against the door and it opened, and I saw the Oklahoma players right there walking by," says Carroll. "And I remember thinking that they were going to be all jacked up because we are so cocky. I thought, 'Man, we're going to blow it.'"

He needn't have worried.

---

[1] She was off-key and slightly behind the music. It was so bad that the Orange Bowl crowd booed when it was over. To be fair, there were apparently significant technical issues that prevented Simpson from hearing anything on the stage.

The Trojans took their first drive of the second half eighty-five yards down the field and scored on another Leinart touchdown pass to Smith. It was Leinart's fifth of the game, in which he would throw for 332 yards. After USC scored that touchdown, Holmes passed Larry Birdine, the defensive lineman who had been talking shit before the game, and asked him, "Is [Leinart] still overrated?"

"We were celebrating on the sidelines by the third quarter," says the punter Tom Malone.

USC locked down the Oklahoma offense. Peterson was held to eighty-three yards and White threw three interceptions. Mike Patterson—one of the most underrated players of the Carroll era at USC—was a big factor in shutting down the run, and he also put pressure on White while dominating the Outland Trophy winner Jammal Brown.

The combination of Glena Carroll's prayers and the painkillers did the job on White's ankle—he rushed for 118 yards and two touchdowns (and would have surgery on his ankle eight days later). Both Jarrett (one touchdown) and Smith (three touchdowns) had over one hundred yards receiving. USC offensive lineman Sam Baker reported that early in the second half, a member of the Sooner defense had asked him to please keep running the ball so that they could run down the clock and get out of there more quickly. "They quit," says Holmes.

USC won the game and the national title, 55–19. It was one of those rare games when a football team reached something they'd never found before, when they were so connected and so tight that they acted and reacted as one, the word made flesh. It was, in other words, their Long Body game.

With the victory, the Trojans had won twenty-two straight games, and thirty-three out of their last thirty-four.

When the final whistle blew, Chow breathed a sigh of relief. It had worked. It had all worked. He shook his head. *This group of players. My word.* He claims now that he had more talent on that USC team than he did on some of the NFL offenses he would later run. He felt weary. Lack of sleep the night before, a night spent walking the streets. He also felt leery. He'd gotten into a shouting match with Kiffin before the game, about what he couldn't exactly remember. But the shouts were real. And then there was the lingering pain of Sarkisian, his protégé from BYU, who had left USC after the 2003 season but not before, Chow believed, actively trying to undermine him. He could feel it. "Some guys, in order to try to get where they want to go, they step on you," he says. "It made me sad."

When the final whistle blew, Orgeron—the bad cop, the ramrod-straight backbone of the coaching staff, Mr. Accountability—playfully tackled Carroll on the sidelines. It would be their last game together. Orgeron had accepted the head coaching job at Ole Miss, where he would flail around for three years, winning only ten of the thirty-five games he coached, never figuring out the good cop/bad cop dynamic, stuck between trying to emulate Carroll and be himself.

Orgeron's loss would be an almost incalculable one, from a coaching and recruiting standpoint, but also from the standpoint of something less tangible. Orgeron was the last of the full-time on-field assistants from the Hackett era (Seto had been a graduate assistant under Hackett). He remembered how terrible things had once been, the pain of losing, of what it felt like to be part of a program unmoored and adrift. That ache never left. He always kept it close—it's why he pushed himself so hard on the recruiting trail and on the practice field. And now, the last reminder of just how far USC had come, and how much work and sweat and discipline it took to get there, was gone. Carroll would acknowledge the depth of the loss fifteen years later, telling the *Baton Rouge Advocate*, "When [Orgeron] left and went to Ole Miss, I never felt the same. I felt like we really lost something enormous in the program just because of his heart and soul and everything that he brought."

And when that final whistle blew that night in Miami, unbeknownst to anyone at the time, the Trojan horse had already entered the walls of Troy.

At the postgame celebration on the field, Carroll spoke with ABC's Lynn Swann (a USC graduate) as Leinart stood to the side, firing oranges into the crowd around the field. Carroll talked about how his team had "left no doubt." He spoke about sustaining greatness. And, at the end of the interview, he looked up at the Trojan fans still in the stands and yelled, "I wanna make sure all of those people up there stay here. We're gonna have a party tonight!"

"I was probably a little full of myself that night," says Carroll.

The party unofficially kicked off when, early on, Malone, the punter, tackled Brennan Carroll through a partition wall and knocked over a bar. And, as it turned out, thousands of those fans in the stadium took Carroll's invitation literally and showed up at the Westin to try to get into the postgame party. Many of them succeeded. "That party was the highlight of my career," says Tessalone.

At one point, deep into the early hours of the morning, Carroll took over DJ duties, telling partygoers, "No one sleeps tonight! Not until the sun comes up!"

CHAPTER TWELVE

The Push

Just a few weeks after USC's commanding win over Oklahoma, Carroll decided it was time for a drastic change to his coaching staff. At the Senior Bowl in late January in Mobile, Alabama, Carroll had a meeting with Kiffin and Sarkisian, who, at the time, was still the quarterbacks coach for the Raiders. Carroll laid out a plan: he wanted Kiffin and Sarkisian to run the Trojan offense as basically co-offensive coordinators. (Kiffin would get the actual title; Sarkisian would become an assistant head coach and the quarterbacks coach.)

Of course, Carroll already had a very well-regarded offensive coordinator on his staff, one who had just helmed an offense that won two straight national titles: Norm Chow.

That same month, the Carrolls and some other coaches' families went to Cabo as an end-of-the-season thank you. At one point during the trip, Carroll asked to speak to Chow about his job. "He told me that he wanted me in a more senior role and wanted the two young guys to take over the play calling," says Chow.

Chow saw the offer for what it was—he was being asked to step aside. He was caught off guard. "I did not want to leave USC after the Oklahoma game," he says. But now the writing was on the wall. He was out, one way or another. A few NFL teams had contacted Chow about open offensive coordinator positions and now, he realized, he'd better get back to them.

Chow was hired in early February as the offensive coordinator for the Tennessee Titans, and he would go on to coach for another fourteen years as an assistant (in college and high school) and as a head coach (at Hawaii and in the European Football League). His departure from the Trojans was a shock to many. "It was a big deal," says John David Booty, who had been with the program since 2003. Some were unhappy with the news. Among them: Leinart, who, just weeks before, had announced he was coming back to USC to play one more year. Bob Leinart expressed his family's displeasure with the move to the *Los Angeles Times*: "It's disheartening . . . there is no loyalty in this business and that's sad."

Chow, like Orgeron, proved to be an enormous loss. Though he had been forced to adopt the offensive strategies that Carroll wanted, he'd done so with aplomb. He was a gifted play caller, with an instinctive feel for the flow of the game. He was a wizard at halftime adjustments.

But, like Orgeron, it was more than just what he brought to the field. His quiet, reserved, and measured nature was the ballast to Carroll's topsy-turvy energy. "Chow was an awesome coach," says offensive tackle Winston Justice (who was reinstated to the team in 2005). "He didn't yell, but his words were really weighty. When he said something, we listened to him."

"He was tough and demanding and an elder statesman who had been around and seen it all," says Palmer. "He kind of felt like your dad."

For years now, Carroll and Chow have politely tiptoed around the matter of the timing and the reasons for Chow's departure from the team. "I hold Norm in the highest regard," is all Carroll will say about it now. And Chow? "I will always be grateful for Pete. He forced us into a lifestyle where now I can retire."

Though Carroll denies it, there are many who believe Chow's departure had to do with ego. Chow was never one of the "guys" on the coaching staff, never really throwing himself into the rah-rah personality-driven part of being a Carroll assistant, never hanging out after hours and, say, drinking a beer.

But Chow did gain recognition for what he did on the field. In 2002, he won the Broyles Award, given to the nation's top collegiate assistant coach. He was profiled by national media outlets and given plaudits for tutoring three Heisman-winning quarterbacks and for crafting some of the most prolific offenses in the history of the sport. He was given a lot of credit for USC's success, sometimes sharing top billing with Carroll; the conventional wisdom was that USC was powered by Chow's offense and Carroll's defense—and the offense, of course, always garnered more attention and headlines. Brian Kennedy, the USC booster, believes it all got to be too much for Carroll. He says that at a USC football awards ceremony at the end of one season, "Norm got a bigger hand than Pete. I saw the look on Pete's face when it happened. It was not pretty."

But there was certainly another factor at play, as well. Carroll, for the first time as a head coach, was finally free from the anxiety of having to fight for his career on a year-to-year basis. And that freedom allowed for change. "After two straight championships, he was basically a god," says Chris Huston. "But I think he felt like it still wasn't perfect, like he won those titles because of the great coaches he had around him and the Hackett recruits." And, like Tiger Woods, who changed his swing a few times amid his dominating years in golf, Carroll sought out a new challenge for himself, almost bored with the tried-and-true. "He wanted to dominate by doing it his way," says Huston. "You started hearing more about his philosophies and the new age stuff and the positivity. He wanted to create a mood around the program that reflected, up and down, his philosophies."

Carroll does not disagree. "I did like to challenge myself to stay competitive and curious and focused," he says. And pushing out Chow and installing Kiffin and Sarkisian, as risky and unpopular as it might have seemed to some, was a way of doing that. "I didn't care that they were young," says Carroll. "I thought they could encapsulate and express what we were trying to do with flair."

And what Carroll was trying to do now at USC had changed a bit. His overriding philosophy was no longer "I'm in." It was now "Win forever." It was the idea he had gotten from John Wooden, that once you figured out your philosophy and stuck with it and could communicate it, you could go about "having a blast, having fun, enjoying the heck out of it by finding out how good you can be," as he wrote in his book, and then making it all come to life. He differed from Wooden in that he became unsatisfied and started to change things, perhaps finding, as many do, that it can be more stimulating and animating to desire something than it is to actually have it.

Because what he was also trying to do, at least in that 2005 season, was win three national titles in a row—what some in the media deemed a "Three-Pete"—which was something never accomplished in the modern era of college football.[*]

Though it doesn't look like it now—not after Kiffin and Sarkisian have proven themselves to be two of the brightest offensive minds in football as head coaches (at Ole Miss and Texas, respectively)—the move to let go of Chow and put the young duo in charge of the offense was risky at the time. And, indeed, both men traveled a bumpy path and had to conquer personal demons to get to where they are today. Many of those bumps were initially encountered at USC.

---

[*] Minnesota was the last to do it, back in 1936.

Kiffin and Sarkisian were very young when they arrived at USC, and it was hard for some of the players to erase memories of the duo's early years in the program. "There's something about a young coach," says Marcell Allmond. "They're just too young at a certain level, and the players are like, 'How does he know anything I don't?'"

The players had mixed reactions to each. "Sarkisian lived and breathed football all the time," says Tom Harwood, a backup quarterback in 2005. "He was fired up all the time, a screamer." Jacob Rogers says Sarkisian was "a little more blue collar than Lane." Billy Hart, another backup quarterback, says Sarkisian "dedicated all of his energy to USC football."

Kiffin, says Fred Davis, "did a lot of things that seemed immature. He was brash and would talk shit to the guys. That was his way of trying to get the best out of them." Rogers says, "I didn't consider Lane to be a leader back then even though he was clearly a good coach. I don't think he was quite ready and was there only out of Pete's loyalty to Monte. I called him 'silver spoon.'"

Harwood says one day in practice, he and his receivers were beating the defensive backs in drill when Kiffin started taunting, well, everyone. "We've got this kid from the band beating your asses!" he yelled at the defensive backs.

"I wasn't even in the band," says Harwood.

The young duo was "really hungry and eager to learn and worked really hard," says Palmer. "You could tell they didn't just want to be the tight ends coach and the quarterbacks coach, that they wanted to be head coaches."

Both men "could recruit their asses off and listened to the same music the players did and knew all about pop culture," says Hancock. "It was like Norm was Mr. Miyagi and Sark and Kiffin were both Daniel-son."

Off the field, the duo also acted their age. They had cocktails on the plane rides home from games. "They would go out in Manhattan Beach," says Hancock. "You'd see their wives out. They were a wild bunch."

"I was trying to sneak into bars in Hermosa and Manhattan Beach, and I'd get in and they would be there," says Collin Ashton. "I look back and realize they were in their twenties still, so young."

"Sark in particular liked to go out and come back and tell us about it or about going to the pier," says Harwood. "Things I wouldn't have talked about at that age."

The other coaches saw the good and the bad. "Sark and Kiffin both got a little full of themselves as they gained power. It really showed with Kiffin," says Pat Ruel. "But they were tolerated because of their obvious incandescent talent. They were already good at their jobs and demonstrated the promise that they would get better."

Kiffin was made recruiting coordinator, replacing Orgeron. He turned out to be very good at it, nabbing multiple five-stars in every one of his classes. But in this endeavor, too, he had to learn to grow up a bit. On a trip to see Ted Ginn Jr.—an über-talented receiver who also wanted to run track in college—USC's sprint coach accompanied Kiffin on the team plane to provide some more firepower for Ginn's recruitment. But Kiffin spent the flight berating and belittling the coach—telling him football players shouldn't run track—instead of game planning for the recruitment or extending any gratitude to him for helping out. (Ginn Jr. ended up at Ohio State, helping them get to a national title game.)

Chow's offenses were surgical, methodical. He maximized the efficiency of the offense, picking apart a defense. He liked to stay in base personnel (two wide receivers, a tight end, a fullback, and a halfback). He utilized his stable of talented fullbacks he had over the years—David Kirtman, Webb, and Hancock—in the passing game, where they usually forced a mismatch when guarded by a slower linebacker. He liked to use White and Bush together on the field, sometimes lining up Bush as a receiver, which forced the defense into an unwinnable quandary: Spread out and cover Bush with a cornerback? Or load the box to try to stop White?

"Sark and Kiffin were always pushing Chow to open things up," says Palmer. "Kiffin wanted to put everything in and run it all. Chow wasn't of that mindset."

But now the duo had their chance. Kiffin would craft many of the plays, which were communicated and translated to the players and other coaches by Sarkisian. The two collaborated on play calling, with Kiffin taking the lead from the booth and Sarkisian on the field. In his first meeting with the offensive players, Sarkisian declared that in every game, the Trojans were going to pass for at least 300 yards and rush for at least 200 yards. They nearly pulled off that ambitious goal. The offense Kiffin and Sarkisian created was explosive—in 2005, they scored more than fifty points in seven of their games—and aggressive. Kiffin and Sarkisian liked big statistics, so they ran up the score against lesser opponents. They also rarely lined Bush up as a receiver, which some thought was done to better his Heisman prospects. (The Heisman voters, it was believed, seemed to prize a big rushing year over a big total-yards-gained year.)

And like young men drawn to fast cars, their offense was, unlike Chow's, very much geared to the pyrotechnic. "They always wanted the big play down the field," says Fred Davis. And that, combined with the aggression, put pressure on the stars— Leinart, Bush, White, and Jarrett—especially against the better teams. And that pressure on the stars would come to a head a few times that season in big moments.

The players—even Leinart—would come around on Sarkisian and Kiffin. "It turned out Chow had two great understudies," says Booty. It also helped that the duo took over what was one of the best offenses in college football history. Leinart, the reigning Heisman-winning quarterback, had two stellar receivers in Jarrett and Smith, both of whom started the season on the watchlist for the Maxwell Award, given to the nation's best receiver. The offensive line featured Ryan Kalil, Deuce Lutui, Sam Baker, and Winston Justice, who would all play in the NFL. The backfield had the bruising White.

And then, of course, there was Bush.

Carroll had a tradition every year after National Signing Day, when the next season's recruits were all locked into coming to USC. He would gather the returning players on his team and show them highlights of those incoming players. It fed into the competitive environment Carroll had fostered. *These are the guys coming in to compete for your jobs. What do you think?*

There is one tape the players of that USC era still talk about: the one that showed the highlights of Reggie Bush.

When Carroll put on Bush's tape, "We were like, 'Wow! That's *really* impressive,'" says Billy Hart. "And then Carroll told us it was just the tape from one game. I was floored." On one play, Bush lined up as the team's punter. Carroll would later quip, not necessarily in jest, "That's why he's our backup punter."

But there was one play in particular that left the coaches and players speechless. Bush, in his Helix High School green jersey, was running down the sideline toward the end zone when a defender caught up to him. (The USC players would find out later that Bush was hurt in that game, which was the only reason he was caught.) As Bush was being dragged to the ground, he instinctively chucked the ball over his head, a perfect lateral to an oncoming teammate, who caught it and ran in for a score. That play would be remembered a few years later, in the last game of the 2005 season.

Bush supposedly had 300 yards from scrimmage in his first Pop Warner game and then 500 yards in a game later in that same season. When he arrived at USC, he was quiet and soft-spoken, with traces of a childhood lisp still present. He made good grades in high school. He worked hard on and off the field—he arrived at USC weighing 185 pounds and left weighing 200, while somehow getting faster.

Bush was rated as the number one running back recruit in the nation as a high schooler. His fellow 2003 running back recruits—Chauncey Washington and White—were rated number eight and number nine, respectively.

When Bush first came in, he received a lot of direct coaching from Carroll, who had him study videos of Gale Sayers, the NFL great. Carroll also sent Chow to the St. Louis Rams to study how they utilized their do-everything back, Marshall Faulk. Kennedy Pola, Bush's position coach when he arrived, noticed that Bush, in his high school tapes, did a lot of improvising before he hit the line. Pola wanted him to change a bit— not to stop improvising but to put his foot on the ground and make a cut, blast through the line, and *then* get creative when he got to the second level and faced the linebackers and defensive backs. That way, Bush could avoid plays that might result in lost yardage.

Bush followed Pola's advice for the most part. But he never stopped improvising, no matter where he was on the field. In fact, he was the king of improv and had a theatrical flair that turned seemingly all of his runs and returns into cliffhangers. Bush had a kinesthetic sense, total control of his body, and so often did what Barry Sanders had once done on the football field—create something spectacular out of nothing. Bush would run one way, only to find that the door was closed. So he would turn and run the other way, shifting the field, and somehow find a new unseen-until-then door that was open. "He would run out of the backfield and go anywhere, and it didn't really matter," says Chow.

"I think I'm dangerous everywhere [on the field]," Bush told the media once, a rare bit of self-analysis from someone who at that time was usually unwilling to talk about himself. "I feel like wherever I am, the other team has to be watching me and keeping an eye on me. That also opens things up for other people on our team. I just like getting the ball in my hands any kind of way."

Bush didn't make an immediate splash in 2003, his freshman year, but showed flashes of his dazzling talent when returning punts. He was viewed by the coaches as not as durable as Washington and White. But Washington got hurt, and Bush was thrust into more playing time than was initially planned for him. He had his breakout game against Washington in the eighth game of his first season, when he had eighty-one yards rushing and caught five passes for 132 yards and two touchdowns. He finished that year as a first-team Freshman All-American.

The next year he finished fifth in the voting for the Heisman. And by 2005, his junior season—his last in college and one he prepared for by working out with NFL superstar running back La-Dainian Tomlinson in the offseason—it was crystal clear that he was the most electric player in the game and, perhaps, one of the best collegiate players ever. One writer called him "the human one-play eighty-yard drive." Another described him as "upset insurance." Snoop just called him "the president."[†]

Of course, Bush wasn't the only potent running back during this time at USC. Hershel Dennis would have his games. Washington would fight through injuries and academic problems to become a productive runner after Bush left for the NFL. But Bush's true brethren in the backfield—really, his peer—was LenDale White.

[†] George W. Bush was in the White House for all but the last year of the Carroll era at USC.

White grew up in the projects of Denver. When he was eleven years old, his father died of HIV. His single mother, working for minimum wage, raised him. An uncle helped out.

It seemed like a familiar story—kid from a rough background who uses the game of football as a way out of the vicious cycle his life seems headed for. Except White didn't love football—not right away. In fact, in his Pee Wee and Pop Warner leagues, he tried to quit. But his mother and uncle wouldn't let him. He only started to shine when he got to Denver South High School, becoming a star running back, with his uncle calling the plays.

But one day at a Denver South practice, a brother of one of the coaches showed up at the field with a gun. He didn't shoot it, but White told the *Los Angeles Times*, "It was one of the craziest things I've seen in my life." He transferred to Chatfield High School, located in a suburb of Denver half an hour away, and blossomed into one of the best high school running backs in the country, recruited by Texas, Michigan, and, of course, USC. Kiffin went after him hard and, even though White knew he'd be competing with the two other star backs in his class—Bush and Washington—Kiffin got him, posting yet another out-of-state recruiting win. "At the time, I was just thankful that Pete took a chance on a kid from Colorado because he had so much talent in California already," says White.

White had his breakout in the fifth game of his freshman season, running for 140 yards (and two touchdowns) against Arizona State, breaking the USC freshman single-game rushing record. He would add two more hundred-plus yard games that season. The next year, he broke the hundred-yard mark in five games and gained 1,103 yards for the season, earning 61 percent of those yards after contact. In both of his first two seasons, he outgained Bush. And he outrushed his backfield mate in both BCS Championship games they played in together.

In 2005, White's junior year and last season at USC, he rushed for more than one hundred yards in six games. In four of those games, he eclipsed the 150-yard mark, including a 197-yard game against Arizona State.[†] He also had a nose for the end zone. By the time his three-year career at USC was over, White would own the school record for rushing touchdowns with fifty-two, more than USC luminaries Marcus Allen, Charles White (no relation), and OJ Simpson.

The White and Bush backfield would be given the nickname "Thunder and Lightning." Though perhaps lacking a bit in creativity, the nickname worked. Bush's lightning strikes on the field were often followed by White's concussive thunder, and the closer the electrical storm got, the more screwed the other team was. The duo decimated teams in tandem. When Bush was on the field—particularly under Chow, when he lined up all over the place—his mere presence opened up opportunities for White by occupying the minds and bodies of defenders and giving defensive coordinators ulcers. White also created opportunities for Bush and never really got the credit he deserved for his role in Bush's success. Because of White, the smaller Bush didn't have to go through the wear-and-tear of being an every-down back. White slammed his 235 pounds into the line, over and over, loosening up and tiring out defenses, which helped Bush. But White also had surprisingly nimble feet and was adept at making defenders miss. His nickname among his teammates was "the Law" because he kept defenses honest. "If our offense was a courtroom," USC offensive tackle John Drake told the *Los Angeles Times*, "then LenDale is the gavel." White ran with a fury and a nastiness that

---

[†] Arizona State was happy to see White leave for the NFL. In three games against them, White rushed for a combined 405 yards and an average of more than seven yards a carry.

fit his personality. "LenDale was a bully. He had an edge to him," says Carroll.

White could also be a thorn in Carroll's side. He didn't have the best work habits, but that was tolerated because of his production. "I may not have worked out as hard as Carroll wanted, but I still got the reps and playing time," says White. In that 2003 game against Arizona State, when he broke the USC freshman running record, White wanted to stay in the game and put the record out of reach. But during what would turn out to be USC's last drive—with just over three minutes left in the game—Carroll took White out and gave the carries to Whitney Lewis, Dennis, and Bush. White walked by his head coach on the sidelines and said, loud enough for his teammates to hear, "Fuck you, Pete."

"I didn't give a damn," says White. "I always just spoke my mind when something needed to be said. I did it for my teammates, too."

Somehow, the USC coaches were able to make the backfield time share—between two highly competitive players who both wanted to be on the field and get the ball on every snap—work, for the two players and for the team. Chow says White was the primary reason. "Reggie was a good guy, but selfish," he says. "LenDale came to me numerous times and said, 'Don't worry, do whatever you have to do to make Reggie happy.'"

But there was some tension between the two and it bubbled up on at least one occasion. "LenDale thought he was a gangbanger and Reggie, early on, could be a crybaby but he wasn't a punk," says Lee Webb, the fullback who blocked for both of them. One day in the locker room, Bush apparently got fed up with White's tough-guy talk and confronted him, referencing the two significant Los Angeles gangs at the time. "Reggie stood up to LenDale and said, 'You said you were a Blood when you came in and now you're a Crip?'" says Webb. "And LenDale rushed him. They fought for a while and then we broke it up."[5]

Ironically, it would be the soft-spoken Bush who would be the one to become more fascinated with LA gangs . . . and cause the biggest headache for USC.

USC's 2005 recruiting class, which still had Orgeron's finger-prints all over it, was ranked first in the country and included two linebackers who would become stars—Rey Maualuga and Brian Cushing—and a five-star quarterback from Mission Viejo High School named Mark Sanchez. Carroll was on the phone with the recruits in the class right after the title win over Oklahoma, something many believed to be insane—*he should just enjoy the moment!*—but something that makes undeniable sense. In fact, there may be no better time to call a recruit. Carroll now had the collective pitch (*Come to USC and win a national title!*) and the individual one (*Come to USC and get drafted into the NFL!*), with many high-profile players becoming top-round picks. He told re-cruits that NFL teams always found the best collegiate players, but they spent more time looking for those players on the best team in the college game.

The Trojans had some toe-stubs before the season began. A handful of starters were forced to miss spring practice because of poor grades—White, Manny Wright, Frostee Rucker, and Dominique Byrd among them.[6] Byrd, the tight end, had the double-whammy of also having his jaw broken . . . by a teammate. Byrd and the receiver Steve Smith got into a fistfight over money

---

[5] Later in their USC careers, the two running backs would befriend and align themselves with two figures from the rap world who didn't get along—White with Snoop and Bush with Suge Knight.

[6] By the way, when is the last time you heard of a big-time college athlete being academically ineligible?

while playing a video game. Carroll disciplined neither player, equating it to a fight between siblings.

All the academically ineligible players would make it back before the season. But one member of the team would not. In March of that year, Eric Wright—who was one of the most talented cornerbacks of Carroll's USC days—was accused of sexual assault. And when the police searched his apartment, they allegedly found 136 Ecstasy pills and charged him with drug possession. Wright was suspended from the team immediately. Both charges were eventually dropped when the alleged victim declined to testify. But, facing an almost certain expulsion from school, Wright opted to transfer (he ended up at UNLV).

USC opened the 2005 season on the road against Hawaii. They left the island with a 63–17 win. They next faced another Southeastern Conference (SEC) team—this time, Arkansas—that, like Auburn two years before, featured two excellent running backs in the freshmen Darren McFadden and Felix Jones. On the third play of USC's first possession in the game, Leinart handed the ball to Bush, who followed fullback David Kirtman out of the backfield. "We called Kirtman 'the surgeon,'" says Pat Ruel. "The guy just had a knack for picking off a backside tackle or defensive end." And on the play, Kirtman did just that, destroying a pursuing defender and setting Bush free on a seventy-six-yard touchdown run.

USC scored touchdowns on its next five possessions, and on nine of its first ten possessions. A Trojans pass for a touchdown with one minute and twenty-five seconds left in the game finished the utter demolition of the Razorbacks, 70–17. The piling on in the blowout win was part of the young offensive coordinators' thirst for statistics (USC had a total of 736 yards in the game, and an average of eleven yards a play). But it was tolerated by the head coach in that game because of a long-simmering grudge. Back in the 1998 season, when Arkansas had a coaching vacancy, Carroll had called the school to inquire, thinking his connection to the school—the year there with Lou Holtz—at least warranted a chat. But the Arkansas athletic director, Frank Broyles, never returned Carroll's call. And Carroll never forgot the slight.

The Trojans rolled through their next three games, beating Oregon, Arizona State, and Arizona. Next up: a trip to South Bend.

Charlie Weis's football coaching career started at a New Jersey high school. He later got a job at South Carolina in the mid-1980s, went back to high school for a year, and then found his footing in the NFL as an assistant to Bill Parcells on the Giants, Patriots, and Jets, winning a Super Bowl as an offensive assistant on the 1990 Giants team.

During his years in the NFL, Weis became very familiar with Carroll and his defenses. In 1994, he was the tight ends coach for the Patriots when Carroll was the coach of the Jets, and he was the offensive coordinator for Parcells at the Jets during the three years Carroll helmed the Patriots. After Carroll was fired by New England, Weis was hired by his replacement, Bill Belichick, to run the Patriots' offense. And with Tom Brady as his quarterback, Weis earned three more Super Bowl rings.

At the end of the 2004 season, after USC had, for all intents and purposes, ended the Tyrone Willingham era at Notre Dame, and after Urban Meyer had turned down the Notre Dame job to coach Florida, Weis was hired by the Irish. He had graduated from the school in 1978.

And in his inaugural season at Notre Dame, he was off to a successful start. Going into the game against USC, the Irish were 4–1, having beaten three ranked teams—Pittsburgh, Purdue, and, most impressively, Michigan, which had been ranked number three at the time. Notre Dame's only loss was to Michigan State, by three points in overtime, and the Irish had risen to number nine in the rankings.

The 2005 USC–Notre Dame game was the seventy-seventh in the rivalry, which had begun in 1926 when Notre Dame coach Knute Rockne put his team on a train to Los Angeles to play the Trojans.** USC had lost to Notre Dame in Carroll's first season in 2001, after the ill-fated tours of campus. But they had won the next three, all in lopsided fashion, by an average score of 43–12.

Notre Dame had a bye week before the 2005 game, giving them extra time to prepare, which Weis believed necessary. "We knew, talent-wise, they were better than we were. They were great on both sides of the ball, had outstanding coaching, and were used to winning," says Weis. "We knew we had to wear them down, control the ball, and play well in all three facets of the game to have a chance."

Weis used psychological ploys to get his players fired up during the two weeks leading to the game. "I played the Trojan fight song every day at practice just to piss my players off," he says. The Notre Dame students got into the mood, as well. They put photos of Carroll, Leinart, and Bush in mostly unflattering places all over campus, like on the floor of the cafeteria and in urinals.

The Trojans—number one in the country and on a twenty-seven-game winning streak—flew into South Bend on the Thursday before the game. Instead of staying in town, they went to a Holiday Inn in Michigan City, which was some forty-five minutes away from South Bend *and* in the Central Time Zone. (South

---

** The Fighting Irish won that game, 13–12. The two teams play for a "trophy" called the Jeweled Shillelagh, which is, in actuality, a Gaelic war club. It is constructed of oak and blackthorn saplings from Ireland, which are said to be "the only things tougher than an Irish skull."

Bend was in the Eastern Time Zone.) "I remember the smell of the chlorine in the indoor pool in that hotel," says Rocky Seto.

The next day, the Trojans boarded two buses to go to Notre Dame Stadium to do their usual walk-through on the field, a normally fairly sedate affair. But when the buses (offense in the first one, defense in the second) pulled onto campus, they were greeted by thousands of Notre Dame students. The students screamed at the Trojan players, chanted "Let's go Irish!" *clap . . . clap . . . clap-clap-clap*, and held up signs with Leinart's face with a red circle around it and a red slash through it and signs with the mugshot of OJ Simpson with the word "MURDERER!" underneath it.

There was no security anywhere in sight. And suddenly, the students descended on the buses and started rocking them back and forth.

Keith Rivers was a sophomore linebacker on the team that year. His position coach, Ken Norton Jr., had given him the nickname "the Shark," telling him that he was a nice guy off the field, but a savage animal on it. Rivers did not like the fact that the Notre Dame students were rocking the buses. "I was getting really pissed," he says. "We were the number one team in the nation. We'd just won two national championships. It all felt really disrespectful."

So Rivers stood up and unleashed a primal scream and then started trying to rock the bus himself. "I guess I became the Shark before the game this time," he says. His teammates on the defense's bus took the cue and joined him, and the bus began to rock back and forth, not because of the students, but because of the fired-up players within it. The offense's bus caught on and started doing the same. "Thousands of pounds of meat, side to side, the buses nearly toppling over," says Brandon Hancock.

"I was thinking we were going to tip over, too," says Pat Ruel. "The driver in our bus started saying, 'Oh my God,' over and over again. Pete was up in the front, just sitting there, smiling. Those kids outside suddenly went quiet. It was like they'd stirred up a hornet's nest."

A few of the USC coaches began to worry that one of their players might snap, drunk with the emotion, and take it too far by hopping out of the bus and attacking a student. But the buses eventually made it to the secure area around the stadium without further incident. And the players walked onto the field only to find that Weis was attempting to play a psychological game with them, as well. "That grass, man. It was long. Really long," says Collin Ashton. Long enough to be above the players' cleats when they stepped on it. "I was having dinner with some friends that night in Chicago," says Tim Tessalone. "The grass was so long that I pulled some and put it in my pocket. I had to show them." The players were forced to change from their normal molded cleats to ones with metal screw-ins.

Weis had been a student at Notre Dame in 1976, when the team intentionally grew the field's grass long to try to slow down the University of Pittsburgh's star running back, Tony Dorsett. It hadn't worked—Dorsett gained 181 yards in a 31–10 win. But Weis apparently thought it was worth trying again. "We didn't do anything intentionally. It just didn't get cut that week," says Weis, with a telling laugh. "It was too wet to cut."

During the walk-through, the strength coach, Chris Carlisle, as was his tradition, told a story to the team. This time, it was about Alexander the Great. "I'll never forget it," says Rivers. "As he came to the end of the story, he said Alexander the Great came up with the phrase *veni, vidi, vici* ["I came, I saw, I conquered"], and those words echoed throughout the empty stadium."[tt]

[tt] This may have been Carlisle's Bluto-from–*Animal House* rallying cry moment ("Was it over when the Germans bombed Pearl Harbor?"). Julius Caesar, and not Alexander the Great, is the man credited for uttering *veni, vidi, vici*.

Weis had a few more tricks up his sleeve. Notre Dame traditionally held a pep rally the night before a game. Usually, around 10,000 people showed up, so the rally was held in the basketball arena. But Weis made a big deal of this one, bringing in the Irish legends Joe Montana, Tim Brown, and Daniel Ruettiger (better known as "Rudy") to participate, and attracting 50,000 people to the football stadium.

The pep rally was televised. And back in their hotel rooms at the Holiday Inn, the Trojan players and coaches all watched it. "They even had a guy up there on the stage dressed up like Jesus," Carroll says. "Robes and everything."

Kickoff finally arrived at 3:40 p.m. EST on Saturday, October 15. It was sixty-two degrees and sunny, a near-perfect Indian summer day. NBC, which had owned the rights to Notre Dame regular season home games since 1991,[‡‡] had Tom Hammond and Pat Haden (who had won two national titles as USC's quarterback in the 1970s) on the call in the booth and Lewis Johnson down on the field, and was very pleased with the hype before the game between the number one and number nine teams in the country. *College Gameday*, ESPN's weekly pregame show, was in South Bend. Various media outlets had branded the clash as "the Game of the Century." And while most of the games given that moniker rarely live up to the billing, this one exceeded it.

As the teams warmed up on the field before the game — Notre Dame in their home blue jerseys, USC in white tops and gold pants — there was already a palpable buzz in the stadium. After the teams went back into the locker rooms for final preparations, USC came out first, standing in the tunnel before taking the field for an extra beat, as if to ratchet up the already deafening chorus of boos showering down on them.

[‡‡] And still does.

And then Weis unveiled his last psyop. When the Notre Dame players reappeared on the field for the start of the game, they were no longer in their blue jerseys but now wearing their supposedly lucky green ones. It was a gambit the football team had first pulled against USC in 1977, when the Joe Montana–led Irish beat the Trojans, 49–19, on their way to a national title. "We were like, 'Whatever. This is just another team trying to pull out everything to beat us,'" says Ashton.

Though the Irish had been down in recent years, they had some talented players. The combined eight members of their defensive line and secondary would all play in the NFL. The running back, Darius Walker, ended up rushing for 1,196 yards that season. Brady Quinn, the quarterback, would play in the NFL for seven years. And he had weapons at his disposal: a big tight end, Anthony Fasano, who would play in the NFL for twelve seasons, and two excellent receivers in Jeff Samardzija and Maurice Stovall.

But the Irish were facing a USC juggernaut that was especially potent on offense. Coming into the game, the Trojans were averaging 640 yards and nearly fifty-two points per game. Leinart was throwing a touchdown pass once in every twelve passes. Thunder and Lightning were living up to their billing: Bush had rushed for more than one hundred yards in the previous four games. White had done the same in the previous three games and rushed for 197 and 179 in his last two.

Notre Dame got off to a nervy start in the game. On the first play of their second series, Weis called for a flea-flicker. But Quinn, after collecting the ball, was hit on his arm by USC defensive lineman Frostee Rucker as he threw, and the ball fluttered into the hands of Keith Rivers for an interception. Two plays later, Bush hurdled an Irish defender on his way to a thirty-six-yard touchdown run. Notre Dame, finding composure, answered with an eighty-yard drive that ended in a touchdown. And then USC scored again on a three-yard touchdown run by White, his sole highlight in the game, in which he ran for only twenty-six yards on ten attempts, a level of production from the big back that was usually not a good sign for the Trojans.

In 2005, with the replay review system in its first year of use across college football,[§§] the decision about whether or not it was to be employed in a non-conference game was made by the visiting team. And Carroll opted out of it for this game. "I just thought it disrupted the flow of the game back then," he says.

That decision had consequences on two plays during the game.

On Notre Dame's first drive of the second quarter, they faced a third and ten. Quinn threw a pass to Samardzija on the sidelines for a first down. But in slow-motion replays, it appeared that the receiver may not have had a foot down in bounds. The game moved on, though, and four plays later, Quinn hit Samardzija on a moon ball. "Samardzija did a stutter step and go, and then Quinn just let it go," says Justin Wyatt, who was covering Samardzija well on the play. "There's an awesome picture on Google of Samardzija catching the ball on me." It shows Samardzija hauling in a thirty-two-yard touchdown pass.

14–14. The home crowd in full throat.

On the Trojans' next drive, they were forced to punt, something that happened only thirty times in their twelve regular season games that year. The funny thing was that they had an All-American punter in Tom Malone. His nickname was "the Bomb," and a USC student had started a "Malone4Heisman" campaign during the punter's junior season. Malone described himself as "a punter on a team that never really needed to punt."

He punted from the USC nineteen. The ball traveled forty-one yards, a decent punt for most college kickers, but a substandard one for Malone. Tom Zbikowski was the Irish's undersized but

---

[§§] The Big 10 had started using it the year before.

big-hearted safety, a throwback player who had once been a boxer and who was now in the midst of the game of his life. He fielded the punt, ran to his right, and then just bulldozed his way straight ahead, breaking the tackles of three USC players, including Malone, for a sixty-yard touchdown return that put Notre Dame ahead, 21–14. "Zbikowski was a football player, man," says Wyatt.

On the ensuing kickoff, the Irish kicked away from Bush and to the Trojans' other returner, Desmond Reed, who was an all-around special teams ace. The ball went over Reed's head. As he turned to retrieve it, his right knee buckled. His ligaments had been shredded, so badly that he would end up with permanent nerve damage. "I really don't think I would have got hurt if the grass wasn't long," he told the *Los Angeles Times*. (The tall grass bit both teams: Irish defensive lineman Chris Frome also blew out his knee in the game.)

On that drive, Leinart was intercepted in the end zone, on a deflected ball meant for Steve Smith. Going into halftime, Notre Dame retained its 21–14 lead.

"Weis had gone away from all of his tendencies we prepared for," says Wyatt. "They were playing ball control. They would have a third and fifteen and instead of throwing it to Samardzija, they'd run a draw and gash us."

At halftime, Carroll told his defense that he believed Weis "had a bead on me," and that they were not going to worry about trying to decipher Notre Dame's tendencies but would instead run their base defense for the rest of the game. "He said, 'I know you guys are better players than they are, so we're just going to play football and play what you see,'" says Wyatt.

Then Carroll addressed the entire team. "I feel really good about where we are," he said. "They've given us their best punch. If we stay ready, we will win."

As the teams took the field for the second half, NBC's Lewis Johnson tracked down Carroll for a quick interview. "We'll see what we're made of. We'll see if we can come back out there and execute like we have been," he told Johnson. He smiled. "We're kind of counting on it." And then he jogged away.

Carroll had ample reason to be confident. USC had trailed at the half in two games already that season and then won the second halves by a combined score of 70–7. And they'd outscored Notre Dame a combined 68–0 in the second half in the previous three games against them.

On the first drive of the second half, "Big Balls Pete" made his first appearance of the game. The Trojans faced a fourth and one on their own nineteen-yard line. Carroll decided to go for it. Leinart took the snap and snuck the ball forward, barely making the yard needed. It was not exactly a confidence-building sneak. A few plays later, Leinart threw his second interception of the game, his first game in the last twenty with more than one interception. He appeared to be a little out of sorts.

That state of being wasn't helped by what happened on the next Trojan drive. Leinart handed the ball to White, who took it one way and then suddenly reversed direction. Leinart then realized he was in position to block for White, and he did. But White ran up his back and, in doing so, inadvertently kneed his quarterback in the head. On the next play, a woozy Leinart handed the ball to Bush, the one-man game-saver, who hesitated behind the line for a moment and then, looking like he was shot from a cannon, ran forty-five yards for a touchdown to tie the game at twenty-one. At the end of his run, Bush slowed down, enough for Zbikowski to nearly catch him from behind. It appeared, at first glance, that Bush had been showboating. But, in fact, he had felt a slight twinge in his knee.

The USC sidelines became a MASH unit. Leinart sat on the bench, clearly unsteady, while his backup, John David Booty, began tossing warm-up throws. And Bush was lying on his back on the ground, with a trainer leaning on one leg that was crossed over his waist. "That's not allowed in certain parts of Utah," Haden said as the NBC cameras hovered over the entanglement of Bush and the trainer.[¶]

Notre Dame made a field goal and then missed one early in the fourth quarter. Down 24–21, USC's defense was obviously beginning to tire. The sunny Indian summer day had retreated into the gloaming. With a little more than seven minutes left to play, USC had the ball on their own thirty-two. At this point in the game, USC had gained 331 yards, and Notre Dame had gained 330. USC drove the field, with Bush capping it off with a nine-yard touchdown run to put the Trojans back on top, 28–24. "Bush was the best player on the field that day," says Weis. Bush would end the game with 160 yards rushing for three touchdowns, a firm grip on the Heisman Trophy, and one heads-up play that saved the day.

Around that same time, NBC showed some scores from around the country. In one notable game, Texas, the second-ranked team in the country, had thrashed number twenty-four, Colorado, 42–17. Texas quarterback Vince Young had passed for two touchdowns and run for three more.

With just more than five minutes to go in the game, Notre Dame started their drive at their own thirteen. NBC cameras cut to the USC sidelines, where Leinart was getting some attention from the trainers. Quinn led a drive, hitting Samardzija[***] for two

---

[¶] Haden and Hammond, clearly having a good time calling the game, had some other memorable quips during the broadcast. At one point they were bemoaning the use of handheld devices, like the at-the-time-ubiquitous Blackberry. "Who would want emails following you around everywhere?" Haden asked, incredulous. Well, Pat . . .

[***] Samardzija was an excellent receiver—tall, deceptively fast, with great hands. But he never played in the NFL, spending thirteen years as a pitcher in Major League Baseball instead.

big gains and then Stovall and then the right end Fasano. And then Darius Walker gashed an exhausted Trojan defense on three straight runs to get the ball inside the USC ten-yard line.

On second and goal from the USC five, with two minutes and nine seconds to go in the game, Weis called a quarterback keeper. Quinn dropped back as if to pass and then dipped his shoulder and ran to the right. He was dragged down (with one arm) by Rivers, but he extended the ball over the goal line as he fell. The referees signaled a touchdown. But the slow-motion replay showed that Quinn's knee may have been down before the ball crossed the plane of the goal line. With no replay review, however, the touchdown stood. Ironically, it very likely would have benefited Notre Dame if Quinn had been stopped just short on that play. The Irish would most likely have scored anyway and, of course, they would have been able to run some precious time off the clock. As it was, they left two minutes and four seconds for USC, which turned out to be a few seconds too many. "I knew we might score on that play and leave some time on the clock, but it was the best call to make at the time," says Weis. With that touchdown, Notre Dame became the first team to score more than thirty points against USC since Cal had in the fourth game of the 2003 season—more than two years prior—the last time the Trojans had lost a game.

And then came one of the most memorable drives in college football history.

With just over two minutes remaining in the game, Bush returned the Notre Dame kickoff to the USC twenty-five. "The place was absolutely berserk then," says Carroll. On the broadcast, as Leinart and the USC offense took the field, Haden said, "I've never heard it this loud here, Tom. Ever. And that means, I think, you have to be careful with audibles. I think you have to go with what you called."

On first and ten, Leinart tried a pass on the right sideline to Jarrett but overthrew him. Jarrett would later admit that he was in no condition to be on the field by then. On an earlier play, he'd gotten hit by a Notre Dame cornerback. The hit had forced his helmet down his face and jabbed him in the eye. "My vision was blurry," he later told the *Los Angeles Times*. "I was seeing double vision. I was out there playing with one eye."

The stadium was so loud that Leinart had to jog over to the sidelines to get the next play call from Sarkisian.

Second and ten, one minute and fifty-four seconds left. Leinart dropped back to pass. No one was immediately open and, on a stunt, Notre Dame's 305-pound defensive tackle Trevor Laws blew through the Trojan offensive line and sacked Leinart for a nine-yard loss.

Third and nineteen. One minute and forty-four seconds left. Ball on the USC sixteen. Carroll called a timeout. He instructed Kiffin and Sarkisian to make sure they at least got back half the yardage needed for a first down. The duo told Leinart to take a quick look downfield on the third down play and if it wasn't immediately there, to check it down to Bush coming out of the backfield.

Leinart snapped the ball. He had excellent protection, but nothing was open downfield, so he did, indeed, dump it to Bush, who gained ten yards. Fourth and nine.

Carroll called his final timeout with one minute and thirty-two seconds left on the clock. "Lane is in the booth, and he tells Sark on the sidelines, 'Tell Matt we're running 60-Sam-Y-Option,'" says Carroll. "It was a play designed to go to a tight end. It was one of our favorites."

Leinart got the call and started to walk back to the huddle. "And then Lane says to Sark, 'Wait, remind him about the blitz automatic!'" says Carroll. "Matt came back, and I told him, 'If you see a blitz, check the play and throw the slant.' It was a protection call. The tight end would stay in and block and every receiver route changed." The alternate play, if needed, was known as "82-Stay-Sluggo-Win."

Leinart stepped up to the line, under center. Kiffin, in the headset, told Carroll and Sarkisian: "We've got the look. Matt should check it."

Easier said than done. "That place was as loud and as amped as a place could be," says Carroll. "Matt sees what Kiffin sees, but he now has to communicate it to the rest of the players." So Leinart, contrary to Haden's advice, called the audible, screaming it to the linemen in front of him and pointing to the receivers on either side of him. "Matt was so cool," says Carroll. "He did it all perfectly, the checks and the snap."

"In hindsight, I wish we had not blitzed," says Weis.

Leinart dropped back—*one, two, three, four steps*—and let a touch pass go to his roommate, who was streaking down the left sideline, right in front of the USC bench. Ambrose Wooden Jr., the Notre Dame cornerback, ran stride-for-stride with Jarrett, nearly perfect coverage. Nearly. "And then the ball goes underneath [Wooden's] elbow," says Weis.

Jarrett, still having trouble with his eyesight, caught the ball by squeezing it with just his left arm against his rib cage. And then he was off. Sixty-one yards later, Wooden caught him from behind at the Notre Dame thirteen.

One incomplete pass and two Bush runs later, and USC had a first down and goal on the Notre Dame two-yard line. USC was out of timeouts, but the clock stopped momentarily on the first down. Twenty-three seconds remaining.

Then things got truly wild.

With an empty backfield, Leinart dropped back to pass. He drifted to his left and, with no one open, decided to try to run for the left corner of the end zone. But he was met, violently, by Corey Mays, a Notre Dame linebacker. Mays's helmet hit the football, which popped free and landed out of bounds.

And from that point on, everyone, save for the still-woozy Leinart, seemed to lose their minds.

The side judge appeared, at first, to want to raise his arms and signal a touchdown, but he successfully fought back the urge and pulled them down just in time. He then pointed to the ground and, finally, signaled for the clock to stop. But neither the clock operator nor anyone else appeared to have seen him.

The crowd went crazy because the clock kept moving . . . 5 . . . 4 . . . 3. As it ran down, a USC coach sprinted down the sideline, all the way to the end zone and well outside of the coaching box, and signaled desperately for a timeout, though USC was out of them. That coach was Carroll's son, Brennan.

The crowd got even louder . . . 2 . . . 1.

The clock hit zero.

The Irish players began to celebrate. Samardzija ran to the USC sideline and screamed "Suck it!" while grabbing his crotch. The referees all looked around at one another, as if waiting for someone to step up and explain what the hell was going on. Weis raised his arms in triumph and began walking onto the field. "I thought the game was over," he says. Students dropped down from the stadium's walls—first in singles and then in a deluge—and rushed the field. "Notre Dame has won!" Hammond said on the broadcast.

There was no big screen in Notre Dame Stadium at the time and, thus, no way for those in the stadium—the referees, fans, players, and coaches—to see the play again. No one had a clue what was going on. All anyone knew was that the clock said no time was left in the game.

The run was over. Some of the Trojan players began to cry.

But wait.

The referees huddled in the middle of the field, having finally come to their senses. They discussed what had happened and made the ruling. The ball had been fumbled out of bounds at the one-yard line with seven seconds left on the clock. Because the ball had gone out of bounds, the clock would not start again until the ball was snapped.

"It's mayhem, especially in the college game, when the clock hits zero," says Dean Blandino, a longtime director of referees for the NFL and the current director of instant replay for the NCAA. "But they made the correct call on the field, and they just had to get on the mic and put everything back together." The referees did exactly that, communicating with the booth. The public address announcer asked everyone to clear the field. Everyone did as told.

Everyone except for Weis.

As the two teams began to line up at the one-yard line, Weis remained in the middle of the field. He couldn't seem to believe that the game was not already over. His khaki pants were pulled up over his rotund belly. His nose had begun to run in the cooling air. As he finally started to walk off the field he appeared, for a moment, like a little kid who was being forced, after the loss of some game, to leave the playground. The delay he caused by not leaving the field right away had given the Trojans precious moments to regroup.

The NBC camera panned to Carroll. He was yelling "Spike!" and motioning his arm and hand to the ground, as if instructing Leinart to ground the ball to stop the clock. "That's Pete Carroll saying down it," Hammond said. Haden agreed. Confusion still hung in the air.

In reality, there would be no reason to spike the ball because the clock wouldn't start until the ball was snapped. But also in reality, Carroll *did not want* Leinart to spike the ball at all.

The truth was the Trojans had practiced for this moment all season long. "Every Friday during walk-throughs, the offense would do a two-minute drill on air, a full drive," says Rocky Seto. "And the drive would always end with the last play at the one-yard line. And the quarterback would sneak it in."

The signal for that play? Carroll making the "spike" motion. And when Leinart saw that, he was supposed to ignore him and key in on Sarkisian. And if Sarkisian pointed at Leinart, that meant, if the quarterback saw a good look, he should run the sneak.

Leinart would later say that, in the moment, he looked at Carroll just to make sure about the call and even pointed at himself as if to ask, "Are you sure?" Carroll, Leinart said, just shrugged.

The referees were still trying to restart the game as Weis took his time getting off the field. The stadium had a weird feel and sound—no yelling or screaming from the fans, just a collective "What is happening?" murmur. The Trojans began to line up, get in their stances, but there had not yet been a whistle from the refs to officially start the play clock. Given the time, Bush moved forward and sidled up to his quarterback and had a conversation, which the duo would, years later, recall on a Fox college football special:

"What are you going to do?" Bush asked Leinart.

"I think I'm going to go for it," Leinart replied.

Oh, damn, Bush thought. And then he said, "All right. I got you."

Notre Dame lined up with all their big boys on the line. They knew exactly what was coming. "Matt got up to the line and thought, 'Holy shit, they're all in there,'" says Carroll.

The crowd found its voice again.

The whistle blew.

Leinart received the snap and pushed straight forward. Two Notre Dame defenders knocked back their blockers and stopped his progress. So he rolled his body to the left, his back now to the end zone, making no headway . . . until Bush arrived from behind him. He hit his quarterback in the chest with his head and hands and then pushed him, fully extending his arms. Leinart instinctively reached the ball over his head. Receiver Chris McFoy—standing in the end zone—grabbed Leinart's shoulder pad with his left hand and gave him a tug. And Leinart fell, backward, into the end zone for a touchdown.

"The stadium had been so loud," says Winston Justice. "And then it went quiet."

USC 34, Notre Dame 31.

Leinart would say later he didn't know exactly what had happened on the play until Bush told him later, "I pushed your ass in there." The play became known as "the Bush Push." And it was illegal at the time. "No other player of [the ballcarrier's] team shall grasp, *push*, lift or charge into him to assist in forward progress," read the 2005 NCAA Football Rulebook.

"That rule was just never called," says Blandino.[†††]

One rule that *was* called on occasion was when a coach wandered far out of the designated coaches' area, as Brennan Carroll had done after Leinart fumbled the ball out of bounds. "That's one thing that's never talked about," says Weis. "That could have been a fifteen-yard penalty, and they would have probably had to settle for a field goal try [to tie the game]."

Brennan Carroll had also been signaling for a timeout that his team did not have. "When a coach does that in football, you just ignore it and there is no penalty. It isn't like basketball," says Blandino. As for being out of the coaches' area? "That's at the discretion of the official," Blandino says. "Most of them would just tell the coach, 'Hey, get out of here.' I wouldn't want to flag a coach for fifteen yards in that moment." In his assessment, Weis also

---

[†††] The NCAA, for all intents and purposes, formally legalized the play when they took the word "push" out of that sentence in the 2013 rulebook.

seems to conveniently forget that, moments earlier, he, too, was well out of his designated area and in the middle of the field.

Weis, though, is gracious about the actual Bush Push. "Though it was technically illegal, I thought it was a heads-up play, to tell the truth, and I would hope that my players would have done the same thing in that situation."

After the touchdown, the game wasn't officially over. USC was flagged for excessive celebration (who could blame them?), and the extra point attempt was moved back fifteen yards and missed, which left the game 34–31, USC, with three seconds left. USC still had to kick the ball off. "We put Reggie on kickoff coverage, just in case," says Seto.

Notre Dame fielded the squibbed kick and tried three laterals before being tackled on their own fifteen-yard line.

And then, finally, it was done.

Carroll made his way to the middle of the field to shake hands with the stunned Weis, then did a short interview with NBC's Johnson, which ended with this: "The players really believe they're gonna win. They didn't give up on the thought that they were gonna win. . . . It's a great day to be a Trojan. See you later!" And then he ran into the scrum of players on the field.

"The thing about Pete is that you never think you're out of a game," says Ruel. "The staff would get down and think we really screwed this up and he'd always say, 'We're all right. We just need to score on this drive.' Comebacks don't happen unless you have a coach who really stays positive. It's too easy to fall into the negative part of it. Pete would never let us do that."

One person who was not immediately jubilant was Leinart. After this touchdown, instead of celebrating with his teammates, he sat on the bench by himself, his head in his hands, crying. He cried later in the locker room, as well. They were not tears of joy, he would say. They were tears of relief. The burden of the winning streak, the attempt at three titles in a row, the aggressive offense that put such a heavy burden on its stars, had all gotten to him.

After Weis spoke to his team in his locker room, he told his twelve-year-old son, Charlie Jr., "Come with me. I want you to learn something."[†††] They walked over to the visitor's locker room and knocked on the door, asking to see Leinart and Bush. The two players came out of the room and Weis asked them if he could address the Trojans. "They invited me in and gathered up the team and I told them that although we'd lost and were crushed, I just wanted to congratulate them on winning an epic game that will forever be remembered," says Weis. When he was done, the USC players gave him a standing ovation.

The game remains among the most memorable in college football history.

[†††] Charlie Weis Jr. is currently the offensive coordinator at Ole Miss. His head coach and boss there: Lane Kiffin.

CHAPTER THIRTEEN

Reaping the Whirlwind

On the field, there appeared to be no sign of a hangover from the high of the Notre Dame win. The next week, USC traveled to Seattle and pummeled Washington, 51–24, with Bush scoring on an eighty-four-yard punt return. The week after that, in a 55–13 win over Washington State, the Trojans made forty first downs while racking up 745 yards of total offense. USC next destroyed Stanford, 51–21 (Bush had a forty-two-yard touchdown run) and then defeated Cal, 35–10.

The Notre Dame win appeared to be an inflection point, the springboard to the greatest season in college football's history by what some were already calling the greatest team in the sport's history.

The hype and hoopla heightened every week. Instead of shying away from it and becoming more conservative, Carroll embraced it and used it as a platform to dive even deeper into his philosophies. He spoke of his "freedom within boundaries" mantra, likening his players to dancers or jazz musicians who mastered their skill to the point that improvisations—within the boundaries—flowed out of them so they could express themselves and become the best they could be. His way stood in stark contrast to the traditional football coaching methods. "The authoritarian way of coaching has always been the most popular way in football," he says. "It eliminates freedoms that can be distracting." He likened that way to being in the Army, where everyone shaved their heads and wore the same uniforms and spoke the same words. "It's 'Shut up and do what I tell you.' It's the easiest way to lead a group of people," he says. "I'm on the other end of the spectrum. I'm coaching my guys like special forces. They aren't infantry. I'm trying to find the extraordinary levels of performance people can generate when they're allowed to tap into all they can offer."

By the time Golden Pat Ruel* arrived at USC in 2005, he'd worked for eleven different head coaches. None of them, he says, were like Carroll. He used one of his former bosses to draw the distinction. "I've worked with Nick Saban," he says. "With Saban, there was a border, and you couldn't draw outside of the lines. But Pete always wanted a player to keep his uniqueness. He never wanted to turn them into robots. He always thought that you don't have to make people miserable to win, you don't have to turn the program into a prison. You could draw a little bit outside the lines with Pete."

Carroll always wanted his players and coaches loose, and he encouraged them to come up with new and fun ways of doing the same old things. The Trojan Walk was a good example. But other activities were smaller in scale. "Some of the guys once came up with the idea of playing *Jeopardy!* to learn our plays," says Ruel. "We'd get the offensive lineman together, or the entire offense, and it was like, 'I'll take backside blocking for $200.'

"It always seemed like it was going to be a fun day with Pete."

And sometimes the fun involved something a bit more elaborate.

On Halloween Day in 2005, USC was beginning its week of practice for the ninth game of the season, against Stanford. Carroll

---

*Yes, that's his real name.

sensed that some of his players, and even some of his coaches, were getting a bit uptight and maybe burdened by the winning streak and the media attention. It made for a perfect time, he thought, to reach back into his old bag of tricks to liven things up. "I always wanted to make practice a special place, somewhere that when everyone came, they weren't sure what was going to happen," he says. "It's like when you were in school and there was that classroom down the hall and you could hear the music, the laughter. You wanted to stick your head in and see what was going on. I tried to make it a thriving environment that was fun to be a part of, so we could ask them anything in terms of involvement because they knew they were going to get a great experience."

And one of his favorite ways to make practice a fun and thriving environment was to pull a prank.

That Halloween, Carroll called Ruel aside and enlisted him as a coconspirator. He tried to recruit Bush, as well, but the running back declined. So he approached White instead, who was game. No one else was in on it.

During the stretching portion of practice that day, White suddenly began to yell and curse at his teammates and coaches, complaining about his lack of carries and having to share the ball with Bush.

His complaints grew louder and louder, and he began to direct them at Carroll and Kiffin specifically. Carroll walked over to him. They screamed at each other. Then White tore into Kiffin. Kiffin yelled back until his face turned red. Then, just as suddenly as he'd begun, White stormed off the field, telling the team that he'd quit (and telling a Fox Sports reporter on the sidelines the same thing). Jethro Franklin, who had taken over for Orgeron as the defensive line coach, put his arm around White as he walked away, trying to coax him into apologizing and coming back to practice. White just shrugged him off.

That White was already known as a sometimes-surly hothead, and that he brought to the surface the issue of splitting time and carries with Bush—which was an issue both the coaches and even some of the players worried about—made everything more believable.

As a last gesture, White threw his football gloves dramatically to the ground, got into a golf cart, and headed away.

Carroll turned to his team and told them to ignore the distraction, and the session resumed.

Near the end of practice, Carroll brought the team together. He told them, "We have won with LenDale, and we will win without him."

And just at that moment came the voice of White, who was yelling, with anger, "I hate football!"

Ruel pointed to the top of a nearby six-story building, where White's voice was coming from and, just as the players turned to look, a body wearing White's jersey came flying off the roof. It was, of course, a mannequin, the tried-and-true prank that Carroll had first learned from Monte Kiffin back in their days at the Vikings.

Most realized what was going on right away. But not everyone did. "I bet 20 percent of the players were legit scared," says Collin Ashton. One of the 20 percent was Bush, who, Ashton says, "almost pulled me down as he gasped." (Though Bush was in on the prank, the reason he declined to participate was that he was afraid of heights.) And one of the Ting twins—Carroll can't remember which one—"broke down in tears," he says.

White eventually returned to the field, laughing. "It was fun because I got to cuss out the coaches," says White. "And some of what I said was true."

"You'd never get away with that in this day and age," says Ashton. "But that shit was awesome."

Carroll says that afterward, he got "hammered in the media because of suicides on college campuses. It really wasn't well thought out by me." But it appeared to work. Carroll's Trojans stayed loose and played well.

The Notre Dame game was an inflection point for another reason: fame.

The popularity of the USC football team—already at unsurpassed heights in 2004—grew even more in 2005. The Trojans broke more attendance records at home games. And, as attested by the epic Notre Dame game, their magnetic pull was just as strong in their opponents' stadiums, as well—people showed up in droves to root against them or just to lay eyes on them. USC practices were filled to capacity with fans and celebrities. "The practice crowds were crazy, the size of a big-time high school football game," says the linebacker Clay Matthews. Everyone and anyone wanted to somehow be associated with the show.

Something had changed in 2005, something that had caused an upswelling that bordered on frenzy. That change: the USC players themselves had become *the* celebrities—bigger ones than some of the famous actors and musicians who came to watch them. This was especially true of Bush and Leinart, who sometimes had to be escorted off the field after practice by security guards so they wouldn't get mobbed by fans.

Bush had blown up because he was in the midst of what would become a Heisman Trophy–winning season. Charlie Weis called him "the reincarnation of Marshall Faulk." Pat Haden likened him to Barry Sanders. ESPN described him as "Shakespeare . . . gifted with speedy brilliance and flourish." *The San Diego Union-Tribune* said he "runs like a witch flies." His teammate Shaun Cody said attempting to tackle him in practice was "like trying to chase a rabbit around."

Bush's captivating play on the field, combined with his winning smile and seemingly humble demeanor off it, fueled his fame. He was, in 2005, the premier athlete in the city of Los Angeles. And yet, his fame paled in comparison to that of his teammate.

"Reggie was a star, there's no doubt about it," says Tim Tessalone, who, as the sports information director, oversaw the fielding of media requests for the team. "But Matt was a real celebrity. He transcended the sports star."

Leinart didn't even have to be at USC that season. In fact, many believed he had been foolish to stay, even though he had one more year of eligibility left, thanks to the redshirt he took his freshman season.

After his Heisman-winning season in 2004, and his spectacular five-passing-touchdown performance in the BCS title game, it was projected that Leinart would be selected high in the first round of the 2005 NFL Draft, perhaps even with the first pick, which was owned by the quarterback-needy San Francisco 49ers.[†]

Less than two weeks after the win over Oklahoma in the championship game, Leinart held a press conference at Heritage Hall and announced that he would be staying at USC for another year, much to the joy of the 500 or so students in attendance—who broke into a giant roar—and his coach, who gave him a high-five at the podium and whose first words after his quarterback's pronouncement were, "Okay, I'm smiling."

At the press conference, Leinart did not mention the tendonitis in his throwing elbow, which would require offseason surgery, or his sports hernia, which would require offseason rehab, as reasons

---

[†] Bush's old high school teammate Alex Smith went first to the 49ers in that draft. Leinart's old foes on the field—Aaron Rodgers and Jason Campbell— were the next two quarterbacks drafted that year, by the Green Bay Packers (at twenty-four) and the Washington Redskins (at twenty-five).

for coming back, though he would later admit that he was worried about his ability to throw for NFL scouts because of the injuries. He also didn't mention the Lloyd's of London insurance policy that his parents had taken out to cover any losses of income if he were to be injured in 2005, or if his position in the 2006 NFL Draft dropped significantly. Instead, he talked about the motivation of trying to win another title, a third in a row, and said, "I realized the opportunity to support my family by going to the NFL early, but to me, I think college football and this whole atmosphere of being here with my friends and teammates that I have been with for four years is ultimately more satisfying and will make me happier than any amount of money could make someone happy. . . . Being in college is the best time of my life."

Yes. Yes, it was.

Leinart's fame began to blow up after the 2004 season, with the championship and the Heisman. He was the subject of feature stories in GQ, *Playboy, Rolling Stone, ESPN the Magazine, US Weekly,* and *Sports Illustrated,* back in a time when print magazines still held much of their powerful sway over public opinion. He threw out the first pitches for both the Dodgers and the Angels. He was encouraged to stop signing autographs for fans after practice because many of those "fans" were part of a secondary market, taking the autographs straight to eBay to auction them off. Voters on ESPN.com named him the "hottest male celebrity." He was a guest on *Jimmy Kimmel Live.*

But what set Leinart apart from any college athlete, perhaps ever—and even most professional athletes at the time—was that "he actually lived in that celebrity world," says Tessalone.

Leinart was initially provided access to that world through his friendship with a man named Josh Richman, an actor, producer, event planner, and nightclub owner who was known as "the Godfather of the LA Club Scene." Richman introduced Leinart to

Nick Lachey, a member of the boy band 98 Degrees, who, at the time, was married to Jessica Simpson. Soon enough, Leinart was hanging out with Vince Vaughn, Tiesto, Justin Timberlake, Leonardo DiCaprio, and Chris Rock, always at the best table in the club, thanks to Richman. He got hammered with Kid Rock. "I went out with Leinart and man, when you're young and can do whatever you want in Hollywood, there's nothing like it in the world," says White.

He was romantically linked with Lindsay Lohan, Paris Hilton, Alyssa Milano, Britney Spears, and Kristin Cavallari. When asked about these supposed romances, Leinart would always claim to be "just friends," though in a 2023 podcast, Cavallari admitted to dating Leinart during his last season at the school. (Brynn Cameron, the USC volleyball player who gave birth to Leinart's child in October 2006, told *The New York Times* that she and Leinart dated until near the end of the 2005 season.) And Fred Davis says he "saw Paris Hilton at Matt's apartment a few times."

Richman threw Leinart his twenty-second birthday party in the spring of 2005 at the club, Mood. In attendance: Lachey, Simpson, Vaughn, Milano, Fred Durst, and Jake Gyllenhaal. "That was the time before camera phones," Leinart told an interviewer. "There was no worry." The only cameras around were in the hands of paparazzi, which hounded him to the point that he often went out in the familiar celebrity disguise of a hoodie over a baseball cap pulled down over his eyes.

In October 2005, just before USC's game against Washington, Leinart went to a Victoria's Secret party attended by other celebrities. And "other celebrities" is the correct way to frame it. Leinart's name appeared in the gossip pages along with the others and, in some ways, his shone brightest. "Matt Leinart is probably the biggest celebrity in LA," White told ESPN at the time. One day after a practice, Leinart and Will Ferrell went to lunch. A student approached the table and asked for Leinart's autograph and ignored Ferrell.

Two things happening at around that time helped boost Leinart's celebrity status. One was the arrival of TMZ, the celebrity gossip website, which launched in the fall of 2005. TMZ was the internet's answer to *People, US Weekly,* and other tabloid magazines, but was much faster and more sensational and salacious than any printed form. It was no coincidence that TMZ's rise coincided with the rise of the "holy trinity" of bad girls back then—Hilton, Lohan, and Spears—who all very publicly cavorted about, often appearing inebriated, and who would all, in the span of a few months, forsake underwear and flash their private parts for paparazzi cameras as they got out of cars. And they all hung out with Leinart.

The second was the popularity of the HBO series *Entourage,* which was the fictional story of an actor, Vincent Chase, who moved to Hollywood with some friends from back home in Queens. The group lived the Hollywood life—male fantasy version—eating at Spago, having sex with models, getting high, driving Ferraris. But what made the show work was the portrayal of genuine friendship among the characters. Leinart, with his dark features and stubble-lined chin, looked like Adrian Grenier, the actor who played Vincent Chase. And, like Chase, Leinart lived the Hollywood lifestyle but was kept somewhat grounded by his own band of brothers—his football teammates.

The good news for Leinart was that during the 2005 season, he had plenty of time for both football and nightlife. He had graduated in 2004, as a sociology major. But he needed to be actively enrolled at USC to fulfill NCAA stipulations for student-athlete eligibility. So he enrolled in one class: ballroom dancing. The class met one night a week and was taught by a choreographer of the movie *Dirty Dancing.* Among his classmates: Brynn Cameron and a then-redshirt freshman quarterback, Mark Sanchez.[‡]

When asked if he was worried about the celebrity statuses of his star running back and star quarterback in 2005, Carroll answers, "Constantly."

He worried about the distraction and the possibility that their priorities might slip. "I was always trying to keep them on task," he says. "I was never scolding but just trying to get them prepared for what was happening." Unsurprisingly, Carroll also liked the fact that they were celebrities and the attention it garnered. It was good for the program's image. It was good for recruiting. And it was, Carroll says, good for Leinart and Bush. "Here's the thing. They were full of themselves, but that was part of the program, part of being in the spotlight. The idea was to get them to live in that mentality, so it became normal. So that when they played Notre Dame, they were ready. Not ready to play the game of their lives. But ready to play like they always did."

Though Leinart would end the 2005 season with statistics very similar to his Heisman-winning season the year before, he struggled a bit, particularly at the beginning of the season. He hit on only 59 percent of his passes against Oregon and Arizona State in the third and fourth games of the season—below his usual 65 percent—and told the media that he didn't feel completely right mentally. And though he won the Notre Dame game with his sneak, he only completed 53 percent of his passes in that game and uncharacteristically threw two interceptions. "I think at times I've lost track of just having fun and not thinking too much," he

---

[‡] Maybe Leinart learned the spin move he made in the Bush Push game in that class?

told the *Los Angeles Daily News.* "I'm a kid who is twenty-two years old going through what I'm going through."

Carroll chalked it up to the pressure of following up on a Heisman-winning season. "In the early part of that year, he felt it. He would say, 'I can't hit anything.' He was a natural worrier," says Carroll. "We had to help him through it by kicking his ass a little bit and building him back up by saying, 'Shut the fuck up. You're awesome.'"

But was it also that he was recovering from the injuries he had in 2004 and rehabbed over the summer? Or was it the offense that put so much pressure on its stars to always perform at their highest level? Or the aggressive downfield passing scheme that had him holding on to the ball a bit longer and, thus, taking some bigger hits, like a massive blow to the head he received against Arizona State?

Or was he distracted by fame? How could he have not been? His teammates say that though he was the same guy in the huddle in games and in practice, he was harder to reach that season. He was on a different plane. He was, well, a celebrity in their midst. "That season, you felt like you couldn't just go up to him and ask to borrow five bucks," says one teammate. Opponents sometimes also used Leinart's celebrity status to try to get in his head. Before the Arizona State game that year, Sun Devils quarterback Sam Keller told the media, "I don't need to have Jessica Simpson running around or anyone like that to make me happy."

Whatever it was, after the Notre Dame game, Leinart got back into rhythm for the rest of the season.

"We own this city when we do it right, boys," Carroll once told his team. "And it's huge. It's LA. Hollywood! It's all that. It's the Trojans!"

He was correct. And it wasn't just Leinart and Bush who did so.

Trojan players were invited—and went—to the Playboy Mansion in Los Angeles. They attended parties at the homes of Jamie Foxx and Will and Jada Smith. They saw what one player described as "weird, creepy shit" at P. Diddy's house parties. Reggie Bush was hanging out with Kim Kardashian. Frostee Rucker dated a woman who was on the Disney Channel. Hershel Dennis dated the actress and model Meagan Good. ("All of us dated a B- or C-list celebrity at one time," says Fred Davis.) White and a few other players hung out, fairly regularly, with Snoop in his studio. The players went to restaurants like Mastro's, Mr. Chow, and Nobu. When they were out, Tyrese Gibson, Owen Wilson, Jonah Hill, and people in the cast of the television series *The Hills* would stop whatever they were doing and come over to say hello. They never had to stand in line at Club Lax. "We would go to clubs and be let in before players on the Chargers were, guys who were making millions, like Shawne Merriman [an All-Pro linebacker]," says Fred Davis. "They would be so upset."

If they were ever pulled over by the police, they flashed their USC IDs or the business card of LA sheriff Lee Baca and got off with a warning. When linebacker Rey Maualuga allegedly knocked out a man at a USC party and an onlooker threatened to call the police, Maualuga reportedly responded, "I own the police." (He was arrested anyway.) Even the players who rarely saw the field received attention, just from association with the program. "Girls wanted to be your friend and sleep with you," says Dominique Wise, a walk-on offensive lineman. "This one girl came up to me and said she wanted to make a sex tape with me and some teammates. It was nuts." Some people—students and nonstudents—even wore USC gear out on the town and pretended to be on the team, hoping to catch some vapor trails.

Brandon Hancock, the fullback, describes a typical night out:

> We'd go to the White Lotus, or whatever the hottest place in town was. It's pretty tough to get eighteen to twenty Black and white dudes with no IDs and underage into a club, but we had a way of pulling it off, with Josh Richman and those guys. We'd walk in and there was [David] Hasselhoff dancing on a table, and Britney Spears in the corner, Adam Sandler, Eve the Rapper. There were nights when there'd be ten A-list celebrities there, just kicking it. They'd see our swarm of big dudes come in. And as soon as they found out who we were, they'd come over.
>
> One of our people would get the first bottle for free. And then a coach might come by, and you'd think, "Oh shit, what am I doing here, I gotta get out of here, some of these guys aren't even legal." And the coaches would be like, "Let's get another bottle." And we'd keep going. And then there'd be a third bottle.
>
> When you're a champion, that's what LA is all about. They don't care unless you're a winner. We had a Heisman winner and another guy who was going to win a Heisman on our team. Players are dating celebs. Paris Hilton is hanging out. You're hanging out with Kid Rock and Tiesto. There's a crossover effect. Now there's paparazzi when you're leaving the club. It just wasn't happening like that anywhere else in college football. Dude, it was like the road was paved with gold.

"When you find success in LA, you have to be an extremely strong person," says Omar Nazel. "LA has fair-weather fans from the tech world, the music world, Hollywood. They now descend on your product because it's a beacon for them and their interests, separate from football. Then there's the money, women, drugs, and the biggest thing, fame. We were kids. And all that stuff is there."

And sometimes, it was even found within.

Owen Hanson grew up in a broken blue-collar family in Redondo Beach in the 1980s and 1990s, back before that town became gentrified. After his mother and sister left the family, Hanson lived with his father, a maintenance man and construction worker.

Athletics were Hanson's ticket out. He was six foot three and 215 pounds, a good enough volleyball player to earn a partial scholarship at USC. When he arrived on campus in 2001, Hanson immediately realized there was a stark difference between himself and the other students there. "I was around all of these spoiled kids driving Mercedes and Escalades," he says. "And I was driving a 1990 Toyota Camry that I got from my grandfather when he died. I was so embarrassed. And I thought I needed to do something."

He figured out what he needed to do when he noticed the kids in his fraternity were buying hundred-dollar bags of cocaine nearly every night. He remembered some old acquaintances in Redondo, members of a Mexican gang, and he made a deal with them. They supplied him with cocaine, and he took it back to USC and undercut the competition, selling his bags to his fraternity brothers for twenty bucks apiece. Later, he added Xanax, Adderall, and Ecstasy to his offerings. And within a few months, he, too, was driving a Mercedes.

In Hanson's sophomore year, he says, his volleyball coach notified him that an All-American player was coming to the team and would be taking his place. The coach told Hanson he would be redshirted, and that he needed to improve his vertical jump and the strength in his shoulders and arms if he wanted back on the team.

So Hanson began to work out religiously. He supplemented and boosted those workouts with steroids, which he procured from a veterinary clinic in Tijuana. Soon enough, he had put on ten pounds of muscle.

Hanson says that he was working out in the USC athletics gym one day when a strength coach from the football team saw him. Impressed, the strength coach told him he should try out as a walk-on for the football team. "I was like, 'Are you crazy? I've never played football,'" says Hanson. "And he was like, 'Well, you never know.'"

A week later, Hanson went to the open tryout. There were around fifty students there, most of them former high school or former Division II or III players looking for a shot at glory. Hanson did not own a pair of cleats. He showed up to the tryout in his volleyball shoes.

The hopefuls were put through various exercises—the forty-yard dash, vertical leap, bench presses, and agility drills. Hanson says he ran the forty twice, clocking in with a 4.62 as his best time. He says he then bench-pressed 225 pounds twenty-five times. He went out for five passes during the tryout and managed to catch three of them.

A week later, he was again in the weight room. The strength coach who had first talked him into trying out told him that the outcome of the tryout was posted on Carroll's door at Heritage Hall. Hanson went to look. There was one name listed: his. He made the team as a tight end. His coach: Brennan Carroll.

In his first practice with the team, Hanson put his shoulder pads on backward.

With zero football experience and only two years of eligibility left, Hanson was an odd addition to the Trojans, even if all big-time college programs need practice bodies. During his two-year career on the USC football team, he didn't make much of an impact on the field. He played a total of two downs, both in a blowout win in 2004 over Washington, and was on the sidelines for the entire national title win over Oklahoma that year.

It was off the field, where he got the nickname "Dr. O-Dog," where he made his presence felt.

Hanson continued the dealing of cocaine and Ecstasy he had done with his fraternity brothers and added some new clientele: some of his teammates. "I gave a lot of guys on the team their first line of cocaine," he says. By his estimate, he supplied around half the team. "Everyone partied at SC," he says.

But the narcotics weren't the only drugs he provided. "Guys saw me in the locker room and asked what I was doing to get so big," says Hanson. Soon, he claims, he was supplying steroids to around one-third of the team. "I won't say who," he says. "That's ratting." Hanson would go to Tijuana to procure the steroids, walking—rather than driving—back across the border with "pills and vials" taped to each leg under bulky sweatpants. He says he coached his fellow players on when to take the steroids—summer was best—and when to stop and how to cleanse so they wouldn't fail a steroid test.

Hanson says his coaches "just turned a blind eye" to it all. That there were, allegedly, steroids in the USC program shouldn't come as a surprise. The unspoken truth is that performance-enhancing drugs are part of nearly every professional and big-time college program, and, by that time, players had become knowledgeable about how to beat the testing system. During the Carroll era at USC, there was only one recorded positive test for steroids, though there were rumors of others. According to the *Los Angeles Times*, safety Brandon Ting failed a test in the winter before the 2006 season. He and his brother, Ryan, left the team in the summer before the season began.[§]

In 2005, Hanson graduated from USC with a degree in business and shook Neil Armstrong's hand as he received his diploma.

[§] The Tings' father was Barry Bonds's orthopedic surgeon and was called to testify to a grand jury in the famous BALCO steroids scandal.

After school, he went on to garner more attention than he could ever imagine. But all for the wrong reasons.

After graduation, Hanson got his real estate license. His real "business" was something else entirely, though. He got into sports gambling, associating with notoriously shady gamblers in Central America, and soon was managing a multimillion-dollar international business that concealed its true activity with fake bank accounts, and harassed its customers who failed to pay on time with threats of violence. With that money, he invested in what would become an international drug-trafficking organization. According to the FBI, Hanson "routinely shipped large quantities of cocaine from Los Angeles to Australia . . . and sold recreational and performance-enhancing drugs to professional athletes." Hanson grew more and more paranoid as the years went on and, as he took on bigger debts, he took bigger risks with his deals until he was arrested in September 2015 after he did a drug deal with an undercover agent.

Hanson was found guilty of operating what the FBI described as "a violent international drug trafficking, sports gambling, and money laundering enterprise that operated in the U.S., Central and South America, and Australia." In late 2017, Hanson was sentenced to twenty-one years in federal prison and ordered to pay $5 million and give up, among other things, luxury vehicles, vacation homes, and a sailboat. Within the report, the FBI stated that Hanson "sold recreational drugs and steroids to his teammates" while at USC.

In 2024, Hanson entered a halfway house, released from federal prison early for good behavior. And late that year, he published a book about his life, titled *The California Kid: From USC Golden Boy to International Drug Kingpin*. On the cover of the book is a figure clad in a USC Trojan football uniform surrounded by bricks of cocaine and bundles of cash. Along with the book, Hanson says there is a documentary in the works about his life, produced by Mark Wahlberg.

Hanson's old teammates—many of whom are in photos with him that he keeps in his phone—are not thrilled with the book and the unflattering attention it has placed on the Trojan teams he played on. "It's an unfortunate situation," says Alex Holmes.

When asked about Hanson, Carroll, at first, says, "I didn't know what he was doing. He was such a unique character. I guess I wouldn't be surprised if he was involved in that. Maybe that's how he got to be as athletic as he was."

But after some reflection, Carroll changes his tune. "He's just a guy trying to profit on our team. He shouldn't even be talked about."

The season after Hanson left, another player filled his void, at least on the recreational drug side. (The player prefers to remain unnamed: "I'm not seeking attention," he says.) Like Hanson, this player arrived at a school of conspicuous consumption and affluence with very little himself. "Everyone else was going out to dinner all the time," he says. "I couldn't afford it. So I figured out a way to make some money." That way was by providing cocaine to his teammates, getting supplied, he says, "from my hood" in downtown Los Angeles.

The player says that he and many of his teammates "did cocaine Monday through Thursday. And then we'd lock in and stop on Friday before the game. Then we'd whoop ass in the game, and everybody would meet up and do it again. We were the NFL team in town, and we did what NFL players did. I saw [a USC player] snort coke off of [a famous woman's] titties."

Even with the drug use, the player says there was accountability. "We lived and partied like rock stars, but we always handled our business working out and at practice. We'd stumble out of the club at five a.m. but then be on the line at practice throwing up, still getting it in. If you went out partying and didn't make it to practice, the players would get on you. You had to show up."

While the steroids and recreational drugs were certainly not endorsed by Carroll and the coaching staff, they were, perhaps, inevitable by-products of the adulation, the winning of gladiatorial games, and the Los Angeles lifestyle lived by the Trojan players. But the rest of it—the fame, the glamour of LA, the celebrities prowling the sidelines—*was* embraced, for strategic reasons. USC had become a behemoth. What was happening off the field fed it, made it more powerful, helped it perpetuate itself. But to paraphrase William Blake, how do you know what's enough until you find out what's too much?

There comes a time in the life of a championship team—or, maybe more precisely, in any given endeavor in which winning becomes the norm—when the highs of victories are far outweighed by the lows of losses. In a sense, all of those connected to the team—its fans and boosters, the media, its players, and even its coaches—begin to resemble opioid addicts, seeking the minimal highs of wins to stave off the devastating lows of losses. Winning becomes its own narcotic.

And in the pursuit of that high, there are often some things that are ignored, things that are, perhaps, growing to the point that they are out of control.

It was certainly beginning to feel like too much to many outside of the program by that time. "I got a lot of calls back then, from anxious folks at the conference and the NCAA and rival schools and even from other major schools across the country," says Keith Miller, the compliance director. "Sideline control was what they called it and what they were worried about most. This isn't supposed to be the Lakers game with Jack Nicholson on the court, or the Knicks with Spike Lee, but that's what it was turning into, even the practices. The verbiage they used was 'tone it down.'"

There was a sense from the other schools and the NCAA that the Trojans had an unfair advantage and that they were, therefore, breaking the rules, that they were somehow in violation of the "amateurism" that was supposedly at the heart of the sport. "Envy never comes to the ball dressed as envy," wrote Martin Amis. "It comes dressed as high moral standards or distaste for materialism."

There were also those close to the program who worried that things were in danger of spinning out of control. "I remember being in the Foundation Room [a VIP area] at the House of Blues and seeing players but also assistant coaches there partying, and thinking, 'This is not normal,'" says Petros Papadakis. "I've seen it all, but that curled my toes. I'm not a pearl-clutching church lady, but whatever lack of institutional control is, that's probably it.

"The entire celebrity thing, the players hanging out with them, the players becoming one of them, seemed out of hand. I mean, it all seemed to become about Matt Leinart's dick."

And even some within the building began to sound the alarm. Chris Huston, the assistant sports information director, was one of them:

> We had the most liberal open-practice policy in football, with a team that became one of the brightest shining teams of all time, filled with stars, and people were just hanging around them all the time. We had people who weren't in the program just hanging out all the time. Our players would practice and then go back to Heritage Hall. They'd shower and get treatment and then come out and there would be reporters and people seeking autographs waiting for them. And I told Tim [Tessalone], "We have to start buttoning this up, it's starting to get to be a little much. Don't close practice,

but make sure there's nobody lurking around here." And it only got worse. You could see things starting to get out of control. Carroll thought he could handle it, thought he could handle any situation. The power of positive thinking.

CHAPTER FOURTEEN

The Third Wheel

After the convincing 35–10 win over Cal on November 12, the Trojans were 10–0. They had three weeks left in the regular season—Fresno State at home, followed by a bye week and then UCLA at home.

Fresno State had been, for years, a team that big programs loathed playing. Coached by Pat Hill, they were scrappy, always seemed to finish with a winning record, and, on occasion, sprung an upset over a ranked opponent, something they'd done twice the year before, beating Kansas State (ranked thirteenth) and Virginia (ranked eighteenth). That scrappiness had a finer point on it when it came to playing USC: many of the Fresno State players were from California and had been overlooked by the Trojans, which left them with chips on their shoulders.

Fresno State came into the Coliseum averaging forty points a game and ranked number sixteen in the country at 8–1 (their only loss was by three points at Oregon). Kickoff was at 7:15 p.m. PST. The game would turn out to be a precursor of what would become known as a "PAC-12 After Dark" game,* a back-and-forth contest of promiscuous scoring and unlikely plays. A game in

---

*The PAC-10 became the PAC-12 in 2011, with the addition of Colorado and Utah.

which Goliath could be done in by a lucky shot with a sling and a stone. A game during which, up late on a Saturday night on the East Coast, you might call a buddy and say, "You watching this?"

It was also the game in which Reggie Bush locked up the Heisman Trophy.

Fresno State's opening touchdown, which gave them a 7–0 lead, was the first indicator that this was not going to be a normal game. The touchdown play began on the USC thirteen-yard line, when the Bulldogs quarterback Paul Pinegar[†] completed a pass to his receiver, Devyn McDonald, who ran the ball all the way to the USC one-yard line. There, he was hit by Trojan safety Scott Ware. The ball popped loose, straight up into the air, and landed right in the hands of another Fresno State receiver, Jermaine Jamison, for a touchdown.

Pinegar would menace the Trojans all night, throwing for 317 yards and four touchdowns but also, critically, four interceptions.

At the half, the Bulldogs led, 21–13, not an unfamiliar position for the 2005 Trojans, who had also trailed Oregon, Arizona State, and Notre Dame at halftime.

And, predictably, USC came out of the locker room for the second half on fire, scoring twenty-one unanswered points.

Fresno State finally answered with a Pinegar touchdown pass late in the third quarter to close USC's lead to six, at 34–28.

And then Bush happened.

This was Bush's game. During film study, Kiffin had deduced that while Fresno State was very good at stopping runs up the middle—between the tackles—they weren't very good at pursuing runs to the outside. And so he put Bush in a position to exploit that. In the first quarter, Bush had popped off a sixty-five-yard

[†] Pinegar is number two on the Fresno State all-time passing touchdowns list, behind Derek Carr and ahead of David Carr.

scamper. He had a forty-five-yard run for a touchdown in the third quarter. And then, with one minute and twenty-seven seconds left in the third, with USC at midfield, he performed one of the signature plays of his college career.

He took a handoff from Leinart and burst through—of all places—the middle of the line and then ran down the left-hand sideline. At the Fresno State twenty-five-yard line, a multitude of Bulldog defenders closed in on him. And Bush did what very few, if any, running backs in the game could ever do—he stopped, completely, and briefly tucked the ball behind his back with the flair of a matador. In a seamless motion, he then accelerated out of that stop as his pursuers, unable to perform the same maneuver, rolled like tumbleweeds by him. Bush then ran to the end zone. He had not been touched on the play.

Bush ended up with 513 total yards on the night—the second-highest number of yards gained in a game in NCAA history at the time—with 294 of those yards coming on the ground.

His score made it 41–28, USC. It was usually at this point in games during the Trojans' remarkable run since 2003 that the opposing team folded. But Fresno State decidedly did not. They were the pest that wouldn't leave. The Trojans' vexation became visible. Once, after getting sacked and driven into the ground, Leinart punched the turf in frustration. *Who are these guys?* Carroll paced the sidelines, gum-less, his face betraying bewilderment instead of the usual smile. The Fresno State players talked trash to the Trojans all night. And they backed it up.

With ten minutes left in the game, Pinegar threw another touchdown pass to cut USC's lead to six at 41–35. And on the ensuing kickoff, Bush—the man of the match—made his only mistake of the evening. On the kick return, he ran with the ball carried cavalierly in his right hand, well away from his body, and it was knocked from his grasp. It was his first fumble of the season, ending a remarkable run where neither he nor White lost a fumble in a combined 452 touches. Fresno State got the ball on the USC eighteen. They scored one play later to take a one-point lead, 42–41, with nine minutes and forty-seven seconds to go.

The Trojans then eased their way eighty-nine yards down the field—with Bush accounting for seventy-two of those yards—and scored on a two-yard White touchdown run. The two-point conversion attempt failed. Now it was 47–42, Trojans.

USC tacked on a field goal after defensive end Lawrence Jackson sacked Pinegar and forced a fumble that was recovered by freshman linebacker Brian Cushing.

Fresno State got the ball back with just over three minutes to play and drove down to the USC twenty-five, converting a fourth and seven along the way. And then, with one minute and thirty-seven seconds left, Pinegar threw his fourth and final interception, to Darnell Bing in the end zone. USC escaped with the win, 50–42. But the warning light in the finely tuned sports car was on.

The game was one of the few since midway through the 2003 season in which the USC starters had to stay in for the entire contest. On defense, at least, they did not show well. USC gave up 427 yards of total offense to Fresno State and, if not for some timely turnovers, the game might have ended differently. "Our defense that year was not the suffocating defense it had been in the past," says John David Booty. Indeed, the Trojans would end the regular season with the thirty-ninth-ranked defense in the country, uncharacteristically poor for a Carroll-led team. "We were pretty banged up on D by the end of the season," says Carroll, which may be why linebacker Rey Maualuga didn't miss a game even after he was arrested for allegedly punching that man at the party in the middle of the season (no charges were ever filed). There were other problems in the Fresno State game, missed assignments and personal fouls, that had kept the Bulldogs in the game. "They had beaten us emotionally," Lawrence Jackson said after the game. "We just outscored them."

And playing poorly and winning can be a coach's nightmare. "Guys just don't want to respond," Nick Saban once said. "They look at you like, 'Hey, Coach, we won the game. Why you upset, making us practice and all that?'"

Fourteen days later, after the bye week, USC appeared to have its "get right" game against rival UCLA. The game was effectively over early in the second quarter after USC scored on its first four possessions to take a 24–0 lead. The Trojans ended up winning, 66–19, over a team that was ranked number eleven in the country and had taken USC down to the wire the season before in USC's 29–24 win. The Trojans had 679 yards of offense on the day, 430 of which came on the ground. Bush gained 260 yards rushing and scored two touchdowns, and White ran for 154 yards and had two touchdowns.

The victory put USC in the BCS Championship game in the Rose Bowl against the team that was also undefeated and had been ranked number two all season: Texas.

But two Trojans had one more stop to make before then: the Heisman Trophy ceremony at the Nokia Theater in New York City.

At the conclusion of the 2005 regular season, only three players were invited to the Heisman ceremony—Reggie Bush, Matt Leinart (who had, of course, won the trophy the year before), and Texas quarterback Vince Young. Leinart would later say that he "was just along for the ride." He was confident he knew who was going to win.

The three players met before the ceremony. They walked from Forty-Second Street into the Nokia Theater but then were sent out to do it again—the Heisman video producer wanted another take. Backstage, as they waited for the start of the ceremony, Leinart snapped a photo of his own portrait, which hung on a wall among the other sixty-nine winners of the Heisman. Bush killed time by printing out notes for his upcoming exams. The three players were cordial, but Young couldn't help but feel like a third wheel. And there was something else, an unspoken tension that hung in the air between him and the two Trojans, representatives of the two teams that would be facing off for the national title in less than a month's time.

When the trio entered the theater, Bush took a seat between the two quarterbacks. And when the running back, who had rushed for 1,740 yards (and a nearly nine-yard-per-carry average) and sixteen touchdowns, was announced as the winner (with 92 percent of the total vote[‡]), he immediately turned to his left and hugged his teammate. Young, who had finished second, offered a quick handshake as he stared, stonily, over Bush's shoulder.

Bush became the seventh Heisman winner from USC. More impressive: he was the school's third in the past four years, an unprecedented run. "That comes along with winning," Carroll told the *Los Angeles Times*.

Bush, in a dark blue pinstriped suit with a vest, took the stage and gave a three-minute speech. He thanked his mother, Denise. And he broke up when he spoke of his stepfather, LaMar Griffin. "You took me in at the age of two," Bush said. "It takes a man to do something like that." And he added, "When I'm long gone from this earth, the Heisman will still be there," a statement that would turn out to be true, but not without some drama along the way.

That night, Bush met Leinart and White at the Marquee, a club in New York. Later on, he and Leinart shared a table at Club Butter with Jay-Z. The next day, Bush read the Top Ten List on *The Late Show with David Letterman*.

Young had a very different experience after the ceremony. "Right now, it feels like I let my guys down," he told the media.

[‡] Which included Leinart's. As a Heisman winner, he was also now a voter.

"Right now, it feels like I let my family down." He later admitted that he had wept when he didn't win.

Young felt slighted and didn't hide it. Back in Los Angeles, Leinart told his teammates that in the limousine, on the ride back to the hotel after the ceremony, Young was "pissed."

The slight he felt was about more than just the Heisman. It was also about his team. On the day before the ceremony, Young had attended a Texas–Duke basketball game at Continental Airlines Arena in the Meadowlands. A reporter asked him how he felt about the upcoming national title game. He responded:

> Right now, yeah, I'm very confident about it. They [the Trojans] come in the game off a high winning streak, and everybody's blowing them up, you know, and they think we're the underdogs and we're not going to come to play. I know that we are. We're going to come and show them the Texas football team. . . . Everybody likes Reggie, and everybody likes USC because they've been winning for so long. . . . It's going to be a lot of fuel for us if I lose [the Heisman].

Bush was asked later about Young's comments. "I don't know what it is about us that people just feel like they need to just lash out and say stuff out of the ordinary," he responded.

The stage was now set.

CHAPTER FIFTEEN

Texas Holds 'Em

The hype.

It began in early December 2005, when the matchup between the undefeated number one and number two teams in the country was confirmed. It continues to this day.

USC was, of course, the better-known quantity. The two-time defending national champions came in riding a thirty-four-game winning streak that stretched back to their loss to Cal early in the 2003 season. That mark tied the Miami Hurricanes teams of 2000 to 2002 for the longest winning streak in Division I in a major conference in the modern era—a mark that still stands today.* Matt Leinart had more national titles than losses at that point in his collegiate career—he was 37–1 as a starter—and the team also had more Heisman winners than losses in that thirty-eight-game stretch (two to one). The Trojans were on the verge of joining the ranks of the greatest dynasties in the sport—the USC teams of the 1970s (three titles in 1972, 1974, and 1978) and the Miami Hurricanes of the 1980s and 1990s (four titles in 1983, 1987, 1989, and 1991)—but they were going to accomplish it in a greater, more

---

* Oklahoma has the record, with forty-seven straight wins between 1953 and 1957.

dominating style, with an unprecedented three championships in a row.

All eyes in the sports world were on them. Pundits pointed to the reasons for their success: great coaching, great recruiting. An explosive, high-powered, star-laden offense. And opportunistic defense that led the NCAA in 2005 with thirty-eight takeaways.[†]

ESPN spent the weeks leading up to the game going through hypothetical matchups that pitted the 2005 USC team against the greatest college football teams of the modern era, like the school's own 1972 team, the 1995 Nebraska Cornhuskers, and the 2001 Miami Hurricanes. Other talking heads went so far as to wonder if this USC team could beat the Houston Texans or the New Orleans Saints, the bottom-dwellers in the NFL that year.

Even the USC players really only paid attention to themselves, as Carroll had coached them to do. "Texas?" says Winston Justice. "We didn't think about them. Not at all."

And yet, Texas certainly warranted attention. A lot of it. They, too, were 12–0 entering the game. And they had their own impressive streaks: The Longhorns had won nineteen games in a row and twenty-three of their last twenty-four. Vince Young was 29–2 in his career. And their 2005 season was every bit as impressive as USC's.

The pivotal game for the 2005 Longhorns happened in their second week of the season, when they'd traveled to Columbus, Ohio, to play Ohio State in front of a then-record Buckeyes home crowd of 105,565. The game went back and forth until it was eventually won on a drive late in the fourth quarter—led by Young and the freshman running back Jamaal Charles—that ended with a

---

[†] Carroll's players had taken his admonition about it being "all about the ball" to heart. At that point, the Trojans' turnover margin since he took over in 2001 was plus-eighty-four.

Young touchdown pass to receiver Limas Sweed. After escaping that game with a 25–22 win, the Longhorns blew through the rest of the season, winning their remaining games by an average score of 53–15 (they scored sixty or more points four times in 2005). In their last game of the regular season, in the Big 12 Championship game, they'd beaten Colorado 70–3.

The reason for Texas's success was, of course, that they had serious talent on both sides of the ball. The defense, which ranked sixth in the country, was strongest in the secondary, which featured cornerbacks Cedric Griffin, Tarell Brown, and Aaron Ross, and the safeties Michael Griffin and Michael Huff, the latter of whom was an All-American and winner of the Jim Thorpe Award, given to the nation's best defensive back. The linebacking corps was underrated, but solid, led by Robert Killebrew. And the defensive line featured Brian Robison, Rodrique Wright, and a redshirt freshman named Brian Orakpo.

The offensive side also had weapons, with two solid receivers in Limas Sweed and Billy Pittman, an excellent tight end in David Thomas, and a running back rotation comprised of two veterans—Ramonce Taylor and Selvin Young—and Charles, the dynamic freshman.

But the leading man, of course, was Vince Young. Going into the title game, he'd thrown for 2,679 yards and twenty-six touchdowns (with ten interceptions) and had run for 850 yards for another twelve touchdowns. He had introduced himself to the nation in the previous year's Rose Bowl, when he'd rushed for 192 yards and four touchdowns (and thrown for another one). On all four of his touchdown runs in that game—of twenty, sixty, ten, and twenty-three yards—he'd gone virtually untouched. After that game, he told the fans at the Rose Bowl, prophetically, "We'll be back."

Young grew up in Houston, raised primarily by his mother and grandmother (his father missed most of his early football career because he was in prison). He was an outstanding athlete in high school, the star of the football, basketball, and track and field teams, and a good baseball player to boot. After redshirting his freshman season at Texas in 2002, Young shared the quarterbacking duties the next year before being named the starter for the 2004 season. That year, he had more rushing touchdowns (fourteen) than passing ones (twelve), and he had a poor touchdown-to-interception ratio (he threw eleven interceptions) because he was prone to mistakes if his first receiving option wasn't open. So, before the 2005 season, Texas offensive coordinator Greg Davis designed a simpler passing offense that often sent Sweed deep and provided Young with two dump-off options—the tight end or a running back—if Sweed wasn't immediately open. And if Young ever found himself in doubt, he was instructed to do what he did best: fix a broken play with his legs.

By the 2005 season, Young had become very comfortable as the leader of the Longhorns. Comfortable enough to try to loosen up his sometimes-uptight head coach, Mack Brown. Young joked around at appropriate times in practice. He appeared loose in games, smiling, confident, and upbeat,[‡] and he played rap music in the locker room. Brown and the rest of the team went along with it. Like Carroll, Young helped serve as a reminder that the game was supposed to be fun.

As part of the championship-week festivities, both teams visited Disneyland at the same time. There was, for a brief moment, a stare down between the two squads, that puffery that's involved in the silent sizing up. As the players walked by one another, Young nodded to Leinart. He did not do the same for Bush. Later, the three Heisman finalists met up again for a promotional photo

---

[‡] After his career was over, Young would admit that the appearance of looseness was a façade masking his nerves.

with a person in a Mickey Mouse costume. Bush and Leinart held golden footballs and stood to the left of Mickey. Young stood by himself on the other side, playfully wearing a pair of Goofy's super-large hands.

And, even when given the chance, Young didn't back down from his comments during the Heisman weekend. When asked if he and his teammates were intimidated by USC, he responded, "Intimidated by what? They haven't seen the guys on our team who are gangster."

Unlike the USC players, the Longhorns *had* kept tabs on their title game opponents. In fact, they'd followed them religiously. "The first big moment I remember us all keeping a collective eye on them was in the locker room after we beat Colorado [42–17] in the regular season," says Drew Kelson, a linebacker on the 2005 Texas team. The Longhorn players watched the end of the USC–Notre Dame game on television. They screamed when USC won on the Bush Push. "They won that game. They found a way. It was dramatic. It was every bit of what made USC special during that era," says Kelson. "And we were sitting in that locker room thinking, 'When? When do we get to play them?' They were the way. They earned the hype. They were one of the best teams of all time. But we wanted to play them, and we wanted to beat them."

From that point on, the Longhorns kept a chart where they tracked USC's statistics, comparing them to their own. "We had no fear. We embraced it," says Kelson. "I don't think people at the time realized that we had been doing the same things that year, that maybe *we* deserved to be feared." The Texas players also embraced what they perceived to be a snub of Young by the Heisman voters. "We all felt slighted," says Kelson. "We took it personally."

During the week leading up to the game, the constant chatter about the greatness of that USC team grew to be too much for some of the Longhorn players. In his hotel room, Young turned off ESPN in favor of the Cartoon Network. But the USC hype wasn't too much for their coach. In fact, he welcomed it. In his final press conference before the game, Brown thanked the media for all their coverage of the Trojans' greatness. "You made my job easy," he told them. "I don't have to say anything to my guys to get them ready for the game."

Young was the obvious worry for the Trojan defense. He was on the vanguard of the trend of more mobile quarterbacks in major programs in college football. These types of quarterbacks posed problems for Carroll's pro-style defense. "In fairness, they cause problems for all defenses," says Nick Holt. "They're just hard to defend." A defense can do nearly everything right—a good pass rush and blanketed defense in the secondary—and a mobile quarterback could ruin it all by squirming out of the pocket and heading downfield past the defensive line while the linebackers and secondary players all have their backs turned. In 2005, USC's defense had shut down Isaiah Stanback, the Washington quarterback who was known for his decent running ability. But Young was on an entirely different level.

What made Young different—aside from his speed and uncanny vision as a runner—was his size. He was six foot five and 233 pounds—basically the same weight as White, USC's thumper back, and three inches taller. In the practices that led up to the game, Carroll had his six-foot-four, 260-pound tight end, Fred Davis, play Young as the scout team quarterback, as much for the visual effect as anything else. "I tried to do my best," says Davis.

Carroll, who before the game received a five-year contract extension at nearly $3 million a year, says now that he was pleased with his team's preparation for the game. "It was exactly what we wanted it to be. I felt like we were primed and ready."

His players weren't so sure that was the case. "It was a perfect storm and not in a good way," says Chris McFoy. "Everyone was hyping the hell out of us, comparing us to NFL teams, and not saying a word about Texas. That gave them motivation right there. No respect. And we felt pressure, but it didn't have to do with playing Texas. It was the pressure of the three-peat. It took us a little off track in terms of focusing on Texas."

And maybe at least some of the players had started to believe what the media was telling them. "I thought we were going to kick their ass," says linebacker Keith Rivers. "We watched the film of Vince, and I was like, 'That dude is slow. We're going to beat the living shit out of them.'"

Something else was going on as well. "The week before the game, guys were hitting the strip clubs, staying out late, missing bed checks," says Brandon Hancock.[s] "It sounds super conceited to say, but we played in the Rose Bowl every other year [against UCLA], and we'd already played there for a championship against Michigan. It was almost like, 'Been there, done that. Who cares about going to Lawry's Steakhouse, Disneyland?' It was all old news. And then there was all the talk about how we were going to handle them in the game.

"There were some cracks, for sure. We got over our skis."

Five days before the game, it began to rain in Los Angeles and didn't stop for seventy-two hours. The storm ended up dropping six inches of rain, which, in normally bone-dry Southern California, felt biblical. The traditional Rose Bowl Parade carried on through some of the worst of the storm, rained on for the first time in fifty-one years. Four floats broke down.

And then, the day before the game, the rain stopped. Though the playing field in Pasadena had been covered in tarps, Rose Bowl authorities arranged for six helicopters to fly into the stadium and

---

[s] Remember, Orgeron, the bed-check enforcer nonpareil, had left the team after the 2004 season.

hover over the field to hasten the drying time with their whirring blades. The grass was trimmed one last time, at five-eighths of an inch, four inches or so lower than the length of the grass in Notre Dame Stadium three long months before.

And, before the game, the BCS did something that the NCAA—a separate organization that the BCS relied on but was not part of—had not been able to do: it tapped the brakes on USC's celebrity machine. The BCS issued a directive that sideline credentials "should be distributed only to individuals who have responsibilities that require their presence on the field," essentially enforcing an NCAA rule that had been trampled on for years. BCS administrators said they wanted a "more collegiate" atmosphere and limited the teams to five "wild card" passes each, which were intended for former players only. Though the rule formally applied to the three other BCS games (Orange Bowl, Sugar Bowl, Fiesta Bowl) as well, it was clearly aimed at the title game and, more pointedly, at USC. In case the directive wasn't clear enough, BCS administrator Bill Hancock added, "People here to watch should be in the stands."

Snoop, according to LenDale White—his best friend on the Trojans—found a way around it, though, by exploiting a loophole. Through ESPN Hollywood, he was "miked up" and officially "working" on the sideline. Matthew McConaughey and Roger Clemens just ignored the edict and spent time on the Texas sidelines early on in the game.

The game was the last Rose Bowl broadcast under the ABC Sports brand, which would be integrated into its sibling company and known as "ESPN on ABC."[¶] It was also, as mentioned, the

---

[¶] Both channels were owned by the Walt Disney Company and remain so to this day.

final game called by the iconic announcer Keith Jackson, who had been with ABC Sports since 1966. He had worked the Olympics and *Monday Night Football* but was known best for doing the play-by-play of the game he loved most, college football.

Jackson was *the* voice of the game. He coined the term "the Big House" for the University of Michigan's stadium and peppered his broadcasts with other signature phrases, like referring to linemen as "big uglies" and describing a runner, as the play unfolded, as "rumblin', stumblin', bumblin'" down the field. He savored calling the Rose Bowl, which, in his phrase, was "the grandaddy of them all." And there was, of course, his most well-known exclamation, "Whoa, Nellie!" which he had borrowed from his Georgia farmer father and saved for the biggest moments of games—a punt returned for a touchdown, an acrobatic catch, or a momentum-changing interception. Jackson seemed to inhabit and embody the best parts of the sport—the pageantry, the emotional drama felt by its fans, the tribal nature of its rivalries. And by January 2006, at the age of seventy-seven, he had the ease and the gravitas of a Southern grandfather, a voice at once authoritative, wise, and breezy, inflected with subtle hints of a bourbon on the rocks.

At the end of the 1998 season, weary from traveling the country every football season, Jackson decided to retire. ABC countered with an offer that would allow him to work only the games on the West Coast, close to his home in Sherman Oaks, California. And so, for his last eight years as a broadcaster, Jackson had done just that, and his voice had become synonymous with the warm late fall/early winter sunlight that splashed onto the Saturday afternoon games of parts of the West Coast. It turned out to be fortuitous timing—Jackson was front and center for the rise and apex of Pete Carroll's USC Trojan teams and, by narrating it game by game and bestowing upon it his imprimatur, he helped augment the era.

Jackson had called fourteen Rose Bowls in his career. The 2006 game was the first he had done that featured a number one versus number two matchup.

Jackson was joined in the booth by Dan Fouts, the Pro Football Hall of Famer who had played fifteen years for the San Diego Chargers, and who had an underrated career as a football color analyst. He was born and raised in the San Francisco Bay Area. In Pee Wee football, he had played on an all-star team with Pete Carroll.

Asked now if the USC–Texas game stood up to its billing as one of the greatest football games ever played, Fouts says, "There are a handful of games you can say that about, and this one would be in that handful."

Pregame warm-ups took place in the last bit of daylight. The USC receivers briefly exchanged unfriendly words with the Texas defensive backs. ABC played a pregame message taped by Matthew McConaughey and Will Ferrell.

The sun dropped behind and silhouetted the San Gabriels. The haze of pollution lit up the last bit of sunlight, painting a vivid belt of orange on the horizon. The USC and Texas bands took turns playing. A few "Three-Pete" signs dotted the stands. Snoop looked like he was already celebrating on the USC sidelines. McConaughey, wearing a brown leather jacket, looked like he'd engaged in a healthy pregame ceremony. Carroll paced, wearing a white USC golf shirt over a long-sleeved mock turtleneck. Brown, on the Texas sideline, stood in place, calm, arms crossed over his Longhorn windbreaker. Vince Young, a silver necklace with a football pendant hanging out of the top of his jersey, hopped around like a little kid, helmet in hand, encouraging his teammates.

At midfield, soon-to-be-retiring Supreme Court Justice Sandra Day O'Connor** flipped a large coin. After a few rotations in the

---

** She left office on January 31, 2006.

air, it landed on the turf, Longhorn side up. Texas deferred to the second half. "We're going to play some football . . . yippee!" said Jackson.

The Texas kickoff specialist Greg Johnson booted the ball two yards into the end zone. Bush caught it and ran it out and was swarmed and stopped at the USC twelve. And then one of the supposed greatest games ever got off to a very sloppy start.

USC went three and out and punted. Texas fumbled the ball during the return, at their own forty-six-yard line. From there, the Trojans drove the field, helped by David Kirtman's twenty-three-yard catch, in which he was leveled by a helmet-to-helmet hit—which wasn't called, as was the norm then—but held on to the ball. Two plays later, White rumbled into the end zone for his twenty-second touchdown of the season, which led the NCAA. He would later admit he thought the game was already over then.

7–0, USC.

Texas received the kickoff and drove to midfield and faced a fourth and one. Brown opted to go for it. His running back, Selvin Young, was stopped for a one-yard loss. Trojans' ball on their own forty-nine.

With nine minutes and twenty-five seconds left in the first quarter, the stadium's game clock conked out, and the officials were forced to keep the time on the field.

The Trojans methodically worked their way down the field. On a nine-yard run, one of Bush's shoes—new Nike Superbads—flew off. It would happen again later in the game. He eventually had them taped onto his feet by a USC equipment manager.

The Trojans now faced their own fourth and one, at the Texas seventeen-yard line. Carroll decided, initially at least, to go for it. Leinart lined up behind the center. And then Carroll seemed to change his mind—he suddenly raced down the sidelines, asking for a timeout. It was too late, though. Leinart received the snap, lost his footing, and came up short. Longhorns' ball.

Texas drove close to midfield when the freshman running back, Jamaal Charles, fumbled the ball. It was recovered by a teammate—Texas had remarkable luck with the ball on the ground that season, losing only eight of their thirty-one fumbles. Though recovered, the fumble took all the heat out of the drive. Texas punted.

So, to summarize the first quarter: two fumbles (one lost), two botched fourth-and-one attempts, a shoe failure, and a clock malfunction (the clock came back on with five minutes left in the first quarter).

But the biggest blunder of the night was still a few minutes away.

For Brad Walker, USC was family. His uncle had played center for the program in the mid-1980s. His cousin was Norm Katnik, the Trojan center from 2000 to 2003, and another cousin, Kurt Katnik, had played tight end at USC in 2003. Walker was not particularly big or fast, but he walked on to the team as a receiver in 2004.

That year, he appeared in five games, mostly on special teams. During the 2005 season, though, Walker flashed as a good downfield blocker, and he appeared in every game, on special teams but also on offense, where he had been slotted into some scripted plays, like draws or screens, plays in which he could utilize his talent for blocking.

The second play of the second quarter of the BCS title game was one of those scripted plays. Walker came into the game and lined up out wide to Leinart's right. Leinart snapped the ball and faked a handoff to Bush, who ran through the line. Then Bush stopped and turned around, and Leinart dumped the ball to him. A classic screen pass, with blockers out in front ready to pick off the defenders down the field.

Bush ran straight then made a jump cut and was off. Thirty-seven yards later, at the Longhorn eighteen-yard line, three Texas defenders converged on him. Bush suddenly looked up and to his right.

Walker had been trailing the play, trying, but thus far failing, to catch up to Bush so he could help with the blocking. As the three Texas players got closer to Bush, the USC running back finally did slow down enough for Walker to draw nearly even with him. But before he could get there, Bush did something completely unexpected.

He tried to lateral the ball to Walker.

"It's fair to say that I did not see that coming," says Walker. "When you're a walk-on and you're out there trying your hardest, you do not expect the best player in the world to try to pitch you the ball."

Complicating matters was the fact that it was not a well-tossed lateral, pitched behind Walker as his momentum was taking him down the field.

Needless to say, Walker did not catch the ball. Texas recovered it. The play likely cost the Trojans at least three points, if not seven. "Reggie tried to be President Bush on that play when all he needed to be was Reggie," says Fred Davis.

Walker is, wrongly, still blamed by many for the play. "It's been nearly twenty years, and I still hear about it. And a lot of times when people talk about it, they'll say, 'And there was a walk-on who should never have been on the field,'" says Walker. "And that kind of bugs me. I ended up playing for four years and earning a scholarship. I had the respect of my teammates and coaches. You don't want to be known for something like that. It has definitely changed my life in some ways. All the time people come up and say, 'Are you the guy Reggie pitched the ball to?' And I'm like, 'Oh my God.'"

"I think we would have won that game nine times out of ten. In Vince, they had the better player. But we had the better team. Was the pitch the deciding factor? Who knows?"

"Brad was my roommate in the hotel for that Rose Bowl, and I thought we'd have to put him on suicide watch that night to make sure he didn't go to the balcony," says Mark Sanchez. "He kept saying, 'I should have caught it.' And I was like, 'Dude, you didn't lose that game. We didn't practice that.' That was exactly what we were coached not to do."

For Carroll, the play evoked a lesson he'd learned during his time at the Minnesota Vikings. "That was a great example of trying to do something outside of yourself, which Bud [Grant] used to talk about," says Carroll. "Whatever you do in games, you have to do in practice. You don't make up stuff in games. If you do, it's not likely to work out."

Carroll was not happy at all with Bush. As the USC coach left the field for halftime, he told an ABC sideline reporter, "I don't know why Reggie flipped that ball back. We were in pretty good shape there." Right after the game, Carroll went even further, describing the play as "shocking." A few months later, in an interview for a USC entrepreneurial studies class, he would say about the play: "That was such a divergent moment. Reggie was so far out of his head to do that. It really struck us all. . . . It was an indication that his head was in a different place. It's hard to imagine the pressure and scrutiny he was under. . . . It was really disruptive and sent a ripple through us."

These were unusually candid words for a coach who, to that point in his career, had never spoken poorly of his players in public. Not too long afterward, Carroll would find out why Bush may have been "out of his head" that night.

A lateral, though, was not totally out of Bush's purview—the attempt against Texas harked back to the famous one on his high school highlight tape that his future coaches and teammates fawned over. And Chris McFoy says a lateral was, at the very least, discussed between the two of them at practice. "I was probably the best blocking receiver, so I was in on a lot of Reggie's plays," he says. "Leading up to the game, we'd run through a play and then Reggie would lateral the ball to me. And one day he pulled me aside and said, 'If it happens in a game, just be ready.' The thing is, I wasn't in on that play [in the championship game]. I had just done two or three plays in a row, and one was a long-ass run. They subbed me out and put in Brad. I don't know if Reggie knew I was out of the game or not. When he did the lateral, I was like, 'Oh shoot, he thought I was in there.' I feel bad for Brad. If Brad had been aware, he might have taken it to the house."

Indeed, had it worked, it would have gone down as one of the greatest improvisational plays in the history of the game. But, instead, it backfired. Drew Kelson, the Texas linebacker, got credit for the "forced" fumble, merely because he was the closest Longhorn defender to the play. "I was in shock that Bush did that, like 'What was he thinking?'" says Kelson. "And I remember thinking, 'If this is how they won against everyone else, this is how they will lose against us.' They had a sense of confidence that once they got things rolling in a game, it would keep rolling. And that led them to do some things in that game that didn't make sense."

After the play, Bush walked off the field with his head down. He was greeted on the sidelines by his position coach, Todd McNair, who threw an arm around his shoulders. Bush looked up for a moment, his eye black with "619"[††] visible, and then put two hands

---

[††] The area code for San Diego.

on his head, as if he had an excruciating headache. McNair continued to talk to his running back as Texas moved the ball down the field. "Great players can get creative and sloppy," says Pat Ruel. Carroll never minded creativity — in fact, he encouraged it. But it had to be within the confines of discipline. Bush had drawn too far outside the lines.

Young drove the Longhorns down to the USC fifteen and then completed a pass to Ramonce Taylor that lost a yard. On the next play, Taylor took a handoff from Young. USC linebacker Oscar Lua burst through the line and knocked the ball from Taylor's grasp. But Texas continued its remarkable luck with fumbles and fell on the ball. Two plays later, Longhorn placekicker David Pino connected on the forty-six-yard field goal.

So, instead of being up 10–0 or maybe even 14–0, USC's lead had now been cut to four at 7–3.

The Trojans seemed to recover from the mistake quickly, taking the next possession down the field with cool precision, powered by Leinart's arm and White's legs. Then, on second and nine from the Texas twenty-five, Leinart threw a high-arching ball to the front left corner of the end zone, where Steve Smith had broken free. But at the last possible moment, Texas safety Michael Griffin appeared and jumped the route, snatching the ball out of the air. On the field, the officials called Griffin out of bounds. But a replay review reversed the call, Leinart's first interception in his last eighty-three passing attempts. Texas ball.

Replay had helped the Longhorns then. On their ensuing drive, a *lack* of replay would help them, too.

Six plays later, Texas had driven the ball to the USC twenty-two. On the next play, Young took a shotgun snap on a designed run to his left. He ran to the ten and, just as he was being tackled, he managed to pull off what Bush hadn't been able to do a few moments before: he lateraled the ball to his running back, Selvin

Young, who was trailing the play and who ran it in for a touch-down . . . except that television replays showed that Vince Young's knee was clearly down on the turf *before* he pitched the ball to his running back.

Both Jackson and Fouts—and everyone else watching the tele-vision broadcast—thought for sure that the play was coming back to the ten and that the touchdown was coming off the board.

But it didn't.

As Texas lined up for the extra point attempt, Fouts was incred-ulous: "I can't believe they're not reviewing this one," he said. "This is huge. This should not have been a touchdown."

Pino, the Texas kicker, perhaps aware that he'd better speed up so the replay officials wouldn't have time to look at the previous play, rushed the kick and missed, wide right.

Later, well after the game was over, the official word from the BCS administrators was that there had been an equipment mal-function in the replay booth at the time, and the replay officials had been unable to look at the play. Apparently, they'd had the wrong feed on their monitor.

Moments after the play, ABC cameras panned to the replay booth. The three replay officials were seen looking at the monitor and talking to one another. The official closest to the monitor raised a hand and appeared to shrug.

On the ensuing Trojan drive, Leinart, who had gotten hit hard on a pass play in the beginning of the second quarter, appeared flustered. On first down, he didn't notice that he had twelve men in the huddle. Five-yard penalty. White then ran for three yards. Leinart then threw an incomplete pass to Jarrett, who was covered by two Longhorns. Leinart hung his head as he stood next to Sar-kisian to get the next play, his eyes and face blank as he returned to the huddle. On third down, Leinart was slow getting his team out of the huddle and to the line of scrimmage. Delay of game and another five-yard penalty. On third and seventeen he again threw incomplete to Jarrett, who, again, was in double coverage.

Now the Trojans' Heisman-winning quarterback, just like the Trojans' Heisman-winning running back, seemed to be, in Carroll's words, "out of his head." Bush's botched lateral, Leinart's interception in the end zone, Young's lateral for a touchdown — the Trojans had been hit by a series of haymakers and appeared staggered.

On the sidelines, Carroll spoke to Leinart's backup, the sophomore John David Booty. He told him to get warmed up. "I thought I was going in at that point," says Booty.

Young and the Longhorns smelled the blood in the water. It took them four plays to drive forty-nine yards for another touchdown on a run by Ramonce Taylor, which put them ahead, 16–7.

USC got the ball back on their own twenty with two minutes and thirty-four seconds to play in a half that they'd rather forget. And they nearly committed another major blunder.

On the second play of the drive, Leinart threw a deep pass to Bush, who was covered by Kelson, on a play designed by Kiffin and Sarkisian. A linebacker covering Bush usually meant disaster for the opposing defense. But Kelson — playing the game of his life — stayed glued to Bush's hip and then turned and grabbed the ball out of the air. Leinart and the Trojans dodged a bullet when the ball popped free as Kelson hit the turf and the officials decided that he didn't have possession for long enough to qualify as an interception. (Both Jackson and Fouts felt it should have been called as an interception.)

About the only good news for the Trojans was that several Texas defenders were going down with cramps. Kiffin and Sarkisian seized on this development and had Leinart pick up the tempo of the offense. USC moved the ball smoothly for a bit, until Leinart did his best Young impersonation and took off on a run, gaining fourteen yards. But as he went down, Texas cornerback

Aaron Ross dove at him and connected, his helmet and shoulder to Leinart's helmet. No penalty was called on the second huge hit on Leinart in the game. And now he was slow to stand, visibly shaken up, taking off his helmet and rubbing his hands on his head and working his jaw. Carroll was forced to take a timeout.

Out of the stoppage, Leinart found Bush on a short pass, and the running back took it to the Texas thirteen with forty seconds left in the half. Leinart was then disastrously sacked on the next two plays, for a combined loss of thirteen yards. Mario Danelo came on to salvage the drive, hitting a forty-three-yard field goal, his longest of the season.

Halftime: 16–10, Texas.

On the half, Leinart was 13 for 21 for 147 yards and an interception. Young was 13 for 15 for 113 yards and had sixty more yards on the ground.

"I won't be surprised if Vince Young takes the football team on his back in the second half," Keith Jackson said as the teams broke for halftime, in what turned out to be a prescient call by the veteran announcer in his last game.

McConaughey, Clemens, and Lance Armstrong visited the Texas locker room at halftime. McConaughey still appeared to be unsober. The Longhorn players were loose, hopping around, fired up for the second half. The USC locker room, on the other hand, was eerily quiet.

But the Trojans, as they almost always did, came out in the second half with their hair on fire. They held Texas to a three-and-out and then took a 17–16 lead on a White touchdown run. It seemed like a familiar script was about to unfold. The Trojans had been down at halftime seven times during their thirty-four-game winning streak and had come back to win each time.

The USC offense seemed to finally be on track.

The USC defense was another matter.

On the next drive, Young relied on his legs. He had three good runs on the next drive, and on the last, a fourteen-yarder for a touchdown, he broke a tackle attempt by Brian Cushing—who had a direct bead on him—weaved around an official, and then smashed through USC cornerback Josh Pinkard, whom he outweighed by ten pounds.

23–17, Texas.

The heartbeat of the game had quickened. The end of the game and all the consequences of a win or a loss had come into view, causing an adrenaline spike. The defenses were tiring. The offenses were trading blows. The game had finally begun to live up to its hype.

Midway through the third quarter, USC had 317 yards on offense. Texas had 318.

USC again embarked on a long drive. On fourth and one at the Texas twelve, knowing field goals were unlikely to win the game, Carroll opted to go for it again. This time, though, he would not leave the short yardage play in the hands of his quarterback. Kiffin and Sarkisian called a 27 Power, a power run by White. Bush was not on the field for the play. The play worked perfectly, as it had all night. White, in his forbidding dark visor, burst through the line and ran twelve yards for a touchdown, his third on a night in which he would run for 124 yards and dominate the game on all but one play.

24–23, USC. The fourth lead change of the game, and the third one in the third quarter alone.

A forty-five-yard Young run set the Longhorns up for a thirty-one-yard field goal attempt, which was missed.

The Heisman winner then had his highlight. Bush took a handoff on the Texas twenty-six, made a jump cut, and then sprinted for the edge to his right, getting around the perimeter and launching himself in the air at the Texas five and breathtakingly flipping into the end zone.

31–23, USC.

Next drive: on third and five from the USC seventeen, on a broken play, Young ran up the middle, was hit by Frostee Rucker, and fumbled. And the Longhorns—*again*—fell on the ball. Pino came on for a thirty-four-yard field goal attempt and, this time, he hit it.

31–26, USC.

And then came the moment when the Trojans appeared to do what they had always done, going back to the 2003 season: put the dagger into the opposing team. Since the half, they had been unstoppable on offense, scoring on all four possessions, a field goal and then three straight touchdowns. A fourth was on its way.

With six minutes and fifty seconds left in the game, on a second and one from the Texas twenty-two, Leinart dropped back to pass. He eyed Jarrett, who'd lined up to his right, the entire way. Jarrett cut in on a slant and Leinart delivered a pass, a bit high, but not out of reach for his six-foot-five receiver. As Jarrett leaped to make the catch, two Texas defenders—Michael Griffin and Tarell Brown—tried to tackle him but ended up colliding with each other, hard, instead. As Jarrett reached the end zone, Griffin and Brown were left prone on the turf, their heads nearly touching, both writhing in pain. It seemed like a devastatingly fitting picture. In trying to stop the superior USC, Texas had taken itself out. And all that was left, as they say, was the crying. (Brown would leave the game with a broken arm. Griffin eventually came back into the game.)

38–26, USC, with six minutes and forty-two seconds to play.

The mood on the Trojans' sideline was jubilant, the exact opposite of the gloom they'd felt going into halftime. So jubilant that some USC players began to celebrate. "I remember being on the sidelines then and they put that 'Tequila' song on," says Clay Matthews, then a redshirt freshman who had gotten in the game for a few snaps on special teams. "And I remember seeing one guy—I won't throw him under the bus—he was doing the Pee-Wee Herman tequila dance. In my head I was like, 'What the hell are you doing? Do you not realize who we are playing?' That game felt far from over."

Steve Bisheff, the longtime *Orange County Register* columnist who wrote a book on the Trojans in 2009 called *Always Compete*, forever argued that the touchdown pass to Jarrett was, paradoxically, perhaps the worst thing that could have happened to USC at the time. It left too much time on the clock. A longer, more methodical drive—even one that ended in a field goal instead of a touchdown—would have likely won the game. The score—up by twelve—and the aftermath of the play, with the two Longhorn defenders lying injured on the turf with their team metaphorically defeated, gave the Trojans a false sense of security, made them feel as if the game was already over.

But it wasn't. Not even close.

Carroll knew at this point that he and his defense had little chance of stopping Young. But, just maybe, they could slow him down enough to take plenty of time off the clock and ensure that, even if he led a touchdown drive, he wouldn't have time to lead another.

Because of injuries, Carroll was playing with a bit of a weakened hand on defense. The Ting brothers—twins Ryan and Brandon—were backup safeties at the beginning of the season, both undersized (five foot ten, 180 pounds). But in the championship game, they were both getting solid minutes on the field. And reserves Ryan Powdrell (at linebacker) and Travis Tofi saw more playing time than usual, as well.

Carroll had a choice on his defensive play calls—he could rush more than four players to try to put pressure on Young, or he could sit back and zone and maybe allow some short passes, but hopefully prevent bigger gains, in the air and on the ground. For the time being—on what would end up being the Longhorns' second-to-last drive of the game—Carroll opted for zone. And Young picked it apart, completing five of six passes on the drive, including two to David Thomas, his tight end/safety blanket, who would end the night as the Longhorns' leading receiver, with ten catches for eighty-eight yards.

Young's one incompletion on that drive, though, was his one big mistake of the game. But he got away with it, perhaps due to the inexperience of Ryan Ting, who batted down the Young pass that he could have tried to catch. "That ball should have been intercepted by Ryan Ting," Fouts said on the broadcast. If it had, the game would likely have been over.[‡‡]

A few plays later, on a second and four from the USC seventeen, Young took the snap and drifted to his left, looking for an open receiver. Not finding one, he stopped and changed direction. He slipped and nearly fell down for what would have been a ten-yard loss and then recovered his balance and ran to his right, pump-faked one defender, and then sliced his way to the end zone.

38–33, USC.

"So it's now . . . kinda cozy," Jackson said.

The Trojans started their drive on their own thirty-four, with four minutes to go. Getting two first downs would have effectively iced the game.

First down: White rushed up the middle, where he was met by a swarm of Longhorns who drove him, headfirst, into the turf after a four-yard gain. White stayed down, cradling the ball and rolling from his side onto his knees, with his forehead still on the ground. He remained in that position for a few moments, then slowly propped himself up, one leg at a time. He appeared hurt.

[‡‡] Ting later told Scout.com that he received death threats because of that play.

Jarrett wiped some grass from the back of his uniform. White stayed in the game.

Second and six: Leinart rolled to his right, a designed play and one that can be difficult for a left-hander. He pumped once and then found Jarrett for a nine-yard gain. Leinart had bounced back from his struggles in the early part of the game, ending his Trojan career by going 16 for 19 for 218 yards and a touchdown in the second half. The catch was Jarrett's eighth of the second half. And it would be the last pass and catch between the roommates.

First down: handoff to White, who started up the middle and then darted to his right for three yards. Again, he got up slowly.

Second down: Leinart faked a handoff to White and stepped back to pass. But Drew Kelson came off the right side of his line, unblocked—a foreshadowing of a play to come, as it turned out—and forced Leinart into a rushed throw to his fullback, Hancock. The pass fell short.

The clock stopped at 2:22.

Third down and seven.

Chants of "Dee-fense . . . Dee-fense" from the Longhorns fans reverberated around the stadium, who seemed to outnumber the fans of the Trojans. "It was like a home game for them," says Fred Davis.

Handoff to White. He had a little room to run this time before he was tackled. But there was an odd scrum at the end of the play. Replays showed that White had fumbled the ball—he hadn't lost a fumble all season. The ball had popped straight up, and Steve Smith, who was trailing the play, plucked it out of the air and plunged forward and down, like a kid diving into a pool.

The fumble cost the Trojans a yard and a half. So, instead of fourth down and inches, it was fourth and two at the Texas forty-five. Texas took a timeout, to save some time if they got the ball back. Two minutes and thirteen seconds left in the game.

"We're going for it," Carroll told his coaches on the headset. It was, of course, part of Carroll's persona to push forward in these situations, to take the initiative, to be the predator and not the prey. And in this situation, strategically, it made all the sense in the world. USC did not want to punt the ball and give it back to Young, even deep in his own territory. The flow of the game— Young toying with the exhausted and undermanned Trojan defense—made it a virtual no-brainer. A first down conversion would have pretty much iced the game, and the Trojans' third title in a row.

Kiffin was up in the booth. He sported a goatee for the game. It was not fully grown in—he still didn't look old enough to accomplish that—and, thus, it had missed, perhaps, its intended effect. He called the play into Sarkisian on the sideline: 27 Power. "I wasn't surprised," says White. "We'd been killing them on that play all game long."

"That was LenDale's play," says Kiffin. "It had never been stopped." In fact, White had already scored his three touchdowns on that very play, on which he was averaging eight yards a carry. "During the season, even when LenDale had been stopped [on the play], he just fell forward and got the yardage," says Kiffin.

Reggie Bush had not made an appearance on the field during the drive. His coaches had opted for brute force and submission as opposed to the theatricality of their Heisman winner, which had potential for a big reward but carried with it a definite higher risk for lost yardage. Perhaps they were still spooked by Bush's improvised lateral in the first half that had gone terribly wrong. Or perhaps they realized that White had been so ruthlessly effective on the play during the game—and the season and during his USC career—that it appeared almost rote.

The Trojans lined up. The crowd noise began to build into a crescendo. Bush remained on the sidelines. He had his helmet on. His face was blank. He put a hand on his right hip and chewed on his mouthguard.

Jarrett lined up to the left. Directly behind Leinart was David Kirtman, "the surgeon," the heat-seeking blocking fullback. Behind Kirtman, flanked a bit to the left, where the play was obviously going, was White.

Leinart snapped the ball quickly, perhaps trying to catch the Longhorns off guard, and handed it to White, who ran full speed and headfirst, as straightforward as a lead pipe.

And he was stoned. Officials brought out the chains for a measurement. Bush jogged down the sidelines and got into a crouch for a better view. One official pulled the chain tight, over the ball, and placed the down marker on the grass. The tip of the football was about six inches short. The Texas players went wild, jumping and dancing and screaming as they left the field.

Texas's ball on their own forty-four with two minutes and nine seconds left in the game.

"I would have run the same play again," says White.

On the official play-by-play readout on the University of Texas football website, the safety Michael Huff is given credit for the game-changing tackle on White. He was an All-American and winner of the Thorpe Award. He'd already had an incredible night and would be named the game's defensive MVP. He was one of fifty-two players on the two teams who would play in the NFL (twenty-nine for USC, twenty-three for Texas).

But a closer look at the play reveals that it was one of the few players on the field that night who would not go to the NFL who had the most impact on the play. That player was the linebacker Drew Kelson.

Kelson was, by that point in the game, exhausted. As the weakside linebacker, his duty had been to cover Bush all night. Near the end of the first half, he had been cramping so badly that he'd limped off the field and gone into the locker room early to get an IV. And while he had not completely shut Bush down, he had been successful in slowing him, just a bit. "Going into the game, Chizik [Gene Chizik, the Texas co-defensive coordinator] told me that we couldn't let Bush have the highlights like he'd done all season," says Kelson. "I knew exactly where he was at all times. He still had his plays, but we were adamant about him not being the guy that night."

On that fourth and two, Kelson was happy to see that Bush was not on the field. That meant he had no distraction. "When they lined up, we knew what play they were going to run," says Kelson. "Everyone in the stadium knew what play they were going to run." His teammate Aaron Ross agreed, telling the University of Texas website, "With them having Reggie Bush on the sideline, all of our focus could be on LenDale."

"We hadn't stopped that play all night," says Kelson. "But we stopped it then."

Kelson was lined up on the right side of the Texas line. On the snap, he ran diagonally to the middle of the field. His fellow linebacker Rashad Bobino shot through the USC offensive line from the opposite side, forcing White to the right side of the Texas line. As Texas defensive end Brian Robison cut under the USC offensive line to bother White's feet, USC's Kirtman contacted Kelson, but Kelson pushed him off and staggered White with a hit to the midsection and then held on for dear life as his teammates helped bring the big USC running back to the ground.

Eighteen years later, Sarkisian—who was by then, in a twist of fate, the head coach of Texas—was asked by a Fox reporter, "What's the worst play call of your career?"

"I know exactly what it was," Sarkisian replied. "Fourth and two, USC playing Texas in the national championship. . . . Play calls are good when they work. They are bad when they don't. . . . That play I'll never forget."

One reason the play to White didn't work was that it wasn't executed correctly.

Winston Justice, the USC tackle, was back with the team in 2005 after sitting out the year before on suspension. That suspension, Justice says, "started a change that needed to happen." Justice had an excellent 2005 season, and he would be selected in the second round of the NFL Draft and play for eight seasons as a pro.[§§]

But on that play, according to his position coach, Justice missed his block. "I don't know what happened to Winston on that play, but he slid down instead of cutting," says offensive line coach Pat Ruel. "He was supposed to cut that linebacker coming in, but he only got a forearm up and the kid bounced off it and right into where LenDale was running and forced him to bounce a little bit to his left. If that doesn't happen, LenDale makes it easily.

"That game devastated me because my player did not do what he was supposed to do. That falls on me."

And yet, it's also possible that the play itself was the problem.

Leinart was not a mobile quarterback—Carroll, at the time, prized the pocket passer over the scrambling runner. Leinart had been adequate on quarterback sneaks that season, though he'd needed the push against Notre Dame and had failed on a fourth and one early in that game against Texas. With two yards to go, a quarterback sneak was probably out of the question as a play call, as was a designed quarterback run. (Ironically, Young, with his dual threat capability, would have been the perfect quarterback for that fourth-and-two situation.)

[§§] He would also later get an MBA and now runs his own private wealth management firm.

But the eternal question on that play is, *Why wasn't Bush on the field for it?* His coaches, after all, knew the value of his presence on the field. "A lot of defensive coordinators only play certain defenses against him," Kiffin had told the media earlier in that season. "There are some defenses that guys don't want to play because of matchup issues, so he limits the calls you have to face."

So, again, *why not just have him out there?* Bush would not have had to even touch the ball. White could have still taken the handoff on the power run. USC would have maybe lost a blocker. But Kelson would have had to, at the very least, take the possibility of Bush getting the ball into account. Part of Bush's superpower was that his mere presence caused insecurity and doubt and stress on the defense.¶

But the result is all that matters. And, in the end, the Longhorn defense beat the USC defense on that play. They stopped them by six inches.

Vince Young now had the ball, with the game in his hands. Many years later, Longhorn running back Selvin Young told *Texas Monthly* that when Vince Young popped into the huddle for what would be his team's final drive, he uttered a phrase that he

---

¶ In the end, one can look at that USC call on fourth and two and view it as underthought. The presence of Bush, even as a decoy, maybe adds the winning wrinkle. Later in Carroll's career, he and his staff would come to a similar juncture, in the Super Bowl at the end of the 2014 NFL season, when Carroll's Seattle Seahawks had the ball on the one-yard line of the New England Patriots, down four points with twenty seconds left in the game. Instead of handing the ball off to the Seahawks' running back Marshawn Lynch—who had been bludgeoning the Patriots—Carroll and his staff opted for a pass, which, of course, was intercepted and cost them the game. That play, one could argue, was the opposite of the White play in that it was overthought. And one can't help but wonder if there was some correlation between the two plays, even if subconscious.

apparently used all the time to loosen up his offense: "All right, it's time to let your nuts hang, bitch."

And now it came down to Carroll's defense.

Before the game, the Trojans knew, of course, that Young was the key. They wanted to make him feel uncomfortable. They wanted to take away, or at least minimize, his running and force him to stand in the pocket and make him go through his reads in the passing game. Make him hesitant, indecisive. But Young, apart from the one nearly disastrous throw that Ryan Ting had knocked down, had played pretty much a flawless game. "We knew he was good, but we didn't think he was the best quarterback," says Collin Ashton. "We'd watched film from the year before, when they'd played Michigan, so we knew what he was about. But on that field that night, he was a freak, faster and bigger than we were expecting, especially when he took off to run. On the play when he pitched it back and his knee was down, I hit him, and I swore I gave him a good shot. But I saw a clip of the play later and I just fell off him. I might as well have been playing Pop Warner."

Carroll opted for aggression early in the Longhorns' final drive, with the Justin Wyatt blitz that resulted in a two-yard loss and the Brandon Ting blitz that forced an incompletion. On third and twelve, Wyatt came again and forced a quick completed pass that fell short of the first down and would have brought up fourth and five. But Darnell Bing was flagged for a face mask, which gave Texas a critical first down.

Another blitz. Young threw a nine-yard completion.

Carroll then dialed back the pressure. Young ran for a first down and then connected with his receiver, Ryan Carter, for seventeen yards to the USC thirteen. First down. Forty-five seconds left.

A corner blitz. Incomplete pass. Another corner blitz, a five-yard run by Young. Third and five. Texas timeout. Thirty seconds left. Carroll called over Ashton and, after asking him if this wasn't the coolest thing ever, he gave him the play call: "Double B-Dog," which meant two blitzers—Ashton and Pinkard—up each B gap, which is the space between the offensive guard and tackle.

On third down, Young snapped the ball and went back to pass. The pressure came and he rushed a throw to Limas Sweed, which harmlessly fell to the turf.

On that play, Texas running back Selvin Young had stayed in the backfield to pick up the pressure coming for his quarterback. That allowed USC defensive end Frostee Rucker to drop back on his left side and spy Young and deter him from running.

"The play worked, so I called it again," says Carroll.

Football is like a chess match with animate pieces that are large, fast, and violent. Coaches play to their team's strengths, try to cover for their own weaknesses, and look to exploit the weaknesses of the opposing team. They use studied tendencies to make educated guesses about what the other team will call on any given play. Luck, timing, the fact that the players are human and are prone to both brilliance and foible, and the oddness of the spheroidal ball all come into play, as well.

In this instance, Carroll was in a chess match with Texas offensive coordinator Greg Davis.

Davis says that during the nearly monthlong preparation for the BCS Championship game, he installed most of the Longhorns' offense while practicing at home in Austin—the week in Los Angeles before the game, he knew, would be too busy to accomplish anything more than minor tweaks.

On the team's last practice in Austin before leaving for Los Angeles, Davis called Young over and told him they had one last thing to work on. "I gave Vince a scenario, that he had one play to win the ball game, from the five-yard line," says Davis. "I told him to give me his call, and I would give me mine. His call was a quarterback draw. My call was a pass. And I said, 'Listen, my call is better than yours for one reason.' He said, 'What's that?' And I said, 'You'll turn it into a draw if it's not there.'"

During the timeout before the last two plays of the last Texas drive, "Vince told Mack [Brown], 'We've got this. We've gone over this exact situation,'" says Davis.

Like Carroll, Davis called the same play for both downs. But there was one difference between his two calls, a tweak, and an unintentional one at that. "On the first play, Selvin was supposed to release if the defensive end [Rucker] dropped," says Davis. "And he did drop. But Blalock [Justin Blalock, a Texas tackle] was late getting to the linebacker, so Selvin stayed in to help block. The second play had the same protection, but it was executed properly. Blalock got the linebacker, so Selvin released."

And that release made all the difference. On the play, Selvin Young ran toward Rucker and then to the inside of him. And Rucker, instead of being able to spy on Vince Young, was forced to follow the running back.

Carroll says he doesn't regret the call. "We'd always take a chance on him throwing the ball," he says. "We just needed to make a tackle."

Davis says the fourth down play, like the third down one, was designed for a pass. "But we knew if it didn't pop immediately, Vince would pop it for a run. We wanted the ball in his hands. Michael Jordan takes the last shot."

That last shot . . .

Fourth and five, USC eight-yard line, twenty-six seconds to go.

The high-water mark of the USC dynasty. Cemetery Ridge reached but not cleared.

Young snapped the ball. Pressure came from his left. He looked to his right and saw the lane that had been cleared by Selvin Young releasing. And he ran.

Rucker was left on an island, with all his momentum moving to his right, in pursuit of Selvin Young. He tried to reverse himself, to run back to Vince Young. He even made a dive and nearly clipped Young's heels—the only Trojan who had a shot at him on the play. But Young skipped over him.

Jackson made the last great call of his long and distinguished career.

"He's going for the cornerrrrrr . . . he's got it!" [Holds a beat.] "Vince. Young. Scores!"

Young's momentum took him through the back of the end zone, right by the stands. He disappeared momentarily, lost to the field and the cameras.

When he reappeared, he was cradling the ball. No outward sign of emotion. The Texas mascot ran over and gave him a hug. Some of Young's teammates did the same. Young didn't celebrate at that moment, never even put an arm in the air, even though he had just put the finishing touches on one of the greatest—if not *the* greatest—performances in a national title game. Thirty for 40 passing, for 267 yards. Nineteen rushes for 200 yards and three touchdowns.

39–38, Texas. Nineteen seconds left.

Texas lined up for a two-point conversion attempt, to try to go up by a field goal. The Trojan defense was confused and signaled for a timeout, their precious last one. Carroll was displeased on the sideline. The timeout didn't work anyway. Young ran the ball in for the conversion.

41–38, Texas.

One last gasp for USC. The Longhorns squibbed the kick. USC linebacker Rey Maualuga picked it up and ran to his own thirty-one-yard line.

Bush was back in. Leinart threw him the ball, and he ran for twenty-seven yards, to the Texas forty-two. A small ray of hope. A field goal would tie it, sending the game to overtime. "We thought we were going to win that game and kept thinking we were going to win it until we didn't," says Justice. "I know that might not seem true, but we really felt that way."

"There was always a sense that we could do it, pull it off," says Rocky Seto. That optimism came from their head coach. *Something good is about to happen.*

Except this time, it didn't.

Eight seconds. No timeouts.

Leinart was flushed from the pocket. He ran around. Time kept on slipping into the future. He threw the ball over his roommate's head and out of bounds.

And at 9:26 p.m. PST, the Rose Bowl clock hit three zeros. Game over.

The enduring image of that game—one that remains iconic even in our overflooded infotainment age—was of Young, just moments after the clock ran out. He was standing tall on a bench on his sideline. The camera was behind and below him. His helmet was off, his all-white uniform emblazoned on the back with his name and number in burnt orange. He finally displayed some emotion, his right arm raised, the forefinger and pinkie on his right hand extended—a gesture meant to mimic the horns of a steer—as confetti fell from the dark sky like softly blowing snow.

In that moment, he appeared as a statue, one of a conquering general who has won a famous battle. He had, indeed, almost singlehandedly halted an empire in its tracks. For it was this moment, in retrospect, when the fall began for Pete Carroll and his USC Trojans, one that, like the old saw about going bankrupt, began gradually and then ended suddenly.

Was it "the greatest game ever played"? Fouts probably has it right—it's among the candidates. What was for sure, though, was that it was the last great game before the diminishing effects of the internet era were truly realized and felt. Facebook had launched two years before the game. YouTube was a year old. Twitter would start two months after the game. Instagram was only a few years away. The sports world—and the world, in general—was not as fragmented. It felt like *everyone* in the country had watched.

"To this day, those USC teams were some of the greatest in history," says Kelson. "I don't care about the wins that were later vacated. They were great. But the most important and impactful part of their story was their downfall. They could have tied the knot on the claim of the greatest team ever, but they had a blemish. They lost to another great team that they didn't see coming."

On the field, after the game, the two head coaches shook hands. Carroll told Brown that he hated that they lost, but they had lost to a great champion.

Bush and Leinart, now headed to the NFL, their college careers complete, graciously went to the Longhorn locker room to offer their congratulations.

In the Trojan locker room, Brad Walker sat by himself, still thinking about the lateral he didn't catch. "It was a pretty somber scene," he says. "Reggie came over and kinda said, 'That was on me, I'm sorry.' I played at USC for another two years and never really talked to anybody else about it."

Ruel was haunted by decisions made by himself and other coaches. "I had so many second thoughts on that fourth and two play," he says. "Should we have made a run-pass option with the quarterback on a naked bootleg? All these situations came up in my head. Maybe we should have done this or done that. I think that game affected me more than any in my life, even more than the Super Bowl we lost." (Ruel was an assistant coach on the Seahawks team that lost Super Bowl XLIX on the interception on the goal line.)

In the locker room after the game, Carroll addressed his team: "We came nineteen seconds away from winning a third consecutive national title. To put all the work we put in, there is no way that nineteen seconds can define us. . . . Give Texas all the credit in the world, but you're still champions."

Now, nearly twenty years later, he says, "For years I preached that if we played the way we're capable of playing and all did what we were counted on to do, we were going to be really hard to beat, and it would take an extraordinary game that someone would have to pull out of their butt to beat us. And, boom, there's Texas. That's exactly what happened. Young was just over and above what we could handle that night."

Justin Wyatt walked out of the stadium, to the north side, where USC had a tent set up on a golf course for what was supposed to be the postgame celebration. "I remember everything was a blur until I got to the parking lot, and I looked back at the stadium and broke down," he says. "I was like, 'Was that it? Did it end like that?' I went down to my knees and cried, damn near in the fetal position."

"I went to the tent," says Fred Davis. "It felt like a funeral."

White went to Snoop's studio after the game. "He was making a song that night with Charlie Wilson and Pharell [Williams]," says White. "I just remember that we were all just heartbroken."

Young was exhausted. He went to Roscoe's and ate chicken and waffles. Later, when a limo came to the hotel to take him and his teammates out on the town, he cramped up and decided not to go. He ended up staying in his hotel room and going to sleep.

Leinart, the great bon vivant of LA, didn't have it in him that night, either. He went to Carl's Jr. and ordered a double western bacon cheeseburger and a shake and then went home.

After the game, Fouts and the rest of the ABC Sports crew gathered in another hospitality tent. "It hit us then that this was Keith's last game," he says. Jackson had brought along a case of wine with him to the game. So, instead of mourning, Fouts says, "We had a good time."

The next day, ESPN asked Will Ferrell how he felt. "I slept in my car," he replied.

Six inches.

That was it. It's the distance, give or take an inch, that separated Carroll and the Trojans from immortality and winning what some still call the greatest college game ever played.

It's the distance that kept USC from winning three national titles in a row and the claim of being the greatest college football program of all time.

It's the distance, too, that may have staved off—or, at least, softened the blow of—the eventual fall from grace.

That Trojan horse that had been sitting there inside the city walls for the past fourteen months?

Its doors were about to blow wide open.

CHAPTER SIXTEEN

Surviving Greatness

One day in April 2006, Charles Robinson, a reporter for *Yahoo Sports*, drove up a hill in the town of Spring Valley, California, a pretty suburb of San Diego, and pulled over at the corner of Apple Street and Luther Drive. He noticed the rolling brown humps of the Jamul Mountains in the distance and the nice view the hill afforded of the Sweetwater Reservoir.

He also noticed that someone else was already there. That person was Jason Cole, a sports reporter at the *Miami Herald*. The two men knew each other casually from covering the NFL. "I'm like, 'Holy fucking shit,'" says Robinson. "We knew we were both here for the same thing. And we were like, 'Oh well, might as well do this together, because there's only going to be one shot at this thing.'"

"We just stood there in front of the house, looking at it," says Cole. "We knew who lived there."

A few months before—at the Senior Bowl in Mobile, Alabama—Robinson had been talking to an NFC scout when the subject of Reggie Bush, who by then was the presumed first pick in the NFL Draft, came up.

"You should poke around a little bit on that," the scout told Robinson. "There's something weird going on there."

"Weird how?" Robinson asked.

"Well," said the scout. "This is going to sound wild, but there is some Indian chief involved with Reggie and there is the threat of a lawsuit from some guys who were giving Reggie money while he was at USC."

Though Robinson says the story sounded "completely bizarre," he did start to poke around. Most people he contacted had no idea what he was talking about. And then he ran into a man who was doing some scouting for the NFL but was also deeply involved in college recruiting. "He instantly was like, 'It's really messed up,'" says Robinson. "He gave me two names—Michael Michaels and Lloyd Lake. And he mentioned a house."

Robinson began to search real estate records and figured out where Bush's mother, Denise, and his stepfather, LaMar Griffin, lived in Spring Valley. "I pulled the deed for their house and saw it was owned by Michael Michaels and thought, 'Holy shit, this is real,'" says Robinson.

Michaels had purchased the house in March 2005 for $757,500. Robinson looked into Michaels and discovered that though he was not a chief, he *was* a member of the Sycuan Band, a Native American tribe. He looked into Lake and discovered that he had a criminal background and, in fact, was in prison at the time. And he found out that the two men had been trying to start a sports marketing agency that involved Bush. "And once I had that information, I knew I had to get out there [to the San Diego area] and start asking questions," says Robinson. But before he left, he called around to a few NFL agents. One of them mentioned that he'd heard that a fellow agent, Michael Ornstein, had been giving money to Bush at USC, as well.

Meanwhile, Cole had also been approached by a source about Bush. "I think the same one who talked to Charles," he says. "He told me Reggie had taken money from an Indian chief and now

the chief wanted to scalp him." Cole says he did some further reporting and he, too, found the house. "I knew what Reggie's parents did for a living and I was like, 'There's no fucking way they
can afford the rent on this house,'" says Cole. "They'd lived in a
small apartment before." (Remember, Bush's mom was a prison
guard, his stepfather a school security guard.)

Cole called David Cornwell, a lawyer representing Bush at the
time. "Cornwell basically said that the other side didn't have anything," says Cole. "He was very aggressive in a way that felt like
an obvious attempt to get me off the scent." Cole then called the
Sycuan Band and asked some questions. In response, he says, he
and the *Miami Herald* received a fax that threatened to sue if they
wrote anything about the tribe being involved with Bush. "That
was an alarm bell that there was something going on," says Cole.
"It had exactly the opposite of its intended effect."

Cole says he told his editors that he'd heard that Robinson was
already out in the San Diego area looking around. "There was a
lot of smoke there," says Cole. "My editors finally said, 'Go.'"

And that's how Robinson and Cole found themselves standing
together in front of the 3,000-square-foot house on the corner of
Apple and Luther in Spring Valley.

The duo presented a mismatched pair, almost like they were
cast for contrasting effect in a buddy movie. Cole was the older of
the two, a hard-bitten reporter who had the demeanor and shape
of a bulldog. Robinson had the appearance of a gentle giant, six
inches taller than Cole, with a warm bearing and friendly smile.

Though Robinson and Cole knew who lived in the house, they
also knew they had to be absolutely sure. "This was a story we
both knew we had to be careful with," says Cole. "We had to nail
every little detail." At one point Cole suggested looking in the
mailbox. But Robinson pointed out that doing so was a felony and
they could get arrested. So they continued their vigil.

And then Cole noticed something in the driveway. "I looked down and in the cement of the driveway it says, 'Griffins '05,'" he says. "They didn't even own the house. You just couldn't make this shit up."

But no one appeared to be home at the time, so Robinson and Cole left. Though they were in separate cars, "we were basically following each other, too freaked out about what each other knew," says Cole.

They made a stop at the Sycuan Band to ask some questions and then, later in the afternoon, ended up back in front of the house again, standing in the driveway. This time, someone was home.

Bush's mom, Denise, came out of the house, walked over to them, and asked what they wanted.

"Charles starts to make small talk with her, just chatting," says Cole.

"I'm trying to finesse it, ease into it to try and see where we could get," says Robinson.

"But I got impatient," says Cole.

"Jason was like a bull in a china shop," says Robinson. "He butts in and says, 'So we want to ask you about the house.' And I'm like, 'Dude, what are you doing? We're going to get shut down.'"

"At that point, her eyes fluttered, like she has no idea what to say, like she knows this is a serious conversation and she's busted," says Cole.

Denise Griffin, standing not too far away from where her last name was etched into the concrete of the driveway, said nothing. And then she walked away.

Cole had a flight back to Miami that night. "I wrote the story on the airplane, submitted it, and then it went through a couple days of vetting," says Cole.

Robinson stayed behind in San Diego. He filed the story from his hotel room in the Courtyard Marriott. The *Yahoo Sports* investigation unit was in its infancy at the time. "This story was unlike anything they'd even handled before," says Robinson, with its heavy accusations and the attendant risks that came with getting anything wrong. His editors were gun-shy, and they spent the morning going back and forth with Robinson, checking and double-checking the material.

At one point while he was on the phone with his editors, Robinson received a text from a source. "The guy told me that there was a moving truck in front of Reggie's parents' house," says Robinson. "And I was like, 'Holy shit, this is their reaction?'"

Robinson immediately drove to the house, where he watched as items were being taken from it to the moving truck. "I called my editors and told them that we had to get this story up now," says Robinson. "I rewrote the first couple of paragraphs and then they posted it."

The story hit on April 23, 2006, six days before the NFL Draft. It detailed the housing arrangement and mentioned that Michaels and Lake had been involved in the creation of a sports marketing company, called New Era. "I kept looking for Jason's story at the *Herald* to drop and saw nothing," says Robinson. "And I started to get anxious that I'd missed something big."

But a few days later, the *Miami Herald* finally published Cole's story. "My editors were being cautious, and then Charles dropped the bomb, and we ran our story," says Cole. The imprimatur from the print stalwart gave the story full legitimacy.

"The Trojans were the sexiest, most glorified, most high-profile football team in the history of Los Angeles," says Cole. "The Rams were boring. The Raiders had won a Super Bowl in 1983, but they were carpetbaggers. UCLA had its moments. But nobody had what USC had, not even in their own glory years with the Marcus Allen and OJ Simpson teams. None of them were like that.

"And then this happened."

"When this is all said and done, everybody will see at the end of the day that we've done nothing—absolutely nothing wrong," Bush said in a hastily arranged televised interview on ESPN two days after the story broke.

And yet further reporting only served to make things look worse for Bush. The attorney for Michaels claimed that Bush's stepfather, LaMar Griffin, was part of New Era, which planned to have Bush as its anchor client, and that Bush himself had sat in on meetings. The lawyer also alleged that Bush and his family had taken money and gifts from Michaels and had failed to pay rent on the house. He told the media that Michaels was preparing a $3.2 million lawsuit against Bush. Cornwell, Bush's attorney, told the *Los Angeles Times* that Bush was being extorted.

The PAC-10 and the NCAA announced they were instigating investigations into the matter. At issue was the question of whether Bush had broken any NCAA rules regarding student-athletes or their families and friends accepting benefits from an agent or "any other person associated with an agency business" or accepting benefits from "anyone who represents any individual in the marketing of his or her athletic ability."

When asked about the story by the *Los Angeles Times*, Carroll said, "I don't know the details of it, so I have no comment about it."

A few months after the initial story broke, *Yahoo Sports* hired Cole away from the *Miami Herald*. He and Robinson were paired together and tasked with doing a full investigation of the Bush story. "We were like, 'Let's take our time and do it right,'" says Robinson. And the bulldog and the gentle giant did just that.

In September 2006, just as football season had begun, Robinson and Cole dropped another bomb: they reported that Bush and his family had, indeed, received gifts from Michaels and Lake, including airfare, limousine rides, hotels, clothing, and weekly payments, going back to the 2004 season.

They also reported that Bush had been receiving gifts at around the same time from the NFL agent Michael Ornstein and hinted that USC possibly knew all of this was going on.

Bush again denied any wrongdoing. And Carroll again told the media, "I didn't know anything."

The Bush story was just the opening scene in what would become a horror movie week for USC football.

Three days after the Bush story dropped, redshirt freshman quarterback Mark Sanchez was arrested for an alleged sexual assault on campus. According to the *Los Angeles Times*, the nineteen-year-old Sanchez had arrived at a bar at a little after eleven p.m. one night, getting in with a fake ID. At around 1:30 a.m., he helped two students push a car that had run out of gas. One of the students said Sanchez was "loud and appeared as if he had been drinking alcohol." The alleged assault took place a few hours later.

The next day, Sanchez and linebacker Brian Cushing were led away from their residence by the police. Cushing was released on site. Sanchez was taken to the police station and then released after posting a $200,000 bond. The university placed him on an "interim suspension" while the allegations were investigated.

And three days after that came the NFL Draft. On the surface, it looked like a winner for the Trojans. Eleven USC players were selected, five of them in the first forty-five picks. But closer inspection revealed several disappointments. Bush, the projected first pick, fell to the New Orleans Saints at number two, his new off-the-field problems perhaps playing a role. Leinart, who had been projected to be the number one overall pick had he left USC after the 2004 season, fell to the Arizona Cardinals at number ten, behind Vince Young, who was drafted at number three by the Tennessee Titans (where Leinart's old offensive coordinator, Chow, worked in the same capacity). White and Justice, two presumed first-round picks, both fell to the second round, reportedly for character issues. (White also ended up at the Titans, joining Young and Chow.)

And on that same weekend, USC announced that it was investigating the prior year's living arrangement with Leinart and Jarrett. It had come to light that Jarrett had paid far less than half of the $3,886 monthly rent at the duo's apartment at the Medici complex in downtown Los Angeles. Leinart's father said that his son moved into the more secure building because of the fans who had showed up at his previous residence, which was closer to campus. "I was freaking out for his safety because people were following him home," Bob Leinart told the *Los Angeles Times*. "He would walk out of his front door and people were waiting there for autographs." Jarrett and Leinart had each paid $650 a month, and Bob Leinart had covered the rest. A few months later, the NCAA declared that Jarrett had indeed violated a rule against extra benefits, and the star USC receiver was declared ineligible for the 2006 season.

At the end of the week, Carroll was contacted by the *Los Angeles Times* columnist Bill Plaschke. In an interview, Carroll said it was "the worst week since I've been here, yeah. It's been very difficult. . . . We needed to see this coming, and we didn't. It's gone beyond all the heads-up, all the alerts, all the education we give these kids. We need to do more. Our guys are marked guys, they have had success and there's people trying to get in on that, and we need to do a better job of making them understand the problems there."

It appeared that in the wake of the Texas loss, all the glitz and hype that had worked to USC's advantage for so many years had exacted a toll, that something that had helped make the program so great in the first place had become its Achilles' heel. That like all classical heroes—no matter how strong or wise—they had, embedded within them, the seeds of their own downfall.

Carroll told Plaschke that he would not change his style of coaching, but that he would work harder to protect his players from those who would do them harm. "We have moved into a different territory now, all the hype, all the distractions, all the people who want to influence us, and we will be more aware of that," he said. "We will work harder to control that."

"As this week has taught Carroll and the Trojan nation, the hard part is not achieving greatness," Plaschke wrote in his column. "The hard part is surviving it."

Luckily for Carroll, he had, by this time, earned an enormous amount of goodwill and leeway. He was the unquestioned Prince of LA. He was adored not only for reviving the USC program and being the best coach in college football, but also for his efforts off the field, which felt genuine and sincere. During his time at USC, Carroll had incorporated Ryan Davidson—a young boy suffering through several bouts with cancer—into the team and had made him an honorary captain and hosted him as a special guest at practices and games.*

He had also taken a dive, headfirst, into an issue that many professed to care about, but few had the courage or will to actually do anything about.

One morning in 2003 while driving to work, Carroll was listening to the radio when he heard that yet another kid had been killed in a gang-related incident. Gang violence was an issue that Carroll had thought a lot about before—it was difficult not to, with USC's campus being adjacent to some neighborhoods that had experienced long-standing gang problems. One study published that year showed that because of gang violence, kids in south central Los Angeles exhibited stronger post-traumatic stress

---

* Carroll would do the same thing for Jake Olson in 2009.

disorder than kids in Baghdad, Iraq, which was in the midst of a war.

Carroll believed that gangs themselves worked somewhat like football teams. They had leaders, they were tribal, and they often operated as units. Carroll also believed that gang violence was akin to terrorism, that it made those caught within and even those around it exist merely in survival mode, the lowest level of the pyramid that Maslow had described in his hierarchy of needs. Finding a way to get people out of that survival mode could not only save some souls, he thought, but could also provide some keys to unlock positive potential. For years, he had talked about the issue with one of his gurus, Lou Tice, a motivational speaker and corporate coach who had founded The Pacific Institute, which described itself as "dedicated to human fulfillment."

"That morning, I heard about the killing on the radio, I called Lou from the car," says Carroll. "I told him that there's a lot of shit happening and now was the time to do what we'd been talking about. Let's get the gang leaders and the kids and law enforcement together and see if we can coach them up like we do our players. And Lou said he was in."

Shortly thereafter, Carroll and Tice scheduled a meeting on a Wednesday night in the Trojans' team room to discuss their idea. "Somehow, word got out all over the city and we had an amazing turnout," says Carroll. "Maxine Waters [a member of the US House of Representatives] was there, and so was the chief of police."

During the meeting, Carroll says, one kid from a troubled neighborhood stood up and told the room that he "knew he was either going to die or go to jail, so what the fuck does it matter?"

"And that, to me, became my understanding: that when you have a vision of your life, whether it's good or bad, it had a pretty good chance of coming true," says Carroll.

So Carroll and Tice set out to change that vision through an organization that would work with former and current gang members and law enforcement on the idea of creating influencers and essentially coaching them in the same way Tice coached CEOs. They would preach positive self-talk, excellence, and having a high regard for not only themselves but the people in their communities. The idea was that the transformation of one person, particularly a person in a leadership position, could spread. They called the organization "A Better LA."

A Better LA formed partnerships with the Los Angeles mayor, Antonio Villaraigosa, and the city's sheriff, Lee Baca. They held marches attended by city councilman Bernard Parks and then–San Francisco mayor Gavin Newsom. They brought Henry Winkler in to give talks to inner-city schoolchildren. ("One of the most amazing things I've ever done," says Winkler.) They brought in a police sergeant named Curtis Woodle, who had worked as a gang liaison, and Bo Taylor, a former gang member, and Aquil Basheer, a professor who specialized in violence intermediation. It was all about "connecting people on the streets to law enforcement, sitting across the table from each other, and trusting each other," says Carroll.

"Gang violence at the time was something that no one with power or money paid attention to," says Woodle. "But when Pete stepped in there, people started to pay attention and even put their hands in it. At that point, Pete became my hero. He stepped in there with his name and recognition. He was like a conductor, bringing everyone together."

The most symbolically powerful thing Carroll did was what he took on himself. Once or twice a month, accompanied by Taylor, he would venture into some of the most troubled neighborhoods in the city at night. "We'd drive in and get out and walk around, talking to people," says Carroll. He would help people carry groceries into their homes. He would "hang and shoot the shit," as he describes it, with members of the Crips and Bloods. People talked about their lives, about their constant fear, about the "ghetto birds" (police helicopters) that endlessly flew overhead. Carroll dispensed advice, helped them get leads for jobs, and freely handed out his cellphone number. And he did all of this without a security detail or a gun, both of which he felt would be off-putting given the experiences many in these communities had with the police.[†]

"The people at USC didn't want him to stray into those areas, they weren't good with it," says Woodle. "But Pete being Pete, he did it anyway." (In 2008, Carroll would take 60 Minutes with him on one of these visits.)

A Better LA, along with gang injunctions and the work of civil rights lawyer Connie Rice, is widely given credit for the curbing of gang violence in Los Angeles in the mid- to late 2000s. In 2003, the year Carroll and Tice founded the organization, there were 505 homicides in Los Angeles. By 2009, after a steady annual decrease, that number had dropped to 300.

"That stuff was real, man," says Carroll.

And Carroll's efforts earned him even more love in the locker room, especially from players who grew up in neighborhoods like the ones he visited. It earned respect from his coaches, too. "Pete always thought he could save everyone," says Pat Ruel. "And he usually did."

As the 2006 season neared, the troubles of the offseason gradually began to resolve. Over the summer, the Bush revelations disappeared from the front pages of the nation's newspapers. Neither Carroll nor Mike Garrett believed much, if anything, would

---

[†] Unlike many football coaches at big southern schools, like Nick Saban, Carroll eschewed the use of state troopers to escort him off the field after games, and the odd and disquieting pageantry of power that the act displayed.

come of them, and Bush was in the NFL, preparing for his first season.

In early June, the charges against Sanchez were dropped for a lack of sufficient evidence, and his suspension was lifted. And in the beginning of August, the NCAA reinstated Jarrett. His punishment: paying $5,352—what the NCAA determined as a just amount of backpay for his rent—to the charity of his choice.

The Trojans were not in rebuilding mode going into the 2006 season. They still had one of the most talented rosters in the country. "We were stacked," says offensive lineman Charles Brown. "In '05, there were so many blowouts that the backups got a lot of playing time. '06 felt like a chance for people to step up."

The Trojans had a talented defense coming back, with an embarrassment of riches at the linebacker position in Keith Rivers, Rey Maualuga, and Brian Cushing, and a freshman five-star safety named Taylor Mays, in whom Carroll and his coaches saw some of Polamalu's ferocity.

Carroll had brought his former linebackers coach, Nick Holt, back into the fold and made the rather surprising move of naming him the Trojans' defensive coordinator, giving up the reins he'd held for the first five years at USC. Holt says he thinks Carroll relinquished his role as defensive coordinator because "after the Texas game he was frustrated and down in the dumps and maybe fed up and wanted to take a break." But Carroll says of the decision, "I just wanted to shake things up and give some guys authority and responsibility." The new arrangement wouldn't last the season.

On offense, the receivers Jarrett and Smith were back, as was the tight end Fred Davis. And the offensive line was anchored by Sam Baker and Ryan Kalil, who would both be first-team All-Americans at the end of the season.

The question marks on the team were in the backfield. Bush was gone. So was White, even though Carroll says they'd tried to convince him to stay another year and make a run at the Heisman. "They didn't try very hard," says White. "Pete called me and asked if I was coming back, and I said I thought I was going pro. And then he got pissed and said, 'If one man steps out of the band, what does the band do? It keeps marching,' and then he hung up on me."

To try to compensate for the loss of Bush and White, Kiffin put together a recruiting class that included six running backs, three of whom were five-stars (Stafon Johnson, C. J. Gable, and Allen Bradford, a linebacker whom USC would convert to running back), which added to the stable of two former four-star prospects—Hershel Dennis and Chauncey Washington—who were already there (USC had ten running backs on its roster that season). The 2006 recruiting class was ranked first in the country for the third time in a row, but in the end, it would not come close to living up to that billing, the opposite of USC's 2003 class.

The other big shoes to fill were those of Leinart. But Carroll and his coaches were confident they wouldn't miss a beat with John David Booty, who had come to USC as a higher-rated recruit than his predecessor and had already spent three seasons within the program.

Booty was born and raised in Shreveport, Louisiana, and played football at the powerhouse high school Evangel Christian, where he followed in the footsteps of his brother, Josh, who played at LSU, and Brock Berlin, who played at Miami. (Both Josh Booty and Berlin played in the NFL, as well.) In his sophomore and junior seasons in high school (2001 and 2002), Booty threw a combined eighty-eight touchdowns and led Evangel Christian to two straight state championships.

Booty was recruited by Orgeron, his fellow Louisianian, who once brought a replica Heisman Trophy to his house, plopped it on the dining room table, and said, "This is going to be yours." Booty says he loved USC right away, loved the "energy and enthusiasm" of Orgeron and Carroll, and the smarts of Chow (who was then still there) and Sarkisian and Kiffin.

The Trojan staff loved Booty, too. But, at least for a while, they loved another quarterback more.

Kyle Wright was a California kid, from Danville, and was considered the top-rated quarterback recruit in the 2003 class. In 2002, Wright visited USC on Junior Day, impressing Carroll, who told his staff that Wright "could play in the NFL right now," the same language he used for Whitney Lewis. Wright narrowed his choices down to USC, Miami, and Tennessee. The USC staff believed he would sign with them. But he opted for Miami instead.

Miami had also offered Booty, and the school was at the top of his list, "only because I thought Kyle was going to USC," says Booty. But USC had been his first choice all along. And, because of Wright's decision, he got his wish.

Booty left Evangel Christian after his junior year to enroll at USC (he had enough credits to graduate) becoming the first high school football player to "reclassify," that is, change their graduation year. He was part of the 2003 class, alongside Bush, White, Sam Baker, and Steve Smith.

Booty, at the age of eighteen, began the 2003 season as Leinart's backup and mopped up in five games, including the UCLA game, in which he broke his wrist. In 2004, he suffered a preseason elbow injury and sat out the season as a redshirt. The next year, he was back to the number two spot behind Leinart and again did mop-up duty, this time appearing in ten games. Throughout his years as a backup, he says, Orgeron and Carroll called his father every week or so during the season to provide an update. "They didn't have to do things like that," says Booty. He says he always felt comfortable with his role on the team and was okay waiting for his time.

And that time was now.

The Trojans began the season ranked number six in the country, behind Texas and Notre Dame, among other teams. Their first game was on the road, against an Arkansas team that would finish number fifteen in the country. The Trojans blew them out, 50–14, behind three touchdown passes from Booty and a rushing touchdown each by three of the freshmen running backs.

USC returned home and, after a bye week, defeated Nebraska, 28–10. Booty again had three touchdown passes and the defense held the Cornhuskers to just sixty-eight yards rushing. USC rose to number three in the country after the win. The following week, in Tucson, the Trojan defense smothered Arizona in a 20–3 win, allowing a total of only 154 yards.

The 2006 Trojans looked like a natural continuation of the previous three years. They resembled the 2003 title team, with a new quarterback and stifling defense. But the season suddenly changed in tenor as the offense began to commit inopportune turnovers and the defense struggled, becoming less aggressive and more penalty- and error-prone.

USC squeaked by a mediocre Washington State team, 28–22, thanks to a last-second interception by the freshman safety Mays near the goal line. The next week at home another narrow win (26–20) over another mediocre team (Washington) in a game whose outcome was in doubt until the clock expired with the Huskies driving on the USC fifteen-yard line. At home again, this time against Arizona State, Booty struggled (12–25 for 148 yards and two touchdowns, an interception, and a fumble) as USC blew a 21–0 lead and needed a late fourth-quarter touchdown to pull out a 28–21 win.

That game was USC's fortieth victory in its previous forty-one games, and fifty-first in its last fifty-three. The Trojans were 6–0 heading into another bye week, and second in the BCS standings (behind Ohio State), putting them in line for an appearance in the national title game. But things felt a little shaky.

For their seventh game of the season, the Trojans traveled to Corvallis to play Oregon State, a team coached by Mike Riley, who had, of course, spoken to Daryl Gross about the USC job back in late 2000 before Carroll took it. The Beavers were 4–3 coming into the game, slowly improving as the season progressed. That improvement went into overdrive early on against USC.

With just under five minutes left in the third quarter, the Beavers led the Trojans by a stunning 33–10 score. USC was a disaster, plagued by their continuing bad habits—turnovers (four in the game) and penalties (eleven to Oregon State's six).

Behind Booty, though, the Trojans stormed back. He hit Fred Davis for a touchdown in the last seconds of the third quarter and then Steve Smith for a thirty-seven-yard score in the beginning of the fourth. Down 33–25. USC got the ball back at their own twenty with two minutes and thirty-nine seconds left in the game. Booty coolly led the team down the field and threw a touchdown pass to Smith—who had 258 yards receiving on the day—with seven seconds left.

The Trojans needed a two-point conversion to tie the game. On the conversion attempt, Booty spotted an open Jarrett to his left, but his throw was tipped at the line by an Oregon State defender. Jarrett seemed to blame Booty after the game, saying, "I had the guy beat. I had the guy on my hip. . . . The ball just didn't get there."

Oregon State recovered the onside kick attempt, and their fans rushed the field. The 33–31 Oregon State win was only the

Beavers' third victory over the Trojans in the previous thirty-nine years. The loss ended USC's twenty-seven-game winning streak against PAC-10 teams.

"From the get-go, something wasn't right about that game," says Booty. "We had a couple of games with Matt and Reggie like that in years past, but at the end of the game, we'd pull it out."

Indeed, Bush's sixty-five-yard punt return in the fog in USC's last trip to Corvallis in 2004 had ensured there would be no upset that day. But those players were gone.

To be sure, Booty did not appear to be the problem. He did not have Leinart's star power off the field, partly by design. "I still had my fun and even hung out with some of the same stars Matt did, but my personality was to keep it much more private," he says. But on the field, Booty had "a commanding leadership role on the team," says Garrett Green, who played quarterback and safety. In the 2006 season, Booty's numbers nearly matched Leinart's from the year before.[‡]

The problem with the Trojan offense in 2006 was that there wasn't the corresponding productivity from the rushing attack. Bush and White, with their running, opened up the entire offense. The Trojans in 2004 and 2005 ran to set up the pass. Now, it seemed, despite a few good games by their rather large running back committee, the pressure was squarely on the passing game.

Hershel Dennis hurt his knee before the season began. Chauncey Washington hurt his hamstring before putting together some solid games. C. J. Gable had flashed early—he became the first true freshman running back to start the first game of the season (against Arkansas) in USC history. But he faded after that until finding his stride again late in the season. Emmanuel

---

[‡] 2005 Leinart: 3,815 yards, twenty-eight touchdowns, eight interceptions. 2006 Booty: 3,347 yards, twenty-nine touchdowns, nine interceptions.

Moody gained 130 yards in the Arizona win but later sprained his ankle and missed the last four games of the season.

The fall off in the USC running game was stark. In 2005, USC rushed for 3,598 yards and scored fifty-one touchdowns. By the end of the 2006 season, the running backs had a combined 1,879 yards and eighteen touchdowns. In that season, USC would lose two games by a combined six points. A more productive running game very well could have made up for that difference.

One of the things that would dog the rest of Carroll's career at USC would be his futile quest to re-create Bush and, to a certain degree, the Bush-White combination. While USC's teams from 2006 to 2009 would feature some fine running backs, they would never again come close to replicating Bush or the "Thunder and Lightning" backfield.

Another problem was Carroll's frustration with the defense. The unit had started the season extremely well, giving up an average of nine points a game in USC's first three contests. But in the next four games, culminating in the Oregon State loss, they gave up an average of twenty-four points per game.

Carroll needed his defense to cut down on mistakes. And he wanted it to be more aggressive. So, after the Oregon State loss, he retook the job as the defensive coordinator.

The defensive change and the shock of the loss to Oregon State seemed to wake up the Trojans.

They destroyed a winless Stanford team, 42–0. They beat then-twenty-first-ranked Oregon, 35–10. They followed that up with a 23–9 win over number seventeen Cal, in which they shut down the Golden Bears and their explosive offense (led by receiver DeSean Jackson and running back Marshawn Lynch). That win clinched at least a share of the PAC-10 title, USC's fifth in a row.

Next up was the Bush Push rematch. While the Trojans were missing some of their stars from the game the year before, the Irish were not—Brady Quinn and Jeff Samardzija were back.

Jarrett once again showed up against Notre Dame, catching seven passes for 132 yards and three touchdowns. Desmond Reed, who'd torn up his knee the year before in the tall grass, returned a punt for forty-three yards. Gable was effective on the ground, running for 107 yards. The 44–24 win made Carroll 20–0 in the month of November. It was the Trojans' fifth straight win over the Irish, and it put them back in the number two slot in the BCS rankings.

The USC juggernaut, it appeared, was back, having moved past any lingering hangover from the Texas title game, the mayhem with Bush, and the hiccup against Oregon State.

Though the 2006 Trojans were missing their celebrity players in Leinart and Bush and, to a lesser degree, in White, there was still substantial buzz around the team. The practices still bustled with fans and celebrities. Home attendance at the Coliseum broke a record for the fourth year in a row. And the media was already salivating over what would be USC's third straight appearance in the BCS title game, and its fourth straight appearance in a game with national title implications.

All USC had to do was beat UCLA, a team they'd won seven straight against, a streak that included the 66–19 beatdown the year before.

USC's week of practice leading up to the UCLA game was a mess—flat and unfocused. "There seemed to be a feeling of, 'Hey, we're better than they are, so we're going to kill them,'" says Alex Parsons, who played defensive tackle in the 2006 season and later became an offensive lineman.

Ruel says there were other things at play, as well. "Kiffin spent that week trying to get a job with the Raiders, and he was also sick," he says. The Trojans had no healthy fullbacks for the game, and Ruel says he needed to know what Kiffin's plan was to address it. "Kiffin just said, 'Let's move linebacker Thomas Williams in there,'" says Ruel. "I wanted to play with two tight ends. But Kiffin didn't have time to meet because he was so busy trying to get the job and we didn't solve the problem."

Carroll sensed that something was off during the week, so he reached into his bag of tricks: he gave his team a surprise day off from practice. "It kind of felt like we should have practiced even though I didn't want to," says backup offensive lineman Dominique Wise. This time, the gambit didn't work.

Meanwhile, across town, the UCLA defensive coaches had been at work. The team was 6–5 coming into the game, having lost four of its last six games. But DeWayne Walker, UCLA's defensive coordinator, and Todd Howard, the Bruin defensive line coach, believed they had a solid game plan for USC. Walker was very familiar with Carroll—he'd worked with him at the Patriots and had been his first hire at USC, coaching the Trojan secondary for one season. It helped that the Bruins had the extra time of a bye week to prepare. It also helped that UCLA had two All-American defensive ends in Bruce Davis and Justin Hickman. "We had a bead on their running game and what each of their running backs had for plays, and their receiver route concepts," says Walker.

"We guessed that they wouldn't change their game plan from the previous week," says Howard. "They liked to run outside on the perimeter, and our game plan was to be really aggressive on the edge with Davis and Hickman and have our guys in the middle, who weren't great players, just hold their own so we could play press man coverage."

On the morning of the game, the UCLA players and coaches met at the team hotel and watched a film. "They showed USC beating us for seven years in a row," says Howard. "They showed the hype before the game and then our guys with their heads down on the field after they'd lost. By the time our guys got off the bus at the stadium, they were seething."

On the Trojan side, the mood was different. "On the bus ride to the stadium I really honestly felt in my gut that we were going to lose," says Wise. "We'd all been talking about going to the title game and we'd beaten UCLA by a lot the year before, but it didn't feel right. The energy was wrong. We weren't locked in."

Booty agrees. "Everyone seemed lethargic and tired."

The game kicked off at the unusually early start time of 1:40 p.m. PST.

The Trojans were back in the Rose Bowl for the first time since their loss to Texas in the national title game.

UCLA set the tone on defense early on, with Davis and Hickman dominating and frequently getting into the USC backfield. "I was under duress from the first play of the game," says Booty. Halfway through the first quarter, UCLA quarterback Patrick Cowan, a two-star recruit who had been born in Canada and had only learned three days prior to the game that he would be starting, led a drive that made him a Bruin legend. And he did it with his legs, with runs of twenty-nine, sixteen, and nine yards, and then a one-yard plunge for a touchdown that capped a ninety-one-yard drive. "We hit him really hard on the sidelines during that drive, and he just stood up like nothing happened," says Charles Brown. It wasn't the only hit Cowan took that day. Later, in the second quarter, Cowan was running for the boundary when the 250-pound Rey Maualuga launched himself and crushed the quarterback with a helmet-to-helmet hit. After the game, Lou Holtz, who was commentating for ESPN, described the hit as "the most violent tackle I've ever seen on a football field." Cowan stayed in the game.

USC scored on a safety and a Gable touchdown run in the second quarter and went into the half leading, 9–7.

But they wouldn't score another point. "We usually came out of halftime totally jacked," says Fred Davis. "But in that game, we were flat." UCLA tacked on two field goals to take a 13–9 lead. The Trojans got the ball with five minutes and fifty-two seconds left in the game on their own twenty-nine-yard line. And Booty, finally finding enough time to set his feet, passed USC down the field, all the way to the UCLA eighteen. It felt like the dormant giant had finally awoken, and that this would be the drive that sent USC to the national title game.

On third and four from the eighteen, with just over a minute left in the game, Booty dropped back to pass. Steve Smith was open on his right, for what would have been a first down and another step toward what felt like the inevitable game-winning touchdown. Booty let the ball go. UCLA linebacker Eric Mc-Neal suddenly seemed to appear out of nowhere. He leaped, both hands extended over his head, and tipped the ball high into the air. And then—his eyes never leaving the ball—he turned 180 degrees and caught his own tip, an incredible display of athleticism.

And the game was over.

Two heartbreaking losses in a row in Rose Bowl Stadium, which had become a house of horrors for the Trojans.

UCLA had won despite gaining only 235 yards on offense and not completing a pass of longer than twenty-one yards. USC had been done in by the twin bugaboos that had haunted them at different times during the season, problems that never seemed to get fixed. They gained only fifty-five yards on the ground. And they were penalized nine times to UCLA's three.[5] The loss snapped the Trojans' sixty-three game streak of scoring twenty or more points. "I remember walking into the locker room with Pete after the game," says Tim Tessalone. "And he turned to me and said, 'Did that just happen?'"

---

[5] The win was UCLA's only one in the rivalry from 1999 to 2011.

"There was just silence in the locker room afterwards," says Charles Brown. "Carroll didn't give a speech. It was like he was only prepared to give a winning speech."

The loss knocked the Trojans out of the national title game. Instead, they returned to the Rose Bowl yet again, to play Michigan. They exorcised some demons: Booty threw for four touchdowns in a 32–18 win. USC would finish the year ranked fourth in the nation. A great season by most teams' standards. But an undeniable letdown and missed opportunity for the Trojans.

Florida took USC's place in the title game and thrashed Ohio State, 41–14. That victory confirmed what the Texas title had indicated the year before: that the white heat of the game of college football had left the West Coast and settled once again in the South. It would stay there for a good while, with schools from that region of the country winning fifteen of the next sixteen national titles.

CHAPTER SEVENTEEN

The Needler and the Damage Done

At the end of the 2006 NFL season, the owner of the Oakland Raiders, Al Davis, decided he needed a new football coach. Always the iconoclast, Davis wanted someone young after years of allowing mediocre middle-aged men to run his team. Like the rest of the country, he was enamored with the only football team in Los Angeles and its high-powered offense. So he called Pete Carroll. He knew Carroll wasn't going anywhere at the time. But he wanted to inquire about the availability of one of his young offensive assistants, thirty-two-year-old Steve Sarkisian, with whom he was familiar from Sarkisian's one season as the Raiders' quarterback coach.

Carroll loved it when his assistants moved on to head coaching jobs—and, by that point, seven of his former assistants at USC and his jobs at the Jets and Patriots had done just that. Carroll viewed himself as a mentor and liked having a coaching tree and the prestige of being a head coaching factory bestowed upon his program. He helped his coaches network and helped them prepare for interviews by giving them the same advice for interviewing that Jim Valvano had once given him.

Davis offered Sarkisian the Raiders' head coaching job. "But Sark knew who Al was from his year there, knew how fucked up it was there, and turned down the job," says Carroll. But then,

Carroll says, he had an idea. "I got on the phone with Al and said, 'I know what just happened and we're high on Sark but, you know, Lane is amazing, too. They're like peas in a pod.'"

A few days later, Davis hired Kiffin, then thirty-one, to be his new head coach. "It was the craziest hire ever," says Carroll.* "By that time, Lane was so full of himself he thought he could do it. It blew up quickly—they were like oil and water. But that's how high and mighty we were. That's how far we had come."

Kiffin's tenure with the Raiders got off to a rocky start when Davis introduced him as "Lance" at his first press conference. And it would mark the beginning of a turbulent ten-year period in Kiffin's coaching career that included resignations, firings, outraged fan bases (complete with death threats), and reportedly being called a "narcissist" by Nick Saban, who was one of Kiffin's bosses. That period ended when Kiffin found success as Florida Atlantic's head coach in 2017 and then, eventually found even more success at Ole Miss, where he landed in 2020 (and remains today).

After Kiffin left the Trojans, Sarkisian became the team's sole offensive coordinator. Brennan Carroll added Kiffin's title as recruiting coordinator to his role as the tight ends coach, and John Morton, a longtime NFL assistant, was hired to coach the wide receivers.

USC's recruiting hot streak continued in 2007. That class, Kiffin's last, included five of the top twenty high school prospects in the country. Though the brand Carroll had created recruited itself at this point, he sometimes received help from his commits. Chris Galippo, a five-star linebacker from Anaheim, committed early to USC that year and then became, he says, "their biggest recruiter."

---

* Carroll would be hired by Al Davis's son, Mark, to be the head coach of the Raiders in 2025.

He did much of his work at the All-American Bowl, an annual game played by the best high school recruits in the nation. "I remember USC told me that Joe McKnight [a running back] was going to be there, and he wasn't committed yet, and that we had to get Everson Griffen [a defensive end]," says Galippo. "I made it a point to bond with them during the week of the game. I played video games with them and shot the shit, not really pitching as much as becoming friends." Both of those players ended up committing to the Trojans.

That recruiting class, ranked number two in the country, was part of the reason expectations were so high for USC going into the 2007 season. Every poll had the Trojans ranked number one. All twelve of the ESPN "experts" had USC winning the national title. To be sure, their optimism had plenty of justification. The Trojans were coming off a season in which they finished fourth in the country. Booty was going into his fourth year in the offensive system and his second year as a starter and was an early favorite for the Heisman. The Trojans had added two more five-star running backs, which gave them an astounding *ten* running backs on the team who had been high school All-Americans (and eleven running backs in total). Jarrett had declared for the NFL early, and Steve Smith had graduated, but USC appeared to have plenty of receiving talent on hand, with the six-foot-five Patrick Turner playing the Jarrett/Williams role, and the five-star recruit Ronald Johnson coming in. And most of the key parts of the defense—which had smothered teams in the latter half of the 2006 season—were returning. The *Los Angeles Times* ran a preseason story titled "Talent Pool Has Never Been Deeper," within which Carroll—not one prone to hype—said the 2007 Trojans were "the most competitive team we've had."

Maybe true, but all the preseason hype was dampened by what had happened over the winter.

On the morning of January 6, 2007—just five days after USC's Rose Bowl win over Michigan—the body of Trojans placekicker Mario Danelo was found at the bottom of a seaside cliff in San Pedro, minutes from his family home. He had last been seen leaving the house at around two a.m. to go on a walk, after a night of partying with friends.

An autopsy report found his blood-alcohol level to be nearly three times the legal limit. Police ruled out foul play, deeming Danelo's death as either an accident or a suicide. His teammates were certain it wasn't the latter. "He was a likable guy, a great teammate, and, obviously, a great kicker," says Booty.

Danelo had been a walk-on who earned a scholarship in the 2005 season, when he became the Trojans' primary kicker. In his two seasons in that role, he'd made twenty-six of twenty-eight field goals and had set the NCAA record for extra points made (eighty-three) and extra points attempted (eighty-six) during the 2005 season.

At the funeral service—attended by more than 2,000 people—Carroll delivered a eulogy. He told the congregation, which included one hundred USC players, that Danelo was "big-time about living life and having fun. . . . He leaves us with a tremendous gift, about this life he led."

Carroll ended by asking the congregation to stand up. "I want him to know how much we love him. I want him to hear the cheer of the crowd that we all play for, that we've all been around in the game of football we love so much."

And with that, the congregation erupted in cheers. "It went on for like a minute," says Brad Walker. "It was pretty powerful.

"I don't know if Mario's death affected our football, but it certainly affected us as people."

A player on the team later came up with an even more power-ful tribute to Danelo.

On September 1, 2007, in the first game of the season, USC hosted Idaho at home, a night game in front of 90,000 fans. On their first possession, the Trojans worked their way eighty yards down the field, scoring on a four-yard rush by sophomore running back Stafon Johnson. The kicking unit took the field for the extra point attempt. The line set up to block. The holder went down on one knee in the backfield, ready to receive the snap.

But there was no kicker on the field.

The players stayed in their positions. The clock ticked down. The crowd, confused at first, eventually realized that what they were seeing was a tribute to Danelo, and their cheers rose and swelled throughout the stadium. The play clock hit zero and USC took a delay of game penalty.

The idea for the tribute had come from Will Collins, the long snapper who had been good friends with Danelo. He'd brought it to Carroll, who loved it. "It was really an amazing moment in the Coliseum," says Carroll. "That place had some real fucking magic."

The Trojans beat the outmanned Idaho team, 38–10, a good but not great start—USC had turned the ball over three times and the offense had stalled a few times during the game in which they'd been favored by forty-six points.

The Trojans sailed through the next two games, beating fourteenth-ranked Nebraska, 49–31, in Lincoln (with 313 yards rushing), and Washington State, 47–14, at home (Booty: four touchdown passes). In their fourth game of the season, some of the old problems from 2006 reared their heads—three turn-overs, sixteen penalties—in a tight 27–24 win over Washington in Seattle.

The good news for the Trojans was that up next was a woeful Stanford team in what looked like exactly the type of game they needed. USC was a forty-one-point favorite.

Jim Harbaugh played quarterback in the NFL for fourteen seasons. He got a head start on a coaching career in his last eight years as a pro player, serving as an unpaid assistant for his father, Jack, who was then the head coach at Western Kentucky. After retiring from the NFL, Harbaugh became the quarterbacks coach at the Raiders for two years and then got the head coaching job at the University of San Diego, where he posted three winning seasons.[†] And in late 2006, he was hired as the head coach at Stanford, a program that was six years removed from its last winning season and had gone 1–11 the year before.

Harbaugh did not come into the PAC-10 quietly or meekly. And he set his sights on the biggest dog on the block.

Harbaugh and Carroll had gone head-to-head during Harbaugh's playing days, and Carroll's coaching days, in the NFL. In one memorable game in 1991, Harbaugh led the Chicago Bears to a comeback win over the Jets and Carroll's defense. Harbaugh beat another Carroll-led defense in 1995, when his Indianapolis Colts triumphed over the 49ers. In 1997, the Patriots, with Carroll as the head coach, played Harbaugh and the Colts twice and won both games. In all, as a defensive coordinator and head coach in the NFL prior to his USC tenure, Carroll won five of eight meetings against a Harbaugh-quarterbacked team.

[†] In 2006, Harbaugh attempted to recruit Carroll's son, Nate—a lightly recruited quarterback—to the University of San Diego, even doing a home visit. "Glena was home that day," says Carroll. (Nate ended up enrolling at USC and not playing football.)

In the spring of 2007, just months after taking the Stanford job, Harbaugh, twelve years younger than Carroll, did an in-depth interview with CBS Sports and went right after the USC coach, telling the writer Dennis Dodd, "[Carroll's] only got one more year [at USC]. He'll be there one more year. That's what I've heard. I heard it inside the staff."

When asked to clarify his remarks in a subsequent interview, Harbaugh doubled down. "I definitely said that. I said what I've heard—that he won't be there past next year." And then he added a grandiose flourish to end the interview that may have revealed his true intentions with the remarks about Carroll's job. "We bow to no man," he said. "We bow to no program here at Stanford."

While it was true that Carroll had been offered the head coaching job at a handful of NFL teams during his time at USC, he had no plans to leave USC at the time. "If he's going to make statements like that, he ought to get his information right . . . and if he has any questions about it, he should call me," Carroll told the *Los Angeles Times*, who described him as "miffed." Rumors like that, even if they turn out to be untrue, have a way of damaging locker room chemistry and recruiting efforts.

Harbaugh wasn't quite done, though. That July, during the PAC-10 football coaches media day, he told a roomful of reporters, "There is no question in my mind that USC is the best team in the country and may be the best team in the history of college football."

Asked to clarify the latter half of that comment, Harbaugh again doubled down. "They may be the best team in the history of college football. My opinion."

Carroll, of course, was hounded for a response. "Gotta love Jim, don't you?" Carroll told ESPN's Pat Forde. "There's no way I'd ever try to understand what that's about."

In forcing a reaction from Carroll—in getting Carroll to even acknowledge the coach of a team that had gone 1–11 the year before—Harbaugh had displayed one of his strongest attributes: he is the great needler, an expert at getting under the skin of opposing coaches and teams for his benefit, and even, at times, getting under the skin of his own players, to his detriment.

"What's funny about Harbaugh and Pete is that they are actually so similar in so many ways," says Ben Malcolmson, a walk-on receiver for the Trojans in 2006 who went on to work as Carroll's assistant for the next fourteen years. Carroll was not above talking trash to other coaches, as he had to Washington coach Rick Neuheisel in his second season. "Both of them are competitive and use psychology and like to poke the bear. That's why there is the rivalry between them and why they piss each other off."

Stanford came into the October 6 game against USC with a record of 1–3. A week before, the Cardinal (as Stanford's football team is known) had been trounced by Arizona State, 41–3. A few days before that game, the father of Stanford receiver Mark Bradford—whom USC had passed on to disastrously sign Whitney Lewis—had died of a heart attack, and Bradford had missed practices in the lead-up to the USC game. And a day after the Arizona State game, the Cardinal's starting quarterback T. C. Ostrander had a seizure at a restaurant. That meant that a redshirt sophomore, Tavita Pritchard—who had only thrown three passes in his career—would be making his first collegiate start. Against USC. In the Coliseum.

USC came into the game ranked second in the country with a thirty-five-game home winning streak. The latter had started after a 2001 loss . . . to Stanford.

The forty-one-point spread on the game favoring the Trojans seemed reasonable given all the factors leading up to it and given the fact that USC had beaten Stanford 42–0 the season before.

USC went up, 3–0, in the first quarter, and then Chauncey Washington scored a touchdown midway through the second that put USC up 9–0 (the point-after attempt was blocked).

The Stanford defense, though, was playing well enough to keep the Cardinal in the game. But late in the second quarter, the Trojans started to move the ball, putting together a drive that started at their own forty-eight and had them at the Stanford one-yard line on fourth down with thirteen seconds left before half-time. Carroll decided to go for it, sensing the chance to likely put away the pesky Stanford team. But running back Chauncey Washington was stopped for no gain, and the half ended.

Stanford was hanging around. But USC had a more immediate worry. Late in the second quarter, Booty had badly injured a finger on his throwing hand. "It was a routine throw to Patrick Turner, and my hand came down on the helmet of a Stanford player and shattered my middle finger," says Booty. "I knew it was broken right away."

Booty came to the sidelines and told his coaches that he couldn't feel his hand. They left him in for the rest of the half, but they had a decision to make coming out of halftime. Stick with Booty? Or put redshirt sophomore quarterback Mark Sanchez in the game?

When the Trojans came out for warm-ups after the half, Carroll and his coaches watched Booty throw. "We're watching him throw with Mark [Sanchez], ten yards apart," says Yogi Roth, who was a graduate assistant helping with the quarterbacks at the time. "Booty was spinning it. But one of the biggest things I wish we did was have them stand twenty yards apart."

"It wasn't like a wrist injury where I couldn't push through," says Booty. "It impacted me. I had trouble. But not to the point where I couldn't play. I was telling them I was good to go."

Carroll and Sarkisian put him back in the game. "When he went back in, he looked fine at first," says Roth.

But then, three minutes into the third quarter, Booty threw a ball intended for the fullback Stanley Havili in the flat, but it landed in the hands of Stanford safety Austin Yancy, who returned it thirty-one yards for a touchdown.

9–7, USC.

On the Trojans' next possession, tight end Fred Davis fumbled the ball. Stanford went nowhere on its drive and punted. And then Booty overthrew David Ausberry for his second interception of the game. And the Coliseum fans did something they hadn't done since the 2000 season: they began to boo.

USC responded with an interception of its own, by Taylor Mays, at the USC eighteen.

And it was at this point that Booty and the Trojans looked like they had regained their footing. Booty threw a perfect pass—just over the fingertips of a Stanford defender—to his big tight end, Davis, who rumbled sixty-three yards for a touchdown.

16–7, USC. The boos in the stadium turned to cheers.

But then Pritchard did something he hadn't done all game—he led a sustained drive, one highlighted by an acrobatic thirty-seven-yard catch by Bradford that put Stanford on the USC one-yard line. Two plays later, the Cardinal punched the ball in the end zone.

16–14, USC.

USC got the ball back at their own fourteen. And Booty stepped up again, connecting with a wide-open Ronald Johnson for a forty-seven-yard touchdown.

23–14, USC, with just over eleven minutes left in the game.

By this time, it was clear that USC had the more athletic players on the field.

But better talent doesn't always mean victory. Momentum and adrenaline can sometimes lift even the greatest underdogs.

On Stanford's next drive, Pritchard once again stepped up, completing passes to Bradford and to Richard Sherman, the future star NFL cornerback who, at this point in his career, was a wide receiver. A Stanford field goal closed the gap to 23–17, USC.

USC got the ball back with five minutes and forty-three seconds left, looking to put the game away with a sustained drive. After picking up a first down, Booty was sacked for a nine-yard loss and then completed a pass for no gain. And then on third and fifteen, he overthrew Patrick Turner on a pass over the middle, and the ball was intercepted.[‡]

Stanford had the adrenaline shot they needed. And they seized the momentum.

On what would turn out to be one of the most memorable drives in the history of the PAC-10, USC had plenty of chances to stop the Cardinal and wrap up the win. Pritchard threw a deep ball that Mays nearly intercepted. A few plays later, Pritchard was hit as he threw a ball high and into the middle of the field, but it somehow dropped harmlessly to the turf.

With one minute and twenty-nine seconds left in the game, Stanford faced a fourth and twenty from the USC twenty-nine-yard line. Pritchard would later admit that the Coliseum crowd was so loud that he couldn't hear Harbaugh's play call, so he called his own in the huddle—a Double-Go. "Basically, a backyard football play," he would say on a television special years later. "All right, you guys all go deep."

They did, but neither of Pritchard's receivers on the outside were open. But Richard Sherman, who was coming across the

---

[‡] Turner may have had his own issues in that game. According to Keith Rivers, in practice before the Stanford game, Turner came over the middle to catch a pass and was hit so hard by Rey Maualuga, "he had blood coming out of his eyes."

middle, was. Pritchard let the ball fly, and Sherman caught it, just inches across the first down line, as he got popped by the USC safety Kevin Ellison. Sherman held on, even though the hit cracked one of his ribs.[§]

First and goal from the USC nine. Pritchard scrambled for four yards, then threw a pass out of the end zone and then a fade that was knocked to the ground.

Fourth and goal from the five. Stanford was penalized five yards for having twelve men on the field.

Now, fourth and goal from the ten. Fifty-four seconds left. Three receivers lined up to Pritchard's right. Mark Bradford lined up alone to his left. Pritchard snapped the ball and then threw a high fade to Bradford, who caught it for a touchdown. The player USC had passed over, and the player whose father had just died.

Mayhem and confusion ensued, to the point that the television play-by-play announcer for the game yelled, "Touchdown USC!" as Bradford came down with the ball. And then the color announcer suggested Stanford go for a two-point conversion for the tie—even though the game was already tied—before quickly correcting himself.

USC got the ball back with forty-nine seconds left. After a twenty-six-yard return and a fifteen-yard personal foul penalty on Stanford for a face mask, the Trojans had the ball on their own forty-one. They had no timeouts left.

Booty was sacked for a loss of seven. He spiked the ball to stop the clock. He threw an incomplete pass to Turner. And then, on fourth and sixteen, Booty threw his fourth and final interception of the game, USC's fifth total turnover.

[§] As coach of the Seattle Seahawks, Carroll would later draft Sherman—by then a cornerback—with the 154th pick of the 2011 NFL Draft, the very definition of a "steal," since Sherman went on to a career that will very likely land him in the Pro Football Hall of Fame.

Stanford, the forty-one-point underdog, had won, 24–23.

USC now had the ignominious distinction of playing in the greatest game of the century and in the greatest upset of the century and coming up on the wrong end of both.

As USC left the field, the Coliseum was silent, the fans in too much shock to boo.

Booty has no regrets about the game. "I would do the same thing over again," he says. "We had a shot at the end to win it. My finger was hurt, but to what degree it impacted the game, I don't know. It wasn't like I couldn't throw the ball. The bad one was the pick-six, which was totally my fault. But outside of that, I don't think the finger is the reason we lost."

At the press conference after the game, as the Stanford players, through a concrete wall, could be heard celebrating in their locker room, Carroll said none of the blame should fall on Booty. "I didn't think for a second we were going to lose. I was allowing myself to lose focus a little bit, maybe. . . . If anything really was a factor, it was my cockiness that there was no way we would lose this game. They would never beat us."

Seventeen years later, Carroll would say that he had made a "horrendous mistake" by leaving Booty in the game with a broken finger. His offensive line coach at USC agrees. "What were we doing? We could have had Sanchez in the game and just run the ball and won by two touchdowns," says Ruel. "But we left Booty in there and one interception, two interceptions, three interceptions, four. That might be the worst call of Carroll's career. To lose to Harbaugh! That game was humiliating."

The needler had triumphed. And not for the last time.

All was not lost for the Trojans, though. The 2007 college football season was pure chaos, a riot of upsets. There appeared to be a curse that came with being ranked number two in the country.

USC had been ranked in that spot when it lost to Stanford. Same for Cal when it lost to Oregon State, South Florida when it lost to Rutgers, Boston College when it lost to Florida State, Oregon when it lost to Arizona, and West Virginia when it lost to Pitt.

That was the good news. The bad news was that Booty was out for at least a few games due to his finger. In his place: Mark Sanchez.

Sanchez had a shaky first start—a 20–13 win over Arizona, in which he threw for just 130 yards and one touchdown and two interceptions. The next week, against a bad Notre Dame team, Sanchez played well, throwing four touchdowns in a 38–0 win. The only trouble the Trojans had that week was on the flight there, when their plane hit some turbulence and dropped. "We were free-falling for a couple of seconds," says Alex Parsons. "Anyone not buckled in hit their head on the overhead bins. Guys were shaking and crying." The plane eventually landed safely, but defensive end Lawrence Jackson had to have part of a popsicle stick removed from his mouth.

In what would be Sanchez's last start of that season, the Trojans traveled to play number five Oregon in Eugene. The Ducks had a new offensive coordinator that season in Chip Kelly, who ran a spread offense with run/pass options, something that suited Oregon's quarterback Dennis Dixon and its running back Jonathan Stewart well, and something that drove Carroll and his defense crazy all game. On USC's last drive, Sanchez was intercepted at the Oregon sixteen to snuff out any chance of tying the game, which Oregon won, 24–17.

The loss, for all intents and purposes, dashed the preseason number one Trojans' title hopes. With Booty back, USC swept their last four regular season games and won the PAC-10 for the sixth straight time. In the Rose Bowl, USC blew out Illinois, 49–17, and ended up at number three in the final rankings. LSU defeated Ohio State in the national title game, becoming the first two-loss national champion in the modern era of the game, bringing into stark relief how costly the loss to Stanford had been for USC.

Back in those days, of course, there was a thinner margin for college teams when it came to getting a shot to play for the national title. In either or both of the 2006 and 2007 seasons, the Trojans might have had a chance at the title had there been a four-team playoff (which started in 2014). And they certainly would have made the twelve-team playoff (which started in 2024) by virtue of their ranking and their PAC-10 titles.

That a team can win on "any given Sunday" is a cliché in the NFL for good reason. Randomness is part of any football game—injuries, weather, individual mistakes, and bad officiating can doom the better team. But in the NFL, by design, all teams have talented rosters (they draft the best players in college, the draft is flipped so that the worst teams get the higher picks, etc.).

The college game, though, is generally a bit less random, the differences in roster talent level starker. (Remember the Saban line about being able to recruit "ten players with first-round talent every year"?) Even though 2007 was a big year for upsets, back in the mid-2000s, "any given Saturday" wasn't really a thing.[1] The teams Carroll fielded from 2002 to 2008 at USC almost always had far more talent than their opponents (with the possible exception of the Vince Young–led Texas team and the 2007 Oregon team, with its Chip Kelly offense).

And viewed through that prism, the 2006 and 2007 Trojan teams failed to live up to their expectations when, twice in two years, they were caught flat-footed and lost to teams with much less talent. The 2007 Trojan team alone boasted thirty-five players who would be drafted by NFL teams.

---

[1] The ability for college football players to capture name, image, and likeness money, as well as the open transfer portal, appears to have leveled the playing field in the college game at least a bit.

Though Booty didn't quite have the skill set that Palmer and Leinart had, he wasn't the main reason for USC's failure to live up to its talent level in those two years. Booty went 21–3 in his two years as a starter. ("And all people want to talk about are those three losses," he says.)

There were other culprits, as well.

There was the practical. While the 2006 and 2007 Trojans were excellent college football teams, they didn't quite stack up to the 2003 through 2005 teams. The lack of a consistently explosive running game is one reason—even with an improvement of the running game in 2007 over 2006, the team still finished 1,000 yards and thirty touchdowns below the bellwether 2005 year. But there is another statistic that truly stands out and separates the 2006 and 2007 teams.

In Carroll's first meeting with his USC team, he had held up a ball, a visual illustration of the importance of his team preventing turnovers of their own and causing them in their opponents. From 2001 to 2005, USC averaged plus-seventeen in turnover margin per season. From 2006 to 2007, the Trojans' average turnover margin was zero. (Plus-four in 2006, minus-four in 2007.) One reason for that: the defenses in those two seasons, while excellent, also seemed to be missing players who had a knack for game-changing plays. "Before, we'd always had somebody who would make a play, like a Lofa [Tatupu] interception, always someone," says Keith Rivers, the linebacker who graduated after the 2007 season. "In my last two years, we just didn't make those plays."

One of the primary reasons it's so hard to maintain a dynasty in any sport is that teams become victims of their own success. Expectations become unrealistic, with fans and the media viewing any season that doesn't end with a championship as a failure.**

** Case in point: After John Wooden coached UCLA to the 1975 national title, an alum of the school supposedly approached him and said, "Congratulations,

It's no coincidence that all of USC's losses in 2006 and 2007 were to PAC-10 teams. "Pete's USC teams were so well-coached and had so much talent," says Mike Riley, who led Oregon State for all but two years of the Carroll era. "And that was good for everyone on the West Coast and a great time for the conference. Pete set a new bar, and you had to either rise up or be left in the dust." Other PAC-10 teams, motivated to beat USC, attracted great coaches, like Riley, Chip Kelly (who was Oregon's offensive coordinator from 2007 to 2008 and became the head coach in 2009[††]), and Harbaugh.

During the Carroll era, too, USC "was everybody's biggest game on the schedule every season," says Brandon Hancock. "SC was the biggest show in town wherever we were. Those away stadiums were always full. Even if you're the much better team on paper, it's difficult to get your dick hard week in and week out when facing everyone's best punch."

And what made finding that level of intensity for every game more difficult as time went on was that, with each subsequent season, the program got farther and farther away from its foundation, its unbending backbone. Which was, as Alex Holmes describes it, "the turning point class" of Hackett recruits who had charged into and wholly embraced the opportunity and excellence of the Carroll era without ever forgetting—and, really, always being driven by—the pain and misery of the Hackett era. "We all committed to doing it right," says Holmes.

"We'd seen it all and we were like, 'Nah, we're not going back,'" says Omar Nazel. "Carroll's later recruiting classes never

---

Coach. You let us down last year, but this made up for it." Wooden's 1974 UCLA team had made the Final Four, losing in double overtime, and had won the national title in nine of the last ten seasons before that.

[††] Perhaps mindful of the trouble Kelly's Oregon offenses once gave his USC defenses, Carroll hired Kelly in 2025 to become his offensive coordinator with the Las Vegas Raiders.

experienced obstacles. They were better athletes, but the mentality of the player wasn't a dog. In those earlier years, the talent was maximized. The effort was maximized. But when every single game you play is the other team's Super Bowl and you don't put in maximum effort, you will lose some of those games no matter how talented you are."

"With all the glitz that came, it's hard not to get rat poison," says Jacob Rogers. "Those guys who came along in the later years [of Carroll's era] just knew the good times."

Even the coaches agreed. "Over time, you get disconnected from where you came from," says Seto. "Leinart and that group were closely connected to the wounds of the previous era."

Recruiting reflected that disconnect. Though the Trojans pretty much only signed four- and five-star players, many of them failed to live up to that billing. Fit and behavioral issues were the main problems. In the highly touted 2006 class, eight players didn't make it past one season or transferred out of the program.

Another reason those five-stars might not have lived up to their potential: they weren't coached well enough. "It's hard to control five-stars," says Keith Rivers. "A guy like Eddie O could do it."

A natural by-product of success is turnover on the coaching staff. "The makeup of the coaching staff became a big part of it all," says Holmes. "Norm and Ed's departures were major things." The influx of new coaches meant that the staff, too, lost the connection to that old pain and misery. They also lost something when it came to player development. "The biggest thing that can't be underestimated was the amount of talent USC had on that coaching staff in those first four or five years," says David Newbury, the USC kicker who covered the Trojans as a television analyst. "Coach Chow and Coach O and all of those guys became head coaches. They were gifted recruiters and incredibly gifted at developing those recruits. They turned terrific athletes into great football players. New coaches have to learn the system. It takes a lot of energy to bring them up to speed."

"Guys like Chow and Orgeron had been around college football a while," says Chris Huston. "They kind of served as a check on Pete's laissez-faire way."

When those coaches with big personalities left—and when Carroll purposely challenged himself and put barriers in his own way to stay energized and engaged—the program revolved solely around Carroll and his personality. He and Yogi Roth—who had played football with Brennan Carroll at Pitt—came up with the idea for a blog they named USCripsit.com (a takeoff on a surfer term). The blog, which was run by Ben Malcolmson, gave an inside look at the program. "It was a way for us to get people to check the website more often," says Malcolmson. "I just posted stuff Pete said and did, and gave a look at the program, all day. It was a bit like tweeting." The blog became, in some ways, a primary source of information for Trojan football news (it was quoted on ESPN at times), a precursor to the way college and pro teams divulge and control news today.

Carroll, through Malcolmson, was also an early adopter of Twitter and Facebook, where he posted things like movie reviews and his song of the day. (Carroll was way ahead of the curve on this, as well.) Carroll, too, offered memberships for his fan club on his website. For fifty dollars, one could get a signed photo and a T-shirt that read, "Do it better than it's ever been done."

Carroll also became freer with sharing the Zen-like psychological underpinnings of his philosophy. He gave an interview to the *Los Angeles Times* in which he talked about "clearing the clutter in the interactions between your conscious and subconscious mind," and mentioned Gallwey, saying, "We are trying to create a self-actualized program. It's really about divine nonchalance." A lesser coach would have faced ridicule for such talk.

But Carroll got away with it because, to this point, it had all worked.

Carroll says now, in retrospect, that some of the moves he made with assistants, some of those barriers he erected on purpose, didn't go as intended. "I gave some authority and responsibility to guys, to keep them and promote them, and I thought they could handle it. It didn't work out that well," he says. "I'm pissed at myself. I didn't find what it took to keep the pressure on. I didn't do it well enough in replacing some coaches. Eddie and Lane and eventually Sark, I didn't replace them well enough."

And sometimes a program run on personality can go astray. "When working for Coach, one of his problems is that guys are so impressed with his uniqueness and naturalness that they want to be like him," says Ruel. "The problem is, if we all become like him, it's all creativity, too much, and no hammers."

Carroll and the Trojans, though, would have one more shot to make it all right again and regain the glory of the not-too-distant past.

CHAPTER EIGHTEEN

¡Viva Sanchez!

Clay Matthews III's grandfather (Clay Sr.) played for the San Francisco 49ers in the 1950s. His father (Clay Jr.) was a linebacker at USC who went on to play in the NFL for nineteen years. His uncle (Bruce) also played at USC and starred in the NFL also for nineteen years as an offensive lineman and is a member of the Pro Football Hall of Fame. His brother (Kyle) played safety on the 2003 USC team. And another brother (Casey) played linebacker in the NFL for five years.

Clay Matthews had exquisite athletic genes. They just took their sweet time to manifest.

In his junior year in high school, Matthews was a scrawny 165 pounds and just a hair over six feet tall. He did not start on his football team, even though his father was his defensive coordinator.

Though still undersized, Matthews did put on a bit of weight before his senior season and played well enough to get recruitment letters from Arizona, Arizona State, and Idaho. But he did not get one from his father's (and mother's) alma mater, USC. "They were rolling in five-stars at the time," he says. "I was not surprised or upset."

He applied to the school anyway and was accepted and walked on to the football team in 2004. "I was pretty naïve to think I could hang," says Matthews. "That first training camp was an eye-opener. Physically, I just wasn't as good as the other players."

So, he says, he just kept his head down and followed instructions. "If there was a workout at six a.m., I was there. I never missed a practice. I wasn't very social, didn't go out and party, wasn't in the frat scene. I didn't really have a plan. I just stuck to doing what I was told."

He grew and put on muscle. But he didn't play a down in 2004. Even when he was offered the chance to go into one game that season, a blowout, he declined. "I think the coaches thought I was crazy, but I wanted to preserve my redshirt so I could get the full five years," he says.

That same year, Carroll made a staffing hire that would transform Matthews's career at USC and beyond. Carroll brought in Todd McNair to coach the running backs but also to run the special teams. McNair had scratched out an eight-year career in the NFL as primarily a special teams player. "Todd told me that he used to run down the field and collect beard hairs in his elbow pads. He called it his 'bearded elbow,'" says Matthews. "He had swagger."

McNair saw something in Matthews and put him on special teams in 2005.

Matthews missed the first game of that season, against Hawaii, because of an injury, but played in the second game against Arkansas. "We beat them seventy to something, and I had to run down on kickoff like ten times," he says. "I was gassed. But it was the start of me being able to put something on film and get more time on special teams and, hopefully, on defense."

But he was still a walk-on, a sort of purgatorial position on a college team. "Most people don't understand how hard it is to be a walk-on," Matthews says. "Even though you're part of the team, there is a separation, a negative connotation. I wasn't allowed to eat with the rest of the team."

At the end of training camp each year, Carroll traditionally gave out scholarships to a handful of walk-ons. "The reality was that they gave them out to guys who had been on the team for a few years who could help bring up the team GPA," says Matthews. When he didn't get a scholarship in the 2005 season, Matthews says, "I was so disappointed. And I had a good GPA."*

But in the training camp leading into the 2006 season, Matthews finally got his wish when Carroll gathered his players in the team meeting room and announced that the special teamer had earned a scholarship. "It was pretty cool, one hundred guys jumping up and down, spraying me with water," says Matthews.

Matthews spent that season and the next as a reserve linebacker and continued to play special teams, where he excelled (he blocked two field goals in 2007) and was named co-special teams player of the year in both seasons.

In 2008, his last season of eligibility, Matthews needed to take only one course to satisfy NCAA requirements. Instead of ballroom dancing like Leinart, though, he took a course on weapons of mass destruction and nuclear nonproliferation in post-Soviet Russia.

That season, too, Matthews finally got his chance on defense, though it didn't happen right away—he didn't start until the fourth game of the season. "Clay was a late bloomer," says Nick Holt. "But he hit a growth spurt and worked out and kicked butt. And he flourished once we got him in there. He was intelligent and understood football."

And he became part of what is regarded as perhaps the greatest linebacking group ever assembled on one college team. In 2008, USC featured:

---

* His GPA was a 3.06 and, in 2006, he would make the PAC-10 All-Academic second team and in 2008 would make the conference's All-Academic first team. "I took my academics seriously," he says.

Matthews, an eventual first-round pick in the NFL Draft by the Green Bay Packers who went on to an eleven-year NFL career, winning a Super Bowl and making the All-Pro team.

Rey Maualuga, who was USC's first Chuck Bednarik Award winner (given to the nation's best collegiate defensive player) and an All-American who played for nine years in the NFL.

Brian Cushing, who was also an All-American and was the NFL's defensive rookie of the year in 2009 and played in the NFL for nine years.

And Kaluka Maiava, who, though he was the least heralded of the group, had a six-year career in the NFL.

The four linebackers—whom fellow linebacker Chris Galippo referred to as "our gladiators"—were "all best friends," says Matthews. Cushing, he says, "was a Jersey guy, such a joy to be around, so passionate about being a hard-ass and not phony about it." Maualuga was "this larger-than-life Samoan, menacing because of all of his tattoos and big body." Matthews hosted Maiava on his recruiting trip to USC. "He was so cool, a typical Hawaiian right off the island," says Matthews. "He showed up in board shorts and sandals. He opened me up to Hawaiian culture, the slang. I caught him eating poi in the living room."[†]

Though the 2008 linebackers all had one another's backs, Matthews says, "We were all competing against each other and none of us lacked confidence. We were competing for who would be talked about most the day after games, who got the game ball, who was going to be on the cover of a magazine. It was healthy. We celebrated each other. But we all wanted to be the best."

[†] Poi is a traditional dish from Hawaii that is made from boiling taro roots and mashing them basically into a paste. It is not an appetizing-looking dish to some.

They competed, too, with the offense. Says Matthews about the practices in his first few years:

> Some of the best times we had at practice were during stretching. We would stretch across from the offense. The coaches would chirp at each other to get us going. Norton [by then, the linebacker coach] would get after Kiffin and tell him the only reason he had his job was because of his dad. Kiffin would say something about Norton's dad losing to Ali. And Norton would say, "My dad broke Ali's jaw!" It was all on the verge of going too far. But it would get us fired up. We didn't want to give the offense anything in practice. It felt personal. Carroll loved it and encouraged it and wanted us to take it right up to the point of fighting.

In practice one day in 2008, Cushing blocked the freshman tight end Blake Ayles into a wall. Ayles retaliated by throwing a football at Cushing's head. "Pete came running at me, full speed," says Ayles. "And he said, 'That's one guy you do not want to fuck with.' And I was like, 'Okay. I got it.'"

Under Carroll, USC went from Tailback U to Linebacker U. It had started with Matt Grootegoed and Lofa Tatupu and continued through Keith Rivers. But in 2008, it hit its zenith.

Of that group, Holt says, "I was very fortunate to coach them. It was good getting off the bus with them."

The 2008 Trojan defense also featured a heat-seeking missile at safety in Taylor Mays. Mays was "one of the fiercest animals I've ever seen," says the offensive lineman Garrett Nolan. "He just destroyed everything in his path." Mays paired that aggression with speed—he ran a 4.24 forty-yard dash, which made him the fastest player on the team. "One day at practice, I ran a fade and got past Cushing and saw that Mays was thirty yards away. I thought I was all good," says Ayles. "But as soon as I caught it,

Mays was there, his face mask an inch from mine. 'I would have killed you,' he said. He was thirty yards away! He was a freak of a human."

With that quartet of linebackers, combined with the violent and intimidating Mays, Carroll knew his defense would be very good—possibly great—in the 2008 season. On offense, the line was young but talented, and the team's core running backs and receivers were returning. The biggest question was at quarterback, where, with Booty graduated, the Trojans would have to start a kid named Mark Sanchez.

Sanchez grew up in Orange County, just as Palmer and Leinart had. After his parents divorced, he and his two older brothers lived with their father, Nick, an Army sergeant who became a captain in the Orange County Fire Authority.

Nick, a former junior college quarterback, encouraged his son to play sports and took it upon himself to train him in some unconventional ways. He would quiz Sanchez on the periodic table as he threw him batting practice and make him do multiplication tables as he dribbled blindfolded. Nick wanted to prepare his son not just for sports, but for life.

Sanchez started his high school football career at Santa Margarita Catholic high school, where his idol, Palmer, had played. "I was Carson's ballboy there," says Sanchez. But he then transferred to Mission Viejo, where his head coach was Bob Johnson, the famed quarterback whisperer who had tutored Palmer.

Sanchez excelled there, both on and off the field—in his senior year, he was named the national player of the year, maintained a 3.7 GPA, and was class president. He chose USC over Texas, Notre Dame, Ohio State, and Nebraska, enrolling in 2005 and redshirting in that season. In 2006, he backed up Booty. In 2007, he did the same and started those three games after Booty broke his finger. During that stretch, he learned about the scrutiny and burden put on the starting quarterback at USC during that era.

Against Notre Dame in his second start in 2007—in a game in which he threw four touchdown passes in a 38–10 win—Sanchez wore a mouthpiece decorated with the tricolors of the Mexican flag. It had been designed and given to him by the Trojans' team dentist. Sanchez liked the idea of wearing it to honor his Mexican American heritage (he is a third-generation Mexican American). But a loud minority of fans and bloggers viewed the gesture as political and accused Sanchez of being a radical and advocating for illegal immigration. When approached for comment, Sanchez told the media that everyone was entitled to their own opinions, and he was okay with that and would no longer wear the mouthpiece because he didn't want it to be a distraction. And he said all of it with a smile— Sanchez liked to please, and he never took himself too seriously.

Still, Mexican American fans in the Los Angeles area and beyond embraced him. Many of them came to USC practices and games wearing sombreros, lucha libre wrestling masks, and sarapes and holding signs that read, "¡Viva Sanchez!" Photos of him hung in the kitchens of Mexican restaurants and in taco stands. He gave talks to Hispanic elementary classes.

Sanchez looked the part of the USC quarterback. Like Leinart, he was dark-haired and scruffy, and he resembled Adrian Grenier, the lead actor in the television show *Entourage* (still on the air at the time), even more than Leinart did. But Sanchez wore his looks casually and unassumingly. He did some magazine shoots— which his teammates ribbed him about, leaving copies all over the locker room—and was comfortable in front of cameras, but he did not spend his off-the-field time hanging out with celebrities, preferring a more low-key surfer dude vibe, with his flip-flops and yarn bracelets. He was the starting quarterback at USC, but, he says, "I had outlets where I could hang out and just be one of the guys. I didn't need more than a handful of Hollywood nights

to realize that wasn't my scene." (He was, though, a little less careful with his partying than Leinart was—he had the dropped sexual assault case, and he reportedly was once briefly detained for
breaking a window at a fraternity.)[‡]

His coaches loved him. Carroll addressed him as "Marky."
And his teammates adored him. They nicknamed him "the Mexican Jumping Bean" for his ceaseless energy at practice. Sanchez
called them all "dude." He had some idiosyncrasies—he brushed
his teeth before games and at halftime. "I'd get this weird taste in
my mouth, almost like venom, in the back of my throat when I
played," says Sanchez.

He was "playful and competitive," says Garrett Green.

He was "never too big-time and liked to poke fun at Coach
Carroll," says Ayles.

All this despite being, perhaps, the most famous person on the
USC campus. Garrett Nolan remembers one of his first days at
USC, when the strength coach, Chris Carlisle, introduced him to
Sanchez. The quarterback immediately invited Nolan to walk with
him to a food truck. "So we're walking through campus and every
girl we pass says, 'Hey, Mark,' and he would respond, 'Hey, what's
up?'" says Nolan. "I asked him if he knew the girls and he said, 'Absolutely not.' And I say, 'Is this what it's like being a USC football
player?' And he says, 'It's what it's like being the USC quarterback.'"

Sanchez was unfailingly gracious to everyone he met. "We'd be
on the field after practice in the media scrum with ten or twelve
guys around," says Tim Tessalone. "Mark would do interviews
with them and when they were over, he'd shake each person's
hand and look them in the eye and say, 'Thank you.'"

In the 2008 preseason training camp, Sanchez was the clear-cut
number one quarterback, even though the Trojans had brought in a

---

[‡] Sanchez also ran into a good amount of trouble in the fall of 2025, of course.

transfer named Mitch Mustain, who had gone undefeated in eight starts with Arkansas. But during warm-ups in a practice early on in camp, Sanchez threw a ball to Clay Matthews and then suddenly fell to the turf in agony. He had dislocated his left kneecap. The USC trainers took him to the sidelines and popped his kneecap back in. An MRI revealed that Sanchez had no ligament damage. But his status for the Trojans' first game was very much in doubt.

The 2008 offseason was, for once, devoid of drama. That year's recruiting class fell a bit in terms of rankings, to number eight, but included two five-star offensive linemen in Matt Kalil (brother of Ryan) and Tyron Smith (who would go on to a fourteen-year career in the NFL). Fan interest remained high—22,000 people attended the spring game, up from 15,000 the year before. The Bush investigation, entering its third year, was off the radar screen, and Carroll and Garrett became increasingly confident that it would amount to nothing more than a minor nuisance. "It's more a feeling. If it was going to break and all this stuff was going to come out, it would have come out a long time ago," Garrett told the *Los Angeles Times*. "It could happen in the next three years or whatever, but I don't think there's a lot to it."

In all, there was a loose and fun atmosphere about the 2008 Trojans. The players seemed to be following the lead of their playful yet serious quarterback—his preseason injury notwithstanding— by working hard but having fun.

And Carroll was back in vintage form.

During training camp that spring, some members of the LAPD interrupted a Trojan team meeting. Carroll conferred with them, briefly, his forehead furrowed in concern. And then the policemen walked over to Everson Griffen, a six-foot-three, 265-pound defensive end, and told them he was under arrest. The reason given: "for physically abusing a freshman." As confusion and gasps spread across the room, the police led Griffen out the door.

And then a video popped up on the wide screen at the front of the room. It showed a clip from practice, with Griffen running through the block of freshman offensive lineman Matt Meyer and tossing him to the ground.

Later that season, Carroll staged what would become one of his most legendary pranks. During practice on the day before Halloween, Ruel—once again Carroll's accomplice—suddenly pointed to a cameraman who was on top of a hydraulic lift, presumably filming practice. Ruel began to yell at the man, berating him for "cutting off three fucking plays" in the practice film from the day before. The cameraman began to respond but then lost his balance . . . and fell off the lift, landing behind the fence that surrounded the field. Ruel and some other coaches began to run to the man's aid, when someone started screaming, "Oh my God, they caught him. They actually caught him."

"They" turned out to be Will Ferrell, who suddenly appeared on the field carrying the cameraman (who turned out to be a professional stuntman; he'd landed on a cushion hidden behind the fence). Ferrell was wearing a Lone Ranger mask, an Ironman shirt with bulging fake muscles, and a red Speedo that was stuffed in the front with a hand towel for maximum junkage.

Ferrell told the team his name was Captain Compete. He shook Carroll's hand and then reached into his Speedo, pulled out the hand towel, and handed it to him. "I want you to hold that for me," he said as Carroll took it.

Ferrell gathered the team around and told them, "I'm here to let you guys know that you've always got to compete. When you wake up in the morning, you gotta compete. When you take a crap, you gotta compete. When you go to school . . . yeah, don't worry about competing."

And then, suddenly, another man appeared on the field, this one on fire. Another stuntman. While the stuntman's partners sprayed him with fire extinguishers, Ferrell ran to grab buckets of Gatorade and, without opening the tops, began to dramatically heave them near the man. And then Ferrell, after a performance that fully captured his nonsensical and physical comedy, ended practice by breaking the team down.

The prank, like many of Carroll's, had a dark and morbid tone. Most of his players loved this one, but a few—like fullback Stanley Havili and defensive lineman Armond Armstead—decidedly did not, visibly shaken by thinking they had witnessed a man fall, perhaps to his death.[5]

The pranks, though, were just a part of the reason that Carroll remained beloved by his players.

Charles Brown says that in 2008, he was having problems with his confidence. Carroll pulled him aside after a team meeting. "He gives me what I needed to hear, and, at the end, I remember him saying, 'If you want to do it, just do it. You'll be able to do it.' As he's saying this, he took the gum out of his mouth and tossed it at a trashcan ten feet away and it dropped right in the middle. And then he just shrugged and walked out."

During warm-ups for the Notre Dame game that year, a few fans ran out past the security guards and onto the field. Blake Ayles walked toward the field-crashers and gave them two middle fingers. A cameraman caught the moment—which looked as if Ayles was flipping off the Notre Dame crowd—and the photo went viral on the internet. "People said it was disrespectful," says Ayles. "And I thought I was going to get in so much trouble."

---

[5] Three years later, a Notre Dame student football assistant died after the hydraulic lift he was standing on blew over in a gust of wind.

On the Monday after the game, Ayles was in the training room getting taped up, along with Brown, Cushing, and Sanchez. Carroll appeared. "All the guys are like, 'You're in trouble now. You're going to get ripped apart,'" says Ayles. Carroll walked over to Ayles as the other players backed away. "And Pete leans in and says, 'I would have done the same thing,'" Ayles says. "And then he tells me that if the media asks if I'm in trouble to tell them that I have to do a thousand up and downs. So the media asks, and I tell them that. But I never had to do it. It was like I thought I was in trouble with Dad, and then Dad comes over and gives me approval."

Sanchez recovered from his knee injury during the fall camp, enough to start—and excel—in the Trojans' first game, at Virginia, going 26 for 35 for 338 yards and three touchdowns. The USC defense held Virginia to 187 total yards of offense (and thirty-two yards rushing) in a 52–7 beatdown. USC, which began the season at number three in the nation, ascended to number one.

After a bye week, USC hosted Ohio State, the fifth-ranked team in the country, and a team coming off two straight appearances in the national title game. Sanchez threw four touchdown passes—and entered the Heisman conversation—and Maualuga had an interception return for a touchdown in a dominating 35–3 win. "Tonight, it didn't matter who we were playing," Carroll said after the game.

USC had won its first two games by a combined 87–10 score and gained an average of 453 yards on offense and allowed an average of 197 yards on defense, per game. "You can stop debating the identity of the best team of the coach Pete Carroll era because, in four months, everyone will agree this is it," Bill Plaschke wrote in the Los Angeles Times. He was far from alone in this assessment.

And then came Oregon State.

———

Oregon State was considered a difficult place to play football. Its stadium was small (capacity of 43,000 at the time) but loud, and the loudspeaker played an annoyingly discordant recording of a chainsaw whenever the visiting team faced a third down. Because of a lack of suitable accommodations in Corvallis, visiting teams were forced to stay in Eugene, some forty-five minutes away. They also had to dress for the game in Gill Coliseum—the basketball arena—and then cross a parking lot and walk down a ramp to enter the stadium.

The Beavers came into the game at 2–2 and were a twenty-five-point underdog to the Trojans. In their second game of the season, they'd been throttled by Penn State, 45–14. "But in that game, we found our new running back," says Oregon State coach Mike Riley. That running back: five-foot-seven, 191-pound freshman Jacquizz "Quizz" Rodgers, whose brother, James, was a receiver on the team.

The game kicked off at six p.m. PST on a Thursday night. Oregon State took their opening drive sixty yards down the field, scoring on a touchdown pass to James Rodgers.

On their first drive of the second quarter, the Beavers went sixty-two yards in eleven plays—all but one to a Rodgers brother—which culminated in a two-yard Jacquizz Rodgers touchdown run.

On its next possession, the Beavers drove fifty-eight yards on eleven plays—all but one to a Rodgers brother—and scored a touchdown on a pass that went right through the hands of USC cornerback Kevin Thomas and into the hands of James Rodgers.

At the half, the score was 21–0, Oregon State. And it wasn't a fluke. The Beavers had controlled the line of scrimmage on both sides of the ball and allowed USC only seventy-five yards of offense and three first downs.

But, as they seemingly always did, the Trojans came out of the half humming. Sanchez found Ronald Johnson for a twenty-six-yard touchdown and then Damian Williams for a twenty-nine-yard touchdown. Oregon State's lead was cut to seven.

Midway through the fourth quarter, Oregon State had a chance to add to its lead, but a forty-one-yard field goal attempt was blocked by Matthews.

With three minutes and fifteen seconds left in the game, an Oregon State punt by Johnny Hekker left USC pinned on its own two-yard line. USC managed to get a little breathing room with a first down, but then Sanchez overthrew his receiver, and the ball was intercepted and returned to where the drive had started: the USC two. From there, Jacquizz Rodgers punched the ball into the end zone and the crowd went delirious.

27–14, Oregon State (the Beavers missed the extra point).

USC got the ball back with two minutes and thirty seconds left in the game. Four plays later, Sanchez threw his third touchdown of the day.

27–21, Oregon State.

USC tried an onside kick. It was recovered by the Beavers, who ran out the clock as fans stormed the field.

"Quizz came out of nowhere for them," says Riley. Indeed, Jacquizz Rodgers was the star of the show, with 186 yards rushing and two touchdowns.

Sanchez walked off the field at Reser Stadium, head down. As he neared the tunnel, *Los Angeles Times* writer Gary Klein joined him. "Gary asked me what happened," says Sanchez. "And I'm like, 'We should have won that fucking game, and would have if I didn't throw that fucking interception.' And then I threw my wristband against the wall. We honestly just laid an egg. They were good, but come on, they had no business hanging around with us."

The Trojans didn't just lose — they got physically beaten up, especially on the defensive side, where their stars had a tough night. Mays coughed up blood. Maualuga injured his knee. Cushing broke his hand.

It was USC's fifth loss in the last three seasons. All the losses had been to PAC-10 teams. And in four of the five losses, USC had been favored by more than twenty points. The losses no longer seemed like flukes.

And after a long period of being fawned over by the local and national media, Carroll began to feel some knifepoints. "Do you ever wonder when someone is going to start holding USC coach Pete Carroll's feet to the fire for these inexplicable losses?" Tom Dienhart at Rivals.com wrote. "Yes, Carroll has national championships, but is it OK for the coach with arguably the most talented roster in the country to annually lose games he isn't supposed to? Just wondering."

"The number one Trojans just ruined their national championship chase with another inexplicable gag job against an inferior opponent," college football columnist Dennis Dodd wrote after the game. (Oregon State would finish the season 9–4.)

From that point on, the Trojans showed no mercy to their opponents. They tweaked their defense, installing Matthews as a starter and playing Cushing and him at a hybrid linebacker/defensive end position known as "elephant." "The offenses we played never knew where our guys were coming from," says Holt.

In their last nine games of the regular season, the USC defense gave up an average of just six points a game, while the offense averaged thirty-eight. (The defense only gave up fourteen touchdowns all season. To put that in perspective, USC scored ten touchdowns in that year's game against Washington State alone.) The Trojans had one close call — a 17–10 win over Arizona — but the rest of the games were blowouts and included three shutouts

(28–0 over Arizona State, 69–0 over Washington State, and 56–0 over Washington). They avenged their loss against Stanford and Harbaugh from the year before with a 45–23 win. And in the second-to-last game of the regular season, they humiliated Notre Dame and Charlie Weis in a 38–3 win. In that game, the Irish only gained nine yards in the first half and ninety-one in the entire game. Notre Dame did not have a first down until the last play of the third quarter and could only muster a total of four of them in the game.

But by that game, the Trojans pretty much knew their destiny. Four teams were ahead of them in the BCS rankings—Alabama, Texas, Oklahoma, and Florida—and USC's strength of schedule was weaker than the other teams' were. (Oregon State ended the regular season ranked twenty-fourth.) By the time the Trojans defeated UCLA in their final regular season game (28–7), their fate was sealed. They'd remained fifth in the BCS rankings. Oklahoma and Florida played in the title game, which Florida, led by Tim Tebow, won, 24–14, for its second title in three years. USC, having clinched the PAC-10 title for the seventh year in a row, was going to the Rose Bowl again, to play Penn State.

The Rose Bowl held the promise of being a competitive game. Penn State was 11–1 and had soundly beaten Oregon State during the season. It was also the first and only matchup between Carroll and the Nittany Lions legendary head coach Joe Paterno, who was eighty-two. Carroll was fifteen years old when Paterno began his head coaching career at Penn State.¶

But the game did not live up to its billing. USC rocketed out to a 31–7 lead by halftime and coasted to an eventual 38–24 win. Taylor Mays, the human missile, took out a Penn State player

---

¶ And Paterno still had three more seasons left in his career, which ended because of the child sex abuse scandal at the school.

and his teammate, Kevin Thomas, on a vicious—and, ultimately, illegal—helmet-to-*helmets* hit late in the third quarter. Sanchez, who was 28 for 35 for 413 yards and accounted for all of USC's touchdowns (four throwing, one rushing), was named the offensive MVP of the game. Linebacker Kaluka Maiava was the game's defensive MVP. The Trojans finished the season ranked third in the country.

"I don't think anybody could beat us," Carroll said after the game. "I wish we could keep playing."

"I know I'm biased, but we were the best team in the nation that year," says Matthews. "We should have been in the title game."

From 2002 to 2008, the Trojans went 82–9. The nine losses were by an average of four points.

A few weeks before the Rose Bowl, Sarkisian took the head coaching job at Washington (he stayed with USC through the game). He was one of the last of Carroll's original staff at USC (Rocky Seto and the strength coach, Chris Carlisle, remained). Carroll told the media that he was "proudly sending this guy off to his new job." Sarkisian took Nick Holt, another member of Carroll's original staff, with him to become his defensive coordinator. Did those coaches see something written on the wall? Holt says he left because "I just felt we played as well as we were going to play, and a lot of good players were leaving. It was time."

The departures meant another shuffling of assistants. Carroll hired an old colleague, Carl Smith—who'd been with him in New England and, later, at USC in 2004—to coach the quarterbacks and call the plays. But Smith lasted only two weeks before he bolted for the same job at the Cleveland Browns. So Carroll hired Jeremy Bates, the former quarterbacks coach of the

Broncos, to become his quarterbacks coach. John Morton took Sarkisian's place as the offensive coordinator. And Seto stepped up as the defensive coordinator.

More turnover. More getting people up to speed. A failure to mesh. "I didn't get along with Bates," says Ruel. "He didn't buy into Pete's way of doing things. He was kind of a tyrant."

Finding good assistants was becoming an increasingly difficult task for Carroll.

But the biggest change—and the one that ultimately might have been the breaking point for Carroll at USC—came a few weeks after the victory over Penn State.

During his tenure at USC, Carroll had developed a strategy that had worked very well. He would rebuild the defense when he started an established quarterback, like Palmer and Booty in their last seasons and Leinart in his last two. Conversely, he would feature a strong defense when breaking in a new quarterback, as he did the first seasons for Leinart and Booty.

His quarterbacks, with the exception of Palmer, whom he inherited, all spent time as backups, learning the system, and then had the starting job for at least two seasons.

By 2008, Sanchez had three years in the system. And that year, his first as a starter, the Trojans fielded an all-world defense, which helped him along. Carroll knew that in the 2009 season—with players like Matthews, Cushing, and Maualuga graduating—the pendulum would again swing to the offensive side, led by a confident and poised quarterback in his second year at the helm.

But Sanchez, as Carroll puts it, "broke the chain."

Palmer had come back for his last season with the Trojans because he needed another year of seasoning to improve his NFL Draft stock. Leinart, despite the fact that he likely would have been the first pick in the 2005 NFL Draft, came back for the fun, the chance at three titles in a row, and because he had some injuries.

And now Carroll needed Sanchez, who had one more year of eligibility, to do the same. In fact, he needed it quite desperately. Neither of Sanchez's backups—Mitch Mustain and Aaron Corp—had flashed. Carroll did have Matt Barkley, a five-star recruit, coming in, but he did not want a true freshman at the helm of his high-profile team.

Carroll had good reason to believe that Sanchez would return, especially in the wake of his magnificent performance in the Rose Bowl. After the game, Sanchez told the media it would be "hard to say goodbye to [USC]. I don't think I can do that."

But sometime in the weeks that followed that game, he changed his mind.

Sanchez says that shortly after the Rose Bowl, he started to think over things. "I was like, 'Okay, who do we have coming back? And is Coach coming back?' He said he was, but I didn't know for sure." There were other factors, as well. "I had already dislocated my kneecap and was like, 'Man, what if I get hurt again?' And Sark, who I'd spent a lot of time with, was leaving."

Sanchez says he went back home to Orange County and sat on the beach, mulling his decision. He called Palmer, Leinart, Booty, and even Peyton Manning to discuss the issue. He talked to his father and brothers. "My whole family wanted me to stay at USC for another year," he says.

On January 15, 2009, two weeks after the Rose Bowl, Sanchez called a press conference to announce his decision.

Carroll had begun working on Sanchez and Sanchez's father after the Rose Bowl and believed, at certain points in time, he had convinced his quarterback to stay. The night before the press conference, he went to Sanchez's apartment, still unsure of what Sanchez had decided. The two ate In-N-Out burgers as Carroll made his final pitch. He believed he had a strong case, based on his biggest piece of evidence, which was how poorly college quarterbacks with only one year as a starter under their belt fared in the NFL. "We just went back and forth all night," says Sanchez. "We would talk about the decision and then talk about something else for half an hour and then talk about the decision again. I couldn't say it flat-out to his face. But at the end of the night, I sort of said, 'I think I gotta go.'"

Carroll left Sanchez's apartment at one a.m., still not 100 percent sure of what Sanchez was going to do.

The press conference the next day was among the most awkward and bizarre episodes of Carroll's career as a football coach. It was either totally out of character, or wholly within it, depending on how you look at it.

When reporters were first brought into Heritage Hall, there were two chairs behind the table at the front of the room, with microphones, presumably for the quarterback and his coach. But one chair and one microphone were hastily removed minutes before the press conference was set to begin.

Sanchez entered the room and sat at the table. He described the decision at hand as "one of the toughest of my life," and then told the room that he had decided to declare for the NFL Draft. "It is with heavy heart that I say goodbye to this great university," he continued. And then he reminded the gathered group that he was forgoing his *fifth* year and not leaving school early. (He would graduate that spring with a communications degree.) He thanked the school president, Garrett, Carroll, his teammates, USC fans, and his family as he fought back tears. He ended with: "I will always fight on."

Sanchez stood up. Carroll, who had been standing nearby, gave him a quick and light hug and then took a seat at the table. He was, as the *Los Angeles Times* described him, "visibly unhappy."

After quickly congratulating Sanchez, Carroll delivered something that bordered on a diatribe. "We don't see this decision the same," he said. "Mark is going against the grain on this decision. He knows that . . . coming out early is a tremendous challenge for a quarterback and the stats don't back up that it's easy to be successful in the way he's going about it." And then he added, almost as an afterthought, "We wish him the very best in doing so."

Carroll took a few questions and reiterated that he was "disappointed that the information that we have wasn't compelling enough to make it clear." In all, he spoke for eight minutes, almost double the time Sanchez had spoken. And then he left abruptly, stopping for only a hasty handshake with his now former quarterback.

"Looking back, I hated that I had to say no to him because I love him so much," says Sanchez. "I think the way his feelings manifested themselves was for me, like, 'Woah. Dang. He's upset and actually personally mad at me.' Thankfully, it didn't hurt my draft position. We made up, but it definitely hurt."

"Pete totally embarrassed himself that day," says Petros Papadakis.

Carroll says his demeanor at the press conference is explained by the fact that he was "competing all the way up to the end" to try to get Sanchez to stay.

Even now, a decade and a half later, Carroll is unable to shake what he seems to see as a betrayal. "It was so frustrating when Mark took off," he says. "It was not the right time. He kinda promised me we were in this thing together. It screwed up the whole process."

And then he adds—competing forevermore, and maybe joking, but maybe not—"I'm still pissed at him."

CHAPTER NINETEEN

Not with a Bang

In the first game of the 2009 season, eighteen-year-old Matt Barkley became the first true freshman quarterback in USC history to start a season-opening game. In the game, the Trojans dismantled San Jose State, 56–3, led by the running backs, who combined for 342 yards on the ground. Barkley was proficient, going 15 for 19 for 233 yards and a touchdown.

But the rubber was about to meet the road. In their second game of the season, the third-ranked Trojans traveled to Columbus to play the eighth-ranked Ohio State Buckeyes. Going into it, Barkley says he was "oblivious to the magnitude of the game."

"Oblivious" in that he says he didn't really know that ESPN's *College Gameday*—the pregame show that always broadcasted from the site of the biggest game of the week—was in town and didn't know that 106,000 fans would be in attendance. "Oblivious" in that he says he "didn't know we were both highly ranked teams, and I didn't know who was favored" and didn't know why, when the USC buses made their way down fraternity row, hundreds of students showed up and "threw beer bottles at us and flipped us off."

"I was a naïve freshman," Barkley says. "But it was really more about Pete. He had us dialed in and believing that it was all about us and not them, and that this was just another game."

He quickly discovered that it was not just another game. "It was so loud in the stadium, like being next to the speakers at a concert," Barkley says. "We had to lip-read in the huddle, even during TV timeouts."

Barkley struggled for much of the game, going 15 for 31 for 195 yards with an interception. But he would come through when it mattered most.

With seven minutes and fifteen seconds left in the game, the Trojans trailed, 15–10. They had the ball on their own fourteen. A sack and then a false start put them back on the five. And then Barkley—with help from junior running back Joe McKnight—led the Trojans on a fourteen-play, clock-eating drive down the field, in which he coolly completed three passes and converted a fourth and one on a quarterback sneak. The drive culminated in a two-yard Stafon Johnson touchdown run, and a successful two-point conversion pass from Barkley to McKnight, which won the game, 18–15.

"Leinart had done something like that when he'd played his first game at Auburn. But he'd been with the program already," says Carroll. "For Barkley to pull that out with that crowd was frickin' awesome."

Barkley was a prodigy from early on. He started at powerhouse Mater Dei—Leinart's high school—as a freshman, the first to do so since Todd Marinovich in the mid-1980s. In a high school playoff game that year, Barkley had his collarbone broken on a tackle by Allen Bradford, his future teammate at USC. "Allen came on a blitz and dropped me, and I landed on my shoulder," says Barkley. "Three years later, I would end up handing the ball to him."[*]

Barkley was given the unusual responsibility of calling his own plays in high school. In his junior season, he was named California's Gatorade Player of the Year and was recruited by nearly

---

[*] Remember, Bradford converted from linebacker to running back at USC.

every big program in the country. "I talked to Nick Saban [at Al-abama], David Cutcliffe [at Tennessee], and Jim Harbaugh [at Stanford]," he says.

But USC was always at the top of his list. "I'm a third-generation Trojan and grew up watching the golden era, from Carson to Leinart and Reggie, the national titles, the Heismans," says Barkley. He ended up graduating from high school early and enrolling at USC in the spring of 2009. "I wanted to get into the system and get things started," he says. "I thought I was going to back up Sanchez, and I was ready to put in the time and wait it out. I did not anticipate walking in there and starting as a fresh-man. But when Mark left, that door opened for me. I was fine with that, but I had to adapt."

Garrett Nolan says Barkley came into the program projecting a confidence that he hadn't necessarily earned. "But I don't blame him for that," he says. "He had to."

In the spring and fall training camps, Barkley competed with Mustain, the Arkansas transfer, and Aaron Corp, a redshirt soph-omore. Barkley had his struggles—he threw many interceptions and in one important scrimmage, he only completed five of eigh-teen passes. In the early going, Corp had the upper hand and was presumed to be the starter after spring practice. But late in the summer he injured his leg, and Barkley seized the opportunity. "Near the end of training camp—it might have been the week before the first game—Coach Carroll took me into his office and told me I'd earned the starting job," says Barkley.

His coaches knew, though, that they were in for some turbu-lence. "We'd trained ourselves on having quarterbacks sit for two to three years and then get to play two," says Ruel. "And all of a sudden, we have a true freshman and he's throwing out patterns into Cover Two and I'm like, 'Uh-oh.'"

Carroll was encouraged by what he'd seen from his team in the first two games. The Trojans weren't world-beaters—not yet, anyway—but Barkley had been competent and cool under pressure, and the young defense had played better than expected. The hope was that the next two games—against Washington and Washington State, two poor teams the Trojans had destroyed the year before—would provide Barkley and the defense with time to grow and learn.

But the team's success also hinged on something else: a good running game. In the previous two seasons, USC had employed a "running back by committee" strategy, rotating through its stable of five-stars throughout games and throughout the season, trying to find the hot hand. The Trojans' offensive line coach didn't love the approach. "You can't play them all," says Ruel. "You have to find your warhorse and anoint him so that he buys in and is not trying too hard on each play. A running back might not see [the holes] in the first quarter, but he will see them better in the second, third, and fourth. We were just putting guys in there, trying to make them all happy."

Carroll and the Trojans had spent years signing five-star running backs in an attempt to replicate Bush. Thus far, they had not come close to doing so. But there was hope that in 2009, they finally had.

In the spring of 2003, Nick Saban, then the head coach at LSU, visited John Curtis Christian, a high school in River Ridge, Louisiana, a suburb of New Orleans. He was there to scout some of the team's junior players. But in one drill, J. T. Curtis Jr., the team's coach,[†] put a rising freshman in the backfield. The rising freshman took a pitch on an option, got the edge, and burned past the defenders.

---

† And son of the founder of the school.

"Nick turned to me with an incredulous look and said, 'Who is that?'" says Curtis.

It was Joe McKnight.

McKnight grew up in Kenner, another suburb of New Orleans, located between the Mississippi River and Lake Pontchartrain. Before his junior year in high school, he was forced to evacuate his home because of Hurricane Katrina. He went to Shreveport for a while and then returned home to find that the family house was gone.

McKnight's father wasn't around, having left the family when Joe was young, and his mother moved away after Katrina. So McKnight moved in with Curtis, his football coach. His team played a truncated season in 2005 because of the hurricane and won a state championship and then won another the next season. In the process, McKnight became something of a folk hero, someone people cheered for to take their minds off the terrible devastation of Katrina. He was the best football player in the state. Many also believed he was the best in the nation.

It was assumed by nearly everyone in Louisiana that their native star would attend their native school, LSU, which was then coached by Saban's replacement, Les Miles. McKnight had many suitors, but narrowed his choices down to LSU, Ole Miss . . . and USC. "Joe was a good, levelheaded kid," says Curtis. "Because of his personality, he did not like to be singled out. He wanted to be part of a team. I tried to tell recruiters that, but they didn't listen. They had Joe ride in the coach's car or put him on a separate tour from the other recruits or had a cutout of him posing with the Heisman. Most schools recruited him that way. But USC didn't. They made him feel like a top recruit, but he did what the rest of the recruits did. Carroll made that happen."

Still, Miles, LSU, and most everyone else believed that McKnight wasn't leaving the state. Miles visited McKnight at the last permissible hour in the recruiting process, he thought, to seal the deal.

But the next day, McKnight, at his high school, made his announcement: he was going to USC. There were audible gasps in the audience. A few people left the building in anger. McKnight received death threats. And, ten days later, his high school's float was booed at a Mardi Gras parade. "Joe wanted to get away from Louisiana because he felt like he was going to be pulled in so many different directions by his local friends if he stayed," says Curtis.

The backlash against McKnight and USC intensified after the announcement because of a controversy. On a radio show, McKnight said he had spoken to Carroll and Reggie Bush on a conference call, because he was worried about the possibility that USC would face sanctions because of the ongoing NCAA investigation of Bush. According to NCAA rules, former players were not allowed to speak to recruits. Curtis intensified the controversy when he told the *Los Angeles Times* that "Carroll was talking to Reggie on a speakerphone and Joe was able to listen and hear Reggie Bush's side of the story."

Carroll denied it happened. Informed of that denial, Curtis later told the *Los Angeles Times* that he talked to McKnight and received a clarification: McKnight had merely spoken to Carroll *about* Bush.

The NCAA investigated the matter and ultimately found no wrongdoing.

But McKnight never escaped the shadow of Bush.

His host on his official tour of USC was Thomas Williams, a linebacker who was Bush's old roommate and best friend on the team. Even McKnight's coaches let the comparison slip. In the Rose Bowl game against Illinois at the end of his freshman season in 2007, McKnight had a very Bush-like game, with 206 all-purpose yards (125 on the ground). After the game, Sarkisian called him "Reggie-ish," and Carroll told the media, "We searched to find somebody to take kind of the style of play that we had a few years ago with Reggie. There's no question that Joe can do similar stuff."

The comparison did McKnight no favors. As Curtis says, he just wanted to play and be part of the team and not be singled out.

McKnight struggled with fumbling issues in that freshman year and caught flak for wearing eye black that read "I need $" in a game. In his sophomore year in 2008, he was slowed by a nagging injury to his foot. But he was always a good teammate. Barkley describes him as "quiet." Alex Parsons says he was "a genuinely nice guy and very low-key."

But the comparisons to Bush were burdensome. "It was unfair, and it had an effect on him, from the media and the fans, trying to live up to expectations," says Chris Galippo.

"Joe had a lot of pressure on his shoulders," says the center Michael Reardon.

The USC coaches worried about the company he kept on the team, too, especially with Thomas Herring, an offensive tackle who spent much of his five years in the program injured and in the coaches' doghouse. Herring was a former five-star recruit who had suffered through two knee injuries and an Achilles tendon tear. He was from a rough part of Los Angeles and carried a gun when he went out on the town. Because of his injuries, and because he had not lived up to his billing, his coaches bullied him, he says. They either ignored him or made fun of him—he tore his Achilles when, in one practice, they took him out of offensive line drills and made him run routes with the tight ends. They made him sit in the back of the meeting rooms. The bullying got so bad, Herring says, that he sometimes sat outside of the house of one of his coaches at night. (He won't say if he had his gun with him or not.)

"Joe and I were best friends," says Herring. "He went through a lot in his life, and I was a person he could talk to."

The coaches, Herring says, believed that he was a bad influence on McKnight and was negatively affecting the running back's play on the field. "I got called out of class one day to meet with the coaches," says Herring. "And Coach Carroll and Sark said, 'We don't want you to hang out with Joe anymore. We don't think it's in his best interest.' I asked why, and the room went silent. No one could tell me." Herring says McKnight later told Carroll that if he couldn't hang out with Herring, he'd go back to Louisiana. That swiftly ended that prohibition.

Herring suspects the coaches believed he had a poor work ethic and that it was rubbing off on McKnight, or believed that Herring might somehow get McKnight involved in the gangs in his neighborhood. "But all we did was smoke weed," says Herring. "We both did it for stress. And I was the one who encouraged him to stop smoking it in his last season."

That last season was 2009, and it started with the best rushing game of McKnight's career: 145 yards gained and two touchdowns against San Jose State. In the next game, against Ohio State, he was again the team's leading rusher (sixty yards against a stingy defense) and was an integral part of the fourth-quarter drive that won the game, touching the ball six times and gaining fifty-three yards and catching the two-point conversion. That season, Mc-Knight became the first USC running back to rush for more than 1,000 yards since Bush and White had done it in 2005.

It appeared that, finally, Carroll had found what he'd been searching for.

On September 9, USC traveled to Seattle to meet Sarkisian, Holt, and the Washington Huskies. Washington had beaten Idaho at home the week before, the team's first win in its last sixteen games. The game against USC looked like a mere formality. The

Trojans had beaten the Huskies 56–0 in 2008 and were favored by twenty-one points.

There was one problem, though. Barkley had injured his shoulder in the second half against Ohio State, a bone bruise that made throwing difficult. Just before the Washington game, Carroll told backup Aaron Corp that he would be starting.

At kickoff, the day was gloomy and rainy but the crowd boisterous. Their spirits dampened by midway through the first quarter. The Trojans had a 10–0 lead, and it looked like the game would be a repeat of seasons past. McKnight and Stafon Johnson were running well. "Our game plan had been to run the ball," says Alex Parsons. "We ran this one play four to five times in the first quarter and got huge chunk plays every time. And then we stopped running it, which was confusing, and Corp got nervous and shaky. And then the game felt different."

Washington, behind quarterback Jake Locker and receiver Jermaine Kearse,[†] began to "mop the floor with us," says Galippo. The Trojans had two turnovers—an interception and a fumble—deep in Washington territory. Corp finished an anemic 13 for 22 for 110 yards with an interception. And Locker and Kearse led a ten-play drive that ended with a game-winning field goal with three seconds left. Final score: 16–13, Washington. "We're not good right now," Carroll said after the game. "We were not really good last week, either, to tell the truth."

"Sark knew the personnel to exploit our defense," says Barkley. "He literally went after one of our cornerbacks all night."

And Holt apparently had a bead on the offense. McKnight told the media that Washington defenders were calling out Trojan plays on the field before they happened.

Two days after the loss, USC's student newspaper *The Daily Trojan* offered its first real criticism of the coach who had saved

---

[†] Kearse would play for Carroll a few years later at the Seahawks.

the program, with a story that was headlined "Carroll Is Responsible for the Latest Letdown."

After a bounce-back 27–6 win over Washington State, USC suffered another blow: the running back Stafon Johnson dropped a bar on his throat while lifting weights and nearly died, requiring an emergency seven-hour surgery. He never played another down for the Trojans. His loss was significant—he was the already-shaky team's emotional leader and its second-best tailback.

USC then defeated Cal, 30–3, and, after a bye week, traveled to South Bend to play Notre Dame and held on for a seven-point win (and more or less ended Weis's Notre Dame coaching career). The next week, the Trojans avenged their 2008 loss to Oregon State, winning 42–36.

And suddenly the season again seemed promising for the Trojans. They were 6–1, number five in the nation, and set to face number ten Oregon in Eugene on Halloween night.

The state of Oregon—and its two teams—had become a place of dread for the Trojans, who had lost in their last three trips there (in 2006 and 2008 to Oregon State and in 2007 to Oregon). "I hated the state of Oregon," says Alex Parsons. The 2009 game against Oregon would only reinforce that sentiment.

For a while in the game, it appeared that USC and Oregon were in for a dogfight. They traded blows in the first half. Oregon led 24–17 at halftime. But then the Ducks blew the game open.

The Trojan defense could do nothing to stop the no-huddle, spread-option offense (known as "the Blur") of Chip Kelly, who was in his first year as the Oregon head coach after serving two years as the team's offensive coordinator. Behind the running of LaMichael James (183 yards rushing) and the running and passing of quarterback Jeremiah Masoli (164 yards rushing and 222 yards passing), the Ducks put up forty-seven points and 613 yards of offense on the Trojan defense, the most ever on a Carroll-coached USC team. The 47–20 final score was also the largest margin of defeat during the Carroll era (the previous largest margin had been eleven points in a loss to Notre Dame in Carroll's first year). That record would not stand for too long. "That was a real mess," was how Carroll described it after the game. And it was about to get a lot messier.

After a tight 14–9 win at Arizona State, a game in which USC had nearly as many penalty yards (98) as passing ones (112), the Trojans were set to face Stanford at home, the site, of course, of their upset loss to Harbaugh and the Cardinal in 2007.

Stanford raced out to a 21–7 lead. The Trojans fought back to get within seven, 28–21, near the end of the third quarter.

And then Stanford quarterback Andrew Luck threw a twenty-four-yard touchdown pass to open the fourth quarter. And Richard Sherman, now a cornerback, once again broke the Trojans, intercepting a Barkley pass and returning it forty-three yards for a touchdown. The rout was on.

Later in the game, after Stanford running back Toby Gerhart scored his third touchdown of the day to put the Cardinal up, 48–21, Harbaugh elected to go for two, presumably to reach the fifty-point mark. The Cardinal didn't convert, but the USC players—and their coach—were miffed that they had even tried it in a blowout win. Stanford later added one more touchdown, completing the utterly embarrassing 55–21 triumph over the Trojans. It was Carroll's first loss as USC's coach in the month of November (he'd been 28–0).

The fifty-five points were the most given up by a Trojan team in the program's 121-year history. The thirty-four-point loss was the worst for USC since the 1960s. Stanford ran for 325 yards in total (Gerhart had 178 of them). Luck passed for two touchdowns. Barkley had a nightmarish game, with a fumble and three interceptions. McKnight, with 142 yards rushing, was the only Trojan who had a good game.

As the final seconds of the game ticked off, a dazed Carroll walked to midfield to meet Harbaugh. The two men did a brief, cold handshake and then Carroll asked:

"What's your deal? You all right?"

Harbaugh, with a quizzical look on his face, shot back, "Yeah, I'm good. What's *your* deal?" And then they parted ways.[5]

Carroll was likely wondering about, in specific, the failed two-point conversion but also, in general, Harbaugh's entire vibe since he'd entered the PAC-10 three seasons before.

All the air had gone out of the Trojan dynasty. "I'm not of clear mind right now," Carroll said after the game. "I'm not really sure how to deal with this."

In many ways in 2009, Carroll had tried to do things as he always had. During the fall camp, a man came to practice who said he was a representative of the NCAA and told the team he was there to talk about a shower fungus that had been ravaging locker rooms across the country, "the only fungus that I know associated with bone damage," he said. The man's assistant, a woman, then

---

[5] Not for long, though. The Carroll-Harbaugh rivalry would continue in the NFL a few years later—with Carroll as the coach of the Seahawks and Harbaugh the coach of the 49ers—with some memorable exchanges. Carroll likes to downplay the rivalry, calling it a media creation and saying, "I respected the crap out of him, even if he was loony tunes." Carroll says that once at a cocktail party during NFL meetings, Harbaugh's wife approached Glena and him and said, "Jim won't come over here, but I just wanted to meet you." Carroll says he laughed and asked where he was. "She pointed across the room, and there he was standing there and just staring at us. I said, 'Go get him and bring him over here.' And she said, 'Oh, no, he won't come over here.'" Carroll and Harbaugh resumed their rivalry in the AFC West division in 2025, where Carroll coaches the Raiders and Harbaugh coaches the Chargers.

told the team they would have to start wearing special knee-high shoes in the shower.

The room went completely quiet. And then the man said, "You guys have been punked, big-time."

The man was singer/songwriter Bill Withers (the assistant was his daughter). Carroll had contacted Withers after a video of Trojan freshman Marquis Simmons singing the Withers classic "Lean on Me" to the team had made the rounds on the internet.

Withers brought Simmons up as he sat down at the piano in the room. Withers played a few chords from his song and then asked Simmons to sing it a capella as the team clapped and eventually joined in, arms around one another's shoulders, weaving back and forth as one.

And on a rare rainy practice day, Carroll staged a contest between Ruel and defensive line coach Jethro Franklin—two of his ample-bellied assistants—to see which one could slide the farthest after bellyflopping into a puddle.

But something was off the entire season, his players say. "Pete got a little out of character," says Garrett Nolan. "During practice before the Stanford game, he had us all meet in the locker room, something he never did. You could tell he wasn't feeling comfortable, which made us all feel uncomfortable. He kept talking about getting our heads right. And I was like, 'Why are you doing this here and now and not in the team meeting room?'"

"In hindsight, I think the team started to maybe sense that Pete wasn't as engaged or energetic as he usually was," says Galippo. Parsons agrees: "He didn't have the same intensity as years prior."

Off the field the vibe was different, as well. "Pete by that time wasn't even doing USC booster and alumni events," says Petros Papadakis. "He was putting on his leather jacket and going downtown to LA Live and hanging out with guys like Anschutz [Philip Anschutz, a billionaire who owned an entertainment company and the NHL's Los Angeles Kings] and Tim Leiweke [a businessman who ran Anschutz's sports company]."

And Carroll's relationship with his boss only in name had become frayed, with shouting matches becoming his primary mode of communicating with Garrett. In a radio interview with Petros Papadakis after the season, Garrett publicly called out the coach who had saved his job and made him look like a genius: "I was very dismayed by our whole season," he said. "I don't think we had one good game."

Home crowds diminished—what was once a sold-out Coliseum now had 10,000 empty seats. Celebrities still showed up on occasion—like mainstays Snoop and Ferrell—but their numbers thinned considerably, the Trojans no longer the draw they once were, the buzz magnet having lost much of its pull in LA, where only success attracted the successful.

USC limped into its rivalry game against UCLA but dominated on defense from the get-go. The game was well over by the time USC got the ball on the UCLA forty-eight, up 21–7, with fifty-four seconds to go. Carroll instructed Barkley to kneel on first down, to bleed out the clock. Then Rick Neuheisel, UCLA's coach, called a timeout. An unnecessary one, Carroll believed. So the USC coach did, essentially, what Harbaugh had tried to do to him the game before. "I went over to the bench for the timeout and met Pete and Jeremy [Bates, the offensive coordinator]," says Barkley. "And Pete said, 'Let's call a deep shot and stick it in them.'" And that's just what they did, with Barkley connecting on a deep touchdown pass to Damian Williams to make the score 28–7. The two teams met on the field after the play and nearly came to blows.

After the final whistle, Carroll went to midfield to meet Neuheisel, the same coach—then at Washington—that he had met at midfield in 2001, and said, "Don't get too comfortable at the top. You know, it's not going to take us very long."

This time, according to the *Los Angeles Times*, Carroll said, "We've been saying it for years, living it for years . . . just compete."

"I don't forget very much," Neuheisel replied, perhaps already thinking ahead to a rematch. A rematch that would never happen.

The Trojans' 2009 season ended, fittingly, with a thud, a 21–17 loss to Arizona.[§] USC was selected to play in the Emerald Bowl against Boston College, in Carroll's birth city of San Francisco. For the first time since Carroll's first season in 2001, the Trojans had failed to win the PAC-10. And for the first time since 2002, they finished the season outside of the top four in the season's final rankings.

The Emerald Bowl was to be played on the day after Christmas. The weeks leading up to it were by no means quiet.

Just before USC's last game of the regular season, Charlie Weis was fired by Notre Dame. Weis had made his name—and fortune—off the 2005 Bush Push game, a game that ended up being one of the most significant in Notre Dame football's history, but not in a positive way. Buoyed by the team's performance in that game, Notre Dame had locked up Weis after it in a ten-year deal that reportedly paid between $30 million and $40 million.

Weis would have one more decent season with the Irish, and then everything went south. In his five years as the head coach, the Irish averaged just seven wins a season. When Weis was fired at the end of the 2009 season, ESPN reported that, with his contract and the buyouts, Notre Dame ended up paying him around $50 million. In five tries, Weis never beat USC.

After Weis was fired, he held an impromptu meeting with five reporters. He complained to them about how he'd been portrayed

---

[§] That loss meant that Arizona State was the only PAC-10 team that never beat Carroll.

in the media—60 *Minutes* had done a profile of him that showed him swearing, which caused a stir at his Catholic university. But in particular, he lamented how he'd been portrayed in the media in contrast to Carroll, with whom he'd had a cool relationship dating back to their shared NFL days. Only one of the media members present—Tim Prister of Irishillustrated.com—wrote about it. ("He never said it was off the record," says Prister.)

In the meeting, Weis said:

> Let me ask you this question. You guys know about things that go on in different places. Was I living with a grad student in Malibu, or was I living with my wife in my house? You could bet that if I were living with a grad student here in South Bend, it would be national news. He's doing it in Malibu and it's not national news. What's the difference? I don't understand. Why is it okay for one guy to do things like that, but for me, I'm scrutinized when I swear? I'm sorry for swearing. Absolve my sins.

Weis was quite obviously referring to Carroll,** and the story blew up on the internet. "It's untrue, it's irresponsible, and it's incredible he'd be talking about me like that," Carroll responded.

Weis later tried to clarify that he was using the story as a hypothetical example of how "the rumor mill can affect people's lives," something he'd proven, inadvertently or not, with his statement.

At the NFL Combine that year, Weis saw Carroll and approached him. "He did apologize," says Carroll. "But it was way too late." After Weis said his piece, Carroll walked away without saying a word.

And a week before the Emerald Bowl, USC announced that it was investigating McKnight over the use of a 2006 Land Rover

---

** The roots of that rumor may have stemmed from June 2008, when Carroll was involved in a minor car accident in Malibu.

that he'd been spotted driving, one that was owned by a Santa Monica marketer who had also registered the website domain name "4joemcknight.com." The use of the vehicle would have violated NCAA rules and, of course, compounded any trouble USC might find itself in because of the ongoing Bush investigation. Nothing ever came of the probe into McKnight, but the school's compliance department did not clear the running back for the bowl game. Three other players—offensive tackle Tyron Smith, tight end Anthony McCoy, and defensive tackle Averell Spicer—were also out for the game after being declared academically ineligible.

And on a dreary, rainy, fifty-seven-degree day, the Trojans' season came to an end with a 24–13 win over Boston College. Barkley threw for 350 yards and two touchdowns and ran for another. He ended the season with 2,735 passing yards, fifteen touchdowns, and fourteen interceptions. He would go on to become a four-year starter and, by the end of his USC career, would be the school's all-time leader in passing yards and passing touchdowns.

"I remember being in the locker room after that game and a couple of guys who were underclassmen were basically saying outright, 'I'm going to the league,'" says Galippo. "Whatever it was, there was something in the water that year, with some of our best players basically saying, 'I'm done with this.' That was maybe a sentiment that was felt by a lot more people than we thought at the time, both coaches and players."

McKnight and Everson Griffen were two of the players who decided to leave USC early after that season.[††]

[††] McKnight would be drafted by the Jets and play four seasons in the NFL and one season in the Canadian Football League. He was killed in 2016 in a road rage shooting in Louisiana.

A 9–4 season would be a pretty good one for most teams in the country. But for the Trojans of the Pete Carroll era, given the expectations they'd set for themselves, 2009 was a shocking disappointment.

There were excuses, many of them valid. USC had lost an incredible amount of talent from the year before, particularly on defense. And they'd lost Sanchez, which meant they were forced to start a true freshman at quarterback. The brain and culture drain had continued on the coaching staff when they lost mainstays Sarkisian and Holt. They'd missed out on some recruits, possibly because of the coaching changes—linebacker Manti Te'o was planning on going to USC but switched late to Notre Dame. And they'd had bad luck: two highly touted linebacker recruits, Frankie Telfort and Jarvis Jones, never played a down with the Trojans because of injuries.[‡‡]

But there was more to it. There was a feeling of entitlement. "There became this expectation that we'd at least be in the Rose Bowl every year," says Galippo. "We fell into a bad habit of guys thinking that just because there's a Trojan on their helmet that we would win games."

There was also, possibly, something else at play. "In hindsight, maybe the coaching staff was aware of what was coming down and maybe started looking into the market for where they might end up next," says Galippo.

One of those coaches who might have been looking ahead to some different future was Carroll himself.

[‡‡] Telfort had a heart condition and had to quit playing football. Jones suffered a neck injury his freshman year and was diagnosed with spinal stenosis. The Trojan medical staff wouldn't clear him to play, so he transferred to Georgia and eventually became a first-round pick in the NFL.

Carroll always knew he had something special at USC. "Pete would often stop practice and turn around and tell the players and coaches, 'You know, you guys aren't going to have this forever,'" says Ruel. "'You better enjoy every minute of it.'"

But by 2009, Carroll also realized that things might have run their course. "We got further away from what made it special," he says. "We suffered a lack of humility. The continuity wasn't as good. I didn't maintain the level of appreciation for being there and everyone felt entitled, like 'We're here, we're going to win.' It's really a natural thing that happens. If you let it get away, the guys aren't going to be worth a shit compared to what they could be. They underachieve. I think that's what happened."

College football had changed, too. That season, Alabama won the national title, the beginning of Nick Saban's dominant era there, which would end with six championships. And the PAC-10—thanks mainly to Carroll, as Mike Riley said—had improved dramatically. That climb back up to the top of the mountain had grown steeper, perhaps impossibly so. And that had Carroll thinking ahead to a different challenge, looking for another mountain to ascend. "The part of it that pissed me off even to admit was that it was going to be so hard to get back to there. It was so frustrating and heartbreaking to think back to that Double B blitz for that third title, to something that had never been done before—that was our first loss in thirty-five games—and I didn't know how we could ever get back to that.

"I was just realizing that we had done about everything we could possibly do, and I was open to what else was out there."

CHAPTER TWENTY

Sleepless in Seattle

During Carroll's tenure at USC, there were rumors nearly every year about job offers from NFL teams. Many of those rumors were actually true. The 49ers, after firing George Seifert's replacement, Steve Mariucci, in 2002, wanted Carroll. "Pete told me he got the offer for what was really his dream job," says Seamus Callanan. "I said, 'Congrats.' And he turned to me and said, 'I can't take it. We haven't accomplished what we set out to do here.'"

In 2007, Dolphins owner Wayne Huizenga was so eager to hire Carroll that he flew down to see him in Costa Rica, where Carroll was on vacation after the season. Carroll says now that during his time at USC, he also had interviews with the Atlanta Falcons, Washington Redskins, Houston Texans, and San Diego Chargers. "It had become apparent that I could be an NFL coach, that it could happen again," he says. "I was open to that thought. I was open to the challenge. I always loved the NFL."

But it had to be the right timing. More than that, it had to be the right place and situation. What Carroll wanted—really, demanded—was something he did not have in his first two jobs in the NFL but *did* have at USC: total control of not only the team on the field but also the shaping of the roster.

Given their history, the Seattle Seahawks would have seemed to be one of the last NFL teams to cede general manager-like control to a head coach. After all, they'd tried it just years before and it had failed.

Mike Holmgren, after leading the Green Bay Packers to two Super Bowls—and winning one of them[*]—became the head coach of the Seahawks after the 1998 season. He was also the team's general manager. But the arrangement didn't work out—in Holmgren's first four seasons with the Seahawks, the team went a mediocre 31–33, including 7–9 in 2002. After that season, the team stripped Holmgren of his general manager duties. And then he went on to make the playoffs the next five seasons, including an appearance in the Super Bowl. He retired after the 2008 season, and the Seahawks hired Jim Mora Jr.—Holmgren's defensive backs coach—to replace him.

Mora had a rough season as the coach. The Seahawks got off to an abysmal start to the year, going 3–7. The team's general manager was fired in the middle of the season. And Seattle finished the year at 5–11. Seahawks president Tod Leiweke (brother of Tim Leiweke) and owner Paul Allen were unhappy with the team's record and the dropping home attendance numbers. But they also worried about Mora's maturity level—he'd impetuously called out his kicker in a press conference during the season, among other things. As the season skidded to its completion, Leiweke came under some pressure—he'd been the one who'd recommended Mora and the one who'd fired the team's general manager. Leiweke knew that though his boss, Allen—the polymathic Microsoft billionaire who was fond of big ideas and

---

[*] Beating the Bill Parcells–led New England Patriots after the 1996 season, the year before Carroll took over that team.

unconventional approaches—was a patient man, there were limits to that patience.

Leiweke pondered a change at head coach. He considered talking to some of the usual names, like Bill Cowher and Tony Dungy. And then he wondered: Would Pete Carroll be willing to leave USC?

During the week leading up to the Emerald Bowl, Carroll received a call from his agent, who told him the Seahawks were interested in him. He told his agent that he would speak to Seattle after the bowl game. (By coincidence, the Seahawks' general counsel Lance Lopes was the brother of USC's senior associate athletic director Steve Lopes.)

With Carroll willing to speak, Leiweke now had to convince his boss that the coach, if he accepted the job, would be the right person for the franchise. Which meant, really, that he had to convince Bert Kolde, Allen's old college roommate, who acted, basically, as his consigliere when it came to decisions about his sports teams. (Kolde had advised Allen on his 1997 purchase of the Seahawks and his 1988 purchase of the NBA's Portland Trail Blazers.)

Leiweke arranged a visit with Carroll. He and Lance Lopes and Kolde flew to Los Angeles and met Carroll and his agent for dinner. Leiweke and Lopes were already on board with the hiring. The meeting was all about persuading Kolde, as well as Carroll. And much to Leiweke's relief, Kolde immediately liked Carroll.

As for persuading Carroll, the USC coach was told that while he wouldn't be the Seahawks' general manager in name, he would help hire the person for that position and would have the final say in all football operations, including personnel. Carroll liked the plan, and an informal offer was made to him. Carroll asked for some time to think about the decision while he was with his family on vacation in Hawaii. During that time, he spoke to Allen on the phone. After that conversation, Carroll called Leiweke.

"I'm in," he said.

It was the same phrase he'd asked the members of his first team at USC to use to demonstrate their commitment to his program.

"The Seahawks came around at the right time and it happened," says Carroll.

Rocky Seto remembers the eerie quiet in Heritage Hall the week after the Emerald Bowl. "We had extra time away from each other because we were used to playing a bowl game in the new year," he says. By then, some rumors about Carroll and the Seahawks had surfaced online. "And Pete didn't immediately deny them as he usually did with those types of rumors," says Seto.

Mora was fired by the Seahawks on January 8, 2010, joining Carroll on the infamous list of NFL coaches who were let go after only one season at the helm. Mora told a radio station afterward that he was "stunned" because he had met with Leiweke only a few days before he was fired and had been given a vote of confidence. He had also conducted a postseason press conference, which was usually a sure sign that a coach was returning.

By January 10, the Seahawks had come to an agreement with Carroll. That evening, he called a meeting with some of his USC players and coaches and told them that he was leaving. He likened himself to his players, saying that, just like them, he also dreamed of being in the NFL and now had his chance. His coaches and staff were caught off guard. "I was blown away because Pete gave us all every indication that he saw USC as a place he wanted to be for the duration," says Ruel. "It was a shock to all of us."

"I was like, 'There's no way he's going to leave.' I thought he would be the John Wooden of college football, Saban before Saban," says Ben Malcomson. "When he told me, I was silent, so shocked."

Carroll's players felt the same way. "That was a day I'll never forget," says Barkley. "It was my first lesson in the business of football. The team meeting was a blur. I was like, 'Is this really happening now?' My head was spinning afterwards. I felt like I had been punched in the gut."

"One hundred percent of the team was heartbroken," says Ayles. "We weren't expecting it."

Some players even internalized it and thought maybe *they* were to blame for Carroll's departure. "It was heartbreaking but as an adult I understand it now," says David Ausberry, a five-star receiver in the 2006 recruiting class. "I thought maybe I was part of the reason he was leaving because I was the fastest guy in the country in high school and wasn't panning out. I thought maybe he was leaving because some of us didn't turn out what we were expected to be."

Other players looked elsewhere for answers. "There was a rumor that Carroll had met with the Seahawks ownership sometime around the Washington game that season, that, under secrecy, he'd committed to them," says Parsons. "I heard it from someone who was going to go with him there." Ausberry and Galippo heard the same rumor. (Carroll denies it.)

The day after the team meeting, Carroll held a press conference and announced he was taking the job as the Seahawks' new head coach. He had signed a five-year deal worth nearly $33 million.

ESPN once referred to Carroll's tenure at USC as "Carroll's Camelot." He had won two national championships and seven straight PAC-10 titles. He coached three Heisman Trophy winners. His overall record was 97–19 (a winning percentage of 83.6). The Trojans spent 103 consecutive weeks ranked in the AP poll, with sixty-two of those weeks ranked in the top five and a record thirty-three consecutive weeks ranked number one. There was also the thirty-four-game winning streak, the seven straight BCS bowl game appearances (with six wins), the record sixty-three-game streak of scoring twenty or more points. Under Carroll, USC had thirty-four first-team All-Americans and fifty-three NFL Draft choices (the exact number of players on a full NFL team) and an identical 8–1 record against each of USC's biggest rivals, UCLA and Notre Dame.

But Carroll's legacy was also about how his football program, in becoming the biggest show in the sport, lifted the entire school. USC had $1.4 billion in revenue in 2001, Carroll's first season. By 2007,[†] that number had risen to $2.5 billion. The USC athletics department went from $38.6 million in revenue in 2001 to $76 million in 2007, a gain driven almost solely by football.

And it was about more than just the money. The year before Carroll joined the Trojans, USC (once known as the "University of Spoiled Children") was number forty-two in the *US News & World Report* annual college rankings list. By the time Carroll left, the school had risen to twenty-seven.

If there is an oddity to the Carroll era at USC, it is that many of his most talented and highest-profile players did not pan out as expected in the NFL. Palmer's career was derailed by a devastating knee injury. Leinart started only eighteen games in a seven-year NFL career. Sanchez played for eight seasons in the NFL and took his team to the AFC Championship game in his first two years but ended his career with eighty-six touchdown passes and eighty-nine interceptions. Booty never took a snap in the NFL. Barkley was a career backup. Cassel, oddly enough, arguably had the best NFL career among Carroll's USC quarterbacks—odd, because he never started as a Trojan. Mike Williams and Dwayne

---

[†] The year before the financial crisis, when most entities in the country took a hit to their top and bottom lines.

Jarrett had disappointing stints in the NFL. Bush was never as electric in the pros as he was in college. White had a hard time staying in shape.

There are exceptions, of course. Ryan Kalil was a two-time NFL All-Pro, and so was Tyron Smith (he was also named to the NFL 2010s All-Decade Team). But the best player of the Carroll era at USC—Troy Polamalu, who won two Super Bowls and is a member of the Pro Football Hall of Fame—was recruited by Hackett.

So was it the case that the Trojan stars played in college for a players' coach who made the game fun and then suddenly found themselves on a team—or a level—where the game was more of a business? That they went from an authoritative coach in college to an authoritarian one in the NFL and didn't—or couldn't— make the adjustment?

Or did Carroll just put together such incredible aggregations of talent—talent far superior to all but a few of their opponents— which made the individual players look better than they actually were?

The answer likely lies somewhere within these explanations.

CHAPTER TWENTY-ONE

Crime and Punishment

There was the initial spark that looked like it was not going to catch, not at the beginning. But then came the great gust, and that small flickering fire took hold and gained strength and confidence. And it grew and grew until it produced what felt like the heat of the sun. As it continued to burn, the fire occasionally shuddered, only to recover in strength. It blazed brightly until, finally, starved of oxygen, it engulfed itself and was given over to time, becoming that "great thing that shall be told among men hereafter," as Homer wrote in *The Iliad*.

The Pete Carroll era at USC was over.

But it never really ended.

The NCAA wrapped up its three-year-and-eight-months-long investigation of the Reggie Bush allegations on January 11, 2010 . . . *the exact same day* Carroll was announced as the new head coach of the Seattle Seahawks.

The very next day, Garrett hired Lane Kiffin to replace Carroll. Kiffin had coached the Raiders in 2007 but was fired four games into the 2008 season. He was scooped up by the University of Tennessee in 2009 and finished that season 7–6, with a young team that had showed promise. And now he left that program jilted, on his way back to the Trojans.

Kiffin held a press conference in Knoxville to announce his departure from Tennessee. It was not a good idea. Drunk and angry students—feeling betrayed by their coach—gathered outside of the building hosting the press conference, causing a near riot and burning a mattress. Kiffin was eventually snuck out of the building at three a.m.

He flew to Los Angeles and was announced as the Trojans' new coach. He hired his father, Monte, as an assistant head coach, Orgeron as his defensive coordinator, Kennedy Pola as his running backs coach, and former USC wide receiver Keary Colbert as a graduate assistant. Kiffin knew he'd be in a bit of a tight spot because National Signing Day was only three weeks away. But he had no idea things would only get worse.

The following month, a USC contingent that included Carroll, Garrett, USC president Steve Sample, running backs coach Todd McNair, and McNair's lawyer Scott Tompsett, attended three days of hearings with the NCAA in Tempe, Arizona. Kiffin went along as an observer.

Tompsett says USC asked him to be ready to represent Carroll if needed. But when notified that McNair, and not Carroll, was going to be named in the upcoming report, Tompsett was asked to represent the running backs coach, instead. "NCAA had alleged that Todd knew Reggie was getting money," says Tompsett. "But I had a very strong case for Todd. Their evidence was weak." Tompsett says that at nearly every break in the proceedings, "Kiffin would corner me and tell me what I was doing wrong."

The USC representatives were there to answer questions from the NCAA's ten-person Committee on Infractions, a group that was very secretive—they never released anything voluntarily to the public—and very powerful. The committee included two conference commissioners, a University of Nebraska professor, and a member of Notre Dame's athletic department. It was chaired by a rotund and bespectacled man named Paul Dee, who was, by then, the former athletic director at the University of Miami.

Because he was, by that time, no longer the USC coach, Carroll was not obligated to attend the hearings. But, with his legacy potentially at stake, he did anyway. After the hearings' last day, he met with the media. "We made some mistakes along the way," Carroll said. When pressed for what those mistakes were, he answered, "I wish we would've known what was going on. We didn't even know. Had we known, I wish we'd have taken care of business and done the right thing and stopped it."

When asked about the hearings themselves, he appeared unnerved: "I thought it was done poorly and very irrationally and done with way too much emotion instead of facts."

Even today, Carroll can't shake the feeling he had after the hearings wrapped up. "We came out of there, and it didn't feel good," he says. "It felt dirty."

In 2009, the NCAA had combined the Bush investigation with investigations into USC's men's basketball and women's tennis programs. Trojan basketball player O. J. Mayo was accused of accepting cash and gifts from a promoter, and his coach, Tim Floyd, was accused of giving a handler some money to get Mayo to play basketball at the school. A women's tennis player was accused of racking up an unauthorized $7,535 in international telephone bill charges.

In January 2010, the USC basketball program announced that it had self-sanctioned, which included vacating some wins, instituting a one-year ban from playing in the postseason, and losing two scholarships. The women's tennis team also sanctioned itself, vacating some wins.

The Trojan football team, however, did not impose any self-sanctions. In fact, they struck a pose of defiance. Garrett did as little as he could to help the NCAA investigators. Ruel says the investigators "were so incompetent" that he kicked them out of his office. "And Pete went to play basketball one day when the NCAA people showed up to interview him," says Petros Papadakis.

That defiance, in the end, would turn out to be a grave mistake.

On June 10, 2010—exactly six months after Carroll left for the Seahawks—the bomb was dropped on the USC football program. They have yet to recover from it.

At a press conference, Paul Dee announced that the NCAA had found that Bush had broken NCAA rules because he and his family had taken cash and gifts from Michaels, Lake, and Ornstein. Carroll was not directly implicated, though the NCAA did cite the program for a "lack of institutional control" and alleged that McNair knew about the improper benefits given to Bush.[*] "High-profile players demand high-profile compliance," Dee proclaimed, rather grandly.

The punishment was devastating. The sanctions on the USC football program stopped just short of the so-called death penalty that the NCAA had given to the Southern Methodist University football program in 1987 after uncovering a "pay-to-play" scheme, which shut down the program for two years and nearly destroyed it for good.[†] "The penalties imposed in this case are commensurate with the nature of the violations and the failure of appropriate oversight by USC," the committee wrote in its sixty-seven-page report.

---

[*] Perhaps luckily for Carroll, the NCAA did not implement its "Head Coach Control" bylaw until 2012, which states that the head coach is "responsible for the actions of their staff and for promoting compliance with NCAA rules."
[†] SMU wouldn't reach a bowl game again for twenty-one years; the program finally became nationally relevant again in 2024, when it reached the twelve-team College Football Playoffs.

Those penalties: a ban on playing in the postseason for two years, the loss of thirty scholarships over three years, and the vacating of wins,[‡] starting with the last two wins of the 2004 season—which included the national title game win over Oklahoma—and the entire 2005 season. And the university had to "disassociate" itself from Bush, who was, perhaps, the best player ever to wear a Trojan football uniform. Outside of Bush, McNair was the only person to be directly punished by the NCAA, which issued him a show-cause order, meaning the organization had to approve his potential future hirings for a year.[§]

Just hours after the NCAA announcement, Garrett stood up in front of a roomful of USC athletics boosters in the San Francisco Airport Marriott. He was there, along with Kiffin and the men's basketball coach, Kevin O'Neill (who had replaced Tim Floyd in 2009), on a preplanned coaches' tour. "As I read the decision by the NCAA, all I could get out of it was . . . I read between the lines and there was nothing but a lot of envy, and they wish they were all Trojans." He added that he had told his staff, "I feel invigorated by all this stuff." Garrett—still "Iron Mike," still seeking contact by running straight into the line—received a standing ovation from the crowd. According to ESPN, as he made his way out, a newspaper reporter asked if he was worried about his job. "I'm just worried about your job," Garrett replied as he patted the man on his chest.

[‡] Vacating wins is a rather silly punishment. No player from the 2004 Oklahoma team goes around today proclaiming, "We didn't lose to USC!" An example of the silliness: in its media book for its 2017 regular-season game against Texas, USC absurdly tried to turn the vacated wins to its advantage, writing, "USC is 4–0 in series with Texas (not including 1 loss vacated due to NCAA penalty)."
[§] The NCAA did not further punish the USC men's basketball team or women's tennis team, presumably because of their self-imposed sanctions.

A month later Garrett was ousted as USC's athletic director and replaced by Pat Haden, the former USC quarterback and the man who had done the television color commentary for the Bush Push game for NBC.

In September 2010, Bush voluntarily gave his Heisman back to the Heisman Trophy Trust, saying the scandal should not "stain the dignity of this award." The school gave back its copy of the trophy, as well.

In May 2011, the NCAA denied USC's appeal of the sanctions. And a month after that, the BCS officially stripped the Trojans of their 2004 national title.

As shocking as the sanctions were, it could have all been much worse. Because at one point during the Bush saga, things threatened to spin out of control. Bush may have been the master of his domain on the college football field. But in this case, he was playing with something—and some people—far out of his league.

The nuts and bolts of the Reggie Bush scandal are as follows:[¶]

Lloyd Lake lived in San Diego and was friendly with Bush's stepfather, LaMar Griffin. Lake had spent time in the rap industry and had become acquainted with Marion "Suge" Knight, a rap record executive. Lake had also been affiliated with a gang as a young man and had served time in prison for trafficking marijuana and cocaine. He possessed much personal charm and, after one of his stints in prison, strove to set his life right by becoming

---

¶ Many of the facts of the Bush scandal that were later used in stories by the *New York Times*, *Los Angeles Times*, and Don Yaeger's book *Tarnished Heisman*, among other places, were originally reported by Charles Robinson and Jason Cole at *Yahoo Sports*. This was very much their story from the beginning—they broke it and continued to write about it until well after the NCAA sanctions were announced.

a legitimate businessman. He believed Reggie Bush was the way to do that.

Sometime in 2004, Lake and Griffin came up with the idea of forming a sports marketing agency, which they called New Era. The first client would be Bush. According to Lake, Bush signed off on the idea during a meeting. Lake contacted an acquaintance named Michael Michaels, who was part of the Sycuan Band, a powerful Native American tribe that sponsored many local businesses, including the San Diego Padres, and at one point in the early 2000s claimed $800 million in annual revenue. Michaels went by the nickname "Chief," though that was not his official position within the band.

According to the NCAA report, as time went on, Lake and Michaels began to pay for things—for the Griffins and for Bush. Michaels bought the house that the Griffins lived in, of course. But he and Lake also paid for plane tickets, hotel rooms, and a car for Bush, and paid off the Griffins' credit card debt. All of this was happening while Bush was playing football at USC.

But sometime during the 2005 season, Lake and Michaels felt like they were being played by Bush, because the running back was not fully committing to their sports marketing endeavor. By that time, Bush had taken an internship with another sports marketer named Michael Ornstein.

Ornstein was a colorful character who had begun his career in football working as an administrative assistant in 1975 for the Oakland Raiders coach John Madden. He was eventually let go from that job after getting into a fistfight with a Raiders executive and clashing with team owner Al Davis. Ornstein then went to work for the NFL as a marketer, where he became an acquaintance of then–NFL commissioner Paul Tagliabue and future commissioner Roger Goodell. That job ended in 1996 when Ornstein pleaded guilty to trying to steal $350,000 in a mail fraud scheme. He was sentenced to five years' probation.

Ornstein told *Yahoo* that he was a "good soldier" who "took a bullet for the NFL" in that scheme but declined to elaborate. Lee Pfiefer, a former business partner of Ornstein's, says the marketer was "wearing an ankle monitor when we first started working together.

"Mike could have taken down the NFL," says Pfiefer. "He had some real big stories. That's why they kept putting up with his shit."**

By 2005, Ornstein was back in the sports marketing game. That summer he hired three USC football players as interns—one of whom was Bush—and paid them eight dollars an hour. While it was undeniably unwise on the part of the USC football program to have some of its active players associate with Ornstein, the internship was cleared through the USC compliance office and within NCAA rules. What happened next, according to the NCAA, was not.

Ornstein, as it turned out, *also* wanted Bush as a marketing client and, in order to entice him, the NCAA said, he, too, began paying for flights, clothes, and other items for Bush and his family. At one point in 2005, Ornstein reached out to a New Jersey memorabilia dealer named Bob DeMartino to put together an autograph deal for Bush. Ornstein wanted $500,000 from DeMartino to join Bush's marketing team. "I put a proposal together, but then Ornstein started asking me for the money before the football season was over," says DeMartino. "I told him he wasn't getting a dime until the season was over. I was a licensee, and I didn't want to get my ass in trouble."

But, DeMartino says, Ornstein kept pushing, demanding the $500,000 during the season. "He started threatening me and

---

** In 2011, Ornstein was sentenced to eight months in prison after pleading guilty to conspiracy to scalp Super Bowl tickets. Ornstein passed away in 2024, taking all of his secrets with him to the grave.

finally I said to myself, 'Everyone here is going to get in trouble,'" says DeMartino. "I wouldn't figure out until later why Ornstein was pushing me so hard for the money."

The NCAA alleged that by this point, Bush was essentially double dipping. And Lake and Michaels did not like that and felt that Bush was reneging on their deal. When Ornstein went to the Heisman Trophy ceremony with Bush, the duo realized that Bush was likely no longer going to sign with New Era. So they tried to recoup their money. And here is where things nearly went off the rails.

Perhaps mindful of the power and influence of the Sycuans, Bush settled his debts with Michaels in 2007, reportedly for between $200,000 and $300,000 and with the stipulation that Michaels would not talk to the NCAA. But Lake believed he was owed money, too, for all that he had provided for Bush and his family—$291,600, to be exact. Through LaMar Griffin, Lake asked to be paid back, or at least to get assurances that once Bush signed his NFL contract the repayment would happen. Lake went back to prison in early 2006 for violating his probation order. But he still wanted his money. And Bush, unwisely, ignored him.

"Ornstein was squeezing me because he wanted to use the money to pay back Lake," says DeMartino.

Lake did not go to the media to put pressure on Bush to pay him, and he did not initially engage a lawyer to intervene on his behalf. Instead, Lake got in touch with an old acquaintance to try to make it happen. That old acquaintance? Suge Knight.

Knight is the founder of Death Row Records, a rap company that released groundbreaking records by Dr. Dre and Snoop.[††] But he was also well known for being a tough guy and had earned the

---

[††] Knight and Snoop had a falling-out in the late 1990s, and Snoop told police that he felt he was in "grave danger as a result of leaving Death Row Records."

nickname "the John Gotti of rap." He had been affiliated with the Bloods gang and once claimed that, as a kid, he and his friends in Compton robbed the corpses they found in the neighborhood. He had been to prison numerous times for assault and robbery (he's currently serving a twenty-eight-year sentence for a voluntary manslaughter charge in a hit-and-run). He was not a man to be trifled with.

After being contacted by Lake, Knight—fresh out of prison but still involved in some legal cases—reached out to his friend, the actor and comedian Faizon Love, to handle the situation for him.

Love had known both Bush and Lake for a while by that time. In fact, Love says, when he first heard of the marketing arrangement Bush and Lake had come up with in 2004, he told Bush he shouldn't do it. "Lloyd was a street guy that Reggie shouldn't have gotten involved with," says Love. "But Reggie didn't listen to me."

Love says he had also been in on the conversation that Bush had with Lake about getting a car. "Reggie wanted a Ferrari and I'm like, 'You're crazy, what the fuck is wrong with you? You're still in school,'" says Love. This time Bush listened, eventually getting a tricked-out Chevy Impala instead.

"Suge asked me to help. I talked to Reggie. I talked to Lloyd. I was mad at Lloyd when he told me the whole thing, for getting Reggie involved in this," says Love. "But Lloyd was right in this situation. He just wanted his money back. And Suge told me to recoup it for him and that it seemed like Reggie was taking the money and laughing in Lloyd's face.

"And all of this was happening about three days before the Texas game [for the national title]," says Love. "Reggie had all this on his mind, the house and the Ferrari, and then he did that weird-ass lateral."

Love says the insinuation was that if Bush didn't pay Lake back, Knight would make sure Bush "lost his San Diego privileges," meaning there would be consequences if Bush showed up again in his home city. Another person involved in the matter says, "Things could have gotten really ugly," because Knight told Lake to "break Reggie's legs" if he didn't pay.

By this time, according to David Caravantes, then an NFL agent who was brought in briefly by Lake and Michaels as a possible partner in New Era, detectives from the San Diego Police Department and the Federal Bureau of Investigations were involved in the case. "They'd wiretapped some phones and heard some disturbing shit," he says. Caravantes says he was interviewed about the situation by the FBI.[++]

But still Bush refused to pay Lake.

Before the NFL Draft in April 2006, Bush signed with agent Joel Segal and signed with Ornstein to do his marketing deals. Ornstein reportedly got Bush $50 million in endorsements, with Pepsi, Adidas, and Subway.[§§] After being drafted second overall by the Saints, Bush signed a six-year, $52.5 million deal with more than $20 million guaranteed.

And he still refused to pay Lake.

Lake still didn't go to the media. Instead, Robinson and Cole found him and interviewed him for the first time months into their reporting, when Robinson met with him in jail. But by October 2007—after the story had broken and he still hadn't been repaid—Lake had finally had enough and filed a civil lawsuit

---

[++] Caravantes says he was only involved in the early stages of New Era, never met Bush, and got out of the arrangement quickly. But his name remained on the business plan, which found its way into the hands of *Yahoo* and ESPN, both of whom mentioned him in their reports. "And just like that, my days as an NFL agent were over," he says. "It ruined my career."

[§§] Bush fired Ornstein in November 2007 with no explanation.

against Bush and his parents, seeking to recover the $291,600 he claimed to have spent on them.

And then, a month later, Lake met with NCAA investigators, becoming their primary witness.

In 2010, just months before the NCAA sanctions were announced, Bush finally reached an out-of-court settlement with Lake.

But by then it was too late.

Had Bush just offered to pay Lake after he signed his NFL contract, or even when he got his first marketing deal, there likely never would have been a Reggie Bush scandal at USC. Even if some or all the dealings Bush had with Lake, Michaels, and Ornstein had come to light, Bush could have done with Lake what he'd done with Michaels—pay him back with the condition that he could not talk to the NCAA. NCAA does not have subpoena power and thus cannot compel anyone to testify. And without Lake's testimony, the NCAA would not have had much of a case against Bush, if it would have had one at all. It was a big fumble for a man who rarely did that during his USC career.

So why didn't Bush just settle with Lake earlier, before things got out of hand? Ornstein wanted him to do just that. So, apparently, did Bush's lawyer, David Cornwell. "In the middle of reporting all of this, I called Cornwell and asked him some questions," says Charles Robinson. "And then he hung up. Or thought he hung up. And I heard a voice say, 'Tell Joel [presumably Joel Segal, Bush's agent] this needs to get fucking settled. Pay the $500,000 and get this over with.' And then the line went dead."

But Bush wouldn't budge, either out of pride or something else.

"Something broke with Reggie," says Chris Huston. "Early on, he was such a nice young guy. But somewhere around 2004, he became really arrogant. He was always a really hard worker, but he started to get greedy."

Thomas Herring also says Bush began to change as his USC career went on. "He started to want to be a streets guy, be tied to the Bloods," he says. "That Impala, a lot of people just think it's a cheap car. But back then, it was a hood car. Reggie got it for that image, with the chrome rims and stereo."

The story the NCAA report tells is one of men who got involved with Bush because they saw him as a gold mine. Bush got his share in return—money, plane tickets, hotel rooms, and a car. But it was his stepfather who appears to be the one who took the most advantage of the fact that his stepson was about to receive a gigantic payday. Griffin leveraged Bush's status for a home to live in and his debt to be wiped clean.

Todd McNair is the fall guy in the report, and the only individual within it to truly get hammered. He is depicted as the coach who not only knew what was going on with Bush but helped facilitate it. Because of the report—and the NCAA's show-cause order against him—McNair would not work in football again for the next nine years. It would be a long time coming, but he would get his revenge.

Carroll's name does not show up in the report. But he is implicitly called out for three issues. One is general—a lack of institutional control—but the two others are more specific.

The first stems from 2008, when Carroll quietly employed an NFL coaching veteran named Pete Rodriguez to monitor USC's special teams in practice and in games. The hiring put USC over the permitted number of coaches and, according to the NCAA, gave USC "more than a limited competitive advantage" over other schools. Carroll initially told the Los Angeles Times that he'd cleared the hiring of Rodriguez with USC's compliance office.

The NCAA said he had not. The NCAA report also stated that USC admitted that the Rodriguez hiring broke the rules but believed it to be merely a secondary violation that should go unpunished. The NCAA clearly did not agree with the self-assessment.

The second, which involves Ornstein, perhaps reveals Carroll's exposed flank in the report. The NCAA claimed that it was Carroll who approached Ornstein about getting his players jobs— jobs that were only available to them and not the general USC student body. Carroll admitted to knowing Ornstein but denied asking him for anything on behalf of his players.

But, given his background, even having Ornstein around the program was a stunningly unnecessary risk that Carroll allowed. And letting his star player work for Ornstein was riskier still.

"Hubris caught up to Pete," says Petros Papadakis.

For years, other schools had complained to the NCAA about the advantage USC had because of the celebrities who attended their practices and games. These schools complained mainly because, well, they were jealous.

For years, the NCAA asked the Trojans to tone it down. But USC ignored those pleas.

And now, with everything detailed in their report, the door had been opened for the NCAA to put a stop to it. As the NCAA report stated:

> The general campus environment surrounding the violations troubled the committee. At least at the time of the football violations, there was relatively little effective monitoring of, among others, football locker rooms and sidelines, and there existed a general postgame locker room environment that made compliance efforts difficult. . . . These activities and others referred to during the hearing fostered an atmosphere in which student-athletes could feel entitled to

special treatment and which almost certainly contributed to the difficulties of compliance staff in achieving a rules-compliant program.

The fun, the glam and glitz, the drawing outside of the lines. "Strengths and weaknesses," Steve Jobs once said, "are almost always the same thing."

Agents were part of USC's practice crowds. David Price, the agent who eventually signed Leinart, attended them, as did Leigh Steinberg and people who worked for David Dunn. Ornstein loved them. "If you've ever been to an SC practice, it's nuts," he once told the *Los Angeles Times.* "Four or five hundred people there."

Monitoring those agents—and making sure that they or their runners had no contact with players—was virtually impossible. Pat Ruel despised having them around. According to the *Los Angeles Times,* Ruel stepped out of Heritage Hall one day and, upon seeing a gaggle of agents, said, "I know what cockroaches look like. And I know what agents look like." And then he got angry. "All agents get the hell out of Heritage Hall. Get out of there!" he said, as if clearing the moneylenders from the temple.

It was also the case that some USC players were being paid or being given improper benefits. "It was always understood that some players got taken care of," says Huston. "There were handshakes, boosters who took care of them, let them use their beach houses."

"We all knew," says Chow. "When I first got there, they took us [Chow and his family] to an apartment complex and showed us a nice unit. We couldn't afford it. But some players were living there. We didn't know the particulars of any payments. It wasn't blatant. But we just knew."

LenDale White has spoken publicly about getting paid while at USC. "I definitely got some money," he says. "I got a bag once with maybe $150,000 in it. But I got more than that. I was getting money every month. Other people on the team got paid, too. Everybody knew what was going on."

"At USC, the guys doing the best on the team were being taken care of by agents or boosters," says Fred Davis. "I was struggling as a freshman and sophomore, but once I got into a position to get extra money, I did it."

To be sure, USC wasn't the only team where this happened. Players were getting paid all over college football, at that time and before. Ruel recounts his days working at Texas A&M. "I knew what we did there," he says. "It was, 'If you ain't cheatin', you ain't tryin'.'" He also had friends at the time at Miami, where he played, and "they would tell me, 'Holy shit, Pat, this is a nightmare here. Escorts, money. Just absolutely crazy.'"

What was happening at USC was, perhaps, even less egregious than what was happening at some other big team college football programs at the time. But it *was* happening. And USC, at the time, did not exactly invest heavily in preventative measures.

Keith Miller worked in USC's compliance office from 2001 to the end of the 2005 season. In fact, for the vast majority of the time he worked there, he *was* USC's compliance office, working out of an office that was a converted bathroom. "I was solo for the most part, though we did eventually hire someone else," he says. "We were under-resourced, especially compared to other PAC-10 schools. Our motto was 'We do more with less.'"

His job, Miller says, could be tedious. "I took heat for a lot of little random things that weren't necessarily covered in the rule book." There were complaints about Leinart taking only the ballroom dancing course in his last season at USC. The PAC-10 and the NCAA inquired about the LenDale White prank in which

Carroll had the dummy thrown off the roof and the time Snoop ran a route in practice. "If they alleged that we broke a rule, I'd have to defend how something was within the rules or self-report that it was outside and come up with a penalty for the program that satisfied the powers that be."

There was a time when a booster gave the team crates of oranges to celebrate USC's invitation to the Orange Bowl. "Technically, at the time, that wasn't legal, so I had to write it up," says Miller. There was another time when some players did a reading at an elementary school and Verizon cosponsored the event and hung banners, "which violated NCAA rule 12.5.11," says Miller. "I self-reported it. But on the morning that we were getting ready to get on the plane to fly to play Notre Dame, the NCAA told me that our players were ineligible to play unless they applied for reinstatement by signing some paperwork. Everyone was already on the bus, and they all had to wait like two hours while I got signatures and faxed them in. Pete was not happy."

Miller says he paid particular attention to the program's high-profile players—like Bush and Leinart. He says he met with them "around three times a week" to remind them to "keep everything aboveboard."

He even had what was supposed to be a preventative measure in place: a signed affidavit that supposedly helped the NCAA ensure its amateurism rules were being followed. The affidavit was akin to an honor code—the players had to answer around twenty questions, affirming that they had not gambled and had not accepted illegal benefits, among other things. "It was a sworn testimony, under penalty of perjury," says Miller. All players were required to sign one before bowl games. But just to be safe, Miller asked Bush and Leinart to fill out an affidavit six times a year. "That was the one thing the NCAA didn't go after [in the Bush case], the affidavits, and I was surprised," he says.

Miller was not contacted by the NCAA for an interview about the Bush case until 2008, two years after the *Yahoo* story broke. He says he could tell from the investigators' questions that "it wasn't going well." It felt like, he says, "a narrative was being forced. They were asking questions that were very unrealistic, like, 'Why didn't we check the leases of all the players' parents?' We had every intention of doing things right."

Miller says the NCAA would periodically do peer reviews of compliance offices of its schools. They would send a school president and a school athletic director (each from a different university) to a given campus to conduct interviews with said school's compliance people. During one peer review before the Bush investigation, the person sent to USC to interview Miller was Donna Shalala, who was then the president of the University of Miami. "I remember she sat in my office and said, 'This was a bathroom, wasn't it?'" says Miller. "She asked me some other questions and then said, very clearly, 'You need to get out of here,' basically because we were under-resourced, and she thought things could get out of control. I was like, 'Wow.'"

Shalala's athletic director at Miami at the time: Paul Dee.

"Did she say something to Dee about her visit?" asks Miller. "Did she tell him about the converted bathroom with the rats in the ceiling? I bet she did."

NCAA rules were broken in the Reggie Bush case. Carroll admitted it. "We made mistakes," he told HBO's *Real Sports*. Kiffin did, too. "There is some guilt, but the punishment is too severe," he told the AP. Even Bush came close to doing so when, after giving back his Heisman so as not to "stain the dignity" of the award, he announced he was establishing "an educational program which will assist student-athletes and their families to avoid some of the mistakes I've made," though he did add some time later that giving back the trophy was "not an admission of guilt."

The Bush case is the story of three grown men trying to exploit the stardom of a kid.

It is the story of a stepfather who saw his stepson's athletic gifts as a way out of what had been to that point a life of relative scarcity.

It is the story of a young athlete who allowed all of this to happen and played with fire when he did not pay back his debts.

It is the story of jealousy on the part of other schools.

But mostly, it is the story of how the NCAA once exploited its athletes.

Yes, rules were broken. But they were ludicrous rules to begin with, especially viewed through the prism of today's landscape where, since the summer of 2021, college athletes have been able to make money from their own names, images, and likenesses.

The old NCAA system was, more or less, a form of modern slavery. Yes, scholarship athletes were provided free schooling, room and board, and a stipend (which, back then, was around $800 to $1,000 a month). But the schools and the conferences and the administrators and, yes, the coaches were the entities making the real money from the labor of their unpaid athletes who, at least in the case of football, also happened to be playing what was a dangerous sport.

Money was everywhere but in the pockets of the players. In 2005, total annual revenue for FBS schools were $3.5 billion (it's now $11 billion). That same year, the SEC distributed $111 million to all twelve of its member schools, and the PAC-10, though not the powerhouse the SEC was, still had a healthy $320 million in football revenue. And USC athletics alone generated $35 million, mostly from its football team.

At the beginning of 2005, eight college coaches were making $2 million or more a year, led by Oklahoma's Bob Stoops at $2.5 million. Later in that season, just before the national title game, Carroll was given an extension and raise. According to the

Chronicle of Higher Education, the $4.4 million he made in the 2006–07 fiscal year was four times what the president of USC earned and made him the highest-paid college employee in the nation.

It was the athletes who built all of this, though. "I remember going into the SC student store and there were racks of number five jerseys [Bush's number]," says Clay Matthews. "All the coaches were driving brand-new cars from Fletcher Jones Mercedes, and I was riding a bike with a bent frame."

"The NCAA was a criminal entity," says Alex Holmes. "A multibillion-dollar criminal entity."

Reggie Bush came from a family of modest means. He was the best college football player in the nation in 2005 (and, arguably, in 2004). And yet, he could not be fairly compensated for that talent under NCAA rules.

The only way for Bush to be fairly compensated at the time "was to deal with people like Lake and Ornstein, who were people who operated in the underworld and underbelly of society," says Jason Cole. "Part of the reason you go to college is to be trained as an adult to do things aboveboard, reputable things that will represent yourself and the college, as well."

Robinson and Cole's reporting in all of this was essential. It exposed the hypocrisy and greed of the NCAA. The Bush case helped get the wheels turning toward change in college sports, finally forcing the NCAA to confront the issue of its false amateurism, which the organization and its member schools had avoided doing for its entire existence because it paid so well. And because it avoided the issue, the NCAA was, for all intents and purposes, stripped of its authority, existing now as, essentially, a powerless entity, a shell of what it once was.

Cole, who left *Yahoo* in 2013 to work at the *Bleacher Report* and then write books, remains proud of the work that he and

Robinson did on the Reggie Bush case. Robinson, who is still at *Yahoo*, went on to do other major investigations of schools and student-athletes over the years. But eventually, he stopped doing them and concentrated on the NFL. He does not feel the same way Cole does:

> I got to the point where I was like, "This system is so fucking stupid." This entire subeconomy exists, and everybody knows it exists, and every school is taking part in it, and the under-the-table threat of it helps them control the kids and keep all the money. When I started out, I thought our investigations were exposing the reality of what was going on in the system—which they were. And I thought they were pointing a finger at head coaches and other adults who were involved in creating the system—which they were. But as time went on, I realized that it was kids who were absorbing all the trauma from having to hide what they were doing and then getting punished by the NCAA and crushed by fans if anyone found out. So, over time, I got to the point where I wondered why I was taking part in this. I look back on that work, including the USC stuff, and feel very conflicted about it.

It's not a minor thing to point out that the improper benefits provided to Bush were done so as to lure him *away* from USC and not to get him to play or stay there.

It's also not a minor thing to point out that the head of the Committee on Infractions for the Bush case, who issued those high-and-mighty reprimands, was not above reproach himself.

Just a year after the USC sanctions hit—and before he left the college investigations beat—Robinson uncovered another scandal, this one involving . . . the University of Miami. A booster named Nevin Shapiro, who was already in jail for his role in a $930 million

Ponzi scheme, claimed that from 2002 until 2010, he provided millions of dollars' worth of improper benefits to around seventy Miami athletes, mainly football players. Those benefits included cash, prostitutes, and jewelry.[¶]

The athletic director for seven of those years (until 2008) was none other than Paul Dee. In fact, Robinson reported that Dee once honored Shapiro on the field before a game. Miami self-imposed a two-year bowl ban. After an investigation, the NCAA docked the school nine football scholarships and put it on probation, a much less harsh penalty than the one levied on USC despite what many believed to be far more egregious misconduct by Miami.

In the report, the NCAA used a phrase familiar to any USC fan. Miami, it said, suffered from a "lack of institutional control."

If you squint, you can see a connection between the Bush case and the astonishing demise of the PAC-12 in 2024. In the wake of the destruction of USC's football program, the conference became a weakling. No PAC-10/12 team has won a national title since USC did in 2004. In fact, since USC's appearance after the 2005 season, only three teams from the conference have played in the national title game. Partly as a result, the conference failed to secure a competitive media rights deal. And in June 2022, the dissipation of the conference began when USC and UCLA were lured to the Big Ten with the promise of more money. Eight other schools subsequently left.[***]

As Mike Riley noted, having a powerhouse team in a conference can create a rising tide that lifts all boats. But when USC

[¶] It turned out that Pat Ruel's sources in Miami were onto something.

[***] The conference operated with two teams—Oregon State and Washington State—in 2024 and will add eight more members in 2026, from the Mountain West Conference and West Coast Conference.

sank, the tide in the conference ebbed, and all of the boats fell. If USC had maintained real relevance on the national stage, it is possible that the PAC-12 might have made it in the era of conference realignment and might have secured the media rights package that it needed to survive. It didn't and now no longer exists as the entity it once was.

If you squint, too, you can see a connection between the Bush case and the 2019 Varsity Blues scandal that enveloped USC. The aftermath of the Bush case left behind a discombobulated (at best) USC athletics department, one perhaps vulnerable to becoming swept up in the scandal in which a USC athletics department official and several coaches were arrested and pleaded guilty to playing a role in a payment scheme that reportedly falsified athletic résumés of the children of wealthy families to gain admittance to USC.

One of the injustices of sanctions like the ones the NCAA placed on USC is that the burden of the punishment is carried by people who had nothing to do with the purported wrongdoing. The sanctions from the Bush case were brutal on the players who remained at USC.

One of those players was Matt Barkley, who faced a triple whammy. Carroll left. Garrett was gone. And the sanctions kicked in. Barkley was, as he had been during his freshman season, thrust into a difficult role. "I had to stand up in front of the cameras as kind of the face of the program, and I had to try to lead by example," he says. USC's players were allowed to transfer that offseason without the usual penalty of having to sit out a year. "One of my goals was to keep people here," Barkley says. "We lost a few good players—Malik Jackson [a defensive tackle] to Tennessee—but there wasn't a mass exodus. And there was no doubt that I was staying. I'm a Trojan."

But because of the scholarship reductions, one of the deepest rosters in the sport suddenly became one of its thinnest. "We had to have eight to ten walk-ons who were special teamers and second stringers on offense and defense," says Galippo. "We were sixty-five to seventy college players who had nothing to do with the sanctions and couldn't play in a bowl game. It was a bummer."

The NCAA also effectively ended one of the things that made USC special. "One of the first things they did was no more open practices. No fans, no celebs, just media. That diminished the USC star power," says Galippo. "They shut the party down."

When it came to coaching replacements for Carroll, USC appeared desperate to try to recapture Camelot by hiring coaches who had touched the robe as assistants during the glory years.

Kiffin came in at a huge disadvantage. He was hired before the sanctions were announced and inherited a team that could not play in a bowl game for two years and was down scholarships and morale. He described that feeling as "finally buying the house of your dreams only to move in and discover that everything had been removed."

Kiffin did well initially with what he was left with. In his second season, the Trojans finished 10–2, best in the PAC-12 South Division. But because of the sanctions, his team could not play in the PAC-12 championship game—or a bowl—that year.

Things went south for him and the program after that.

USC went into 2012, Kiffin's third season, ranked number one in the preseason, but thudded to a 7–6 record and ended the season with a locker room brawl after a loss in the Sun Bowl. Five games into the 2013 season, after a humiliating 62–41 loss to Arizona State—which left the Trojans with a 3–2 record—Kiffin was fired by Haden, the athletic director, after the team plane landed in Los Angeles following the game. Kiffin was replaced, on an interim basis, by Carroll's old defensive line coach Orgeron, who led the team to a 6–2 record for the remainder of the regular season. But Orgeron left the team before its bowl game, because USC had hired Sarkisian as its new head coach.[†††]

Sarkisian seemed to have the ship headed in the right direction in 2014, leading the Trojans to a 9–4 record. But then, in the summer before his second season, Sarkisian reportedly appeared inebriated when he addressed a USC booster group. And during a late September game against Arizona State, he allegedly reeked of alcohol and then showed up to an October practice so drunk he was sent home. He was immediately put on leave by Haden and fired the next day.

After Sarkisian, USC finally moved away from the Carroll coaching tree and hired Clay Helton and then Lincoln Riley. Though Helton guided the Trojans to a PAC-12 title in 2017 (their first and only one since 2008), and Riley coached Heisman Trophy winner Caleb Williams in 2022, USC has not come close to reaching its former heights.

In a very real sense, the USC football program has yet to recover from the punishments resulting from the Bush investigation.

"It ruined a couple of decades of USC football. Does all of this misery cancel out the success under Carroll? Was it all worth it?" says Petros Papadakis. "I don't know. Maybe it was."

[†††] Orgeron would go to LSU as the defensive line coach and then become the head coach there, winning a national title in 2019. He left LSU after the 2021 season and has not coached since.

A year after the sanctions were handed down, Todd McNair filed a lawsuit against the NCAA for libel and slander, among other things. In 2012, a judge described the NCAA's treatment of McNair as "malicious." In 2015, as part of the case, emails sent among the members of the Committee on Infractions were made public. Many of them did not reflect well on the NCAA. One member likened the USC case to the Oklahoma City bombing in 1995. Another read, "Individuals like McNair shouldn't be coaching at ANY level, and to think that he is at one of the premier college athletics programs in the country is outrageous. He's a lying, morally bankrupt criminal, in my view, and a hypocrite of the highest order."

In 2019, after being away from the game for nine years, McNair got his first job since USC, as the running backs coach of the Tampa Bay Buccaneers. In 2021, McNair reached an out-of-court settlement with the NCAA for an undisclosed amount of money. That same year, he won a Super Bowl with the Buccaneers. He was fired two years later and remains out of football.

In October 2016, Reggie Bush came back to the Los Angeles Coliseum as a backup running back for the Buffalo Bills, in a game against the Rams. (He had one carry in the game, for three yards.) Three years later, Bush—by then a television analyst—visited again. Because USC was still formally disassociated from him, Bush had to get special permission from the NCAA to work the game. The following year, the university, because of a new NCAA rule, was able to lift its dissociation from Bush.

In August 2023, Bush filed a lawsuit against the NCAA claiming the organization defamed him when one of its spokespeople, upon being asked if the organization would revisit the Bush case in light of the 2021 NIL rulings, said, "NCAA rules still do not permit pay-for-play type arrangements."

In April 2024, the Heisman Trophy Trust gave Bush his Heisman back because of the "enormous changes in the college football landscape."

Bush apparently still feels like he hasn't been compensated enough for what he endured, though. In September 2024, he filed a lawsuit against the NCAA, the PAC-12, and USC for NIL compensation.

Epilogue
The Last King of Troy

He still feels the sting. Even now. Even after he coached the Seahawks for fourteen seasons, making the playoffs in ten of them. After winning a Super Bowl and losing another on a goal line play. After becoming the winningest coach in the franchise's history and proving—beyond a doubt—his different style of coaching not only worked in the NFL, it thrived.

Even now.

"People think I ran," Carroll says. "It looks like shit."

Because of the timing of his departure, Carroll's legacy at USC, to some, will always carry with it a black eye, deserved or not.

So did he run because he knew the devastating sanctions were coming?

LenDale White has long maintained that he did. "He bailed as fast as he possibly could," he said in the 2015 documentary *Trojan War.*

White and Carroll had a fractured relationship by that time. Just a few months after Carroll took the Seahawks job in 2010, he traded a second-round draft pick to acquire White from the Titans. And then, a month later, much to White's surprise, Carroll cut him but didn't do so in person. Says White:

Pete was a father figure. I've known him since I was sixteen. He knew everyone in my family. I stayed at his house in Manhattan Beach and hung out with his daughter and his nieces. I would have thought he would talk to me face-to-face instead of me seeing that I was cut on TV first. To me, that was chickenshit, the weirdest shit ever. But that's why we called him "Sneaky Pete." It ain't like he ain't got his own secrets. It was not like I shouldn't have expected it.

After Carroll cut him, White told the media that his former coach had "handled it like a coward." Carroll gave a half apology to the *Los Angeles Times*: "I am sorry he feels hurt by the situation and truly wish him well."

Several other players and many outsiders also believe Carroll knew what was coming from the NCAA. "I think he had some heads-up of the sanctions," says Ayles. "The team felt like he knew something was going on with them."

"I'm sure he had an inkling," says Alex Holmes. "But I don't think it affected his decision."

Surely Carroll had divined *something* from the questions the NCAA investigators asked of him and his staff. And he likely would have known, at the very least, the nature of the allegations against his program by late September 2009, when the NCAA sent a notice to USC.

But even if he had an inkling, did Carroll know how harsh the sanctions would end up being? He vehemently denies that and says that's not why he left. "I had no idea, and I was shocked," he says. "I would have stayed had I known they were going to be that bad."

Or did he leave because, as he admits, that mountaintop at USC seemed farther and farther away and he felt like he'd done what he could do and was ready for a new challenge?

In the end, these scenarios might not be that different from each other. His time at USC, whatever the reason, was up.

And either way, Carroll says, the sanctions were preposterous. "The whole issue was, 'How much did we know and allow to happen?' And the answer is 'Nothing,'" he says.

Carroll thinks the sanctions were so harsh because of the way he did things at USC. "People thought we were doing something wrong, that we shouldn't be allowed to have that much fun," he says. "We were doing things for exactly the right reasons. We were doing it to have fun. And they passed judgment on that."

In a sense, the NCAA and other programs became a bit like Robert Kraft and Leon Hess. They didn't understand or like the different way that Carroll did things in football.

At the end of the 2009 season, with his team having already played its bowl game, Carroll took part in the television broadcast as an analyst for the BCS National Championship game between Alabama and Texas. "At one point we were standing on the sidelines, and no one knows he's leaving," says Yogi Roth. "And we're soaking in the atmosphere, and I look around and say, 'Look at this place. How will you ever leave this?' And he leaned in and says, 'Yogi, this is every Sunday in the NFL.'"

That Carroll took a job in the NFL was no surprise to those who knew him well. He had an itch that he needed to scratch, that chance to prove to the Krafts and the Hesses of the world that his methods were not just suited for college but could work in the pros, as well. Carroll had told the booster David Bahnsen that he would someday be back in the NFL. He'd said the same to Tim Tessalone. Carroll had unfinished business in the NFL. And the Seahawks situation—the timing, the control, the hunger of the franchise's ownership, and the fact that he would remain located in the more free-thinking and less uptight West Coast—probably could not have been better.

In some alternate universe, LenDale White falls forward on that fourth and two with two minutes and nine seconds remaining against Texas and converts the first down, and USC becomes the first team in modern college football history to win three national championships in a row.

And in that same universe, the Seahawks hand the ball to Marshawn Lynch in Super Bowl XLIX, and Pete Carroll has three national titles and two Super Bowls, the first coach ever to accomplish that feat.

But even in the real universe—the one of near misses—Carroll is one of only three football coaches in history to win a national title *and* a Super Bowl (along with Jimmy Johnson and Barry Switzer). That alone puts him somewhere on the list of coaching greats. His coaching career perhaps doesn't get the attention it deserves because he had the unfortunate historical timing of sharing the stage with Nick Saban, who is considered the greatest college coach of all time, and Bill Belichick, who is considered the greatest NFL coach of all time.

And, of course, he also did it in an unconventional way.

Carroll made his first public appearance at USC in 2014, just months after the penalties from the sanctions ended. He gave a talk about winning and sports and business. Will Ferrell started off the event by punting a football from the stage into the crowd.

The next year, Carroll returned again, this time to receive an honorary degree and to be inducted into the USC Athletics Hall of Fame. The latter ceremony took place in the McKay Center, a building with new coaches' offices, weight room, and training room for the football team. The building was conceived during Carroll's tenure at USC and completed in 2012 at a cost of $70 million.

EPILOGUE

In 2016, Carroll returned to the Coliseum for the first time since he'd left USC, now as the coach of the Seahawks, to play the Rams in that team's first home game in Los Angeles since they'd left after the 1994 season, a departure that helped create the city's football vacuum that Carroll's Trojans filled until it overflowed.

In 2025, Carroll, along with religion professor Varun Soni, taught a class at USC called "The Game Is Life."

It is the late fall of 2024. Pete Carroll should be on a field somewhere, or in a meeting room with his assistants dissecting film, or on a plane headed to a game. But he's not. He didn't officially get fired from the Seahawks at the end of the 2023 season—he was kicked upstairs, made a "senior adviser"—but he is, functionally, no longer with the team.

It is his first year out of football in twenty-three years, since that seminal year in 2000, when he figured it all out. He says he still has the energy, still has the drive. He knows he could still do it. But the opportunities for a now seventy-three-year-old head coach are few and far between, both in the college and in the pro game.

He sounds both wistful and at peace. He spends many of his days at his fishing cabin, on a river deep in the emerald woods of Washington, far away from the hubbub of the cameras and microphones and sports radio and social media and all the cacophony that comes with coaching in big-time sports. Far away from the noise in the Seahawks stadium—a noise that soaks up all that is not its own—and from the tattered grandeur of the Coliseum. He is far away from the practice field, the camaraderie, the pranks, the grass stains, the blood, sweat, and tears, the attempt to throw the ball more yards than his age on his birthday. Now he sits in his cabin, reading, writing, talking on the phone, until that magic hour when the sunlight moves off the river and into the trees, and the mayflies begin to hatch and hover over the water. And then he takes his fly rod and lopes down to the river and makes long, looping casts for rainbow trout, their sides brushed light pink, like the setting sun on the horizon.

"Everything that came together in 2000 is happening again," he says. "I'm recognizing now why it was so crucial for me then. When you step away from the game but stay in it, it's a tremendously rich time for learning and growing. That's what happened then. That's what's happening now. It's fascinating how it works like that."

As the 2024 football season comes to an end, Carroll begins to look for a way back in. In early January he talks to the Chicago Bears, but they opt for a coach nearly half his age. Later in the month he does another interview, this time with the Raiders, a team now owned by Al Davis's son, Mark, and located in Las Vegas, a city built from a dream in the desert. Carroll is offered the job, and he takes it.

He arrives at his introductory press conference. At first glance, one notices a slight hunch at the shoulders, and that he's skinny in the way that some septuagenarians get, and that he seems to wear his glasses full time now.

But then he speaks and everything changes. His face brightens. He moves with alacrity. He suddenly appears to be a man twenty years younger.

This is his last shot. To help his players and coaches remember why they fell in love with this game in the first place. To recapture what he first found at USC, that era that was and will never be again, where the red flame now lives, the story the poets must sing over and over again.

His last shot to try to win forever.

Acknowledgments

I interviewed more than 150 people for this book. Not all of them made the manuscript by name (some by choice), but each and every one of them helped.

Special thanks to Pete Carroll, who took the time to sit for seven interviews.

For research, I combed through countless newspaper stories written about this era of USC football—from commentary to the game and practice reports. I stand on the shoulders of these men and women who tapped out these stories.

My agent, Richard Pine, is *the* rock.

My sincerest gratitude to all of the folks at Grand Central and Hachette—Morgan Spehar, the tireless and wonderfully fastidious copy editors, and the marketing team—but especially to Amar Deol, who came to me with an idea that meshed perfectly with my previous work, cheered me on ("Aces!"), and then deftly edited the manuscript.

I thank David DiBenedetto for his weekly check-in on my progress (or lack thereof).

The Olympians, E-man, and my uncle Charles Gaines continue to inspire and encourage me.

My father's spirit hovers over everything I do, and I see him often in the eyes and deeds of my brothers, Justin and Chris.

ACKNOWLEDGMENTS

My mother, Hansell, taught me the meaning of unconditional love.

My wife, Heidi, and our three daughters are simply the loves of my life and make everything worth it.

Selected Bibliography

Bisheff, Steve. *Always Compete: An Inside Look at Pete Carroll and the USC Football Juggernaut*. St. Martin's Press, 2009.

Carroll, Pete, with Yogi Roth and Kristoffer A. Garin. *Win Forever: Live, Work, and Play Like a Champion*. Portfolio, 2010.

Delsohn, Steve. *Cardinal and Gold: The Oral History of USC Trojans Football*. Crown Archetype, 2016.

Fry, Stephen. *Troy: Our Greatest Story Retold*. Penguin Books, 2021.

Gulati, Ranjay, Matthew Breitfelder, and Monte Burke. "Pete Carroll: Building a Winning Organization through Purpose, Caring, and Inclusion." Harvard Business School Case 421-020, October 2020. (Revised March 2021.)

Hanson, Owen, and Alex Cody Foster. *The California Kid: From USC Golden Boy to International Drug Kingpin*. Turner, 2024.

Wharton, David, and Gary Klein. *Conquest: Pete Carroll and the Trojans' Climb to the Top of the College Football Mountain*. Triumph Books, 2005.

Yaeger, Don, and Jim Henry. *Tarnished Heisman: Did Reggie Bush Turn His Final College Season into a Six-Figure Job?* Pocket Books, 2008.

Index

About the Author

Monte Burke is a *New York Times* best-selling author of *Saban*, *Lords of the Fly*, *Rivers Always Reach the Sea*, *4th and Goal*, and *Sowbelly*. His books have won an Axiom Award for biography; been named one of the best books of the year by *Sports Illustrated*, *Outdoor Life*, *Field & Stream*, and Amazon; and been chosen for Barnes & Noble's "Discover Great New Writers" program. After a fourteen-year stint as a reporter, staff writer, and editor at *Forbes*, he is now a contributing editor at the magazine. He is also a contributing editor at *Garden & Gun* and *The Drake*. His work has appeared in *The New York Times*, *The Wall Street Journal*, *Esquire*, *Sports Illustrated*, and the *Daily Beast*. Burke graduated from Middlebury College with a BA in religion. He grew up in New Hampshire, Vermont, North Carolina, Virginia, and Alabama and now lives in Brooklyn with his family. Connect with him via @monteburke13 or through monteburke.com.